iPod & iTunes *Second Edition*

THE MISSING MANUAL

*The book that
should have been
in the box*

iPod & iTunes *Second Edition*

THE MISSING MANUAL

J.D. Biersdorfer

POGUE PRESS™
O'REILLY®

Beijing · Cambridge · Farnham · Köln · Paris · Sebastopol · Taipei · Tokyo

iPod & iTunes: The Missing Manual
by J. D. Biersdorfer

Published by Pogue Press/O'Reilly & Associates, Inc.,
1005 Gravenstein Highway North, Sebastopol, CA 95472.

February 2004:   Second Edition.

ISBN: 0-596-00658-6

Table of Contents

Introduction 1

    What Is an iPod? 1

    The iPod Family 3

    What You Need to iPod 4

    Mac vs. Windows iPods 4

    About This Book 5

    About MissingManuals.com 6

    The Very Basics 6

Part One: iPod: The Hardware

Chapter 1: Meet the iPod 11

    Parts of the Pod 11

    Charging the Battery 16

    Earphones–Apple's or Otherwise 20

    The Remote Control 21

    The Case 21

    The iPod Menus 22

Chapter 2: The iPod Sync Connection 35

    FireWire 35

    Installing a FireWire Card 37

    USB 2.0 40

    The iPod Software CD 42

    Your Very First Sync 45

    Variations on the Auto-Transfer Theme 47

    The Unspeakable Act: iPod-to-Computer Copying 52

Part Two: iPod: The Software

Chapter 3: Digital Audio Formats 65

    Introduction to Digital Audio 65

    Other Podworthy File Formats 69

    Bit Rates 74

    Free (and Legal) Music on the Web 75

Chapter 4: iTunes for Macintosh and Windows 77

Introduction to iTunes 77
A Quick Tour 79
Ripping CDs into iTunes 83
Importing Other Music Files into iTunes 91
Deleting Songs 92
Playing Music 92
iTunes Administration 96
Internet Radio 102
Playlists 104
Burning a CD or DVD 108
Playing Songs Across a Network 110

Chapter 5: MusicMatch Jukebox for Windows 115

Introduction to MusicMatch Jukebox 116
A Quick Tour 117
Ripping CDs into MusicMatch 120
Importing Other Music Files into MusicMatch 125
Deleting Songs 126
Playing Music 127
MusicMatch Administration 131
Internet Radio 133
Playlists 134
Burning CDs 138

Chapter 6: The iTunes Music Store 141

Welcome to the Music Store 141
A Store Tour 142
Searching and Shopping 146
iTunes on America Online 154
What to Do with Music You've Bought 157
Music Store Billing 161
The iTunes Music Store Song 163

Part Three: Beyond the Music

Chapter 7: iPod as Address Book 167

Introduction to the iPod Address Book 167
Transferring Contacts to the iPod 169
Copying Contacts from Windows 170
Copying Contacts from the Macintosh 174
Manually Deleting Contacts 181
Address Book Settings 181
Even More Organizer Shareware 182

Chapter 8: iPod as Calendar **183**
Preparing the iPod 183
Calendar Formats for the iPod 184
Calendars from iCal (Macintosh) 184
Calendars from Palm Desktop 4 188
Calendars from Microsoft Entourage X 189
Calendars from Entourage 2001 191
Calendars from Microsoft Outlook 191
Calendars from Now Up-to-Date for Mac OS X 192

Chapter 9: iPod Games and eBooks **195**
Games 195
Notes 198
iPod as eBook: The Shareware Way 200

Chapter 10: iSync **205**
The iSync Concept 205
iSync Meets iPod 206

Chapter 11: The iPod as Hard Drive **211**
The iPod's Hard Disk Format 211
Turning the iPod into an External Hard Disk 213
Storing Data Files on the iPod 214
Deleting Data Files 215
Unmounting the iPod Drive 215
The iPod as Startup Disk (Macs Only) 217

Part Four: Extreme iPodding

Chapter 12: Connecting the iPod to Other Audio Systems **229**
Connecting the iPod to a Stereo System 229
Connecting to a Car Stereo 232
Connecting to the Computer 238

Chapter 13: Hot Hacks and Cool Tools **239**
The AppleScripted iPod 239
More Mac Shareware 242
Windows Shareware 244
Linux on the iPod 245
Recording Your Own MP3s 246

Chapter 14: iStuff 251

Cases 251
Speakers 255
Stands 257
iPod Extenders 258
Power Adapters 263
Battery Boosters .... 264Chapter 1: z

Chapter 15: Troubleshooting 267

The iPod's Self-Help Modes 267
iPod Hardware Problems 272
Problems with Song Quality 279
Problems with the Headphones or Remote 280
iTunes Blues 281
Windows Woes with MusicMatch Jukebox 287
Problems with the iTunes Music Store 291
Reinstalling and Updating the iPod's Software 296
Where to Get Help Online 301

Chapter 16: iPod on the Web 303

Points of Interest at Apple.com 303
Software Updates for iTunes 304
Software Updates for MusicMatch Jukebox Plus 305
Fun and Informative iPod Web Sites 306

Part Five: Appendixes

Appendix A: iTunes, Menu by Menu 311

File Menu 315
Edit Menu 318
Controls Menu 319
Visualizer 320
Advanced 321
Window Menu (Macintosh Only) 322
Help Menu 323
Keyboard Shortcuts for iTunes 4 324

Appendix B: MusicMatch Jukebox Plus, Menu by Menu 329

File Menu 329
Edit Menu 331
View Menu 332
Options Menu 335
Help 339
Keyboard Shortcuts 339

The Missing Credits

About the Author

 J. D. Biersdorfer writes the weekly computer Q & A column for the Circuits section of *The New York Times*. She also writes an occasional Circuits feature story and has penned articles for *The New York Times Book Review*, the *AIGIA Journal of Graphic Design*, and *Rolling Stone*. After living all over the country as a former Air Force brat and theater technician, she planted herself in New York City in 1989. In her limited spare time, she plays the banjo and watches far too much CNN Headline News. Email: *jdbiersdorfer@mac.com*.

About the Creative Team

David Pogue (editor) is the weekly tech-review columnist for *The New York Times* and the creator of the Missing Manual series. He's the author or co-author of 30 books, including nine in the Missing Manual series and six in the "For Dummies" line (including *Magic, Opera, Classical Music*, and *The Flat-Screen iMac*). In his other life, David is a former Broadway theater conductor, a magician, and a pianist (*www.davidpogue.com*). Email: *david@pogueman.com*.

Nan Barber (copy editor) co-authored *Office X for the Macintosh: The Missing Manual* and *Office 2001 for Macintosh: The Missing Manual*. As the principal copy editor for this series, she has edited the titles on iPhoto 2, Mac OS X Hints, iMovie 3 & iDVD, Dreamweaver MX, and Windows XP. Email: *nanbarber@mac.com*.

Rose Cassano (cover illustration) has worked as an independent designer and illustrator for 20 years. Assignments have spanned everything from the nonprofit sector to corporate clientele. She lives in beautiful southern Oregon, grateful for the miracles of modern technology that make living and working there a reality. Email: *cassano@uci.net*. Web: *www.rosecassano.com*.

Phil Simpson (design and layout) works out of his office in Stamford, Connecticut, where he has had his graphic design business since 1982. He is experienced in many facets of graphic design, including corporate identity, publication design, and corporate and medical communications. Email: *pmsimpson@earthlink.net*.

Acknowledgments

I would like to thank David Pogue for suggesting this book to me and then for being a terrific editor all the way through the mad scramble of hardware and software updates. I owe a debt of gratitude to the Missing Manuals team for all their work on the project.

On a personal note, I'd also like to extend thanks to all my friends and family who put up with months of vague iPod-related mutterings while this book was under construction, including Mary and Bobby Armstrong, Tom Biersdorfer, my parents, and my grandfather. Other occupants on the thank-you list include Andy Webster for his proofreading prowess, Tom Simpson and his shared playlists, my supportive Internet buddies (the Wonder Women and the gang in Echo's upf_oz), and most of all, Betsy—for being there.

—J. D. Biersdorfer

The Missing Manual series is a joint venture between Pogue Press—the dream team introduced on these pages—and O'Reilly & Associates, one of the most respected publishers on earth.

Thanks, too, to agent David Rogelberg; proofreaders Jenny Barber, Chuck Brandstater, John Cacciatore, and Danny Marcus; Apple's Tracy De Lano and Steve Schiel for assistance in capturing the uncapturable (iPod screenshots); and the other Pogues— Jennifer, Kelly, and Tia—who make this series, and everything else, possible.

—David Pogue

About Pogue Press

Missing Manual books are designed to be superbly written guides to computer products that don't come with printed manuals (which is just about all of them). Each book features a handcrafted index, cross-references to specific page numbers (not just "see Chapter 14"), and an ironclad promise never to use an apostrophe in the possessive word *its*. Current and upcoming titles include:

- *Mac OS X: The Missing Manual, Panther Edition* by David Pogue
- *iLife '04: The Missing Manual* by David Pogue
- *iPhoto 4: The Missing Manual* by David Pogue, Joseph Schorr, & Derrick Story
- *iMovie 4 and iDVD: The Missing Manual* by David Pogue
- *GarageBand: The Missing Manual* by David Pogue
- *Switching to the Mac: The Missing Manual* by David Pogue
- *Mac OS X Hints, Panther Edition* by Rob Griffiths
- *FileMaker Pro 7: The Missing Manual* by Geoff Coffey
- *Dreamweaver MX 2004: The Missing Manual* by David Sawyer McFarland
- *Office X for Macintosh: The Missing Manual* by Nan Barber, Tonya Engst, & David Reynolds
- *AppleWorks 6: The Missing Manual* by Jim Elferdink & David Reynolds
- *Windows XP Home Edition: The Missing Manual* by David Pogue
- *Windows XP Pro: The Missing Manual* by David Pogue, Craig Zacker, & L. J. Zacker

Introduction

Remember the first time you heard about MP3 files? You could take a regular old CD, like *The Essential Johnny Cash* or an album of Strauss violin concertos played by Sarah Chang, put it in your computer's CD drive, and convert all of your favorite songs into the MP3 format. And do you recall your delight when you learned that those MP3 files took up a tenth of the space it would take to copy the CD audio files directly to your hard drive? You could leave the CD at home and play the new files (which sounded *almost* as good as the original CD, come to think of it) and rock out at your desk with your growing collection of freshly "ripped" MP3s.

Having a folder stuffed with tunes on your computer made working at it more enjoyable, but humans are always on the go. By 1998, the first portable MP3 players began to trickle onto store shelves, many offering 32 big, roomy megabytes of memory to store song files transferred from the computer.

Of course, most people wanted more than 30 minutes of music at a time. So later MP3 players came with more room for music, even if they were a little bigger and a little bulkier.

Then came the iPod.

What Is an iPod?

An iPod is many things to many people, but most people think of it as a pocket-size music player that holds 1,000 songs, 10,000 songs, or more, depending on the model.

Like the original Sony Walkman, which revolutionized the personal listening experience when it was introduced in 1979, Apple's announcement of the original

5-gigabyte iPod in the fall of 2001 caught the music world's ear. "With iPod, listening to music will never be the same again," intoned Steve Jobs, Apple's CEO. But even out of the Hyperbolic Chamber, the iPod was different enough to get attention. People noticed it, and more importantly, bought it. By the end of 2003, Apple had sold over two million of them. The iPod was the single bestselling music player on the market, the dominant player; for the first time in its history, Apple got to feel like Microsoft.

And no wonder. The iPod was smaller, lighter, and better-looking than most of its rivals—and much, much easier to use. Five buttons and a scroll wheel could quickly take you from ABBA to ZZ Top, and every song in between.

Gleaming in a white and chrome case slightly larger than deck of cards, the original iPod could hold at least 1,000 average-length pop songs (or six typical Grateful Dead live jams), and play them continuously for ten hours on a fully charged battery. The black-and-white LCD screen offered the song information in type large enough to actually read, and a bright backlight allowed for changing playlists in the dark. And with its superfast FireWire connection, the iPod could slurp down an entire CD's worth of music from computer to player in under 15 seconds.

Beyond the Music

Inside the iPod spins a hard drive, rather than the memory chip found in most music players. That hard drive, of course, is the secret to its massive capacity—but it's also the secret to a whole raft of surprising, little-known features like these:

- **iPod as hard drive.** You can hook up an iPod to your Mac or Windows machine, where it shows up as a disk. You can use it to copy, back up, or transfer gigantic files from place to place—at immense rates of transfer speed, thanks to its FireWire or USB 2.0 connection.

- **iPod as eBook.** The iPod makes a handy, pocket-sized electronic book reader, capable of displaying and scrolling through recipes, driving directions, book chapters, and even Web pages.

- **iPod as PalmPilot.** Amazingly, the iPod serves as a superb, easy-to-understand personal organizer. It can suck in the calendar, address book, to-do list, and notes from your Mac or PC, and then display them at the touch of a button.

- **iPod as GameBoy.** All right, not a GameBoy, exactly. But there are three video-style games and a memory-tugging audio quiz built into the modern iPod—perfect time-killers for medical waiting rooms, long bus rides, and lines at the Department of Motor Vehicles.

You know how Macintosh computers inspire such emotional attachment from their fans? The iPod inspires similar devotion: iPod Web sites, iPod shareware add-ons, an iPod accessory industry—in short, the invasion of the iPod People.

If you're reading this book, you're probably a Podling, too—or about to become one. Welcome to the club.

The iPod Family

Apple's iPods began life as white-and-silver rectangles. But as the family grew and prospered, the case designs changed, shrank, and sported colors. These days, the only thing you can count on in the iPod family is change itself.

- **Original iPod.** In October 2001, Apple unleashed the first, Macintosh-only model with 5 gigabytes of storage and a moving scroll wheel. It worked with Apple's free iTunes 2 software for encoding and organizing music files.

- **10-gig iPod.** Apple, realizing it had a good thing on its hands, announced the 10 GB iPod in March 2002. It still had a scroll wheel that actually turned, and it was still Macintosh-only—in theory. Windows and Linux users were already at work adapting the player for use with their own systems.

- **Windows iPod.** In July 2002, the Windows world got what it was craving: iPods formatted to work naturally with Windows and the popular MusicMatch Jukebox software. Apple also introduced a new, thinner version of the 10-gigabyte iPod whose scroll wheel was an immobile, solid-state "touchwheel" that responded to finger pressure.

- **20-gig iPod.** The iPod got itself a big sibling that same July day in the form of the 20 GB touchwheel iPod. Both of the touchwheel iPods came with a small remote control that hooks into the headphones cord, and a black carrying case complete with a belt clip. In all, there were then three iPod models—in 5 GB, 10 GB, and 20 GB sizes—in separate Mac and Windows formats.

- **2003 iPods.** The third-generation iPods arrived in a flash of music-related announcements from Apple. The new iPod line came in 10 GB, 15 GB, and 30 GB models, each of which could work either with Mac or Windows. The new iPods were thinner; the 15 and 30 GB models even came with a glossy white docking station that held the iPod upright while it charged, connected to the computer, or blasted tunes though the built-in line-out jack to the family stereo. Later in the year, Apple changed the hard drive sizes to 10 GB, 20 GB, and 40 GB—but the iPod's look remained the same. (In January 2004, the hard drive offerings grew again, to 15, 20, and 40 gigabytes.)

- **iPod Mini.** Apple introduced the iPod's first spin-off in early 2004: the iPod Mini, a streamlined, rounded-edged miniature version that can hide behind a business card and looks like the offspring of a lipstick tube and a box of Tic-Tacs. Its smooth anodized aluminum case comes in five bright colors: silver, blue, pink, green, or gold. Within its striking shell, the first Mini contains a 4 GB hard drive that holds 1,000 songs (in AAC format) and includes cables to connect by FireWire and USB 2.0. But while it may look mini on the outside, on the inside it runs the same operating system that lets it do everything a regular iPod can do.

- **The H-Pod.** Apple isn't the only company that will ever sell iPods. Hewlett-Packard will soon sell its own iPod, done up in "HP blue," and will include Apple's iTunes for Windows on every computer it sells. (At this writing, HP doesn't know what it will call the thing. But isn't HPod a great name? Get it? "HP"? And H is the letter before I?)

Clearly, the evolution of the iPod has only just begun.

What You Need to iPod

The iPod is designed to communicate with a Mac or a PC, which serves as the loading dock for tunes. Fortunately, it doesn't have especially demanding system requirements. Here's what your computer must have:

- **A decent amount of horsepower.** For the Macintosh, Apple recommends 256 megabytes of RAM and at least a 400-megahertz G3 processor. For the PC, you need at least a 330-megahertz Pentium-level processor and at least 96 MB of RAM, or 256 MB if you have Windows XP. More memory, of course, is always better.

- **A recent operating system.** For the Mac, you need Mac OS 9.2.2 (to use iTunes 2) or Mac OS X 10.1.5 or later (to use iTunes 4). Of course, if you go all the way to Mac OS X 10.2 or later, you get to use a lot of extra goodies in concert with your iPod, like iCal, iSync, and the Mac OS X Address Book.

  To use Apple's iTunes for Windows software, you need either Windows 2000 or XP. For PCs using the MusicMatch Jukebox software, Windows Me, 2000, or XP will do.

- **A FireWire or USB 2.0 connector.** FireWire, also known as IEEE 1394, is a fast cable connection for transferring data. Most Macs made after 1998 come with built-in FireWire, but FireWire jacks are only now becoming standard connectors on Windows PCs.

  If your PC doesn't have a FireWire connector, you can add a FireWire card to it (Chapter 2)—or use USB 2.0, which is even faster that the original FireWire connection. USB 2.0 is becoming a standard feature on new Macs and PCs, and you can install it into older machines via USB 2.0 expansion cards.

Mac vs. Windows iPods

If they were all hanging out together one afternoon at the beach, it would be hard to tell a Windows iPod from a crowd of Mac iPods. On the outside, they look the same.

But just as Macintosh and Windows computers use totally different formats for their hard drives, so do Mac and Windows iPods. This makes perfect sense, because the iPod *is* a hard drive. (Note for nerds: Mac iPods use a file system called HFS Plus; PC iPods use the unappetizing-sounding FAT32. If you've ever had to back up, reformat, and reinstall your pre–Windows XP system, FAT32 may sound familiar: it's the system Windows used for years.)

So how, then, can Apple claim to sell a single iPod model that, out of the box, comes formatted for either a Mac or a PC?

It doesn't really. The current iPod models are all preformatted for the Mac. But if you run the CD installer software that comes in the box, and it detects that it's running on a PC, it quietly reformats the iPod hard drive with the FAT32 system. Details on this process, and on the cabling differences between Mac and PC, begin on page 35.

Software Differences

These days, both Mac and PC fans use the same software to manage and organize what's on the iPod: a free program called iTunes. It works almost precisely the same in its Macintosh and Windows versions. Every button in every dialog box is exactly the same; the software response to every command is identical. In this book, the illustrations have been given even-handed treatment, rotating among the various operating systems where iTunes is at home (Windows XP, Mac OS X 10.2, and Mac OS X 10.3).

If you're a PC fan and you don't have Windows 2000 or XP, however, you can't use iTunes. Therefore, this book also describes the Windows software that preceded iTunes: MusicMatch Jukebox. It, too, can manage and move music to the iPod, copy songs from CDs to your hard drive, organize and play them, and burn blank CDs with playlists of your favorite songs. And like iTunes, it can automatically transfer your music library to the iPod whenever it's hooked up.

About This Book

The tiny square pamphlet that Apple includes with each artfully designed iPod package is enough to get your iPod up and running, charged, and ready to download MP3s.

But if you want to know more about how the iPod works, all the great things it can do, and where to find its secret features, the official pamphlet is skimpy in the extreme. And help files that you have to read on the computer screen aren't much better: You can't mark your place or underline, there aren't any pictures or jokes, and you can't read them in the bathroom.

This book is one-stop shopping for iPod reference and information. It explores iPod hardware and software, for both Macintosh and Windows, for all iPod models. It takes you on a joyride through the iPod subculture. And it guides you through all the cool musical and nonmusical things you can do with your iPod, from looking up phone numbers to checking the weather report. You'll also find heaping helpings of the Three T's: tips, tricks, and troubleshooting.

About→These→Arrows

Throughout this book, and throughout the Missing Manual series, you'll find sentences like this one: "Open the System folder→Libraries→Fonts folder." That's shorthand for a much longer instruction that directs you to open three nested folders in sequence, like this: "On your hard drive, you'll find a folder called System. Open it.

Inside the System folder window is a folder called Libraries; double-click it to open it. Inside *that* folder is yet another one called Fonts. Double-click to open it, too."

Similarly, this kind of arrow shorthand helps to simplify the business of choosing commands in menus, as shown in Figure I-1. That goes for both your computer and your iPod, whose menus feature arrows > like > these that lead you from one screen to the next.

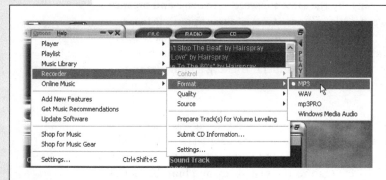

Figure I-1:
In this book, arrow notations help simplify menu instructions. For example, "Options→Recorder→Format→MP3" is a more compact way of saying, "From the Options menu, choose Recorder; from the submenu that then appears, choose Format; and from its submenu, choose MP3," as shown here.

About MissingManuals.com

At the *www.missingmanuals.com* Web site, click the "Missing CD-ROM" link to reveal a neat, organized, chapter-by-chapter list of the shareware and freeware mentioned in this book. (As noted on the inside back cover, having the software online instead of on a CD-ROM saved you $5 on the cost of the book.)

The Web site also offers corrections and updates to the book (to see them, click the book's title, then click Errata). In fact, you're invited and encouraged to submit such corrections and updates yourself. In an effort to keep the book as up to date and accurate as possible, each time we print more copies of this book, we'll make any confirmed corrections you've suggested. We'll also note such changes on the Web site, so that you can mark important corrections in your own copy of the book, if you like. And we'll keep the book current as Apple releases more iPods and software updates.

The Very Basics

To use this book, and indeed to use a computer, you need to know a few basics. This book assumes that you're familiar with a few terms and concepts:

- **Clicking.** This book gives you three kinds of instructions that require you to use your computer's mouse or trackpad. To *click* means to point the arrow cursor at something on the screen and then—without moving the cursor at all—to press and release the clicker button on the mouse (or laptop trackpad). To *double-click,* of course, means to click twice in rapid succession, again without moving the cursor at all. And to *drag* means to move the cursor *while* pressing the button.

When you're told to ⌘-*click* something on the Mac, or *Ctrl-click* something on a PC, you click while pressing the ⌘ or Ctrl key (both of which are near the Space bar).

- **Menus.** The *menus* are the words at the top of your screen or window: File, Edit, and so on. Click one to make a list of commands appear, as though they're written on a window shade you've just pulled down.

- **Keyboard shortcuts.** If you're typing along in a burst of creative energy, it's sometimes disruptive to have to take your hand off the keyboard, grab the mouse, and then use a menu (for example, to use the Bold command). That's why many experienced computer mavens prefer to trigger menu commands by pressing certain combinations on the keyboard. For example, in most word processors, you can press ⌘-B (Mac) or Ctrl+B (Windows) to produce a **boldface** word. When you read an instruction like "press ⌘-B," start by pressing the ⌘ key; while it's down, type the letter B, and then release both keys.

- **Operating-system basics.** This book assumes that you know how to open a program, surf the Web, and download files. You should know how to use the Start menu (Windows) and the Dock or menu (Macintosh), as well as the Control Panel (Windows), Control Panels (Mac OS 9), or System Preferences (Mac OS X).

Tip: If you're lost on these topics, there are Missing Manual titles that cover Windows Me, Windows 2000, Windows XP Home, Windows XP Professional, Mac OS 9, and Mac OS X. But enough sales pressure.

If you've mastered this much information, you have all the technical background you need to enjoy *iPod & iTunes: The Missing Manual.*

Part One:
iPod: The Hardware

Chapter 1: Meet the iPod

Chapter 2: The iPod Sync Connection

1

Meet the iPod

E ven before you extract it from its box, the iPod makes a design statement. Its
shrink-wrapped cardboard cube opens like a book, revealing elegantly pack-
aged accessories and software nestled around the iPod itself.

The first part of this book will familiarize you with the hardware portion of this
parcel.

Parts of the Pod

In addition to the nicely nestled iPod itself (Figure 1-1), the package's compart-
ments hold all the other stuff that comes with various iPod models: earbud-style
headphones and their foam covers, the connection cable for your computer, power
adapter, dock, carrying case with belt clip, remote control, and software CD. All you
get by way of instructions, though, is a small square folder, including the short iPod
User's Guide. Good thing you have the book in your hands to fill in the gaps.

You'll probably blow right past the warranty information (basically, you're covered
for one year) and the software agreement (the usual legalese that makes most people's
eyes glaze over like fresh Krispy Kreme doughnuts). The software agreement includes a small section about making digital copies of music, whose sentiment is
echoed right on the iPod's cellophane wrapping: *Don't steal music.*

The Screen

The monochrome LCD screen is your window into the iPod's world. You can use it
to navigate the menus, see how much of a charge the battery has left, and view the

name of the current playlist or song. The display, whose resolution is 160 x 128 pixels, also comes with a white backlight, so you can still use your iPod in movies, concerts, and coal mines.

Tip: The iPod screen uses the Chicago font, which should be familiar to Macintosh veterans.

Figure 1-1:
After the outer sleeve (top) is removed, the artfully designed packaging opens up to reveal the inner iPod. (Don't be deceived by the black-looking iPod photo. That's supposed to show what the thing looks like in the dark. There's no such thing as a black iPod—at least not yet, although a company called Colorware will sell you a hand-painted Pod at www.colorwarepc.com. (And you can always indulge your color whims with an iPod Mini.)

The iPod comes with all the hardware and software you need to get up and running, but the choice of music to put on it is up to you. If your iPod model didn't come with all the accessories shown, you can probably find most of them for sale on the Web.

WORKAROUND WORKSHOP

The Fingerprint Magnet

The full-size iPod's shiny chrome and white acrylic may be gorgeous and perfect the day you open the box. But like a white sofa in a house full of Labrador retrievers, it's not the best combination for disguising dirt, detritus, and especially fingerprints.

Cleaning with a soft, lint-free cloth can take care of most of them. For dark smudges, the iKlear solution and special cleaning cloth from Klearscreen (*www.klearscreen.com*) can also shine up your iPod.

The Scroll Wheel

The concentric ring on the iPod's face is the scroll wheel, which you use to navigate up or down lists of menu options on the screen. It lets you jump to a specific playlist, album, artist, song, or even a certain part of a song.

When a song is playing, you can also use the scroll wheel to adjust the iPod's volume: Spin the wheel counterclockwise to turn the volume down, or clockwise to increase the sound.

Figure 1-2:
Pressing any button turns on the iPod. The original iPod design (left) had the control buttons around the scroll wheel. On later iPods (middle), the control buttons are above the scroll wheel. The iPod Mini (right) puts the controls on a springy "click wheel" that combines the tactile response of the original iPods with the smooth surface of the wheel.

Of course, "spin" may not quite be the right word. The wheel on the 2001 iPods actually turned. But on the 2002-and-later iPods, including the iPod Mini, the turning wheel gave way to a stationary *touchwheel,* which you operate by dragging your finger around the ring. You've got one less moving part to go bad.

Tip: Want to personalize your Pod forever? Say it with lasers—laser engraving, that is. You can immortalize the chrome backside of your iPod with a short, two-line message of your choosing for an extra $19 when you order an iPod at *store.apple.com*.

Just don't make a typo.

The Buttons

The first generations of iPod had raised, contoured control buttons—Menu, ▶❙❙, and so on—hugging the outer edge of the wheel.

Beginning with the 2003 iPods, Apple made all the buttons nonmoving, touch-sensitive parts (Figure 1-2). This design offers two advantages: It keeps sand and dirt from derailing the iPod's parts, and it lets a red-orange glow backlight the names of the buttons when it's dark out. Many iPodders complained, though, that the new layout makes it more of a thumb reach to hit the ❙◀◀ and ▶▶❙ buttons without bringing in a second hand.

Owners of the iPod Mini don't have to worry about *that;* its buttons are actual, clickable spots on the 12, 3, 6, and 9 o'clock positions *on* the scroll wheel. If you're old enough to own an iPod, your thumb can probably reach them.

In any case, no matter which model you have, no matter where the control buttons have migrated, they all work the same way once you find them.

Starting from the center, here are the controls:

• **Select.** The big white button in the center of any iPod is the Select button. Like clicking a mouse on a desktop computer, you press Select to choose a highlighted menu item. When a song title is highlighted, the Select button begins playback.

• **Menu.** On early-model iPods and on the Mini, the Menu button is at 12 o'clock, up at the top of the circle. On current full-size iPods, Menu is the second button in the row of controls.

Pressing the Menu button once takes you to the iPod's main screen, which gives you five options: Playlists, Browse, Extras, Settings, and Backlight. They're described in more detail later in this chapter. (If you haven't updated your iPod's system software in a while—see page 296—you may see a slightly different list. See Chapter 15 for more on software updates.)

The Menu key is also your ticket home: If you've burrowed deep into the iPod's menu system, pressing the Menu key repeatedly takes you back one screen at a time until you're back where you started.

Tip: The Menu button also controls the white backlight for the iPod's display screen. Hold it down for a few seconds to turn the backlight on or off. Of course, you can also scroll to the Backlight item on the iPod's main menu (as found in iPod system software 1.3 and later) and select Backlight there, too.

• **◄◄ and ►►.** You press the Next/Fast-forward button (represented in this book by this symbol ►►) once to advance to the next song on the playlist. You can also hold it down to fast-forward through the current song to get to the good parts.

The Previous/Rewind button (◄◄), of course, does the opposite: Press it once quickly to play the current song from the beginning; press it repeatedly to cycle back through the songs on the playlist. Hold it down to rewind through the current song, just like the Rewind button on your old tape deck.

Tip: Here's another great way to navigate the song that's now playing: Press the Select button and then use the scroll wheel to zoom to any part of the song you want. This technique, called *scrubbing,* gives you more control and greater precision than the ◄◄ and ►► buttons.

• **►II.** The Play/Pause button, marked by a black triangle (►) and the universal Pause symbol (II), plays or stops the selected song, album, playlist, or library. It's also the iPod's Off switch if you press it for three seconds. (The iPod also turns itself off automatically after two minutes of inactivity.)

Tip: These buttons, used in combination, also let you reset a locked-up iPod. Details in Chapter 15.

Places for Plugs

Here are the various switches and connectors you'll find on the top and bottom of your iPod, as shown in Figure 1-3:

- **FireWire port.** This is where you plug in the FireWire cable that came with your player. In most cases, you can connect the iPod directly to the computer's Fire-Wire connector both to charge the battery and to download music and data. (Some iPod models come with a white plastic cap that covers the FireWire port.)

  You'll find much more detail on this syncing business in Chapter 2.

Note: When you're away from the computer, there's another way to charge up your iPod: Attach the cable to the included AC power adapter and plug it into the wall. You *have* to use this technique, by the way, if the FireWire adapter card for your PC doesn't supply power.

Figure 1-3:
The headphone jack in the center and the Hold switch on the right side have remained up top in all generations of the iPod, but the FireWire port has roamed.

The original 2001 iPod (top) is wider than later models and has no plastic cover for the FireWire port like the 2002 iPod (middle) does.

The 2003 iPod (bottom) and the iPod Mini (not shown) has a remote jack closely aligned with the headphone port in the center. The Hold switch is still off to the right, but the FireWire port has changed shape and migrated to the bottom of the device.

The 2003-and-later iPods, including the iPod Mini, have a nonstandard connector for supplying power to the iPod. It's still a FireWire cable in most cases, but it has a flat connector that can plug right into the bottom of the iPod—or into the spiffy dock that comes with certain models.

- **Headphone port.** On the iPod's top, you'll find the jack where you plug in the earbud-style headphones that come with your iPod.

  Fortunately, this is a standard 3.5mm stereo plug. In other words, you're free to substitute any other Walkman-style headphones, or even to play the music on the iPod through your home sound system (Chapter 12).

- **Remote control jack.** On the 2003-and-later iPods, including the Mini, there's an extra little port right next to the headphone jack. This small oval notch is for the remote control, which is a two-pronged affair.

- **Hold switch.** With all the control buttons on the front of the iPod, it's easy to hit one accidentally while you're taking it in or out of your pocket or purse. To prevent such unintended button activity, slide the iPod's Hold switch over to reveal a bright orange bar. You've just disabled all the buttons on the front of the unit, preventing accidental bumps. (A small lock icon appears on the iPod's screen when the Hold button is on.) Slide the switch back to turn off the Hold function.

Note: A common moment of iPod panic occurs when the device's control buttons don't seem to be working. Check the top to make sure the Hold switch isn't on. If your iPod model includes a remote control, check the Hold button on the remote as well.

Charging the Battery

Many a cloud of gadget euphoria dies instantly when the new owner realizes that the device must sit in a battery charger and juice up before any fun can happen.

Out of the box, the iPod may have enough juice to turn itself on and get you hooked on spinning the scroll wheel. But you'll still need to charge the iPod before you use it for the first time.

Charging via FireWire or USB 2.0 Cable

In computers with *powered* FireWire jacks (usually the fatter 6-pin FireWire connections, not the little 4-pin connectors found on many Windows machines), you can use the included FireWire cable to plug it into your computer. The battery charges through the FireWire cable as long as the computer is on and not in Sleep mode.

Note: The iPod Mini can charge itself from *either* a FireWire cable or USB 2.0 cable, on both Macs and PCs—a welcome improvement.

It takes about three hours to fully charge your iPod. Note, however, that it gets about 80 percent charged after an hour. If you just can't wait to unplug it and go racing out to show your friends, you can begin to use it after an hour.

During the charging process, you may see either the "Do Not Disconnect" message (if the iPod is also sucking down music from your computer), the "OK to Disconnect" message (if it's done with that), or the main menu (if it's a 2003 or later model).

The Dock

Some iPods come with a cool accessory: the iPod dock. The dock, shown in Figure 1-4, is a plastic stand with FireWire and stereo line-out connections built into the back. To charge up the iPod, you can either plug in the flat FireWire cable right into the bottom of the player, or plug the cable into the back of the dock.

Figure 1-4:
The iPod dock allows for upright charging and a better view of the iPod's screen, not to mention a healthy flow of air around that toasty little battery as it charges. If your iPod didn't come with the dock, you can buy one separately on Apple's Web site for $40. (Alas, the dock doesn't fit 2001 or 2002 iPod models. There is one available for the iPod Mini, though.)

Once the dock is plugged into the computer, place the iPod upright onto the metal connector in the bottom of dock to begin charging it. The iPod trills out a little tweet of joy when it makes contact, and you see the animated "charging battery" icon.

Using the AC Adapter

You can also charge the battery by plugging the iPod's FireWire cable into the boxy white AC power adapter that comes with it (Figure 1-5). With the iPod turned off, a larger version of the animated charging battery icon appears in the middle of the screen.

Note: Even when fully charged, the battery in an "off" iPod slowly drains after 14 to 28 days. If, for some inconceivable reason, you haven't used your iPod in a month or more, you should recharge it, even if you left it fully charged the last time you used it.

Checking the Battery's Charge

The battery icon on the iPod's screen shows the approximate amount of gas left in the tank. When the iPod is connected to the computer, the battery icon in the top-left corner displays a charging animation, complete with tiny lightning bolt.

Battery Life

The iPod uses a rechargeable lithium ion battery. Battery life depends on which version of the iPod you have.

If you let a 2001 or 2002 iPod play all night, you can get about 12 hours per charge. But if you're like most normal people who turn it on and off, tinker with settings, skip around playlists, and turn on the backlight, eight hours is a more likely average.

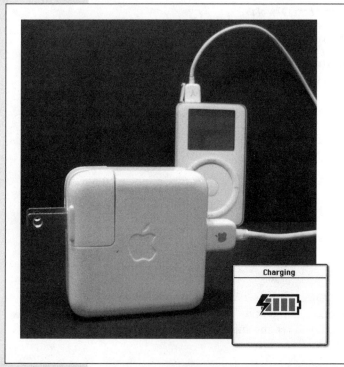

Figure 1-5:
The FireWire cable that comes with the iPod plugs into the end of the AC power adapter. Flip out the electrical prongs tucked into the adapter's end, and then plug it into a regular wall socket. Run the FireWire cable between the AC adapter and the iPod's FireWire port (or charging dock).

Inset: The iPod makes it graphically clear that you're charging its battery— just in case you were wondering.

Charging

GEM IN THE ROUGH

Prongs Across the World

The iPod's AC power adapter can handle electrical currents between 100 volts and 240 volts at frequencies of 50 and 60 hertz. Put another way, it works not only with the voltage in North America, but also in many parts of Europe and Asia.

But although the iPod adapter automatically converts the *voltage* of global outlets, it doesn't convert the *prongs* of the world's various outlets: round prongs, flat ones, prongs in pairs, prongs in threes, and so on.

The Apple Store sells a World Traveler Adapter Kit for the iPod: six plugs that snap onto the end of the iPod's AC adapter to adapt its prongs for electrical outlets in the United Kingdom, continental Europe, Japan, China, Korea, Australia, Hong Kong, and other parts of North America. The World Traveler Adapter Kit costs about $40 at Apple's Web site and stores.

The 2003-and-later iPod is smaller than the previous models, so it contains a smaller battery; same goes for the iPod Mini. Apple estimates that modern iPod models have a battery life of up to eight hours. Again, you can expect shorter life in the real world (see the box below for more detail). If your iPod is conking out too soon, contact Apple Support by phone or Web.

Originally, Apple made the iPod without a replaceable battery, at least until it faced a spate of power cells with early deaths (and user complaints). Apple now offers a $99 battery replacement program and a special AppleCare warranty just for iPods.

Tip: If you don't mind voiding your iPod's warranty—or if it's already expired—and you're up for a little manual labor, you can pry the case open and replace the battery yourself (page 276).

POWER USERS' CLINIC

Maximizing Your Battery's Potential

Battery life varies. Someone inclined to settle into a long playlist and let the iPod go without interruption will enjoy more time between electricity refills than an iPodder who constantly jumps around to different songs and fiddles with controls.

Apple has several recommendations, both environmental and behavioral, for getting the most out of the battery. For example, as better power management is a perpetual goal, the company recommends always having the latest version of the iPod software installed.

While the iPod can operate without incident in temperatures between 50 and 95 degrees Fahrenheit, the iPod (like most people) works best at room temperature—around 68° F. An iPod left out in a cold car all night, for example, needs to warm up to room temperature before you play it; otherwise, it may have trouble waking up from sleep mode. It also may present the Low Battery icon onscreen. (If this happens to you, wait until the iPod warms up, then plug it into its power adapter and reset it by pressing the Menu and ▶ II buttons until the Apple logo appears.)

Using the Hold switch (page 16) can make sure that a sleeping iPod doesn't get turned on, and therefore run its battery down, by an accidental bump or nudge while in a purse or pocket. Pausing the iPod when you're not listening to it is another way to save power, especially if you tend to get distracted and forget that the player is set to repeat songs and playlists over and over.

Jumping around the iPod's music library with the I◀◀ and ▶▶I buttons can also burn down the battery sooner rather than later. Like a laptop, the iPod stores its data on a tiny hard drive, and hard drives can be power hogs. To save power, the iPod lets its hard drive stop spinning as often as possible—by playing upcoming music from a built-in memory chip. Pushing the iPod's buttons to change songs forces the iPod to start its hard drive spinning again, which requires energy.

The iPod's memory cache works best with song files that are smaller than 9 MB. That's plenty for songs in the MP3 or AAC formats (Chapter 3). But if you're listening to AIFF tracks you copied straight from the CD without compression (you know who you are), the larger file sizes may overload the cache, and your battery won't last as long.

That backlight, while illuminating, is also a power drain. Use the light sparingly for better battery life.

What about the iPod's charge when you're *not* using it? Turns out that it quietly sips juice even when it's turned off. In fourteen days (or much sooner), the battery will empty itself completely. In short, treat the iPod as you would a pet snake: Give it a big meal every few days.

Earphones–Apple's or Otherwise

The iPod comes with a set of white earbud-style headphones (Figure 1-6). These aren't just flimsy freebies tossed in the box, either. They're designed with the iPod's amplifier in mind.

Figure 1-6:
You're supposed to wedge the iPod earbuds into your ear canals, preferably after covering each one with one of the included gray foam covers. (You even get two sets of these covers, so you and a loved one don't have to exchange earwax.) As with any type of headphone, excessively loud music can damage hearing, so use the volume controls sensibly.

With a frequency response of 20 to 20,000 Hertz, the iPod can cover a huge range of sounds—comparable to that of a respectable home stereo. In other words, it lets most people hear all the detailed sonic mayhem on a Pink Floyd album. To reproduce this range of frequencies, the iPod earbuds use 18mm drivers with neodymium transducer magnets. (No, you're not expected to know what that means—but it's fun to say at cocktail parties. See the box below.)

While the iPod earbuds are quite robust, they're not for everyone. Some people don't care for the sensation of oversized chunks of foam jammed into their auditory canals. Others lack the wedge of cartilage that keeps earbud-style headphones in place, and can't use the iPod buds without duct tape.

UP TO SPEED

Neodymium and Why You Care

The *driver* is the moving element in any type of speaker system, from tiny headphones to subwoofers. When an amplifier supplies power, the driver vibrates and produces sound waves.

Neodymium—which, from your cramming for that high school test in the Periodic Table of the Elements, you may recognize as atomic number 60—is a rare-earth metal that's used in magnets, lasers, and purple glass. Its name is derived from

the Greek *neos didymos*, which means "new twin" (an appropriate name for a substance used in a pair of earbuds).

Apple claims that its neodymium driver is five times as powerful as the aluminum or cobalt drivers in other earbuds, capable of delivering accurate sound with minimal distortion.

Sounds good so far.

Fortunately, the 3.5mm jack on the iPod's headphone port makes it possible to use just about any type of Walkman-style headphones. If you have truly hard-to-fit ears, for example, Apple also sells a set of in-ear headphones with three different earhole cap sizes that you gently plug into your head for maximum comfort. These in-ear buddies cost $40 at *www.apple.com/ipod/accessories.html*.

Swapping out the iPod earbuds for smaller ones, or even headphones that go over the head and cover the outer ear, is perfectly fine. However, if aesthetics matter to you, finding white earphones that match the iPod may be something of a challenge.

The Remote Control

Some 2002-and-later iPod models include a delicious accessory: a futuristic-looking silver remote control (see Figure 1-7). Complete with a handy jacket clip, the remote replicates most of the main iPod controls including ◀◀, ▶, ▶▶, volume adjustment, and Hold.

With the remote within easy reach, you can pause a song without having to fumble around for the iPod. No longer must you miss out on the beginnings of all those conversations when someone walks up to you and says, "Hey, did you get an iPod?"

The remote does make for a longer earphone cord, though, making cable management more of an issue.

Note: If your iPod model didn't come with a remote, and you're coming down with a serious case of Remote Envy, the remote control and a spare pair of earbuds are available for $40 from Apple's Web site, stores, and retail outlets.

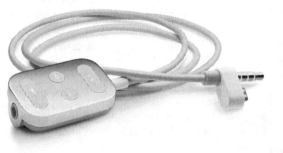

Figure 1-7:
The iPod remote control, included with the higher-priced models of each generation (and optional for other 2003-and-later models like the Mini), has a clip on the back to attach to a lapel or pocket.

The Case

Apple began including a simple black iPod carrying case with the more expensive iPod models in 2002, and continued the tradition with the 2003-and-later family. The case is basically a slipcover with a belt clip on the back. It holds the iPod snugly and protects it from scratches and fingerprints (Figure 1-8). If you're feeling left out, you can buy the case for $40 from the Apple Web site.

The iPod Mini's belt clip snaps onto the player. If you want to wear your music on your sleeve on days when you're going beltless (or when you're working out), $30 at Apple's Web site will get you a wide black armband instead.

Figure 1-8:
Some people don't like the included case because it covers the iPod's screen and makes using the front-panel buttons impossible. When it's on, you must control the iPod from the wired remote instead of the iPod buttons. Chapter 14 describes alternative cases and where to get them.

The iPod Menus

The iPod's menus are as straightforward as its controls. You use the scroll wheel to go down the list of options you see on the screen. Then you press the Select button to pick what you want. Small arrows on the end of each menu item (like this: Settings >) indicate that another menu lurks behind it, so keep pressing Select until you get where you want to go. (If you realize that that is *not* where you want to go, press the Menu button to retrace your steps.)

Figure 1-9:
If you don't see this main menu at the moment, press the Menu button repeatedly until you do. From here, you can drill down into any iPod function.

Note: The menus and screens described here refer to the ones used in iPod system software 1.3 (for 2001 and 2002 iPods) or 2.1 (on third-generation models that first appeared in 2003). If you have an older iPod that you haven't updated in a while, you can update your software by downloading the current version from Apple's Web site. Details on page 296.

The main screen (Figure 1-9) says iPod at the top and offers a choice of five areas to go to next: Playlists, Browse, Extras, Settings, and Backlight. Here's more about what's under each menu item.

Playlists

A *playlist* is a customized list of songs that you create from the tracks in your music library. It's your own personal music mix that you can save, store, and play over and over again on your iPod or computer.

Except for On-The-Go playlists (described next), you make playlists on your Mac or PC using the iTunes or MusicMatch Jukebox software. For example, you can make a playlist called "Go For Baroque" and add all of your favorite Bach and Handel songs from your music library, in the order you want to hear them. You can also get the computer to create playlists for you with the iTunes Smart Playlists feature (page 106).

Once you save a playlist and synchronize your computer with the iPod, the file is transferred to the iPod.

All of the playlists you've created in iTunes or MusicMatch Jukebox Plus appear in the Playlists menu (Figure 1-10). When you want to hear a particular set of songs, choose the playlist's name and press Play. When you finish listening to one playlist, pick another from the Playlists menu to keep jamming.

Figure 1-10:
Left: Scroll to the playlist you want, select it, and press Play.

Right: If you highlight a playlist name and then press Select instead, you see a list of the songs in that playlist.

Playlists are not set in stone. For example, if you made a playlist called "Everything Radiohead Ever Recorded," and Radiohead puts out a new album, you can just rip the new CD to MP3 files on your Mac or PC, drag them onto your existing Radiohead playlist, and update the iPod.

To modify or delete a playlist, use iTunes or MusicMatch; you can't do that kind of thing on the iPod.

Playlists On-The-Go

Before the 2003 iPods beamed in from Apple headquarters, the only way to make a playlist for the iPod was to sit down at your computer and fire up iTunes (Chapter 4) or MusicMatch Jukebox Plus (Chapter 5). Then you had to download the fresh hot playlist to the iPod when it was connected.

This method didn't exactly provide instant gratification. If, while you were bopping around town, you found yourself suddenly wishing you could hear an eclectic mix of tunes from several different albums and artists, you were out of luck.

The Playlists On-The-Go feature fixes that. You scroll through your iPod's music library, select the song you want to add, and hold down the Select button for a few seconds. The song's title blinks three times to acknowledge its addition to a special, modifiable playlist called *On-The-Go*. You're then free to scroll onward to the next song you want to add. You can press and select entire albums, artists, or even other playlists to add to your On-The-Go compilation.

To see your On-The-Go playlist, just scroll to the very bottom of the Playlists menu. Press Select to see the list of songs in it—or press Play to hear them.

Note: The first version of the On-The-Go playlist feature held the song set in its memory *only* until the next time you connected it to the computer. Version 2.1 of the iPod system software fixes that temporal annoyance, and lets you sync your spontaneous mix back into iTunes. To gain this power of preservation, install the latest update to your iPod's software from *www.apple.com/ipod/download*.

If you tire of those tunes before you sync up again, you can wipe out the temporary list by selecting the Clear Playlist option at the bottom of On-The-Go submenu.

Browse

If you don't have a particular playlist in mind, the Browse menu (Figure 1-11) lists your entire music collection, organized in several different ways:

Figure 1-11:
Click Artists to see a list of all the bands and singers in your iPod's music library. Once you select an artist, the next screen takes you to a list of all of that performer's albums. Similarly, the Albums menu shows all your iPod's songs grouped by album name.

- **Artists.** This menu groups every tune by the performer's name.

- **Albums.** This view groups your music by album.

- **Songs.** This is a list of every song on the iPod, listed alphabetically.

- **Genres.** This menu sorts your music by type: Rock, Rap, Country, and so on.

- **Composers.** The iPod displays all of your music, grouped by songwriter. (This option doesn't work on Windows-formatted iPods used with MusicMatch Jukebox on the desktop side.)

Chapters 3, 4, and 5 let you know how all that song information gets attached to your digital audio files in the first place.

Note: If you're a classical music buff, all bets are off when it comes to filing tidy bits of information into the Song, Composer, and Artist slots. As an article in the *New York Times* put it: "Take Saint-Saëns's First Cello Concerto, 'Violoncello in A major,' Opus 33, No. 1, with Mstislav Rostropovich as soloist and Carlo Maria Giulini conducting the London Philharmonic. Whose name should go into the 'artist' slot? And what's the 'song title'?"

Sometimes, you just have to suffer for your art.

Extras

This menu contains all the goodies that make the iPod more than just a music player. Here's what you'll find there (Figure 1-12).

Note: Pre-2003 iPod models lack the Notes feature, Solitaire, Music Quiz, and the Parachute game.

Clock

When you choose Clock, you see the screen shown in Figure 1-12 at right: a live digital clock. This little timekeeper comes in handy if you forget your watch.

Figure 1-12:
Left: Playing music is only one function of today's iPod, as it can double as a personal organizer, time keeper, and palm-sized game arcade.

Right: The Clock gives a whole new meaning to the term pocket watch. *As it turns out, the iPod makes a dandy travel alarm.*

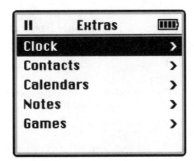

Beneath this display, the latest iPod models offer a tiny menu that lists three other commands, all related to time eternal: Alarm Clock, Sleep Timer, and Date & Time. Here's what they do.

Alarm Clock

The iPod's alarm clock can give you a gentle nudge when you need it. To set the iPod alarm, do the following:

1. **Choose Extras→Clock→Alarm Clock→Alarm. Press the Select button.**

   You've just switched the alarm on (Figure 1-13, left).

Figure 1-13:
Left: Any old alarm clock lets you specify what time you want it to go off. But how many let you specify what song you want to play?

Right: Turn the dial to set the time.

2. **Scroll to Time, press Select, and spin the scroll wheel.**

   As you turn the wheel, you change the time that the iPod displays (Figure 1-13, right). Keep going until the desired wake-up time appears.

3. **Press Select again to set the time.**

   It's time to decide whether you want "Beep" (a warbling R2-D2-like noise that comes out of the iPod's built-in speaker) or music. If you choose to be alerted by music, it will play through your headphones, assuming they haven't fallen out of your ear sockets during sleep.

4. **Scroll to Sound and press Select. Choose Beep (at the top of the list), or highlight the playlist you want to hear at the appointed time. Press Select.**

   The Alarm Clock is set. You see a tiny bell icon on the main clock screen.

When the alarm goes off, the iPod beeps for a few seconds—or plays the playlist you selected—until you press the iPod's Pause button.

If you wake up early and want to prevent the alarm from sounding, go to Extras→Clock→Alarm Clock→Alarm and press the Select button to toggle it off.

Tip: You don't have to burrow all the way to the Clock option just to use your 2003 iPod as a pocket watch. You can ask iPod to display the current time in its title bar whenever music is playing. To do so, choose iPod→Settings→Date & Time→Time in Title. Press the Select button to toggle the Time in Title display on or off.

Sleep Timer

The sleep timer is like the opposite of the alarm clock: It's designed to help you fall *asleep* instead of waking you. The idea is that you can schedule the iPod to shut itself off after a specified period of music playing, so that you can drift off to sleep as music plays, without worrying that you'll run down your battery.

To set the iPod's Sleep Timer, choose Extras→Clock→Sleep Timer. Scroll down to the amount of time iPod should play before shutting down: 15, 20, 60, 90, or 120 minutes. (You can also choose to turn off the Sleep Timer here.)

Now start the iPod playing (press Play) and snuggle down into your easy chair or pillow. The screen displays a little clock and begins a digital countdown to sleepyland.

Your iPod will stop playing automatically after the appointed interval—but if all goes well, you won't be awake to notice.

Date & Time

See page 31; this is a repeat of the command found in the Settings menu.

More Extras

The remaining items on the Extras menu go far beyond music—once you know how to use them. More details about getting the most out of your iPod are revealed in Part 3 of this book, but here's what you have to look forward to:

- **Contacts.** Phone numbers and addresses reside here (Chapter 7).
- **Calendars.** This menu holds your personal daily schedule (Chapter 8).
- **Notes.** The 2003 iPods were the first to come with a built-in text reader program that you can use to read short documents and notes (Chapter 9).
- **Games.** You can play the historic Brick game on the iPod. On 2003-and-later models, you also get Parachute, Solitaire, and a Music Quiz (Chapter 9).

Settings

The Settings menu has more than a dozen options for tailoring how your iPod sounds and looks.

Note: The following list refers to the menu layout on the 2003 iPods. (On iPod Software 1.3—the last update available for the 2001 and 2002 models—the order of the settings is slightly different, and there is no Main Menu item for customizing the iPod's main screen.)

About

The About screen displays the name of your iPod, the number of songs on it, the hard drive capacity of your model, and how much disk space is free. As shown in Figure 1-14, you can also find the version of the iPod system software that your unit is currently running, as well as your iPod's serial number. (The serial number is also engraved on the iPod's back panel.)

Note: On earlier iPods that have not been updated to iPod Software 1.3 or later, this command lives on the iPod's main menu.

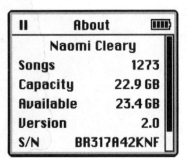

Figure 1-14:
Left: Among other bits of trivia, the About screen shows how much space is left on the iPod, ready for you to fill with songs and files.

Right: The Main Menu settings, just under About, can customize your iPod's main screen.

Main menu

The iPod 2.0 software (introduced on 2003 models) came with a handy personalization feature: The ability to arrange your iPod's main menu screen so that only the items you like show up when you spin the wheel. For example, you could insert the Calendar option onto the iPod's opening screen, so that you don't have to drill down through the Extras menu to get at it.

The iPod 2.1 update adds more options to the display. For example, if you've bought a Belkin Voice Recorder to capture your own sweet nothings in your iPod, the Voice Memos command appears here, right up front.

To customize your iPod's main menu, start by choosing Settings→Main Menu from the main iPod menu (Figure 1-14, right). You see a list of items that you can choose to add to or eliminate from your iPod's main screen: Playlists, Browse, Artists, Clock, Sleep, and so on.

As you scroll down the list, press the Select button to turn each one on or off. You might, for example, consider adding these commands:

- **Clock,** for quick checks of the time.

- **Games,** for quick killing of time.

- **Contacts,** to look up phone numbers.

To see the fruits of your labor, press Menu twice to return to the main screen. Sure enough, in addition to the usual commands described in this chapter, you'll see the formerly buried commands right out front, ready to go.

Note: To restore the original factory settings, select Reset Main Menu at the bottom of the list and Reset on the next screen.

Shuffle

When the Shuffle option is *off,* the iPod plays straight down each playlist as you originally designed it (Chapters 5 and 6). If you turn on Shuffle Songs, the iPod ambles through all the songs on your chosen playlist or album in *random* order. Press Select again to get Shuffle Albums, which makes the iPod mix up the order of the albums it plays (but not the songs within each album).

To set your Shuffle preferences, choose Settings→Shuffle from the main menu. Then press the Select button to cycle through your three options—Off, Songs, or Albums— until you hit the one you want.

Repeat

The Repeat function works like the similarly named button on a CD player: It makes the music you're listening to loop over and over again.

To set your Repeat preferences, choose Settings→Repeat from the main menu. Now, by pressing the Select button repeatedly, you can cycle through these three options:

- **Repeat One.** You'll hear the current song repeated over and over again, like a hippie teenager with a new Beatles 45.

- **Repeat All.** This function repeats *the current list* over and over again, whether that's an album, a playlist, or your entire song library.

- **Off.** The iPod will play the selected playlist or album once, and then stop.

Note: Be careful with the repeat functions. If you set the iPod down (or if it gets bumped when the Hold switch wasn't activated), it will cheerfully play away, over and over, endlessly, until the battery is dead.

Backlight Timer

The iPod screen's backlight is pretty, but can be a real drain on the iPod's battery. Fortunately, you can specify how long the backlight stays on each time you press a button or turn the dial, from 1 Second to Always On. If you *never* want the iPod to light up—for example, when it's in its case and you use the remote control to operate it—you can also turn off the backlight completely.

To set your Backlight Timer preferences, choose Settings→Backlight Timer. Scroll to the amount of time you want the Backlight to stay on when you touch any iPod button: 2 Seconds, 5 Seconds, or whatever, and then press Select.

For example, if you use the iPod in low-light conditions, or have a hard time reading the screen, a ray of backlight for 5 or 10 seconds should be enough time to scroll up a new playlist or album when you touch the controls.

Choose Always On to keep the light shining until you manually turn it off by holding down the Menu button.

Tip: If you're spinning tunes as an iPod DJ in a dark club or other squinty situation, the Always On setting is handy. But run the player from the AC adapter unless you have a really short set list, since the backlight is hungry for battery power.

EQ

When it comes to range of sounds, not all music is created equal. A howling heavy metal rock band produces a wider array of noises than a solo female singer armed with only an acoustic guitar.

Equalization is the art of adjusting the frequency response of an audio signal. An equalizer emphasizes or boosts some of its frequencies, while lowering others. In the range of audible sound, *bass* frequencies are the low rumbly noises; *treble* is at the opposite end with the high, even shrill sound; and *midrange* is, of course, in the middle, and the most audible to human ears.

To save you the trouble of getting an audio engineering degree, the iPod includes a set of equalizer presets, named after the type of music (and the typical musical instruments) they're designed to enhance. Dance music, for example, usually has higher bass frequencies to emphasize the booming rhythm.

By contrast, if you're listening to your playlist of Haydn string quartets, try setting the iPod's equalizer to the Classical preset. This setting softens some of the more screechy higher frequencies while providing firm, sturdy midrange and bass frequencies that make for a mellow cello.

There are more than 20 equalizer presets on the iPod—for acoustic, classical, dance, hip hop, jazz, pop, rock, and other types of music—plus settings than can add or reduce bass and treble sounds. You might not be able to hear much difference, but many people prefer equalized music for the overall sound quality.

To set your iPod's Equalizer to a preset designed for a specific type of music or situation, choose iPod→Settings→EQ. Scroll down the list of presets until you find one that matches your music style, and then press the Select button. The name of the preset is now listed next to EQ on the Settings menu.

Tip: See Chapters 4 (Mac) or 5 (Windows) for more on equalization—and how you can apply it from your computer.

Sound Check

This ingenious setting cuts down on those jarring moments between, say, George Winston's New Age noodling and the latest angry Metallica thrash, by adjusting the overall volume settings.

Note: Sound Check is a feature of iTunes. If you're on Windows and have opted to stand by MusicMatch Jukebox for your desktop software, though, you don't have to put up with sore ears. The program's equivalent feature is called Volume Leveling (page 130). In fact, unlike iTunes, which treats Sound Check as an all-or-nothing deal, MusicMatch Jukebox Plus lets you level *groups* of songs.

Note, however, that Volume Leveling on your PC adjusts the volume of the song files themselves when they're transferred to the iPod.

The key to making this feature work is to remember that you have to turn it on *in two places:* once in iTunes on your Mac or PC, and once on the iPod.

Start in iTunes. Choose Preferences→Effects (⌘-comma on the Mac; Ctrl-comma in Windows), and turn on the Sound Check box. Then, on the iPod, choose Settings→Sound Check, and press the Select button to change the setting from Off to On.

The next time you sync up iPod with the computer, the Sound Check adjustments you made in iTunes get passed along to the player.

If you don't like the Sound Check effect, turn it off *in both places.*

Contrast

You can alter the relative blackness of the text on the iPod screen by pressing the Contrast setting and adjusting the screen with the scroll wheel. (Temperature—either of the iPod or the air around it—can nudge the contrast out of whack, which is why you may sometimes need to adjust it.)

Clicker

Usually, each time you click an iPod button or turn its dial, you hear a little clicking sound from the iPod's built-in speaker. If you prefer to scroll in silence, simply turn the Clicker sound off here.

Some people might think the Clicker noise sounds like ants tap dancing, but others like the audio cue—especially on touchwheel iPods that don't otherwise give much in the way of feedback while you're scrolling.

Date & Time

If you've just flown in from the coast and need to adjust your iPod's clock, you can change the player's date, time, and time zone settings here. These settings are especially important if the iPod needs to be punctual, like when you intend to use the Alarm Clock.

Tip: If you're syncing your iPod to a Mac running Mac OS X 10.2 or later, don't bother setting your date and time on the iPod. The computer does it for you.

To manually set the clock from the Date & Time settings area:

1. **From the main menu, choose Settings→Date & Time.**

   You're going to set the time zone first. Setting the time zone is sort of a moot point if you never go far enough to change time zones. But if you travel a lot and want to change the iPod's clock with a minimum of fuss, this setting saves you from resetting the time when you land in New York after flying in from Los Angeles.

2. **Scroll to and select Set Time Zone. Pick your time zone (or a city in your time zone) from the list. Press the Select button when you're done.**

   You may notice that the iPod's list doesn't match the list of time zones found in a world atlas. Although the standard U.S. time zones are represented (with a Daylight Savings Time option for each), foreign time zones are represented by a list of major cities in each. The list isn't in alphabetical order, but starts at the International Date Line and moves eastward from Eniwetok to Auckland.

3. **Back on the Date & Time settings screen, scroll to and select Set Date & Time.**

   Use the scroll wheel to adjust the highlighted hour, minute, day, month, and year. You can also choose to have the iPod display the time in the standard 12-hour clock with AM and PM designations, or 24-hour clock used by the military and on *M*A*S*H* reruns. Use the Next and Previous buttons on the iPod to skip over fields you don't need to change.

4. **Press the Select button for each part of today's date as you scroll to it, until everything is set.**

   Press the Menu button a couple of times to return to the main menu.

Contacts

This setting lets you change the sorting order of the first and last names of people in your iPod's built-in address book (Chapter 7). See page 181 for full details.

Language

The iPod is the United Nations of digital audio players, in that it can display its menus in most major European and Asian languages.

To set the language for the iPod's menus, choose Settings→Languages from the main iPod menu. Scroll down the list of languages and press the Select button when you find your native tongue (or the one you want to use if you're practicing vocabulary for Swedish class).

The iPod's menus now appear in the new language. To change back, return to the Language settings and scroll to a new language.

Tip: See Chapter 15 if you accidentally change your display language to Korean and can't figure out how to change it back again.

Legal

The Legal menu contains a long scroll of copyright notices for Apple and its software partners. It's not very interesting reading.

Reset All Settings

This command takes all your iPod's customized sound and display settings back to their original factory settings. This feature doesn't erase your music or contacts—just customized tweakings of things like the Shuffle function and Backlight Timer.

To return your iPod to its untweaked state, choose Settings→Reset All Settings. Then scroll to Reset and press the Select button. (There's a Cancel option if you decide to bail out.)

Note: Reset All Settings affects the software only. It's not the same thing as resetting the iPod itself (the hardware). Resetting the iPod involves pushing buttons to reboot the player when the iPod freezes or won't wake up from sleep mode. See page 268 to learn the procedure.

Backlight

The Backlight menu provides a quick and easy path to enlightenment on the main iPod screen: Just highlight this command and press Select to turn the light on or off.

Tip: You can also turn on the backlight by holding down the Menu button for a few seconds, no matter what screen you're looking at.

Figure 1-15:
Now Playing is a little display of the current song, album, and performer. It starts out with a scroll bar "map" that shows how far you are into the song, and how much song is left to play. But each time you press the Select button, the bottom display changes: from a static map of your progress, to a movable "scrubber" indicator, to a screen where you can adjust the rating for the current song (by turning the scroll dial—2003-and-later models only).

When the backlight is activated on a 2003 iPod, the control buttons light up in a glowing red that nicely complements the bright white backlight.

Now Playing

Highlight this command and press Select to call up the main Now Playing screen, shown in Figure 1-15.

The iPod
Sync Connection

S leek and smart as the iPod may be, it can't do much by itself until it meets up
with a computer. Once connected to a Mac or PC, however, the iPod is ready
to accept whatever you want to give it—your whole music library, of course,
but also everything from the complete recorded works of Tom Petty to your phone
book, from news and calendar information to files too big to fit on a burned CD.

This chapter is dedicated to that concept of iPod as Satellite to Your Computer. It
explains FireWire and USB 2.0, and how to use these connections to get songs and
files off the mother ship and onto the ultraportable, ready-to-go iPod.

FireWire

Apart from boosting magazine sales, there's never been much value in sitting in
front of the computer, waiting for large files to copy onto external drives and other
add-ons. In the eternal search for faster data-transfer speeds, Apple developed a new
high-speed cable called FireWire in the mid-1990s. It's easy to use, it's *hot-swappable*
(you don't have to turn off anything before plugging or unplugging the cable), and—
unlike SCSI cables, which came before it—it doesn't force you to go through
configuration acrobatics to get multiple devices to all work properly.

Dozens of other companies, including Windows PC makers, eventually picked up
FireWire. Some gave it other names along the way: IEEE 1394 (its official moniker
from the Institute of Electrical and Electronics Engineers, an industry standards
group) and i.LINK, used primarily by Sony. But whatever the name, it's still the
same speedy connection underneath.

With its ability to move 400 megabits of data per second, FireWire was quickly adopted by a product that needs to get an enormous amount of information from Point A to Point B: the digital camcorder. Other hardware with a need for speed, like external CD burners and hard drives, followed the path to FireWire connectivity.

FireWire's speed makes possible one of the iPod's best tricks: slurping in an entire CD's worth of music from your computer in ten seconds. It's also how the iPod gets its battery charge. That's great if you have a Macintosh, because every Macintosh made since about 1998 has a FireWire connector built right in (see Figure 2-1).

Figure 2-1:
Left: The FireWire icon on cables and ports signals that the computer is equipped with the high-speed standard.

Right: The connectors are wider and less rectangular than those of a USB cable.

If you're a Windows PC fan, however, FireWire isn't such a sure thing. If you bought an iPod and then found out to your horror that your computer doesn't *have* a FireWire port, you have two alternatives.

First, you can add a FireWire card to your computer, as described later in this chapter.

Second, if you have a 2003 (or later) iPod model, you can connect your iPod via a USB cable—a far more common PC connector. See page 40 for details.

Connecting Your iPod by FireWire

If you have a Mac, connecting the iPod is simple: Just plug in the FireWire cable.

If you have a PC, things are slightly more complicated, because there are so many different kinds of connectors your PC might have. For example:

- **FireWire connector, 6-pin.** If the white FireWire cable that came with your full-size iPod fits a socket on your PC's FireWire card, great! Connect the far end to the iPod, and you're ready to rock. (As a bonus, your iPod may even get its power charge from the same cable, depending on which brand of FireWire card you have.)

- **FireWire connector, 4-pin.** The FireWire cable that comes with the full-size iPod has a fattish 6-pin connector at one end. It doesn't fit the smaller 4-pin connectors common on Windows FireWire cards.

Fortunately, you also got a small white 4-pin adapter in the box. It fits over the *end* of the included 6-pin cable (see Figure 2-2). Just snap the adapter onto one end of the cable and plug it into the PC's port. Then plug the other end into the iPod (or its dock, if you have one).

The iPod Mini's FireWire cable has only a 6-pin connector, and it doesn't come with the adapter. You can buy one from a computer store—or you can just use USB 2.0 instead.

Note: Don't forget to connect the AC adapter. You can't charge an iPod from a 4-pin connector.

Figure 2-2:
The FireWire cable adapter included with full-size iPods snaps over the end of the standard 6-pin FireWire cable. The smaller 4-pin end then plugs into the PC. Sony Vaio laptops are among the computers that need the 4-pin adapter. The iPod Mini doesn't include the cable adapter, but you get your choice of a whole 6-pin FireWire cable or a USB 2.0 cable to use instead.

Installing a FireWire Card

Most computer stores, both retail and online, sell FireWire/1394 expansion cards (Figure 2-3); they're available for both desktop and laptop computers. FireWire cards designed for desktop machines fit into one of the computer's spare PCI slots on the motherboard, making the new FireWire ports available on the back of the case along with all the other port connectors.

There are expansion cards for FireWire, USB 2.0, and even combo cards that let you add ports for FireWire *and* USB 2.0 if you really want to go whole-hog toward faster data-transfer speeds. A basic FireWire card generally sells for less than $60, a relatively small price to pay to give your computer the gift of FireWire.

FireWire cards for laptops, which are generally more expensive than the PCI cards, snap into the CardBus slot on the laptop. (CardBus is a ramped-up version of the PC cards used with laptops.) Most laptops manufactured after 1999 can handle CardBus cards, in either FireWire or USB 2.0 flavors.

Before you buy a FireWire card, make sure it's compatible with your operating system and hardware configuration. If you're pressed for time, you can go straight to proven, Apple-approved goods by buying a Belkin PCI expansion card and a PC-ready CardBus FireWire 400 card from the Apple Web site.

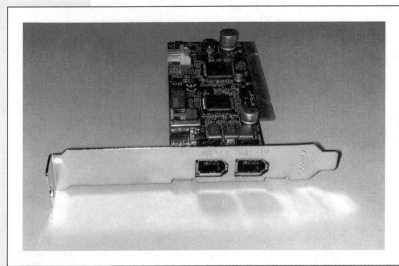

Figure 2-3:
FireWire cards come in all shapes and sizes and can add two, three, or four FireWire ports to a computer. The cards snap into an empty PCI slot on the computer's motherboard. Adding a FireWire card will allow you to use FireWire-enabled devices like digital camcorders, CD burners, and iPods.

Installing the Card

Your package will have instructions on how to install the FireWire card, but the general process is straightforward.

- First, turn off the computer and unplug it. Depending on the design of your computer, you may need to unplug all of the cables and cords coming out of the back in order to get to get the outer case off. You may also need a screwdriver.

- Static electricity is the enemy of an exposed circuit board, so discharge any built-up electricity in your body before poking around the PC. Touching the metal power supply (a big silver box inside the computer) or any metal on the back of the computer should release any pent-up static.

- Remove your new FireWire card from the antistatic bag it came in. Hold the card by the edges, making sure not to get your fingers on the metal connectors that go into the computer slot.

- Locate an empty PCI slot on the computer's motherboard. The PCI slots are usually in the back, rimmed with white plastic the same length as the connector strip on the bottom of the FireWire card. You may have to remove the screw that holds the card bracket to the inside of the computer's case. Remove the bracket and screw and set it aside.

- Line up the metal connectors on the bottom edge of the FireWire card over the empty PCI slot, making sure that the FireWire ports are facing the back of the computer. Press down firmly and evenly on both ends of the card, pushing it into the slot until the card is securely seated, as shown in Figure 2-4.

- Replace the screw you removed earlier, affixing the card in place inside the case. Replace the computer's outer case, reattach the cables and cords, and turn on the machine.

Figure 2-4:
Top: Remove any metal brackets shielding the back of the computer and gently push the FireWire card into the white plastic PCI slot on the computer's motherboard until it clicks onto place.

Bottom: After installation, the exposed FireWire ports are available alongside the rest of your PC's ports.

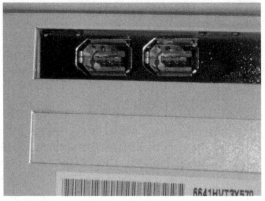

Nudging Windows

Once you've taken the trouble get a FireWire card (and its software) into your PC, you may need to take an extra step to make sure that Windows knows it's there.

- **Windows 2000 and XP.** Right-click My Computer; from the shortcut menu, choose Properties. In the System Properties box that results, click the Hardware tab, and then the Device Manager.

  After the Device manager window opens, look down the list of devices and double-click "IEEE 1394 Bus Host Controllers." If the card is installed correctly, you should see its name in the window. To further examine the card, click the General tab. In the Device Status field, you see a message saying that "This device is working properly."

- **Windows Me (for use with MusicMatch Jukebox only).** Right-click My Computer; from the shortcut menu, choose Properties. In the System Properties box, click the Device Manager tab and then the OK button. Look for "1394 Bus Controller" and double-click it.

  Click Host Controller, then click Properties to get the Host Controller window. You can see the status of the new FireWire card in the Device Status field. If everything is as it should be, you see the words, "This device is working properly."

  If you don't see this message of acceptance from Windows, check to make sure the FireWire card is firmly seated in its PCI slot inside the computer and that you've installed any software drivers that came with the card.

USB 2.0

These days, you don't have to use FireWire as the iPod-to-computer connection. If you own a 2003 or later iPod model, another option awaits you: USB 2.0.

Note: If you have a Windows PC, you can use a USB 2.0 cable for *any* 2003-or-later iPod, including the iPod Mini.

But if you have a Macintosh with USB 2 jacks, you can connect *only* the iPod Mini. Full-size iPod models require a FireWire connection to the Mac.

About USB 2.0

Before USB 2.0 hit the streets, a FireWire connection was the fastest way to transfer big chunks of data onto a computer from devices like digital camcorders, external hard drives, and CD burners. FireWire, which transfers data at 400 megabits per second, whips the plastic off a USB 1.1 connection (about 12 megabits per second).

When USB 2.0 products began to crowd store shelves around 2002, FireWire was left in the dust, speed-wise. USB 2.0 (also known as Hi-Speed USB) can whisk data from device to device at 480 megabits per second. USB 2.0 is also backwards compatible, so people with a box full of USB 1.1 mice, scanners, and other peripherals can still plug in and use their old devices in USB 2.0 ports, even if they don't get the 2.0 speed boost.

Note: Those are mega*bits,* not megabytes. Data transfer speeds are traditionally measured in *megabits* or *kilobits per second*; disk and file sizes are measured in *megabytes* (MB).

There are eight bits in a byte. To put USB and FireWire into more familiar terms, then, USB can transfer files at up to 1.5 MB per second. FireWire can move 50 MB of data per second, and USB 2.0 can shuttle to 60 MB per second.

(FireWire isn't standing still, of course; there's now FireWire 800, which, as you can probably guess, moves data at 800 megabits per second. To add to the confusion, the original FireWire standard is now sometimes called FireWire 400. FireWire 800 is available on high-end Macintosh computers and peripherals, but has not yet made the leap to the iPod.)

Connecting with USB 2.0

If you've got a PC with an USB 2 port, you can skip FireWire altogether. You can sync the iPod with USB 2 instead—if you have what it takes:

- **The proper iPod.** USB 2 requires a 2003-and-later iPod model, including the iPod Mini.

- **The proper operating system.** You need Windows Me, 2000, or XP. Macs with USB 2.0 connectors work, too, but sync only with the iPod Mini.

- **iPod Software version 2.0.1 or later.** To find out what version you have, use the Settings→About command on your iPod. If you don't have the latest, download it from *www.apple.com/ipod/download.* (To learn how to update your iPod software, see page 296.)

- **The proper cable.** If you have a full-size iPod, buy Apple's $20 combo FireWire/ USB 2.0 cable from the Apple Web site or a computer store. This cable has a flat, wide iPod Dock connector plug on one end; the forked far end has both USB 2.0 and FireWire connectors. Plug the flat end onto the iPod (or its Dock) and the USB end into the PC.

  You won't need the FireWire end of the cable until it's time to *charge* the iPod. The FireWire end snaps into the iPod's AC adapter and seeks its power from the nearest electrical outlet.

  If you have an iPod Mini, a USB 2 cable came right in the box. Connect it straight into the Mini or its dock, and plug the other end into a Mac or PC. As a bonus, this cable charges up your Mini whenever it's connected to the computer.

Tip: Technically, you can sync your iPod via regular USB, even if your PC has only regular USB (not 2.0). You can use the same Apple cable. After all, USB 2.0 and USB 1.1 are compatible and use the same connector plug.

Remember, though, that USB 1.1 is very slow compared with 2.0. You may want to plan a day's worth of activities while leaving the PC and iPod to their data-transfer duet. (A performance of Wagner's entire *Ring Cycle* or the Boston marathon should do it.)

The iPod Software CD

The CD that comes with the iPod contains all the software you need to get up and iPodding in no time (Figure 2-5). (There's only one CD in the box of the latest iPod models. The iPod CD installer program is smart enough to figure out what kind of computer you're using and show you only the Mac or Windows installer on the disc.)

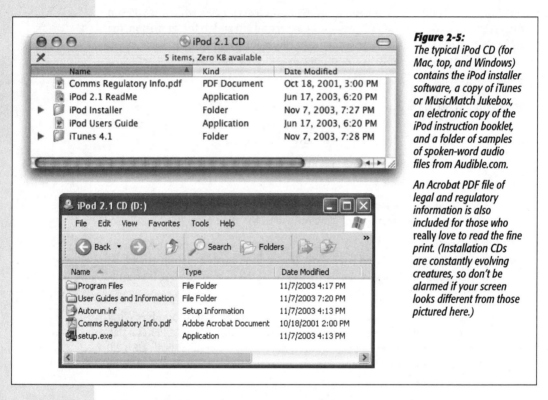

Figure 2-5:
The typical iPod CD (for Mac, top, and Windows) contains the iPod installer software, a copy of iTunes or MusicMatch Jukebox, an electronic copy of the iPod instruction booklet, and a folder of samples of spoken-word audio files from Audible.com.

An Acrobat PDF file of legal and regulatory information is also included for those who really love to read the fine print. (Installation CDs are constantly evolving creatures, so don't be alarmed if your screen looks different from those pictured here.)

The Macintosh CD

Early versions of the iPod CD included software for both Mac OS 9 and Mac OS X. But beginning with the 2003 iPods, Apple expects you to use Mac OS X 10.1.5 or later. Recent versions of the iPod CD come with iTunes 4; if that's not the version you have, download the latest version of iTunes at *www.apple.com/itunes*.

Note: If you're a stalwart Mac OS 9 fan, there's still hope. Some people have reported being able to get a new iPod to work with iTunes 2 and the latest version of Mac OS 9, although sometimes erratically. A few folks have come up with detailed workarounds (like those described at *www.phaster.com/ipod_hacks*), but they're not for the technically faint of heart. If you want to use a new iPod in all its glory—with the iTunes Music Store, iSync, and other goodies described in this book—it's best to do it with the operating system Apple recommends.

To install the software, insert the iPod CD into the Mac. If necessary, install the iTunes jukebox software from the CD or download the latest version from Apple's Web site.

The iPod has an operating system of its own, too (see page 246), but you don't need to install it; it's already on your iPod. However, double-clicking the installer in the iPod Installer folder puts a copy of the iPod installer program on your Mac, so you'll have it handy if you ever need to reinstall the iPod's system software.

Along the way, you'll be asked for your iPod's serial number and your registration number.

When the software installer finishes, put the CD in a safe place. You'll need it if you ever need to reinstall your programs after a hard drive crash.

The first time you connect the iPod to the Mac, iTunes starts right up to greet it.

The Windows CD

If you have a PC, the software installer starts automatically when you insert the CD. (If you or someone you love has turned off the CD auto-start feature on your PC, open My Computer, and then open the icon for the CD-ROM drive. Locate and double-click the Setup.exe program on the disc; you can see this icon in Figure 2-5 at the bottom. Finally, click the Install button to kick-start the installation process.)

The installer gives you all the necessary iPod drivers, plus a handsome piece of jukebox software to organize your music and download it to the iPod:

- **iTunes for Windows.** This free software is arguably the best jukebox software available for Windows. It gives you access to Apple's online $1-a-song music store (Chapter 6) and does a beautiful job of organizing, searching, and playing your tunes (Chapter 4).

  There are only two reasons why you wouldn't want to install iTunes. First, it requires Windows 2000 or XP, and you might have something earlier. Second, you might already be using MusicMatch Jukebox—and love it.

  Fortunately, iTunes isn't your only option.

- **MusicMatch Jukebox Plus.** If you're using an earlier version of Windows, or you're already using MusicMatch and you're perfectly happy there (and don't intend to use the iTunes Music Store), you're in luck. MusicMatch can also talk to, and work with, the iPod—and it, too, is free. Chapter 5 shows you how to use it.

Tip: If your CD came with only MusicMatch Jukebox and you'd *prefer* iTunes, go to *www.apple.com/ itunes* and grab yourself a copy of the latest version for Windows.

When you install MusicMatch, you have to type in the serial number from the sleeve of your iPod's CD (if, indeed, your CD came with MusicMatch Jukebox; the latest iPod CD doesn't). It's responsible for turning the free version of the software to the full version called MusicMatch Jukebox Plus, which includes a speed bump of 25 percent when ripping CD tracks to MP3 format and other goodies for working with CDs.

Tip: If MusicMatch asks whether you want to check its Web site for an updated version, decline the favor. Newer versions may not work with the iPod unless you do some plug-in tinkering; check with the Apple or MusicMatch Web site before proceeding. When in doubt, stick with the version that came on your iPod CD, which is specifically designed to work with Windows-based iPods. Version Hell details on page 116.

By the way, you should note that the iPod can sync with only one program. You must commit to *either* iTunes *or* MusicMatch Jukebox—the sooner the better. If you download and install iTunes after you install MusicMatch Jukebox, the iPod will automatically switch to iTunes with the next sync, and the songs you import from then on will go into the iTunes Music folder.

If you decide that you really liked MusicMatch Jukebox better, you'll have to uninstall iTunes and reinstall the MusicMatch software. See page 116 for details on *that* afternoon of fun.

A Windows Note for Current iPod Models

Back in the Olde Days of the iPod (2002), Macintosh and Windows iPods were pre-formatted at the factory and sold separately as Macintosh iPods or Windows iPods.

Figure 2-6:
It's not quite as dramatic a moment as watching a butterfly emerge, but the transformation of a brand-new iPod into a Windows iPod is beautiful in its own right.

Top: The installer asks whether you want to "configure" the iPod—that is, reformat it with the Windows FAT32 disk-formatting scheme.

Bottom: The iPod set-up process offers you the chance to install iTunes on the PC.

Although you might never suspect it, however, *all* 2003 and later iPods come out of their boxes formatted for *Macintosh*. When you run the setup program on a Windows PC, behind the scenes, it actually reformats your iPod's hard drive for Windows. See Figure 2-6 for details.

Your Very First Sync

For most people, the goal with any new electronics purchase is to get the new toy working right away so the fun can begin. For new iPod owners, getting to The Fun can be a very short wait. After unpacking the iPod and all its accessories, charging it up as described in Chapter 1, and installing the software, you're ready to dive in.

The First Sync (If You Use iTunes)

You may already have Apple's free iTunes program and plenty of songs stored in its music library. If so, the first synchronization between iPod and computer can be astoundingly simple. As soon as you connect the new iPod to the Mac or PC, iTunes opens automatically and begins copying your entire music library to the player (see Figure 2-7).

Tip: If you *don't* want iTunes to appear automatically every time the iPod is connected, you can turn off this option in the iPod Preferences dialog box (Figure 2-9).

Figure 2-7:
The Source list (left side) displays an icon for the iPod whenever it's connected, as well as your music library, list of playlists, songs from the iTunes Music Store, and Internet radio stations. The bottom of the window shows the amount of space left on the iPod, the number of songs, and consecutive days the iPod can play music without repeating songs.

If you don't have iTunes or any MP3 files on your hard drive already, you'll have to install iTunes and snag some music files from your music CDs (Chapter 4) or download some songs from the Web (Chapter 3). Once you have a library of music built up that you'd like to transfer to the iPod, just plug it in, let iTunes open, and watch the two machines talk music together.

The First Sync (If You Use MusicMatch)

Once all the necessary software is installed, connect the iPod to the PC as described earlier in this chapter.

The Portables Plus window

When you plug in your iPod for the first time, MusicMatch Jukebox opens automatically. In a few seconds, another window pops up next to the Library window: the Portables Plus window (Figure 2-8).

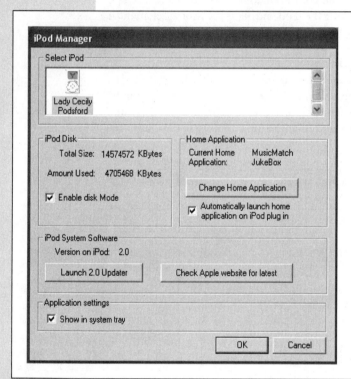

Figure 2-8:
When the MusicMatch Jukebox installation is complete, you'll find a new icon in your Windows system tray (notification area) that opens the iPod Manager program shown here. It lets you adjust some of the Pod's settings—like whether or not it acts as an external hard drive for your PC ("Enable disk Mode") without your having to open MusicMatch Jukebox Plus.

The Portables Plus window (called the Portable Device Manager in the MusicMatch online help) is your portal to managing music on the iPod. If your iPod appears in the list, under the heading Attached Portable Devices, in the left pane of the box, then you know MusicMatch Jukebox has recognized it and is ready to shovel some symphonies the iPod's way.

In any case, if all is well, MusicMatch automatically transfers all of the songs in the PC's music library to the iPod. A status bar in the MusicMatch window keeps you abreast of the transfer situation.

Variations on the Auto-Transfer Theme

The beauty of the iTunes/iPod system is that whatever music you add to your Mac or PC gets added to the iPod automatically, effortlessly, quickly. You've always got your entire music collection with you. Just plugging in the iPod inspires iTunes (or MusicMatch) to open up and begin syncing.

It's conceivable, however, that you won't always want complete and automatic syncing to take place whenever you connect the 'Pod. Maybe you use the iPod primarily as an external hard drive (Chapter 11), so you don't especially care to have iTunes jumping up like a West Highland terrier every time you plug in the iPod. Maybe you want to synchronize only *some* of your music, not all of it.

Fortunately, you're in complete control of the situation.

Stop Auto-Opening iTunes (or MusicMatch)

If you like, you can command your jukebox software to open only when *you* want it to, rather than every time the iPod is plugged in.

- **iTunes.** When the iPod plugged in, click its icon in the Source list. Then click the iPod-shaped icon in the bottom right part of the iTunes window (identified in Figure 2-9). The iPod's Preferences box appears, where you can turn off the "Open iTunes when attached" checkbox.

- **MusicMatch.** Look for your iPod in the Portables Plus box, right-click it, and choose Options from the shortcut menu. Click the iPod tab in the box, and turn off "Automatically launch MusicMatch Jukebox on device connection." Click OK.

Tip: With MusicMatch Jukebox and 2003-and-later iPods, you can also turn off the auto-launch in the iPod Manager box, which appears when you click the iPod icon in the Windows system tray. Turn off "Automatically launch application on iPod plug in."

Transfer Only Some Songs

The auto-sync option pretty much removes any thought process required to move music to the iPod. But if you'd rather take control of the process, or you just want to transfer *some* songs or playlists, you can change the synchronization settings.

To control how this syncing goes, proceed like this:

- **iTunes (Mac and Windows).** With the main iTunes window open, click the name of your iPod in the Source list on the left side of the window. Look at the bottom of the iPod window for the four small buttons along the right side (Figure 2-9). Click the first button, which has a small graphic of an iPod on it, to open the iPod Preferences dialog box.

- **MusicMatch Jukebox.** When MusicMatch Jukebox opens after you plug the iPod in, the Portables Plus box also opens (Figure 2-10). The iPod's name appears in the list on the left side of the window.

There are two ways to open the Options box that lets you change your syncing preferences, as shown in Figure 2-10.

Once the Options dialog box is open, click the third tab, labeled Synchronization.

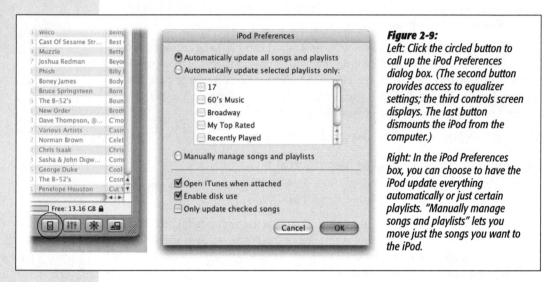

Figure 2-9:
Left: Click the circled button to call up the iPod Preferences dialog box. (The second button provides access to equalizer settings; the third controls screen displays. The last button dismounts the iPod from the computer.)

Right: In the iPod Preferences box, you can choose to have the iPod update everything automatically or just certain playlists. "Manually manage songs and playlists" lets you move just the songs you want to the iPod.

Whether you're using Mac or Windows, the dialog box before you lets you control how the autosyncing of your music library goes:

Complete automatic synchronization

The wording is a little different—"Automatically update all songs and playlists" (iTunes) or "Complete library synchronization" (MusicMatch Jukebox)—but the effect is the same. Your computer's music collection and your iPod's are kept identical, no matter what songs you add or remove from the computer.

If you have a PalmPilot or PocketPC, you may be thinking to yourself: "*Ah, sweet synchronization! I won't have to worry about losing any data, because everything is updated all the time no matter where I input them!*"

There is a difference, however: Unlike a palmtop, the iPod's synchronization with the computer is a one-way street. If a song isn't in iTunes or MusicMatch, it won't be on your iPod. Delete a song from iTunes or MusicMatch Jukebox, and it disappears from the iPod the next time you sync up.

Tip: One exception to that last remark: MusicMatch Jukebox offers an autosync option that never whacks tracks on the iPod, even if you've deleted them from the PC. It's the Ignore Content Deletions checkbox shown in Figure 2-10.

This, of course, is the iPod's system for preventing music piracy. If song copying were a two-way street, people could wander around with their iPods, collecting songs from any computers they came across, and then copy the whole mass back up to their home computers.

On the bright side, the autosync system means that you never worry about which songs are where. With the autosync option, what is in the computer's music library is on the iPod, and that's that.

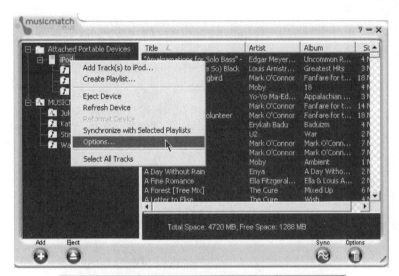

Figure 2-10:
Scenes from Music-Match.

Top: When the iPod is connected and the Portables Plus window is before you, there are two ways to open the Options dialog box. One way is to click the Options button in the lower-right corner. The other is to right-click the iPod icon at the left, and choose Options from the shortcut menu, as shown here.

Bottom: The Synchronization tab lets you change the way your iPod syncs its library to the PC. Turning off "Automatically synchronize on device connections" stops the computer from trying to download the entire music library to the iPod. You can also sync up only the selected playlists. The "Ignore all content deletions" option stops MusicMatch from erasing iPod songs that aren't in its own library.

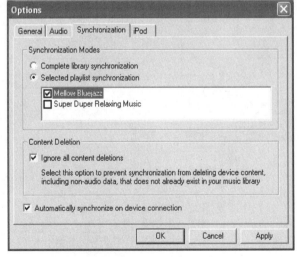

Sync up selected playlists only

Choosing to only sync up only certain playlists can save you some time, because you avoid copying the entire music library each time. This tactic is helpful when, say, you have a workout playlist that you fuss with and freshen up each week. You can choose to update only that playlist instead of waiting around for the whole iPod to sync. (This feature is also handy if you're a multi-iPod household. Each iPodder can maintain a separate playlist.)

Once you turn on "Automatically update selected playlists only" (iTunes) or "Selected playlist synchronization" (MusicMatch Jukebox), you're shown a list of the playlists you've created (see Chapters 4 and 5). Turn on the ones you want synced.

Manually manage songs and playlists

There may be times when you don't want any automatic synchronization at all. Maybe, for example, you've deleted some audio files from your hard drive that you still want to keep on your iPod. If you leave automatic syncing turned on, iTunes or MusicMatch will erase any songs from the iPod that it doesn't have itself.

- **Manual control in iTunes.** In iTunes for Mac or PC, turning on "Manually manage songs and playlists" means that no music will be auto-copied to the iPod. You'll have to do all the copying yourself.

Note: When you turn on this option, iTunes says, "Disabling automatic update requires manually unmounting the iPod before each disconnect." It's telling you that from now on, when you're finished working with the iPod, you'll have to click the Eject button in the lower-right corner of the iTunes window. This action safely releases the iPod from the computer connection.

From now on, you'll have to drag songs onto the iPod manually (Figure 2-11). After you close the iPod Preferences box, click the small triangle next to your iPod in the Source list. It reveals all the songs and playlists on the iPod, which work just like any other iTunes playlists (see Chapter 4).

Figure 2-11:
You can add songs to the iPod playlists by dragging them out of your main iTunes Library list, delete them by clicking their names and then pressing the Delete key, click the New Playlist button (the + icon) to create a fresh playlist, drag playlists onto playlists to merge them, and so on.

To delete songs off the iPod, click its icon in your iTunes Source list. Then, in the main song-list window, click the songs you don't want anymore, and then press Delete. The songs will vanish, both from the iPod's list in iTunes and from the iPod itself.

Tip: The Only Update Checked Songs option in the iPod Preferences box (Figure 2-9) can be useful in this situation. It ensures that iTunes will update the iPod only with songs whose title checkmarks you've turned on. If you have songs that aren't part of your iTunes music library, make sure they're unchecked—and therefore unerased—during an automatic synchronization.

- **Manual control in MusicMatch Jukebox.** To turn off autosync in Windows, connect your iPod. When MusicMatch Jukebox brings up the Portables Plus window, open the Options dialog box (see Figure 2-10 for instructions).

Click the Synchronization tab and turn off "Automatically synchronize device upon connection."

Once you've deactivated automatic synchronization, what's on the iPod is up to you. You can add songs to it by dragging them from the My Library window onto the iPod's track list in the Portables Plus window. Or right-click the iPod icon and choose Add Track(s) to iPod from the shortcut menu. Or click Add at the bottom of the Portables Plus window.

In any case, when you're ready to perform the synchronization that you've lined up like this, click the Sync button in the right corner.

TROUBLESHOOTING MOMENT

"Do Not Disconnect"

The universal symbol for NO!, pictured as a circle with a slash through it (∅), is a common sight when the iPod is connected to the Macintosh or PC. It appears whenever the two drives are busy exchanging music and data (and probably a little hard-disk humor on the side). If you're using the iPod as an external hard disk, or you've turned off the iPod's automatic synchronization feature, you'll see a lot of this Dr. ∅.

Breaking the connection while all this is going on can result in lost files and possibly a scrambled song. So if you need to unplug the iPod and get going for work, be sure to *unmount* it properly (remove its icon from the screen) first.

Macintosh: You can disconnect the iPod by clicking the Eject button in the iTunes window; by dragging the desktop icon of the iPod into the Mac's Trash; or by Control-clicking the iPod icon on your screen and choosing Eject from the contextual menu.

Windows: With the iPod selected in the iTunes Source list, click the Eject button in the lower right corner of the window to safely unmount the iPod. In MusicMatch Jukebox, click Eject in the lower-left corner of the Portables Plus window (Figure 2-9).

When you've ejected the iPod correctly, its screen flashes a large happy check mark (older iPods) or pulls up the standard main menu, ready for action (2003 and later models).

CHAPTER 2: THE IPOD SYNC CONNECTION 51

Tip: You can send a freshly created playlist and its accompanying songs right to the iPod by clicking Send in the MusicMatch Jukebox Plus Playlist window.

To delete songs or playlists from the iPod, right-click the item and choose Remove from the shortcut menu, or click the unwanted material and then click Remove in the Portables Plus window. (Deleting a playlist doesn't remove its songs from your iPod.)

Tip: You can change your iPod's name to something more exotic or memorable than just "iPod" or "[Your name]'s iPod" in a couple of different places. In iTunes, click its icon in the Source list once to highlight it, pause, and click again to open the renaming box. Type away.

In MusicMatch Jukebox, in the iPod Options box (Figure 2-10), click the iPod tab and type in a new handle in the box marked Device Name.

The Unspeakable Act: iPod-to-Computer Copying

The iPod was designed to be the destination of a one-way trip for your tunes: music slides down the cable *to* the iPod, but songs on the player never make the trip back to the Mac or PC.

This design was perfectly intentional on the part of its creators. As noted earlier, Apple's position appears on a sticker on every iPod: "Don't steal music." If the iPod let you copy music both ways, people might be tempted to turn the device into a pocket music-sharing service, capable of copying free copyrighted songs from computer to computer.

The truth is, though, that not everyone who wants to upload songs from the iPod to a computer is stealing music. You may perfectly have legitimate reasons for wanting to be able to do so.

For example, say your computer's hard drive self-destructs, vaporizing the 945 MP3 files that you've made from your paid-for CD collection. You legally own those copies. Shouldn't you have the right to retrieve them from your own iPod?

Most people would answer "yes." Some might even thump their fists on the table for emphasis.

And then they would clear their throats and ask, "Well, how can I do it, should I ever need to copy files off my iPod?"

Note: Once again, the following methods are printed here not to encourage you to steal music, but instead to help you back up and manage the songs that you already own.

The Hidden World of the iPod

Turning the iPod into a FireWire hard drive (Chapter 11) lets you copy everyday computer files back and forth from your Mac or PC. But when it comes to your *music* files, you won't even be able to *find* them. The iPod and its music management programs use a special database for storing and organizing the music files—and it's invisible.

The name of the super-secret invisible iPod music folder is called iPod_Control, and there are software utilities for both the Mac and the PC that can make it visible. Here are a few of the easiest and most reliable.

Copying Files to the Macintosh

A quick search on "iPod" on the VersionTracker.com Web site (*www.versiontracker. com*) or on any of the hardcore iPod fan sites mentioned in Chapter 16, will bring up plenty of iPod programs.

Note: On the other hand, you may find it quicker to download these programs directly from the "Missing CD" page at *www.missingmanuals.com*.

---

iPod Viewer

For beginners, the nicely designed iPod Viewer program (Figure 2-12) makes the whole copying-to-the-Mac procedure very simple. iPod Viewer 2.0 is designed for Mac OS X 10.2 (Jaguar) and later; iPod Viewer 1.5.2 is designed for Mac OS X 10.1. Both versions are available on the "Missing CD" page at *www.missingmanuals.com*.

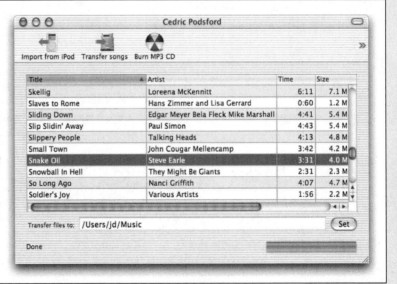

Figure 2-12:
The free iPod Viewer program lets you select all or just some of the songs you want to copy over to the Mac. The program also gives you the option of deciding what folder to put the imported songs into. Just click the Transfer Songs button at the top of the window to start copying. You can also make a CD of the imported files by clicking the Burn MP3 CD button.

Once you install iPod Viewer, open the program with your iPod attached to the Mac; click your Poddy little pal in the list. The program's preferences let you arrange your songs in the order you want. Then, when you click the Import From iPod button at the top of the iPod Viewer window (Figure 2-12), the program pulls in the list of everything on the iPod.

OmniWeb

Yes, OmniWeb is a Web browser. But in addition to surfing the Net with it, you can also surf the hidden contents of your iPod and copy songs back to your computer. The OmniWeb browser sells for $30, but you can download a trial copy from the "Missing CD" page at *www.missingmanuals.com*. (Although paying for a Web browser may seem like a bizarre idea, OmniWeb has some wonderful features like spell-checking, ad-blocking, and automatic bookmark-updating.)

To use OmniWeb to browse the iPod, drag the iPod icon off your desktop and into the browser window. (See Chapter 11 for details on making the iPod appear on your desktop.)

A list of all the files on the iPod appears, including the elusive iPod_Control folder. Double-click iPod_Control, and then the folder within it titled Music, shown in Figure 2-13. You see a list of folders, all starting with F. Within these folders lie your songs. Double-click the songs you want to copy to the Mac; OmniWeb does the rest.

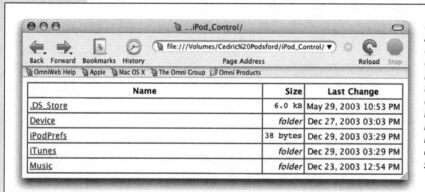

Figure 2-13:
After you drag the desktop iPod icon onto the OmniWeb browser window, the program clearly displays the secret iPod_Control folder. Inside iPod_Control is the Music folder and the iPod's secret stash of songs.

TinkerTool

You know how in those Invisible Man movies, people could only see him if he had a hat or a coat or a mask on, or spilled something on his invisible self? It was all about revealing the hidden aspects.

You can do the same thing with your invisible iPod files with the aid of some helpful freeware by way of Germany. TinkerTool, available on the "Missing CD" page at *www.missingmanuals.com,* is a system utility for Mac OS X that can make hidden files visible.

Once you have installed TinkerTool on your Mac, you'll see an icon for it in System Preferences. Click TinkerTool; in the box that pops up, turn on "Show hidden and system files," and then click the Relaunch Finder button. Figure 2-14 shows the way.

When the Finder restarts, you see all the formerly secret invisible system files right there on your screen, as though someone had spilled paint on the Invisible Man. You see a lot of .DS_Stores all over the place, but step over them and connect your iPod to the Mac. (Make sure you've turned on its FireWire disk feature as described in Chapter 11.)

Double-click the iPod's icon to see all the files that live on it, including the iPod_Control folder that holds all of your music files (Figure 2-14, bottom). You can click through the folders from iPod_Control→Music→F00 (all the iPod's music folders are named F-something) and drag the files you wish to copy to your Mac's own hard drive.

Figure 2-14:
Top: Turn on the box in the Finder options to show hidden and system files in the TinkerTool Finder preferences box, and you'll see a lot more on your iPod after you relaunch the Finder.

Bottom: With the hidden files out in the open courtesy of TinkerTool, you can browse the iPod's contents like any other hard drive.

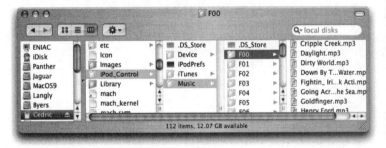

iPod.iTunes

Built for speed, iPod.iTunes keeps the Mac and iPod constantly in sync with each other, and only copies songs *not* found in the iTunes library. In case of a disastrous hard drive crash on the Mac side, iPod.iTunes can fully restore music files and playlists in the iPod, and can even fix those accidents where you mistakenly delete music from iTunes.

The program also makes it possible to *clone* an iPod, making an exact duplicate of its contents, and can synchronize music and playlists together or separately. Once installed, iPod.iTunes walks you through its synchronization procedure in great detail. iPod.iTunes is yet another program available from the "Missing CD" page at *www.missingmanuals.com.*

iPod Free File Sync

Christian Vick, who crafted the iPod.iTunes shareware mentioned above, also has a similar file-copying utility that works on Mac OS 9. It's called iPod Free File Sync, and it's downloadable from *www.missingmanuals.com.* The program works with iTunes 2.

PodWorks

Combining a nice interface with plenty of iTunes-like organizational abilities, PodWorks lets you sort, search, and hear previews of the songs you want to copy back over to your Mac. The program, seen in Figure 2-15, can also copy playlists and On-The-Go playlists. PodWorks costs a mere $8, but you can sample a limited trial version to get a feel for it.

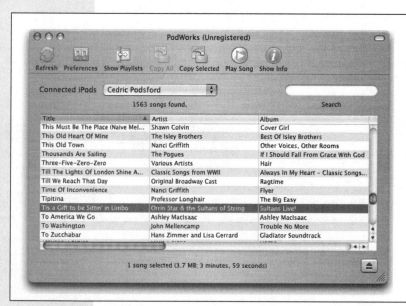

Figure 2-15:
Select all of your songs—or just one—from the iPod's database and click the Copy button to restore the music to your library. A trial version of PodWorks is available (with limited features) so you can sample the 'ware.

iPodRip

Whether it be an operating system upgrade that inadvertently trashes your hard drive and takes your tunes with it or some other hardware calamity, iPodRip can restore both your music and your sanity. The software can excavate your playlists and other supported audio files from the iPod's hard drive and copy them safely back to your Mac OS X 1.2 or 10.3 system. It can even rescue voice memos you've recorded with your iTalk or Belkin Voice Recorder microphone (page 260). The program, shown in Figure 2-16, has a free trial version, but only costs $9 to buy—a small price to pay if you're facing the prospect of re-ripping 500 CDs to restore your music collection.

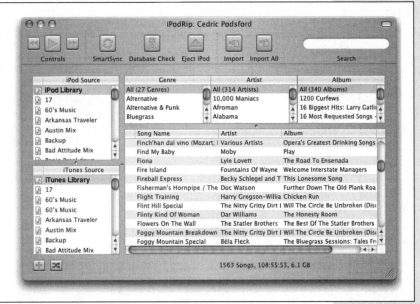

Figure 2-16:
iPodRip offers a rather comforting—and familiar—interface. In the program's preferences, you can choose to import your songs and playlists into iTunes, onto your desktop, or to the disk or folder icon of your choice. It, too, is available from the "Missing CD" page at www.missingmanuals.com.

Copying Files to Windows

Getting songs from the iPod is also possible in Windows. You may not even need to download extra freeware or shareware.

Note: When a free or shareware program is mentioned on these pages, however, you can download it from the "Missing CD" page at *www.missingmanuals.com*.

The free way

Connect the iPod to the PC, and then proceed like this.

1. **Open My Computer.**

   You can do this from an icon on your desktop or your Start menu.

2. **On the list of drives connected to the computer, double-click the iPod.**

   Its icon appears in the list as long as you've turned on the FireWire disk option described on page 213.

3. **Choose Tools→Folder Options.**

   The Folder Options dialog box pops up.

4. **Click the View tab; turn on "Show hidden files and folders." Click Apply.**

   As though by magic, the iPod_Control folder reveals itself, as shown in Figure 2-17 at top.

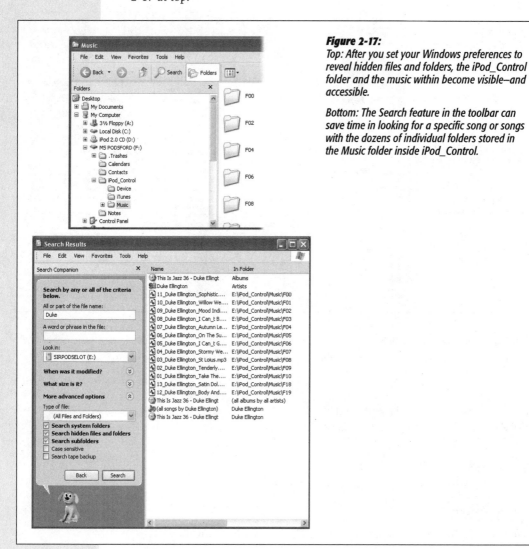

Figure 2-17:
Top: After you set your Windows preferences to reveal hidden files and folders, the iPod_Control folder and the music within become visible—and accessible.

Bottom: The Search feature in the toolbar can save time in looking for a specific song or songs with the dozens of individual folders stored in the Music folder inside iPod_Control.

5. **Open the iPod_Control folder, and then open the folder within labeled Music.**

You see a series of folders with names that only a computer could love, like F07, F08, and so on. If your old hard drive died and took all of your MP3 files with it, copy all the folders over to the PC's new hard drive. Songs can be jumbled and randomly scattered about, so if you just want to retrieve certain songs, click the toolbar's Search button and type in the specific song titles you're looking for (Figure 2-17, bottom).

6. **Drag the songs you want over to the hard drive icon.**

EphPod

Until Apple released Windows-compatible versions of the iPod, the EphPod program was one of the few options PC fans had for using the original Mac-only iPods. Even with the arrival of Windows-blessed iPods, the free EphPod continues to be a superior and beloved Windows utility for managing the iPod.

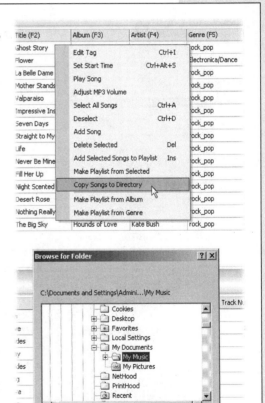

Figure 2-18:
Top: In the Songs area of the EphPod window, right-click the songs you'd like to copy. Then, from the shortcut menu, choose Copy Songs to Directory. The program copies the songs into the PC folder of your choosing.

Bottom: Once you've picked your songs, EphPod copies them to wherever you specify.

Tip: At *www.ephpod.com*, you can even find a thorough description for making the iPod work with Linux systems.

Once you launch EphPod and acquaint it with the iPod connected to your PC, it can show you the songs stored on your iPod. To copy them to your PC, see Figure 2-18.

XPlay

XPlay was one of the first commercial programs to let Windows fans use the original Mac-based iPods. The program's sales suffered once Apple released the Windows-compatible iPods in 2002, but it still offers plenty of management features that can ease the process of using the iPod with Mac or Windows, like drag-and-drop updates for music and Outlook contacts.

You can download the full program for $30 at *www.mediafour.com/products/xplay*. A free trial version is available, too. See Figure 2-19 for instructions.

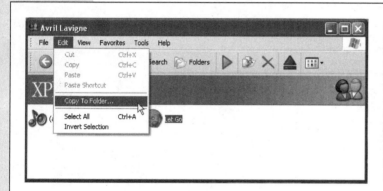

Figure 2-19:
In this exciting XPlay action shot, Avril Lavigne's Let Go *album is on the cusp of getting copied to the computer. If, say, you just want a few songs off an album, double-click it to reveal the songs inside. XPlay can also play the iPod's songs through Windows Media Player, WinAmp, or another program that you prefer instead of MusicMatch Jukebox.*

PodUtil

PodUtil is one of those rare freeware creatures that comes in versions for Mac OS 9, OS X, and Windows 2000 and XP. No matter what version you use, once PodUtil scans your iPod's hard drive, it presents you with a list of songs that you can then copy to your computer.

Anapod Explorer

If you've ever wished you could browse through the files on your Windows iPod as easily as you browse through the files on your PC, take a look at Anapod Explorer from Red Chair Software. This $25 program can serve as a substitute for iTunes as well as get under the iPod's hood and push your music and data files around, even copying them back to the PC.

As shown in Figure 2-20, Anapod Explorer lets you access your iPod's contents from any Web browser and play its music via any MP3 program of your choice. You can even edit song tags right on the iPod. For people who get giddy at the thought of databases, the program has an embedded database engine (AnapodSQL) so you can search the iPod using almost any criteria you can imagine and (*gasp!*) even generate reports in HTML or XML. A limited trial version is available to try before you buy.

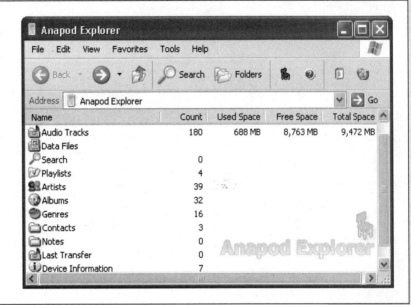

Figure 2-20
Copying files back to the computer is only the tip of the iceberg with Anapod Explorer. It lets you see deep into the heart of your music player, much like you root around in your PC using Windows Explorer. Anapod Explorer works with all versions of the iPod, and Windows Me and later operating systems.

Part Two:
iPod: The Software

Chapter 3: Digital Music Formats

Chapter 4: iTunes for Macintosh and Windows

Chapter 5: MusicMatch Jukebox for Windows

Chapter 6: The iTunes Music Store

2

Digital Audio Formats

Recorded music has appeared in a variety of shapes and sizes over the decades, including fragile discs spinning at 78 rpm, vinyl records in colorful sleeves that were artworks in themselves, pocket-size cassette tapes, and futuristic-looking compact discs. But no music format ever exploded into the public consciousness as quickly and widely as the bits of computer code known as *MP3 files.*

The MP3 format makes it possible to compress a song into a file small enough to be uploaded, downloaded, emailed, and stored on a hard drive. That feat of smallness set off a sonic boom in the late 1990s that continues to reverberate across the music world today.

This chapter tells all about MP3 and other music formats, including the latest iPod-approved format: AAC (Advanced Audio Coding), a copy-protected file type that makes Apple's iTunes Music Store possible.

Introduction to Digital Audio

The era of modern digital audio began in the early 1980s. A new, small, shiny format called the audio compact disc, developed by Sony and Philips, began to appear in music stores alongside albums on tapes and vinyl records. Unlike *analog* tapes and LPs, audio CDs stored music in *digital* form, and produced a bright, clean sound with pristine clarity. (Some audiophiles still prefer the "warmer" sound of vinyl, not to mention the expansive canvas that records provided for detailed album artwork, but many have accepted the CD.)

1985 was a pivotal year for the CD. The format's popularity got a huge boost from its first big seller, *Brothers in Arms* by Dire Straits, and a variation on the audio CD technology called CD-ROM (Compact Disc, Read-Only Memory) edged into the computer market as a way to play multimedia files and interactive programs.

When CD Met PC

Over the years, a CD drive became a standard component of a computer. On most audio CDs, songs are stored in a format called CD-DA (Compact Disc, Digital Audio), which is essentially the same thing as AIFF format.

On a Windows PC, if you inspect the contents of a music CD, you see a screen full of names like "Track01.cda." These turn out to be nothing but 1 KB files that point to the hidden audio tracks, as shown in Figure 3-1. Mac OS X displays the audio tracks in all their hefty glory as AIFF files, right in the Finder window.

Even if you can't see the audio files, you can still *extract* them from the CD with software. "Extracting audio tracks" may sound like an uncomfortable medical procedure, but it means copying them from the CD to your hard drive in a computer-readable format. You may also hear the term *ripping* CDs, which is the same thing.

And while you're digesting new-millennium terminology: Once the music files are on your Mac or PC, you *encode* them into a compressed audio format like MP3 or AAC, so that more music fits on a CD that you burn—or on a music player like the iPod.

Compressed Audio Formats

Up until a few years ago, the MP3 format was the only game in town for playing quality song files on your computer, whether downloaded from the Internet or taken from CDs. MP3 still dominates the Internet, but other formats—like Ogg Vorbis (a new audio format favored by Linux fans and the open-source software crowd; details at *www.vorbis.com*) and Windows Media Audio (WMA)—have dedicated fans, too.

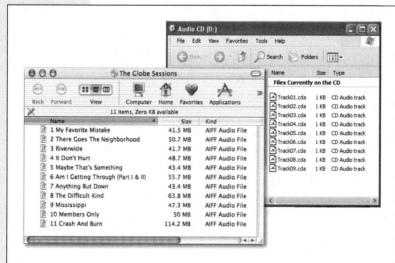

Figure 3-1:
Left: Here's what a desktop window looks like for a music CD inserted into a Mac. It looks just like an MP3 playlist, except that these AIFF files are much larger. Your computer can play these high-quality files, but they eat up a lot of hard drive space.

Right: Audio files are more bashful when a disc is inserted into a Windows drive. The tracks on this Prince CD remain hidden behind tiny pointer files and can be lured out only with CD-extraction software.

Those two aren't on the list of iPod-compatible formats, but many others are, including MP3, AAC, AIFF, and WAV. Here's some explanation of each Podworthy format.

MP3

Suppose you copy a song from a Sheryl Crow CD directly onto your computer, where it takes up 47.3 MB of hard disk space. (This sort of audio extraction is quick on a Mac, somewhat harder in Windows; see page 66.) Sure, you could now play that song without the CD in your CD drive, but you'd also be out 47.3 megs of precious hard drive real estate (see Figure 3-1).

Now say you put that Sheryl Crow CD in your computer and use your favorite encoding program to convert that song to an MP3 file. The resulting MP3 file still sounds really good, but only takes up about *4.8 MB* of space on your hard drive—about 10 percent of the original. Better yet, you can burn a *lot* of MP3 files onto a blank CD of your own—up to 11 hours of music on one disc, which is enough to get you from Philadelphia to Columbus on Interstate 70 with tunes to spare.

How It Works

MP3 files are so small because the compression algorithms use *perceptual noise shaping,* a method that mimics the ability of the human ear to hear certain sounds. Just as people can't hear dog whistles, most recorded music contains frequencies that are too high for humans to hear; MP3 compression discards these sounds. Sounds that are blotted out by louder sounds are also cast aside. All of this space-saving by the compression format helps to make a smaller file without overly diminishing the overall sound quality of the music.

MP3 History

The work on the technology behind the MP3 format began in the mid-1980s at the Fraunhofer Institute in Germany, which got a patent for the MP3 compression format in 1989. The format is flexible and permits different compression levels, but the average ratio was 10:1, meaning that a song can take up a tenth of the space but still retain good sound quality. (Hard-core audiophiles will debate the meaning of the phrase "good sound quality" until the end of time, but for most listeners, "good sound quality" translates into "I can hear all the instruments and vocals really well, and I know that's Peggy Lee singing 'Fever.'")

In the early 1990s, Fraunhofer developed the first MP3 player. By the mid-to-late 1990s, software for encoding and playing MP3 files on a computer was all over the Internet. WinAmp was one of the first programs to become hugely popular for ripping songs from compact discs into MP3 files.

By 1998, portable MP3 players like the Diamond Rio began to appear in electronics stores, allowing music lovers to download their music onto a pocket-size device and take it anywhere. Unlike personal cassette and CD players, the MP3 players had no moving parts to break, and let you create an endless number of *playlists* (song sets sequenced in whatever order you like).

New portable MP3 player models come out all the time, but many people consider the iPod's arrival in 2001 to be a defining moment in the history of MP3 hardware.

Tip: MP3 is short for MPEG Audio, Layer 3. And MPEG stands for Moving Pictures Experts Group, the association of engineers that also defined the specifications for the DVD video format, among others.

NOTE FROM THE LAWYERS

The Law of the Digital Music Land

Years before the iPod was even a twinkle in Steve Jobs's eye, the Recording Industry Association of America sued the makers of the first portable MP3 player. RIAA felt that the player—the soon-to-be-released Rio PMP300 from Diamond Multimedia—could serve as a tool for pirating copyrighted songs. Diamond eventually won the case. The court found that the Rio itself violated no federal music-piracy laws, paving the way for dozens more MP3 players to hit the market.

The Audio Home Recording Act of 1992 says that you can make copies of your own legally purchased music for your personal (noncommercial) use. Even though MP3 players didn't yet exist, the court ruled in the Rio case that consumers have the right to move the music they own onto a playback device—as long as it's for personal use.

The arrival of the MP3 format changed the way people listened to their music—and shared it. Before MP3, nobody thought much about copyright law when they dubbed a song mix to give to a friend or a romantic prospect. (After all, the exchange of the mix tape/CD has been an important part of the young American courting ritual for years.)

But the small size of MP3 files, mixed with the power of the Internet, ripped the lid off a 55-gallon drum of worms. With music being passed freely all over the world and CD sales dropping (maybe as a result of MP3 sharing, maybe because of unrelated factors), industry groups like RIAA have begun looking for new ways to block digital music copying. They're also taking a highly litigious interest in Internet services that make sharing MP3 files easy.

In 1999, a file sharing service called Napster got a lot of attention from music fans and lawyers alike. The Napster software, authored by a teenager named Shawn Fanning, let music lovers search out and share MP3 files with

anybody else on the Internet running the same program—which turned out to be millions of people. Napster traffic became so heavy that at some universities, it actually created a drag on their networks, and resulted in a Napster ban.

While Napster gave people a chance to sample a wide range of music for free, it also sent RIAA on a legal mission to shut down the file sharing service. RIAA eventually prevailed, and in 2002, Napster went to that great Web site in the sky.

(Napster, in its original form, died that day. But in October 2003, it returned in the form of an iTunes Music Store wannabe where music shoppers could legally download tracks for less than a buck apiece. In a further effort to ape Apple, Napster 2.0, as this Windows-only, pay-to-play service was dubbed, even began selling its own iPod clone.)

Although the group's first attempts to squash other file sharing services like Grokster and KaZaA in 2003 were later rebuffed by the courts, RIAA is looking into new technology that can prevent CD tracks from being copied onto computers at all. RIAA has recently begun filing lawsuits against Internet service providers to find out the names of customers who use file sharing services or host music-swapping sites and suing the individuals directly.

Mind you, MP3 files themselves are not illegal. Ripping tracks from CDs that you've purchased over the years for playing on your iPod is legal. Downloading MP3s offered freely by bands and musicians just wanting to be heard is also legal.

Copying copyrighted music that you *didn't* pay for is not legal, and that's why you can be sure we haven't heard the last from the RIAA.

AAC

The Advanced Audio Coding format may be relatively new (it became official in 1997), but it has a fine pedigree. Scientists at Dolby, Sony, Nokia, AT&T, and those busy folks at Fraunhofer collaborated to come up with a method of squeezing multimedia files of the highest possible quality into the smallest possible space—at least small enough to fit through a modem line. During listening tests, many people couldn't distinguish between a compressed high-quality AAC file and an original recording.

What's so great about AAC on the iPod? For starters, the format can do the Big Sound/Small File Size trick even better than MP3. Because of its tighter compression technique, a song encoded in the AAC format sounds better (to most ears, anyway) and takes up less space on the computer than if it were encoded with the same quality settings as an MP3 file. Encoding your files in the AAC format is how Apple says you can stuff 10,000 songs onto a 40 GB iPod.

The AAC format can also be copy-protected (unlike MP3), which is why Apple uses it for the songs it sells at the iTunes Music Store (page 141). (MP3 fans take note: Don't blame Apple. The record companies would never have permitted Apple to distribute their property without copy protection.)

Note: You can think of AAC as the Apple equivalent of WMA, the copy-protected Microsoft format used by all online music stores except Apple's. For better or worse, the iPod doesn't recognize WMA files; it can download $1-a-song music *only* from Apple's iTunes Music Store (Chapter 6).

Since the iPod can play several different audio formats, you can have a mix of MP3 and AAC files on the device if you want to encode your future CD purchases with the newer format. If you want to read more technical specifications on AAC before deciding, Apple has a page on the format at *www.apple.com/mpeg4/aac.*

Note: AAC is the audio component of MPEG-4, a new video format that's designed to get high-quality video compressed enough to travel over computer networks (even pokey old modem lines) and still look good onscreen.

Other Podworthy File Formats

The iPod was designed to handle AAC and MP3 formats the most efficiently, but it's not limited to them. Here are the other types of music files you can play on an iPod:

WAV

WAV is a standard Windows sound format, going all the way back to Windows 95. (Most Macs can play WAV files, too.) Windows fans download WAV recordings for everything from TV-show snippets to start-up sounds and other system alert noises. A WAV song usually sounds better than the same song in MP3—but takes up more room on the iPod.

AIFF

Speaking of big file sizes, the AIFF standard (Audio Interchange File Format) can create sound files that sound spectacular—in fact, these *are* the audio files on commercial music CDs—but they hog hard drive space. For example, if you stick Prince's *Purple Rain* CD into your computer, double-click the disc icon, and drag the song file for "Let's Go Crazy" onto your desktop, you'll soon have a 46.9 MB AIFF file on your hard drive. Although the sound fidelity is tops, the files are usually ten times bigger in size than MP3s.

Apple originally developed the AIFF standard, but AIFF files play on other operating systems, too.

Note: If you insist on putting gargantuan files like AIFFs on your iPod, you'll have to worry about running out of battery power as well as disk space.

A modern iPod comes with a 32 MB memory chip. (Pre-2003 iPods have a slightly smaller buffer.) Yes, it serves as skip protection, because it stores 25 minutes' worth of MP3 or AAC music. For instance, if a jogging bump or your boxing partner jostles the hard drive, the music doesn't skip—because the iPod effortlessly plays the music it's been storing in its memory. But it also serves as a battery-life enhancer, because the hard drive stops spinning whenever the music plays from the memory buffer.

If you have big song files on the iPod, the memory buffer holds less music. When it runs out of music data, the iPod has no choice but to read more information from the hard drive, which runs your battery down much more quickly.

Audible

You can listen to more than just music on your iPod; you can also listen to the spoken word. Not books on tape, exactly, but more like books on MP3—courtesy of *www.audible.com*.

There, you can find over 18,000 spoken recordings to download. These are downloadable versions of the same professionally produced audio books you see in stores: the latest bestsellers in popular genres, children's books, and even old science fiction faves like Neal Stephenson's *Snow Crash*.

If you choose to subscribe, $15 a month gets you one recorded book a month, plus a daily, weekly, or monthly magazine or radio show. Audible.com has everything from vocalized versions of the *New York Times* to programs like National Public Radio's *All Things Considered*. You can hear free samples of most files on the site before you buy.

You can also skip the subscription business and just buy the books you want for a flat fee. Prices vary, but the audio file usually costs less than the hard copy and fits in your pocket better. *The Da Vinci Code,* a popular mystery novel selling for $25 in book stores, was simultaneously $20 on Audible.com.

But you don't have to go to Audible's site to buy many of its wares. The iTunes Music Store sells more than 5,000 Audible audio books in great-sounding AAC format.

Tip: The iPod Software 2.0 CD that came 2003 iPod models included some free Audible.com samples, including a 22-minute excerpt from radio's *This American Life* and the late Douglas Adams reading a chapter from *The Hitchhiker's Guide to the Galaxy.* If you were lucky enough to find that version of the iPod CD in your iPod package, look fro these files in the folder named Audible.com. The samples come in the MP3 format for MusicMatch Jukebox and standard Audible format for iTunes.

If you bought your iPod more recently, you still get a free sample or two, but you have to download them from Audible.com. The details are at *www.audible.com/ipod.*

Formats within formats

Audible.com files that come from its Web site (and *not* from the iTunes Music Store) use the *.aa* file name extension. You can't convert .aa files to MP3, but you can burn them to an audio CD to play on the stereo—and, of course, you can copy them to your iPod.

Most recordings from Audible.com come in a variety of sound resolutions, from low-fi, AM radio–like sound to a really good MP3 quality. The Audible resolutions that work on the iPod are called Formats 2, 3, and 4 (from worst to best quality). Better audio quality, of course, means a bigger file to download.

As shown in Figure 3-2, the 18-hour audio book for *Snow Crash* is split into two files. The first half is a 34 MB download in Format 2, a 63 MB download in Format 3, or a 127 MB download in Format 4. The various formats cost the same, but unless you have a broadband connection, you'll probably want to stick with the smaller file size.

Figure 3-2:
When you buy a title, Audible.com gives you a choice of audio resolutions for your audio book (formats 2,3, and 4 work with the iPod), as well as instructions for what to do with the file once you've downloaded it.

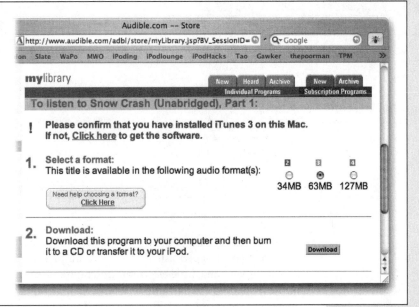

Tip: If you decide you don't like the way a format sounds, you can download your selection again in a different format by logging back into your account on the Audible.com page—a benefit you *don't* get at the iTunes Music Store.

Audible.com for Mac

If you're using iTunes on a Mac, make sure the program is set to handle Audible files. Choose iTunes→Preferences, click the General icon, and next to "Use iTunes for Internet Music Playback," click the Set button. When you download a book file from Audible.com, it shows up right in iTunes.

Before you listen to it, iTunes asks you to type in the name and password you set up with Audible.com, as shown in Figure 3-3 at top. Thereafter, you can listen to it at your desk (Figure 3-3, bottom) or transfer it to your iPod like any other track.

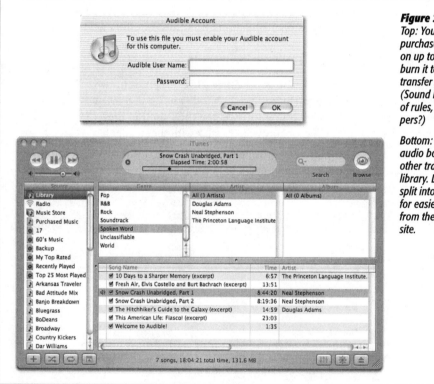

Figure 3-3:
Top: You can play your purchased Audible file on up to three computers, burn it to a CD, or transfer it to an iPod. (Sound like a familiar set of rules, iTunes shoppers?)

Bottom: iTunes plays your audio book just like any other track in your library. Longer books are split into multiple parts for easier downloading from the Audible.com site.

You play them just like regular audio files; the iPod even remembers where in the audio book you stopped listening, so you can pick up where you left off the next time. Better yet, these little electronic bookmarks are synchronized between iTunes and the iPod; if you're listening to a chapter of a book on your iPod while walking home from work, you can connect the iPod to your Mac to transfer the bookmark. Then you can continue listening at your desk, in iTunes, without missing a sentence.

Audible.com for Windows

Audible offers a vast library of books, periodicals, and radio shows beyond the limited sampler in the iTunes store offers. To listen to them on a Windows iPod, you need the free Audible Manager software (available at *www.audible.com/software*).

The AudibleManager software (Figure 3-4) does everything from accessing online Audible.com accounts to transferring purchases to Pods. It shows you what you've downloaded, what you have on deck to move to the iPod, and even how much space is left on the iPod (so you don't max it out by stuffing the 62-hour unabridged version of Tolstoy's *War and Peace* onto the player). The handy AudibleManager toolbar provides a button for just about everything you need to do.

If you use MusicMatch Jukebox, the AudibleManager is the only program you need for wrangling Audible files onto your iPod.

If you use iTunes, though, importing them is a separate step. Choose File→Add to Library, and then navigate to the folder where Audible deposits your files, which is usually the C:→Program Files→Audible→Programs→Downloads folder. Select the folder to pull your audiobooks into iTunes.

Audible realizes this two-step tango is a tad unfair for Windows fans, since Mac folk can buy Audible files right there in iTunes without involving a separate Manager program. The company says that a fix is on the way.

Figure 3-4:
When working with Audible.com recordings, the AudibleManager for Windows takes over file management duties. The control bar (top) provides a button for just about every task, from downloading new files to transferring them to the iPod to burning them to CD. You can sync the Pod to PC and keep track of your place within the audio file as well.

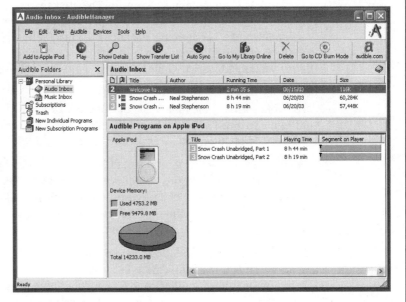

Bit Rates

Bit rate may sound like one of those unbelievably geeky computer terms (which it is), but it plays a big role in how your music sounds when you snag a song from a CD and convert it to MP3 or AAC format. When it comes to sound quality, all digital audio files are not created equal.

The bit rate has to do with the number of *bits* (binary digits—tiny bits of computer data) used by one second of audio. The higher the number of bits listed, the greater the amount of data contained in the file, and the better the sound quality.

Tip: Eight bits make a byte. So why are audio files measured in kilo*bits* (thousands of bits), and not the more familiar kilo*bytes?*

Force of habit. Geeks measure size and storage capacity in bytes, but network speeds and data-transfer speeds have always been measured in bits. When you encode an MP3 file, the transfer and compression of the audio data into the new format is measured in kilobits.

Files encoded with lower bit rate settings—like 64 kilobits per second—don't include as much audio information from the original sound file. They sound thin and tinny compared to a file encoded at, say, 160 kbps.

Just as you can't compare megahertz ratings across different chip families (like Pentium III vs. Pentium 4), you can't compare bit rates between AAC and MP3 files. A 128 kbps AAC file generally sounds much better than a 128 kbps MP3 file. In fact, tests by the group that developed the AAC standard found that a *96* kbps AAC file generally sounds better than a *128* kbps MP3 file. (Your ears may differ.) As a bonus, the AAC version takes up much less space on your hard disk and iPod. You probably don't want to encode AAC files lower than 128 kbps, though, as the sound quality will begin to suffer noticeably.

For both formats, the higher the bit rate, the larger the file size. For example, an MP3 file encoded at 160 kbps sounds a heck of a lot better than one recorded at 96—but takes up over twice as much disk space (1.5 MB vs. 700 KB).

For MP3s, most people find that 128 kbps is a good compromise of file size and sound quality. At that rate, MP3 files take up roughly one megabyte of space per minute of music. The 128 kbps rate is considered high quality for the AAC format—which is why iTunes comes factory set to 128 kbps. (Songs for sale in the iTunes music store are 128 kbps AAC files, too.)

You're not stuck with the 128 kbps rate for your own home-ripped tracks. If you're a classical music fan and want to hear every nuance of a symphony, go for 160 or even 192 kbps. On the other hand, if you're listening to garage rock while strolling city streets, 96 kbps may sound fine, while giving you plenty of room on the iPod.

To make this kind of change, choose iTunes→Preferences on the Mac (Edit→ Preferences in Windows) and click the Importing icon (Figure 3-5, bottom); in Music-Match for Windows, use the Recorder settings box (Figure 3-5, top).

Note: The iPod can also play files encoded in the MP3 *VBR* format, in which sophisticated software has adjusted the song's bit rate *continuously* along the length of the song. (VBR stands for Variable Bit Rate.) The song winds up using more data during sonically complex parts of a song (higher bit rates) and lower settings during simpler parts that require less data. By constantly adjusting the bit rate within the song, a MP3 VBR file conserves space more efficiently than a song encoded at a high bit rate all the way through.

To set up iTunes for MP3 VBR, go to Preferences, select Importing→MP3 Encoder. From the Setting pop-up menu, choose Custom to find the option for VBR encoding.

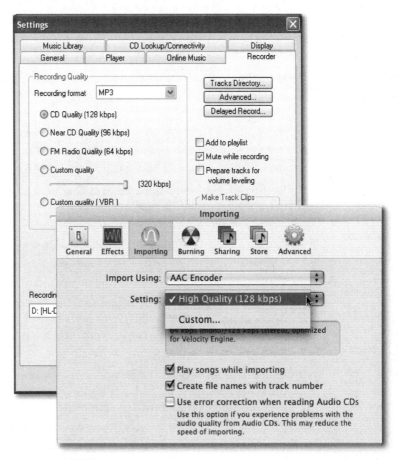

Figure 3-5:
You can adjust the bit rate setting for ripping MP3 and AAC files in the iTunes Preferences dialog box (bottom) and for MP3 and WAV files in the recorder settings in MusicMatch Jukebox (top). In the battle of Sound vs. Size, music lovers can choose to encode audio files at higher bit rates that take up more space (and sound better), or opt for lower bit rates and smaller file sizes (and poorer sound).

Free (and Legal) Music on the Web

MP3 files don't have copy restrictions built into them (as AAC and WMA files often do), which is why MP3 is the format of choice for trading and sharing. Thousands of Web sites offer MP3 files to download, as a quick trip to Google.com will tell you. Some sites offer music posted by bands and musicians who want to make their songs free to anyone who wants to listen. Other sites stockpile copyrighted works and bombard you with pop-up windows for all manner of services (including adult material).

Here are a few sites that offer free and legal MP3 files:

- **Music.download.com.** The venerable MP3.com site was bought and sold, but a free download site from its sister company CNET is on the way. Scheduled to debut in early 2004, the site promises to provide a place for independent artists to share their music freely with once and future fans (*music.download.com*).

- **PasteMusic.** For the mere act of signing up for the Paste mailing list, you can download free full-length songs by the site's featured artists. Why are the songs free? The bands hope you'll get hooked enough to purchase the whole CD, which you can also buy here (*www.pastemusic.com*).

- **FreeSoloPiano.** If you think the sound of ivories being tickled is just the thing for your iPod, the free solo piano works available here could be a gold mine (*www.free solopiano.com*).

- **Vitaminic.** One of Europe's major sites for new music and musicians using the Internet to promote themselves, Vitaminic hosts thousands of free MP3 files that span both the globe and the genre list (*www.vitaminic.com*).

- **Internet Underground Music Archive.** Dedicated to helping new musicians get heard, the IUMA site offers up free tracks of everything from hip hop to New Age (*www.iuma.com*).

- **FreeKidsMusic.** MP3 files aren't just for grown-ups anymore. The FreeKidsMusic site hosts scores of MP3 files just for kids and plenty of information about the artists (and albums) who make them available (*www.freekidsmusic.com*).

- **Peoplesound.** With a search engine that can find music with a similar sound to that of established rock stars, Peoplesound's MP3 collection not only includes pop music, but classical, reggae, folk, urban, jazz, and dance (*www.people sound.com*).

- **Amazon.com.** The once humble online bookseller now hawks everything from consumer electronics to the kitchen sink (really!), and has a collection of free MP3 files from popular artists to download. They reportedly still sell books, too (*www.amazon.com*).

Tip: Be careful out there, Windows fans. If you're downloading any type of file from the Internet, including MP3s, make sure your computer's antivirus software is up to date. Worms, viruses, and Trojan horses could get into your computer and wreak havoc if unleashed. A firewall program is also a good idea in these days of rampant malicious code. (No Macintosh virus has ever been found in these files.)

---

iTunes for Macintosh and Windows

A pple's iTunes software—the ultimate jukebox program for Macintosh and Windows—supplies the software yin to the hardware yang of the iPod. It plays and organizes your music, copies music from your CD collection onto your hard drive, and burns new CDs with music in a sequence you like. It's also an online music store where you can buy a favorite song, legally, for a buck, with just a few mouse clicks.

Note: If you're on Windows, you can still use MusicMatch Jukebox Plus, which first came with the iPod in 2002—but you won't be able to use the iTunes Music Store. If you install iTunes after you've installed MusicMatch Jukebox, be warned that the iPod will switch its syncing allegiance to Apple's software (returning to the mother ship, as it were).

If you try iTunes but want to go back, see page 116 for steps on how to get MusicMatch and the iPod speaking to each other again.

Introduction to iTunes

As the MP3 music craze of the late 1990s swept across the globe, software programs for playing the new music files on the computer began to pop up around the Internet. Many Windows fans fondly remember WinAmp as their introduction to MP3 software; early adopters on the Mac side likely recall programs like SoundApp, SoundJam MP, and MacAmp.

When iTunes debuted in January 2001, Apple reported that 275,000 people downloaded it in the first week. The iTunes software proved to be a versatile, robust all-around music management program made exclusively for Macintosh. And it was *free*.

Even in that first version of iTunes, Mac fans could import songs from a CD and convert them into MP3 files; play MP3s, audio CDs, and streaming Internet radio; create custom playlists; burn audio CDs without having to spring for extra CD burning software; zone out to groovy animated laser-light displays in the iTunes window while songs played; and transfer music to a few pre-iPod, Mac-friendly portable MP3 players.

When the iPod arrived in October 2001, iTunes 2 accompanied it, now with iPod synchronization, an equalizer for enhancing different types of music, a crossfade feature, and the ability to burn MP3 CDs.

Note: Although iTunes 4 is the latest and greatest version of the program, it only works with version Mac OS X 10.1.5 or later and Windows 2000 or later. If you're running Mac OS 9, you'll have to stick with iTunes 2. (Earlier versions of the Mac OS don't work with iTunes or the iPod.) Most of the iTunes features listed in the remainder of this chapter—and throughout the book—refer to iTunes 4.

The marriage of iTunes and the iPod was a match made in heaven for fans of MP3 players, and Apple made the union even stronger in the summer of 2002 when it announced the new iPod models for Macintosh and Windows. iTunes 3 debuted simultaneously, with better integration with Apple's iLife suite (iPhoto2, iMovie 3, and iDVD 3). iTunes 3 also added software goodies like a one-to-five star rating system for favorite songs (page 97), Smart Playlists (page 106), a Sound Check feature designed to smooth out volume levels from song to song, a Join Tracks command that merges several tunes from one album into one uninterrupted track (page 101), and so on.

With the launch of iTunes 4 at the end of April 2003 (October 2003 for Windows), Apple finally brought all the pieces of the digital music puzzle together. Now you can download perfectly legal music files from well-known artists using the Music Store feature and zip them over to your iPod in no time, all from within iTunes and without buying a single CD.

With 500,000 songs within its virtual doors (and counting), and more than 5,000 audio books, the iTunes Music Store is big enough to rate its own chapter in this book—Chapter 6.

iTunes 4 only works with Mac OS X 10.1.5 and later, or Windows 2000 and later. But with iTunes 4, you also get:

- The new AAC format, which can make music sound just as good as the MP3 format but without taking up as much precious space on your Mac, PC, or iPod.

- A music-sharing feature that lets you blast your music *from* any Mac or PC on your home network, *to* any others, all without any setup or configuration. (You can thank Apple's Rendezvous network-discovery software for this feature; it's built into Mac OS X 10.2 and later and provided to Windows by the iTunes installer).

- The ability to burn your music collection to a blank DVD, which can hold 4.7 gigabytes of files.

- A place in the main iTunes window to display artwork or images—like scanned album covers—as your songs play.

- An easy-to-remember place to upload your voice memos if you have one of those handy Belkin Voice Recorder attachments.

- A way to save those On-the-Go playlists you made on your iPod when you were out and about.

Many of the features in iTunes 4 also require Apple's QuickTime 6.2 software or later. (If you need to update iTunes or QuickTime, Apple keeps an area of its Web site devoted to news, updates, and downloads for QuickTime at *www.apple.com/ quicktime* and iTunes 4 at *www.apple.com/itunes.*)

A Quick Tour

The area at the center top of the iTunes window—the status area—tells you what song is playing, who's playing it, which album it came from, and how much playing time remains. To the left are volume and song navigation controls; to the right is a search box for hunting down or looking up specific singers or songs. Figure 4-1 presents a guided tour of the controls and functions on the iTunes screen.

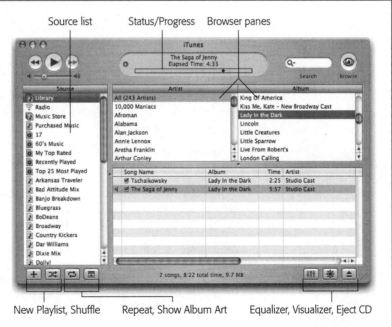

Figure 4-1:
The iTunes window shows all of the current playlists, the various places to find music in the Source list, and even album art on the left side. The main area of the window displays all of the songs on the chosen source. Depending on what you click in the Source list, iTunes displays all of the songs you're currently hearing. In this case, you can see the entire contents of the iTunes library.

The Source panel at the left of the iTunes window displays all of the audio sources you can tap into at the moment. If you have a CD in the computer's drive, for example, it shows up in the Source list, as will a currently connected iPod.

Clicking a name in the Source column makes the main song-list area change accordingly, like this:

- Click the icon of a CD you've inserted; the disc's track list appears.

- Click a playlist (page 104); the contents of that music mix appear in the window.

- Click the Radio icon; a list of Internet radio stations shows up.

- Click the Music Store icon; you jump to Apple's online music emporium where you can browse, preview, and buy songs (Chapter 6).

As shown in Figure 4-1, the iTunes window is brimming with tools for managing your music, all of which are described in detail starting on page 96. But first you'll need some music to work with. The next section explores one of the most popular uses for iTunes—ripping digital audio files from compact discs.

Window Fun

Don't be misled by the brushed-aluminum look of the iTunes window. In fact, you can push and pull the various parts of the window like taffy.

- You can resize the panes within the iTunes window. Look for a shallow dot between panes; it denotes strips that you can drag to resize adjacent panes.

- The main song list is separated into several columns, which you can sort and rearrange. Click a column title (like Artist or Album) to sort the song list alphabetically by that criterion. Click the little black triangle next to the column title to reverse the sorting order.

- Change the order of the columns by dragging them. For example, if you want to have Album right next to the Song Name, drag the word Album horizontally until it's next to Song Name.

- To adjust the width of a column, drag the vertical divider line on its right side.

- To resize all the columns so that they precisely fit the information in them, right-click (or Control-click if you have a Mac) any column title and choose, from the contextual menu, Auto Size All Columns. Double-clicking on the vertical column lines automatically resizes them to fit the text as well.

- To add more kinds of information to your list of columns (or less), right-click (or Control-click) any column title. From the pop-up list of column categories (Bit Rate, Date Added, and so on), choose the name of the column you want to add or remove. Column names with checkmarks are the ones that are currently visible.

Tip: Want to track your own listening habits? Turn on the Play Count in iTunes Options. Now you can see just how many times you have played "I Want You Back" by the Jackson 5 since you ripped that CD of old Motown gems to your hard drive. Checking out the Top 25 Most Played playlist in the Source window (page 79) can also let you know where your ears have been lately.

If you intend to make a *lot* of adjustments to your list of columns, though, it's much faster to make the changes all at once. Choose Edit→View Options to produce the dialog box shown in Figure 4-2, where you can turn columns on and off en masse.

Figure 4-2:
The View Options box from the iTunes Edit menu lets you see as many—or as few—categories for sorting your music as you can stand.

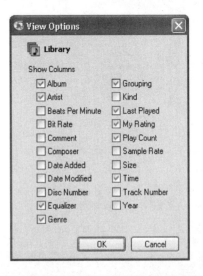

GEM IN THE ROUGH

Arbitrary Groupings

The Grouping column heading (in iTunes 4.2 and later) lets you override the usual sorting criteria and keep together a bunch of songs of your own choosing. (If you don't see the Grouping column, right-click or Control-click *any* column heading and choose Grouping, so that a checkmark appears next to its name.)

Many classical albums, for example, contain different symphonies, concertos, and other musical forms, all on one disc. How can you make sure that all of Mozart's *Concerto for Piano No. 5 in D Major (K 175)* stays together, and doesn't get mixed in with concertos 6 and 8 from the same CD?

Easy. Select all the "songs" that belong together (by ⌘-clicking on the Mac, or Ctrl-clicking on the PC). Then choose File→Get Info. iTunes asks if you're sure you want to edit the file information for all of the selected pieces at once; yes, you do.

In the Get Info box, type *Piano Concerto 5* (or whatever group name you want). Now, when you click OK, you return to the main iTunes list.

To sort your list by grouping name, so that grouped pieces appear consecutively in the list, just click the word Grouping at the top of the column.

Minimizing the window

Lovely as the iTunes window may be, it can take up a heck of a lot of screen real estate. When you're just playing music while you work on other things, you can shrink iTunes down to a svelte display panel that takes up a fraction of the size of the full window.

Figure 4-3:
And what size music would you like today? In both the Mac and the Windows versions of iTunes, you can choose large, medium, or small. (Press Ctrl+M in Windows to get the medium size, which you can then scrunch up into the small player by dragging the resize handle.) Only the large version has the space to serve as command central for MP3s, Internet radio, visual effects, and the kitchen sink.

Box Full of Buttons

The round button up in the top-right corner of iTunes changes depending on what you're doing. Here's what each one means and when you see it.

 The Browse button appears when you click the Library icon to look through your collection or shop in the iTunes Music Store.

 This version of the Burn CD button shows up when a playlist is selected in the Sources area or you have a separate playlist window open onscreen.

 If you have taken iTunes up on its offer to burn a CD by clicking on the previous button, this icon appears as the disc-burning process begins.

 The Import button indicates you've inserted a CD into your computer and are ready to rip some songs into your iTunes library.

 When the iTunes Visualizations are turned on, clicking the Options button lets you adjust the frame rate and other visual settings.

 To check for new radio stations and other live streams available in the iTunes Radio area, click the Refresh button.

In fact, iTunes can run in three size modes: small, medium, or large. Here's how you pull this off:

- **Large.** This is what you get the first time you open iTunes.

- **Medium.** You can switch back and forth between large and medium by clicking the green zoom button at the top- or middle-left corner (or choosing Window→Zoom). If you use iTunes for Windows, press Ctrl+M or choose Advanced→Switch to Mini Player to get the medium-sized window.

- **Small.** If your desktop isn't big enough for even the small iTunes window in Figure 4-3 at lower left, try taking it down a notch. To create the mini bar shown at lower right in Figure 4-3, start with the medium-size window. Then drag the resize handle (the diagonal lines in the lower-right corner) leftward. To expand it, just reverse the process.

Ripping CDs into iTunes

Ripping a CD means "converting its recordings into digital files on the computer." (Too bad recording-industry executives didn't know that when they accused Apple's "Rip, Mix, Burn" ad campaign of promoting piracy, evidently equating "Rip" with "rip off.")

With the proper iTunes settings, ripping a CD track and preparing it for use with the iPod is fantastically easy. Here's how to go about it.

FREQUENTLY ASKED QUESTION

Transferring Your MusicMatch Library to iTunes

Okay, okay! This chapter has already convinced me to switch to iTunes, but I have thousands of songs in MusicMatch Jukebox already. How do I get them moved over to iTunes without missing a beat?

Fear not, gentle Windows friend. Moving your vast audio collection from one program to another can be painless, and you'll definitely have fewer backaches than if you were hefting around boxes of CDs or LPs.

If you haven't downloaded iTunes yet, do so. During the installation process the program asks whether you'd like to search for any music files to add to the iTunes music library. If you agree, iTunes automatically gathers up copies of all MP3 files on your PC.

If you've already downloaded iTunes but skipped the music roundup option, don't worry. Just launch iTunes and follow these steps.

First, open your My Music folder (or whatever folder you've set MusicMatch Jukebox to use for song storage). In its window, you see all of the subfolders that contain your music.

Position the My Music window so that you can see the iTunes program window—specifically, the Library icon on the Source list.

Now drag the songs out of the My Music window and onto the iTunes Library icon. iTunes adds the songs to its music library.

If you want to bring the *playlists* you made in MusicMatch into iTunes, choose File→Import (in iTunes) and navigate to your MusicMatch playlists. You can import any playlists in the .xml, .txt, and .m3u formats.

Phase 1: Choose an Audio File Format

Before you get rolling with ripping, decide which format you want to use for your music files: MP3, AAC, AIFF, or WAV.

To make your selection, choose iTunes→Preferences (Mac) or Edit→Preferences (Windows), click the Importing tab, and choose the format you want from the Import Using pop-up menu (see Figure 4-4).

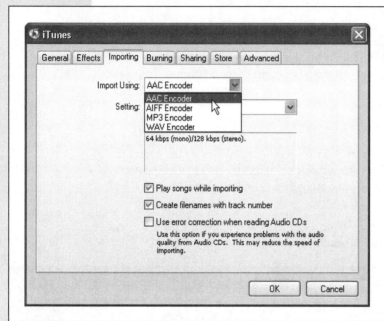

Figure 4-4:
The Importing Preferences box is where you tell iTunes which file format and bit rate it should use when ripping tracks from a CD. Turning on "Create files names with track number" arranges the songs you import in the same order in iTunes as they were on the CD—even if you don't choose to rip every song on the album.

Chapter 3 provides a detailed overview of these formats, and most people use either the familiar old MP3 (.mp3) format or the spunky new AAC (.a4u) encoding option. But here's a quick recap:

- AIFF and WAV offer better sound quality than MP3 and AAC, but result in larger file sizes.

- Both MP3 and AIFF offer good sound quality in the resulting files, but AAC usually creates files that are 30 to 40 percent smaller than an MP3 recorded at the same *bit rate* (page 74).

Before you stack up the CDs next to the computer for an afternoon of ripping, you may want to test your format preferences by ripping test songs as both MP3 files and AAC files. Let your ears tell you which format and bit rate sounds best to you.

Phase 2: Download Song Names and Track Information

When you first insert a music CD into a Mac or PC, you may be disappointed to discover that to the computer, the album is named "Audio CD," and the songs on it are called "Track 1," "Track 2," and so on. It turns out that most audio CDs don't include any digital information about themselves. So if you don't do anything to solve the problem, after you've ripped, say, seven CDs into iTunes, you'll find that you have seven songs called Track 1, seven songs called Track 2, and so on—not the easiest way to organize your music.

There are two ways to remedy the problem: You can type the information in manually, or let iTunes go on the Internet to find out for itself.

The manual method

After you load up a CD, you can type in all of the song information for each track. To do so, click the track's name once to highlight its row, and then a second time to open up the renaming box. Edit away.

Tip: You can edit the information in the Artist, Album, or Genre columns the same way.

You should consider this purely theoretical information, however; you'd be nuts to go about naming your CDs and tracks this way. Read on.

The online way

If you have an Internet connection, choose iTunes→Preferences (or press ⌘-comma) on the Mac or Edit→Preferences (Ctrl+comma) in Windows. The Preferences dialog box opens. Make sure that the settings in the bottom half of the dialog box match Figure 4-5. This setup allows the computer to zip out the Internet to go get the specific song information for the CD you've just inserted.

Behind the scenes, it's consulting a massive, comprehensive CD Database (CDDB), maintained by a company called Gracenote (*www.gracenote.com*). After iTunes sends information from the disc to the Gracenote CDDB servers, the database identifies the album and sends back the song titles and other data for iTunes to display.

Note: Firewall software may interfere with some iTunes functions, like downloading CD track information or listening to streaming Internet radio. If you're using iTunes on a network that uses an *HTTP proxy* (ask your administrator) for security reasons, check the settings in the Network pane of your Mac's System Preferences area or the LAN Settings section on the Connections tab in the Windows Internet Options control panel to make sure you have the information entered correctly.

If you don't have a high-speed Internet connection (cable modem or DSL), you may not want the computer constantly dialing up every time you insert a CD. In that case, turn off the "Connect to the Internet when needed" box. Instead, you may prefer to ask for the CD information when you're already connected to the Internet. Just choose Advanced→Get CD Track Names.

Phase 3: Convert the Song to a Digital Audio File

Once the songs on the CD have been identified, the song and artist names, time, and other information pops up in the main part of the window, as shown in Figure 4-4. Each song has a checkmark next to its name, indicating that iTunes will convert and copy it onto the computer when you click the Import button.

If you don't want the entire album—who wants anything from Don McLean's *American Pie* album besides the title track?—you can uncheck the boxes next to the songs that you *don't* want. Once you've picked your songs, click Import in the upper-right corner of the screen.

Tip: You can ⌘-click (Mac) or Ctrl-click (Windows) any box to deselect all checkboxes at once. To do the reverse, ⌘-click (or Ctrl-click) a box next to a list of unchecked songs to turn them all on again. This is a great technique when you want only one or two songs in the list; turn *all* checkboxes off, then turn those *two* back on again.

Another way to select a single song is to click it in the iTunes window and then choose Advanced→Convert Selection to MP3 (or whatever format you have chosen for importing). You can also use this menu item to convert songs that are *already* in your library to different audio formats.

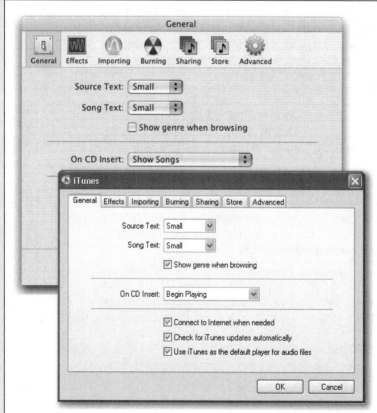

Figure 4-5:
The iTunes Preferences dialog box, shown here in both Mac and Windows, is where you give iTunes permission to go to the Internet to bring back CD information. You can also set the size of the program's display font for the Source and Song lists to either "Small" or "Large," and opt to show the Genre column in your iTunes browser window.

As the import process starts, iTunes moves down the list of checked songs, ripping each one to a file in your Home→Music→iTunes→iTunes Music folder (Mac) or My Documents→My Music→iTunes→iTunes Music (Windows). Feel free to switch into other programs, answer email, surf the Web, and do other work while the ripping is under way.

Once the importing is finished, each imported song bears a green checkmark, and iTunes signals its success with a little melodious flourish. And now you have some brand new files in your iTunes music library.

Figure 4-6:
When you click Import, iTunes converts the selected songs from the CD to MP3, AAC, AIFF, or WAV files on your hard drive (depending on what you've selected in Preferences). The status bar at top shows the song being imported, the amount of time left, and the speed of the conversion. Songs in progress sport a wavy line in an orange circle.

Phase 4: Add Cover Artwork

Songs you download from the iTunes Music Store (Chapter 6) often include artwork, usually a picture of the album cover. iTunes displays the pictures in the lower-left corner of its main window.

But you shouldn't have to be a slave to the artistic tastes of some faceless, monolithic record company; you can install any art you like for any song. If Pachelbel's *Canon in D* makes you think of puppies, you can have baby dachshund photos appear in the iTunes window every time you play that song.

The only stipulation is that the graphic you choose must be in a format that Quick-Time can understand: JPEG format, GIF, PNG, TIFF, or Photoshop, for example. Just keep in mind that the bigger the image size, the bigger the overall file size of the audio file and the more hard drive space you fill up.

Adding an image to an individual song: drag-and-drop method

To add an image file to a song you're listening to in iTunes, click the Show/Hide Song artwork button at the bottom of the iTunes window. The artwork pane appears. As shown in Figure 4-7, faint gray words appear in the pane, telling you exactly where to drag the image file. Just drag any graphics file right off of the desktop (or any other Finder folder) and into this space to install it there.

Tip: If you find an image on the Web that you love, right-click (or Control-click) it and choose Download Image to Disk to save it to your hard drive (the wording depends on your browser). Most browsers nowadays let you drag images off the Web page onto your desktop, too. Either way, you can drag the resulting graphic into the iTunes artwork pane.

Figure 4-7:
To copy a picture into the iTunes artwork pane, just drag it into the designated spot in the corner of the window (after you've selected the song you want to illustrate), as shown here before and after. You can also double-click any image that appears in this panel to view it in a separate window.

Adding an image to an individual song: dialog box method

Instead of dragging a graphic off your desktop, you may prefer to use the Get Info dialog box, where at least you can inspect the image before accepting it. Figure 4-8 shows the way.

Tip: You can even install *multiple* graphics for an individual song. Just drag multiple images into the artwork pane; thereafter, you can click through them with the arrows at the top of the Selected Song bar. If you use the Get Info dialog box shown in Figure 4-8, you can click Add, and then ⌘-click (Mac) or Ctrl-click (Windows) the multiple graphics files to achieve the same result.

If you decide you want to get rid of any artwork or change what's attached to your songs, click the track and press ⌘-I (Ctrl+I). Click the Artwork tab, then click the art in the window. Click the Delete button to remove the image.

Adding an image to an entire album

To select the same art for *all* the songs on an album (or by the same artist), saving yourself a little time, open the iTunes browser (page 97) by clicking the eyeball icon at the top right of the screen. Click the name of an artist or album in the browser, and then press ⌘-I (Mac) or Ctrl+I (Windows) to open the Multiple Song Information box. (You'll see a worrisome alert box from iTunes, asking if you're sure about editing multiple items. Click Yes.)

Figure 4-8:
Click a song and press ⌘-I (Mac) or Ctrl+I (Windows), or choose File→Get Info, and click the Artwork tab. Click the Add button to select a digital photo from your hard drive. You can use almost any kind of photo or image file with your music. If you like the result, click OK.

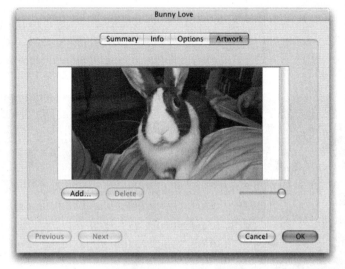

Figure 4-9:
The Multiple Song Information box can save a lot of time because it allows you to change information all at once for all the songs listed in the Artist, Album, or Genre categories. For example, you can assign the Equalizer's "Classical" preset to all your files in the Classical genre, add a picture of a yellow submarine to all of your Beatles tracks, or adjust the title of all the songs at once on a mislabeled album.

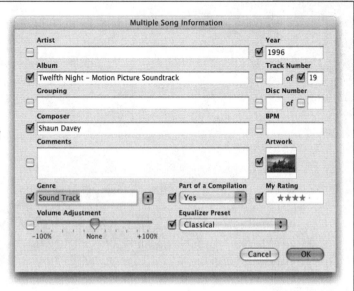

In the Multiple Song Information dialog box (Figure 4-9), turn on the Artwork checkbox, and then double-click in the white area. In the window that opens, navigate to and select the image file you want to use for all the songs on the album, and then click OK. (Of course, you can also drag a graphic into this white box, right off your desktop.) You'll see a progress bar as iTunes applies the artwork and any other group settings you've chosen for the files.

Click OK, confirm your decision one last time, and then enjoy the new album art.

Tip: On the Mac, you can apply the same image over and over again into all the songs in the same *playlist.* Visit *http://malcolmadams.com/itunes* and download a copy of the "Selected Artwork to All in Playlist" AppleScript. The next time you have an image that you want to associate with all the songs on a particular playlist, just fire up Doug's AppleScript (see page 241).

Artwork Made Easy

If you have a scanner, the original CD, and a large amount of free time, you can scan in album cover artwork yourself.

Alas, life is too short already. If that scenario doesn't appeal to you, there are plenty of places around the Web to download pictures of album covers that have been previously scanned and are just hanging out for you to copy.

Amazon.com and AllMusic.com have comprehensive selections, as do most sites that sell CDs. That's still a lot of manual effort, though: looking up an album, Control-clicking or right-clicking its artwork, choosing Copy from the contextual menu, and finally pasting into iTunes.

Fortunately, a great little free Mac OS X program called Clutter can spare you even that effort. (You can download it from *http://sprote.com/clutter.*) After you launch Clutter while playing a song in iTunes, it recognizes the song and

automatically downloads an image of the album cover from Amazon.com.

The program has a pretty good track record, so to speak, for finding pop and rock album covers, but more esoteric fare may come up blank.

The album cover art appears both in Clutter's Now Playing window and the Dock. You can also drag the image onto your desktop to create a sea of tiny, floating album-cover windows, as shown here. When you click a cover, iTunes jumps to that album and starts playing it.

Clutter stores the album images it uses on your hard drive, where you can snatch a copy for use in your iTunes artwork window. To find the images, go to Home→Library→ Images→com.sprote.clutter→CDs and open the folder name of the artist you're looking for. Drag the JPEG file into the iTunes artwork pane to add the image to your song file.

Importing Other Music Files into iTunes

Not all sound files come directly from the compact discs in your personal collection. As long as a file is in a format that iTunes can comprehend (MP3, AAC, AIFF, WAV, or Audible), you can add it to the iTunes music library by any of several methods.

Note: The AAC format includes a copy-protection feature that MP3 doesn't have. Songs you buy from the iTunes Music Store and music encoded from your own CDs with iTunes work, but you may have trouble playing or moving other copy-protected AAC files (like those bought from, for example, LiquidAudio.com).

- On the Mac, you can drag a file or folder full of sound files onto the iTunes icon on the Mac OS X Dock, or onto Mac OS 9's floating Applications palette, to add the music to the library. In Windows, hover the mouse over the iTunes taskbar button without letting go of the song files; when the program window pops open, you can drop the songs on the iTunes window. (The taskbar gets cranky if you try to drop files directly onto the iTunes button.)

- You can also drag the files or folders straight into the iTunes window.

- If menus are your thing, choose File→Add File to Library. In the resulting dialog box, locate and click the file you wish to add, or ⌘-click (Mac) or Ctrl-click (Windows) several files in the list to highlight them all at once. Click Choose to bring it, or them, into iTunes.

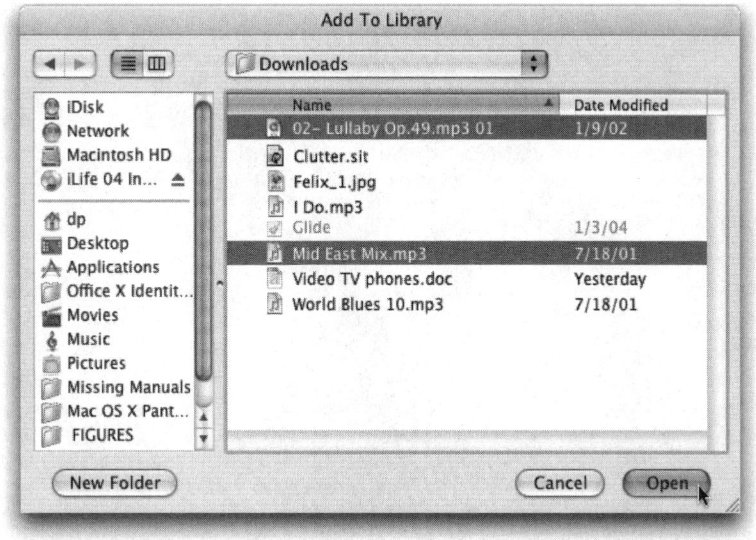

Figure 4-10:
Select the file you'd like to add to your expanding iTunes library with the File→Add File to Library command. If the files you want to add are not in iTunes-friendly formats, you can find scores of shareware on the Web that can convert different audio formats. Some of these sites include MP3 machine (www.mp3 machine.com), the Hit Squad (www.hitsquad .com), and MP3-Converter (www.mp3-converter.com).

Deleting Songs

If you want to delete a song or songs—like when you outgrow your Britney Spears phase and want to reclaim some hard drive space by dumping those tracks from the *Oops...I Did It Again* album—click the title in the Albums pane, select the songs you want to delete from the song list, and press Delete (Backspace).

Tip: Selecting songs works just like selecting files in the Finder. Select a swath of consecutive songs in the list by clicking the first, then Shift-clicking the last. Add or remove single additional songs to the selection by ⌘-clicking (Mac) or Ctrl-clicking (Windows).

When iTunes asks if you're sure you want to delete the music, click Yes. You'll usually be asked twice about deleting a song, the first time for deleting it from a list, the second time about deleting the music file from your iTunes music library altogether. If you want your hard drive space back, click Yes to both.

Playing Music

To turn your computer into a jukebox, click the triangular Play button in the upper-left corner of the iTunes window, or press the Space bar. The computer immediately begins to play the songs whose names have checkmarks in the main list.

The central display at the top of the window shows not only the name of the song and album, but also where you are in the song, as represented by the diamond in the

---

FREQUENTLY ASKED QUESTION

Auto-Playing Music CDs

In Mac OS 9, you could set the QuickTime Settings control panel to play music CDs automatically when they're inserted into the Mac. Can Mac OS X do that?

Sure!

Hey, what about Windows?

Of course! Keep reading.

Mac OS X. First, make sure that iTunes is slated to open automatically when you insert a music CD. You do that on the CDs & DVDs panel of System Preferences (use the "When you insert a music CD" pop-up menu).

Then all you have to do is make sure iTunes knows to begin playing automatically once it launches. Choose iTunes→Preferences, click the General icon, and from the

On CD Insert pop-up menu, choose Begin Playing, and click OK.

Windows. Choose Edit→Preferences, click the General tab, and from the On CD Insert pop-up menu, choose Begin Playing and then click OK.

Before you even get this far, however, Windows XP may fling up the same alert box that it displays whenever it senses a floppy, CD, or removable drive that might contain digital music, video, or photographs. If it does, pick iTunes from the list of programs and turn on the checkbox instructing Windows to always use that program when it encounters an audio CD.

From now on, whenever you insert a music CD, iTunes will open automatically and begin playing.

horizontal strip. Drag this diamond, or click elsewhere in the strip, to jump around in the song.

Or just click the tiny triangle at the left side of this display to see a pulsing VU meter, indicating the current music's sound levels at various frequencies.

Tip: You can also control CD playback from the Mac's Dock. Just Control-click the iTunes icon (or click and hold on it) to produce a pop-up menu offering playback commands like Pause, Next Song, and Previous Song, along with a display that identifies the song currently being played.

As music plays, you can control and manipulate the music and the visuals of your Mac or PC in all kinds of interesting ways. As a result, some people don't move from their machines for months at a time.

Visuals

Visuals is the iTunes term for an onscreen laser-light show that pulses, beats, and dances in perfect sync to the music you're listening to. The effect is hypnotic and wild. (For real party fun, invite some people who grew up in the sixties to your house to watch.)

To summon this psychedelic display, click the flower-power icon in the lower-right corner of the window (see Figure 4-11). The show begins immediately—although it's much more fun if you choose Visualizer→Full Screen so that the movie takes over your whole monitor. True, you won't get a lot of work done, but when it comes to stress relief, visuals are a lot cheaper than a hot tub.

Once the screen is alive with visuals, you can turn it into your personal biofeedback screen by experimenting with these keys:

Key	Function
?	Displays a cheat sheet of secret keystrokes. (Press it repeatedly to see the other shortcut keys.)
F	Displays, in the upper-left corner of your screen, how many frames per second iTunes' animation is managing—a quick, easy way to test the power of your graphics circuitry.
T	Turns *frame rate capping* on or off—a feature that limits the frame rate to 30 frames per second, to avoid sapping your Mac's horsepower when you're working in other programs (not really much of an issue in Mac OS X, of course).
I	Shows/hides info about the current song.
C	Shows/hides the current Visuals configuration (the name of the current waveform, style, and color scheme) in the upper-right corner of the screen.
M	Turns slide show mode on or off. In slide show mode, the visuals keep changing color and waveform as they play. (Otherwise, the visuals stick with one style and color.)

B	Turns on an Apple logo in the center of the Visuals screen.
R	Chooses a new waveform/style/color at random.
Q or W	Cycles through the various waveform styles stored in iTunes.
A or S	Cycles though *variations* on the currently selected waveform.
Z or X	Cycles through color schemes.
Number keys	Cycles through the ten different preset, preprogrammed waveform/color/style configurations.
D	Restores the default waveform settings.

Tip: These are the secret keystrokes for the *built-in* visuals. The Web is crawling with add-on modules that have secret keystrokes of their own.

Figure 4-11:
No matter what you're listening to, the animated full-color patterns produced by the iTunes Visualizations feature can make it a more interesting experience. (This feature works really well with the original cast album from "Hair" or anything by Jimi Hendrix.)

Keyboard Control

You can control iTunes' music playback using its menus, of course, but the keyboard can be far more efficient. Here are a few of the control keystrokes worth noting (Windows fans should substitute the Control key for the Mac ⌘ key, and Alt instead of Option):

Function	Keystroke
Play, Pause	Space bar
Next song/previous song	Right arrow, left arrow

Next source/previous source	Down arrow, up arrow
Louder	⌘-up arrow
Quieter	⌘-down arrow
Mute	⌘-M
Fast-forward, rewind	Option-⌘-right arrow, -left arrow
Eject	⌘-E
Turn Visuals on	⌘-T
Turn Visuals off	⌘-T or mouse click
Full-screen visuals	⌘-F
Exit full-screen visuals	⌘-T, ⌘-F, or mouse click

The Graphic Equalizer

If you click the Graphic Equalizer button (identified in Figure 4-1), you get a handsome floating control console that lets you adjust the strength of each musical frequency independently (see Figure 4-12). (Mac fans can also press ⌘-2 or choose Window→Equalizer to get the console onscreen.

Tip: You can also make an Equalizer pop-up tab appear as one of the iTunes columns. Choose Edit→View Options and turn on the Equalizer checkbox.

To apply Equalizer settings to a specific selected song, press ⌘-I (Mac) or Ctrl+I (Windows) or choose File→Get Info, and click the Options tab, shown at bottom in Figure 4-12.

You can drag the Preamp slider (at the left side of the Equalizer) up or down to help compensate for songs that sound too loud or soft. To design your own custom preset pattern with the Preamp and the other ten sliders, click the pop-up tab at the top of the Equalizer and select Make Preset.

Preventing Ear-Blast Syndrome

No longer must you strain to hear delicate Chopin piano compositions on one track, only to suffer from melted eardrums when the hyperkinetic Rachmaninoff cut kicks in right after it. The Sound Check feature attempts to bring the disparate volumes onto line, making the softer songs louder and gently lowering the level of the more bombastic numbers in the iTunes library. Audiophiles may nitpick about the Sound Check function, but it can be quite useful, especially for times, like bicycling uphill, when constantly grabbing at the iPod's volume controls on the remote or scroll wheel are inconvenient.

The first step using Sound Check is to turn it on. First, connect your iPod and select it from the iTunes Source list when it pops up. Then click the iPod Preferences button at the lower right side of the iTunes window.

In the resulting dialog box, click the Effects icon and turn on the Sound Check dialog box. You also need to turn on Sound Check on the iPod itself: From the iPod's main screen, choose Settings→Sound Check and click the Select button.

Then in iTunes, open the Preferences box (⌘-comma on a Mac or Ctrl+comma on a PC). Click the Effects icon or tab and turn on the box for Sound Check.

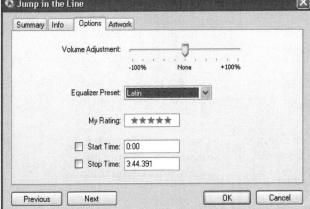

Figure 4-12:
Top: Drag the sliders (bass on the left, treble on the right) to accommodate the strengths and weaknesses of your speakers or headphones (and listening tastes). Or save yourself the trouble—by using the pop-up menu above the sliders to choose a canned set of slider positions for Classical, Dance, Jazz, Latin, and so on. In iTunes 3 and later, these settings even transfer to the iPod.

Bottom: You can also apply preset or customized equalizer settings to individual songs under the Options tab in the song's Get Info box (shown here in Windows).

iTunes Administration

At its heart, iTunes is nothing more than a glorified database. Its job is to search, sort, and display information, quickly and efficiently. Here, for example, are some powerful managerial tasks it stands ready to handle.

Searching for Songs

You can call up a list of all the songs that have a specific word in their title, album name, or artist attribution, just by typing a few letters into the Search box at the top of the window. With each letter you type, iTunes shortens the list of songs that are visible, confining it to tracks that match what you've typed.

For example, in Figure 4-13, typing *train* brings up a list of songs by different performers that all have the word "train" somewhere in the song's information—maybe the title of the song, maybe the band name. This sort of thing could be useful for creating themed playlists, like a mix for a Memorial Day barbecue made from songs that all have word "sun" or "summer" in the title.

Figure 4-13:
The Search box in the iTunes window can quickly find all the songs in the library that match the keyword you enter. To erase the Search box so that you see all of your songs again, click the little circled X button at the right side of the box.

The Browser

The Browse button is the eyeball in the upper-right corner of the window. (It appears only when the Library icon is selected in the source list at the left side of the screen.) It produces a handy, supplementary view of your music database, this time organized like a Finder column view (shown in Figure 4-14).

Tip: Can't get back that full list of albums on the right Album pane after you've clicked on a name in the Artist list in the left pane? Go to the top of the Artist list and click All. The complete album list reappears.

It's worth noting, by the way, that this two-panel Browser can become a *three*-panel browser, much to the delight of people who enjoy the phrase "drill down." Figure 4-15 has details.

Critic's Corner

Although there's no way to give a song two thumbs up within iTunes, you can label each song in your collection with a star rating (one to five). Not only can you, too, now feel like a *Rolling Stone* record critic, but you can also use your personal rating system to spontaneously produce playlists of the hits, nothing but the hits.

To add a rating to a song in the Song list window, first make sure the My Rating field is turned on in the iTunes Options box (⌘-J [Mac] or Ctrl+J [Windows]). Then proceed as shown in Figure 4-16.

Figure 4-14:
When you click an Artist name in the left column, you get a list of all attributed albums on the right side. To see the songs you've imported from each listed album, click the album name. The songs on it appear in the main list area of the iTunes window, beneath the Browser panes.

Figure 4-15:
The Genre pane in iTunes preferences can add another whole layer of categorizing for your music collection. If you don't see the Genre pane when you start iTunes for the first time, you need to turn it on in Preferences. Press ⌘-comma (Mac) or Ctrl+comma (Windows), or choose iTunes→Preferences→General (Mac) or Edit→Preferences→General (Windows), and then turn on "Show genre when browsing."

Once you've assigned ratings, you can sort your list by star rating (click the My Rating column title), create playlists of only your personal favorites (page 106), and so on.

Tip: One the newer iPods, you can even rate songs on the go; your ratings will transfer back to iTunes 4. To rate a song on the iPod, start playing it and tap the Select button twice from the Now Playing screen. Use the scroll wheel to spin across the ghostly gray dots onscreen and transform them into the number of stars you feel the song deserves.

Figure 4-16:
Click inside the My Rating column. The horizontal position of your click determines how many stars you're giving. You can also add a rating by selecting a song title, pressing ⌘-I (Mac) or Ctrl+I (Windows) to open its Get Info box, and then clicking the Options tab.

Editing Song Information

You have a couple different ways to change song titles in iTunes—to fix a typo or other incorrect information, for example.

In the song list, click the text you want to change, wait a moment, then click again to make the renaming rectangle appear. Type to edit the text, exactly as when you change a file name on the desktop.

Another way to change the song's title, artist name, or other information is to click the song in the iTunes window and press ⌘-I (Mac) or Ctrl+I (Windows) to bring up the Get Info box. (Choose File→Get Info if you forget the keyboard shortcut.) Click the Info tab (Figure 4-17) and type in the new track information. This is the way to go if you have several pieces of information to change.

Tip: Once you've got a song's Get Info box up on the screen, you can use the Previous and Next buttons to navigate to the other tracks grouped with it in the iTunes song list window. This way, if you want to rapidly edit all the track information on the same playlist, on the same album, in the same genre, or by the same artist, you don't have to keep closing and opening each song's Get Info box.

Converting Between File Formats

iTunes isn't just a cupboard for music; it's also a food processor. You can convert any song or sound file into almost any other format: MP3 to AIFF, AAC to WAV, MP3 to AAC, and so on.

Tip: If you're going from a compressed format like MP3 to a full-bodied, uncompressed format like AIFF, you shouldn't hear much difference in the resulting file. Quality could take a hit, however, if you convert a file from one compressed format to another, like MP3 to AAC. If you're a stickler for sound but still want the space-saving benefit of the AAC format, it's best just to set the iTunes preferences to encode in AAC (page 69) and re-rip the song from the original CD.

To get the conversion underway, choose iTunes→Preferences (File→Preferences on a PC) and click the Importing button. From the Import Using pop-up menu, pick the format you want to convert to, then click OK.

Figure 4-17:
Lower right: The Get Info box for each is where you can add, correct, and customize information for each song.

Upper left: Click the Summary tab for the lowdown on the song's bit rate, file format, and other fascinating technical details.

Now, in your iTunes library, select the song file you want to convert, and then choose Advanced→Convert Selection to AAC (or MP3 or AIFF or WAV, depending on what you just picked as your import preference).

If you have a whole folder or disk full of potential converts, hold down the Option key (Mac) or Shift key (Windows) as you choose Advanced→Convert to AAC (or your chosen encoding format). A window pops up, which you can use to navigate to the folder or disk holding the files you want to convert. The only files that don't get converted are protected ones: Audible.com tracks and AAC songs purchased from the iTunes Music Store.

The song or songs in the original format, as well as the freshly converted tracks are now in your library.

Joining Tracks

If you want a seamless chunk of music without the typical two-second gap of silence between CD tracks, you can use the Join Tracks feature to stitch together a sonic sampler in one big file. This feature is great for live albums or other CDs that run one song into the next.

To rip multiple songs as one track, pop in the CD you want to use, download the song information, make sure the list is sorted by track number, and then Shift-click to select the tracks you want to join during the ripping process. You can only join tracks that are in sequential order on the CD.

Once you've got the tracks selected, go to Advanced→Join CD Tracks. iTunes displays a bracket around the selected tracks, and indents the names of the tacked-on ones. If you change your mind and want to separate one of the tracks from the group, select it and go to Advanced→Unjoin CD Tracks. (You can Shift-click to peel off multiple tracks from the group, too.)

Click the Import button to rip the selected songs to one big track.

Changing Start and Stop Times for Songs

Most of the time, there's musical interest in every juicy moment of the songs that you download, buy, or rip from CDs. Every now and then, though, some self-indulgent musician releases a song with a bunch of onstage chitchat before the music starts. Or maybe you've got a live album with endless jamming at the end, as a song plays out.

Fortunately, you don't have to sit there and listen to the filler each time you play the file. You can adjust the start and stop times of a song, so that you'll hear only the juicy middle part.

As you play the song you want to adjust, observe the iTunes status display window; watch for the point in the timeline where you get bored (Figure 4-18, top). Say, for example, that the last two minutes of that live concert jam is just the musicians riffing around and goofing off. Note where *you* want the song to end.

Then select the track you want to adjust. Choose File→Get Info to call up the information box for the song, and proceed as shown in Figure 4-18 at bottom.

The shortened version plays in iTunes and on the iPod, but the additional recorded material isn't really lost. If you ever change your mind, you can go back to the song's Options box, turn off the Stop Time box, and return the song to its full length.

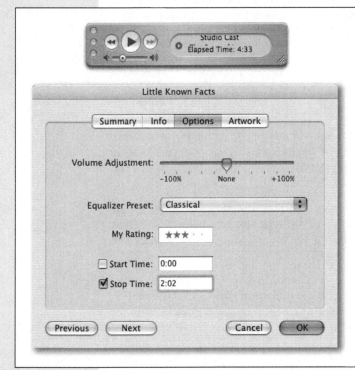

Figure 4-18:
Top: Song too long for your taste?

Bottom: Click the Options tab and take a look at the Stop Time box, which shows the full duration of the song. Change the number to the length of time you want the song to run, as you noted earlier. iTunes automatically turns on the Stop Time box. Click OK to lop off those last two boring minutes of the song. (You can do the exact same trick at the beginning of a song by adjusting the time value in the Start Time box.)

Internet Radio

Not satisfied with being a mere virtual jukebox, iTunes also serves as an international, multicultural radio without the shortwave static. You can find everything from mystical Celtic melodies to American pop to programming from Japan, Italy, Germany, and other spots around the globe.

Computers with high-speed Internet connections have a smoother streaming experience, but the vast and eclectic mix of musical offerings is well worth checking out even if you have a dial-up modem. Just click the Radio icon in the Source list to see a list of stations, as shown in Figure 4-19.

Just like the cars backed up on the interstate right before a long holiday weekend, streaming audio files are also subject to traffic jams while traveling across the Internet. If you find your radio streams are constantly stuttering and stopping, try this:

Choose iTunes→Preferences (Mac) or Edit→Preferences (Windows). In the Preferences dialog box, click the Advanced icon or tab. From the Streaming Buffer Size pop-up menu, choose Large. Click OK.

Figure 4-19:
The Radio list displays the categories and subcategories that can take you around the world in 80 stations with iTunes. Click the Refresh button to update the station list.

UP TO SPEED

Audible.com: Spoken Like a True iPod

You can download any of 5,000 audio books right in the iTunes Music Store, but that's just the tip of the iceberg. If you want to hit the motherlode of spoken-word recordings, head to Audible .com. You can listen to Audible selections on your iPod, including audio books, current newspaper articles, and so on. All you need is iTunes 3 or 4, and iPod software version 1.2 or later.

First, make sure iTunes is configured properly for the task. Choose iTunes→Preferences (Mac) or Edit→Preferences (Windows), click the General icon, and turn on Use iTunes for Internet Music Playback.

Then visit the Audible site (*www.audible.com*), create a user account, and buy an audio file to download. Your Web browser whisks you to a page called My Library, where you can see the files you have selected.

On that page, click the Get It Now button next to each file. The iPod can play Audible files in formats 2, 3, and 4, which indicate the relative audio quality settings. Remember, though, that higher quality files like format 4 take up more space on the iPod.

Click the Download button on the Web page.

Macintosh: The Audible file appears right in iTunes. Double-click it and (if this is your first listen) enter your Audible.com name and password.

Windows: Use the Audible Manager program described on page 73 to get the file into iTunes.

Either way, your spoken-word recording will arrive on the iPod the next time you sync it with your computer.

Having the buffer set to Large may increase the waiting time before the music starts flowing through your computer from the Internet, but it allows iTunes to hoard more music at once to help make up for interruptions caused by network traffic.

Tip: It's possible to save music streams to your computer's hard drive, although the practice dances dangerously close to copyright infringement. Programs like Streamripper X for Mac OS X (from *http://streamripperx.sourceforge.net*) or Audiolib MP3 Recorder (at *www.audiolib.com/recorder*) for Windows let you save radio streams as MP3 files.

Playlists

A *playlist* is a list of songs that you've decided should go together. It can be made up of pretty much any group of songs arranged in any order. For example, if you're having a party, you can make a playlist from the current Top 40 and dance music in your music library. If you're in a 1960s Brit Girl Pop mood, you can make a playlist that alternates the hits of Dusty Springfield, Lulu, and Petula Clark. Some people may question your taste if you, say, alternate tracks from *La Bohème* with Queen's *A Night at the Opera,* but hey—it's *your* playlist.

Making a New Playlist

To create a playlist, press ⌘-N (Mac) or Ctrl+N (Windows). You can also choose File→New Playlist or click the + button below the Source area of the iTunes window.

All freshly minted playlists start out with the impersonal name Untitled Playlist. Fortunately, its renaming rectangle is open and highlighted; just type a better name. As you add them, your playlists alphabetize themselves in the Source window.

FREQUENTLY ASKED QUESTION

A Trip to the Library

Where exactly does iTunes store its music library on my computer's hard drive? Can I move the music library if my hard drive starts to get full?

The music library is the program's personal database. It stores all of the songs you've imported into the program, as well as all of the playlists you created from those songs. This database file sits in your Home→Music→iTunes Music folder (Mac) or My Documents→My Music→iTunes→iTunes Music folder (Windows).

If you rudely drag the iTunes Music folder to a different place without telling iTunes, it will think the songs are gone. The next time you start the program, you'll find it empty.

(While iTunes remains empty but calm, *you* may have heart palpitations as you picture your music collection vanishing in a puff of bytes.)

To move the iTunes Music folder to a new drive, just let the program know where you're putting it. Move the folder to the desired location, then choose iTunes→Preferences (Mac) or Edit→Preferences (Windows) and click the Advanced icon or tab. In the area labeled iTunes Music Folder Location, click the Change button, and navigate to the place where you moved the iTunes Music folder. Finally, click OK.

Exhale.

Once you've created and named this spanking new playlist, you're ready to add your songs. You can do this in two different ways.

If this is your first playlist, opening the playlist into its own window might make it easier for you to see what's going on. To do so, double-click the new playlist's icon in the Source list, which opens a window next to your main iTunes window. From here, drag the song titles you want over to the new playlist window. Figure 4-20 demonstrates the process. (You can also open the iTunes Music Store into its own window with the double-click trick.)

Figure 4-20:
Making a playlist is as easy as dragging song titles from your library window to your new playlist window. The other way to add songs to a playlist is to drag them over from the Songs window and just drop them on the new playlist's icon in the Source list. (If you have a lot of playlists, though, you risk accidentally dropping songs on the wrong icon.)

Don't worry about clogging up your hard drive. When you drag a song title onto a playlist, you don't *copy* the song; you're just giving iTunes instructions about where to find the files. In essence, you're creating an *alias* or *shortcut* of the original. You can have the same song on several different playlists without having to worry that you've now got 16 copies of "The Battle of New Orleans" by Johnny Horton.

Note: Anytime you see an exclamation mark next to a title in the iTunes song list, iTunes is alerting you that it can no longer find that song in its library. The song may have been moved or deleted by accident.

If you think you know where you moved it, double-click the song title and navigate to where you think the song is living. Once you find it, select the song file and click Choose.

Modifying a Playlist

If you change your mind about the order of the tunes you've selected for a playlist, just drag the song titles up or down within the playlist window to reorder them.

You can also drag more songs into a playlist, or delete the titles from the list if you find your playlist needs pruning. (Click the song in the playlist window and hit Delete or Backspace to get rid of it. When iTunes asks you to confirm your decision, click Yes.) Remember, deleting a song from a playlist doesn't delete it from your music library—it just removes the title from your *playlist*. (Only pressing Delete or Backspace when the *Library* icon is selected gets rid of the song for good.)

Tip: If you want to mix up the songs on a playlist but don't feel like thinking about it, iTunes can do it for you. Click the Shuffle button at the bottom of the iTunes window. You'll hear your playlist songs in a random order.

Deleting a Playlist

The party's over and you want to delete that playlist to make room for a playlist for next week's bash. To delete a playlist, click it in the Source list and press Delete (Backspace). (Again, this just zaps the playlist itself, not all the stored songs you had in it. Those are still in your iTunes Music folder.)

Tip: Want to change the name of your iPod? Once you've connected the iPod to the computer, click the iPod's name to select it and then click again to highlight the text. Type whatever name you'd like to call your iPod, and then click somewhere else. If you're using your iPod as a FireWire disk (page 213), you can also click it on the desktop and type a new name for it, just as you can with any file or folder.

Smart Playlists

Just as you can have iTunes vary your song order for you, you can also have the program compose playlists all by itself. Once you give it some guidelines, a *Smart Playlist* can go shopping through your music library and come up with its own mix for you. The Smart Playlist even keeps tabs on the music that comes and goes from your library and adjusts itself on the fly.

You might tell one Smart Playlist to assemble 45 minutes' worth of songs that you've rated higher than four stars but rarely listen to, and another to play your most-often-played songs from the Eighties. Later, you can listen to these playlists with a turn of the iPod's control dial, uninterrupted and commercial-free.

To start a Smart Playlist in iTunes, press Option-⌘-N (Mac) or Ctrl+Alt+N (Windows) or choose File→New Smart Playlist. A Smart Playlist box opens: It has a purple gear-shaped icon next to the name in the Source list, while a regular playlist has a blue icon with a music note icon in it.

Tip: When you press Option (Mac) or Shift (Windows), the + button for Add New Playlist at the bottom of the iTunes window turns into a gear icon. Click the gear button to get a new Smart Playlist to appear in the Source list, all ready for you to set up.

Now you can give the program detailed instructions about what you want to hear. You can select the artists you want to hear and have iTunes leave off the ones you're not in the mood for, pluck songs that only fall within a certain genre or year, and so on. You can make a Smart Playlist using information from any field in the song's tag, like a collection of every tune in your library that's track 17 on an album.

Click the little + sign at the end of each line to keep adding criteria, or click the - sign to remove one. See Figure 4-21 for an example.

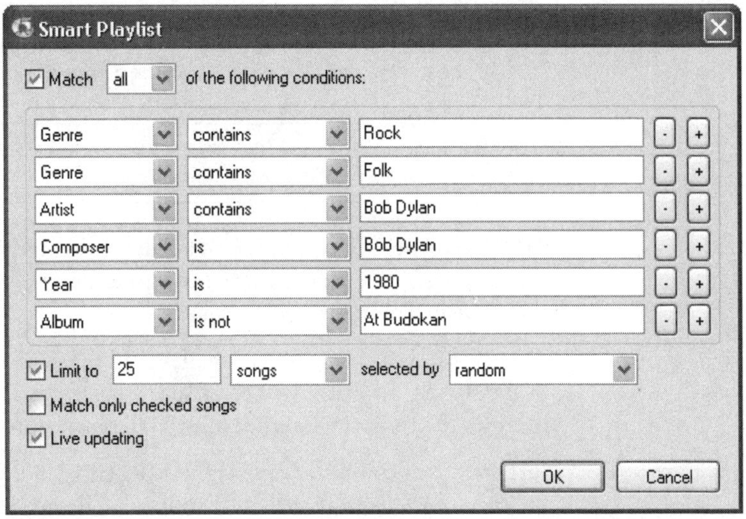

Figure 4-21:
This Smart Playlist seeks out all Bob Dylan songs in your collection, either written or performed by Bob, on albums released before 1980, but not including any songs from the Dylan At Budokan *album. Depending on your music collection, this Smart Playlist would not only include tracks from the height of Bob Dylan's long career, but versions of his songs performed with other musicians, too—provided you have them in your library.*

Then, provided the "Live updating" checkbox is turned on, iTunes will always keep this playlist updated as your collection changes, as you change your ratings, as your Play Count changes, and so on.

A Smart Playlist is a dialogue between you and iTunes: You tell it what you want in as much detail as you want, and the program responds back with what it thinks you want to hear. Once you lay out the boundaries, iTunes pores through the current contents of your music library and generates the playlist.

Tip: If you find Smart Playlists are becoming an obsession, take a browser ride over to *www.smartplaylists.com*. There, you will find many like-minded individuals exchanging tips, tricks, and tales about Smart Playlists, iTunes, and what they'd like Apple to add to the *next* version of the program.

Burning a CD or DVD

If want to record a certain playlist on a CD for posterity—or for the Mr. Shower CD player in the bathroom—iTunes gives you the power to burn. In fact, it can burn any of three kinds of discs:

- **Standard audio CDs.** This is the best part. If your computer has a CD burner, it can serve as your own private record label. (Apple has a list of external CD recorders that work with iTunes at *www.apple.com/support/itunes.*) iTunes can record selected sets of songs, no matter what the original sources, onto a blank CD. When it's all over, you can play the burned CD on any standard CD player, just like the ones from Tower Records—but this time, you hear only the songs you like, in the order you like, with all of the annoying ones eliminated.

Tip: Use CD-R discs. CD-RW discs are not only more expensive, but may not work in standard CD players. (Not all players recognize CD-R discs either, but the odds are better.)

- **MP3 CDs.** A standard audio compact disc contains high-quality, enormous song files in the AIFF format. An *MP3* compact disc, however, is a data CD that contains music files in the MP3 format.

  Because MP3 songs are much smaller than the AIFF files, many more of them fit in the standard 650 or 700 MB of space on a recordable CD. Instead of 74 or 80 minutes of music, a CD-R full of MP3 files can store *10 to 12 hours* of tunes.

  Just about any computer can play an MP3 CD. But if you want to take the disc on the road or even out to the living room, you'll need a CD player designed to read both standard CDs and discs containing MP3 files. Many modern players can play both CDs and MP3 CDs, and the prices are not much higher than that of a standard CD player. Some DVD players and home-audio sound systems can also play MP3 CDs.

Note: You can't easily convert copy-protected AAC files into MP3 files, so you can't burn an MP3 CD from a playlist that contains purchased music. If you're determined to do that, certain workarounds are available. You could use certain frowned-upon utility programs from the Web. Or you could burn the AAC files onto a CD and then rip *that* into iTunes, exactly as described earlier in this chapter. At that point, the songs are MP3 files.

- **Backup DVDs.** If your Mac has Mac OS X 10.1 or later and has an Apple Super-Drive that can play and record both CDs and DVDs, you have another option. iTunes 4 can also back up 4.7 gigabytes of your music collection at a time by copying it to a blank DVD. Most Windows computers with DVD burners can also burn DVDs with iTunes. (The disc won't play in any kind of player, of course; it's just a glorified backup disk for restoration when something goes wrong with your hard drive.)

You pick the type of disc you want to make in the Preferences dialog box (Figure 4-22). Then proceed as follows:

1. **Select the playlist you want to burn. Check to make sure you have all the songs you can fit, in the order you want them in.**

   Consult the readout at the bottom of the window, which lets you know how much playing time is represented by the songs in the playlist.

Note: Although earlier versions of iTunes would stop burning a long playlist once it got to the last full song it could fit on a disc, iTunes 4.2 and later versions ask you to insert another disc if it runs out of room on the first one and then picks up where it left off.

---

2. **When you're ready to roll, click the Burn Disc button at the top-right corner of the iTunes window.**

   The icon changes into a yellow-and-black graphic that resembles the symbol used for fallout shelters in the 1950s.

3. **Insert a blank CD into your computer's drive when prompted. Click the Burn Disc button again after the program acknowledges the disc.**

   iTunes prepares to record the CD, which may take a few minutes. In addition to prepping the disc for recording, iTunes has to convert the music files to the standard format used by audio CDs.

Figure 4-22:
Choose iTunes→ Preferences (Mac) or Edit→Preferences (Windows), and then click Burning. Here, you select the recorder you wish to use, as well as what kind of CD to make: a standard disc that will play in just about any CD player, an MP3 CD that will play in the computer's CD drive (and some newer home decks), or a backup just for safekeeping.

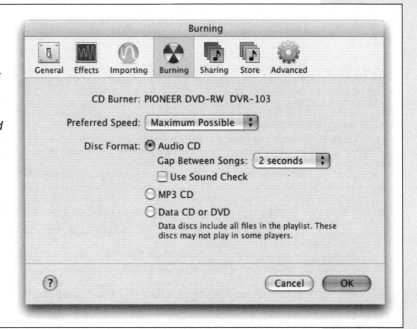

Once iTunes has taken care of business, it lets you know that it's now burning the CD. Again, depending on the speed of your computer and CD burner, as well as the size of your playlist, the recording process could take several minutes.

When the disc is done, iTunes pipes up with a musical flourish. Eject the CD (by pressing the Eject key at the upper right of a Mac keyboard, for example) and label the top of the newly minted music storehouse with a magic marker (or your favorite method).

Tip: You can set up your computer to auto-eject the CD when it's finished ripping—a great hint if you plan to copy a bunch of CDs to your hard drive, assembly-line style.

In iTunes, choose iTunes→Preferences (Mac) or Edit→Preferences (Windows). Click the General icon or tab. Where it says, "On CD Insert," choose "Import Songs and Eject." From now on, each CD spits out automatically when it's done.

Playing Songs Across a Network

If you've taken the trouble to set up a home network so your family can share a printer, an Internet connection, and so on, more treats await. With iTunes 4, you share songs and playlists with up to five networked computers—Macs, PCs, or a mix of both. You could, for example, tap into your roommate's jazz collection without getting up from your desk, and she can sample the zydeco and tejano tunes from your World Beat playlists. The music you decide to share is streamed over the network to the other computer.

Note: In iTunes 4.0, you could even listen to music on Macs *elsewhere on the Internet,* as long as you knew their IP addresses (network addresses). It didn't take long for people to figure out how to exploit this feature and share music all over the Internet in sneaky ways that Apple had never intended.

In response to hysterical phone calls from the record companies, Apple removed this feature (and the Advanced→Connect to Shared Music command) in version 4.0.1. Now you can connect only to other machines on your own office network.

To share music across a network, the machines involved must meet a few requirements:

- The Macs on the network need to be using at least iTunes 4.0.1 and Mac OS X 10.2.4 or later. The Windows computers need iTunes 4.1 or later.

- The computers must be on the same *subnet* of the network. (If you don't know what that means, read on.)

- The iTunes Sharing preferences for each computer involved need to be configured properly.

Preparing to Share

The *Subnet Mask* (that is, the chunk of the network you're on) is identified by four numbers separated by periods, like this: 255.255.255.0. (Nobody ever said networking was user-friendly.)

To check the subnet number of a Macintosh, open System Preferences and click the Network icon.

To check the Subnet Mask on a Windows machines, choose Start→Control Panel, double-click the Network Connections icon, and right-click the icon for your connection. Then choose Properties from the shortcut menu. In the Properties box, click Internet Protocol, and then click Properties to see the subnet information.

Sharing Your Own Music

To "publish" your own tunes to the network, choose iTunes→Preferences (Mac) or Edit→Preferences (Windows) and click the Sharing icon. Turn on "Share my music" (see Figure 4-23). You can choose to share your entire collection, or just selected playlists.

Whatever you type in the Shared Name box in the Sharing preferences will show up in your friend's iTunes Source list. You can also require a password as a key to your own music library—a handy feature if you feel that your colleagues mooch off of you quite enough in other areas of life.

You can share AAC, MP3, AIFF, WAV files, and radio station links with your network buddies, but not Audible tracks or QuickTime files. And sharing means "streaming" here. You can listen to shared music, but you can't burn someone else's music files to a CD, copy them to an iPod, or add them to your own iTunes library.

And one more point of fine print. Remember that songs bought from the iTunes Music Store can play on a maximum of three machines. If you want to listen to such a song across the network, one that hasn't been authorized on your computer, you must enter the Apple account name and user password that was used to purchase the song before you can play it. Your computer now takes one of the three spots on the song's authorized list (see Chapter 6 for details on authorization). If you *don't* type in the owner's name and password for purchased songs, iTunes will skip those tracks.

Listening to Someone Else's Tunes

It's easy to listen to somebody else's music collection; once it's been shared, their iTunes libraries generally appear right in your Source list, labeled with whatever name your benevolent buddy has chosen for the shared collection. (See Figure 4-23, bottom.)

Double-click the desired song to fire it up and play through your computer's speakers. (If your pal has put a password on the shared collection, you'll have to type that in before you can listen.)

Tip: Want to know if a certain song is shared? Select the title and press ⌘-I (Mac) or Ctrl+I (Windows), or choose File→Get Info. If the word "Remote" appears next to Kind in the Summary area, you're looking at a shared file.

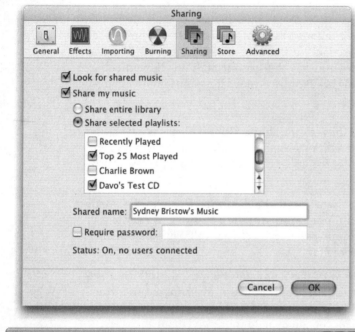

Figure 4-23:
Top: The iTunes 4 Sharing Preferences box lets you share as much of your music collection as you would like with other people on the same network. It also allows you to seek out music on other connected computers yourself. To share your music, you must first turn on the sharing feature and indicate what you want to put out there for others to sample.

Bottom: Once you've decided to share, your subnet pals can sample your collection right from their iTunes Source lists.

If the other person's tunes aren't showing up, choose iTunes→Preferences (Mac) or Edit→Preferences (Windows) and click the Sharing icon. In the Sharing preferences box (Figure 4-23, top), turn on "Look for shared music."

POWER USERS' CLINIC

Freeware and Shareware for iTunes

Just as dozens of friendly little programs have made the iPod easier and more fun to use, music-loving programmers have also come up with some handy tools to enhance iTunes. Searching VersionTracker (*www.version tracker.com*) for the keyword "iTunes" will generate results for over 80 programs. MacUpdate (*www.macup date.com*) is another site that keeps tabs on available programs for the Macintosh. Among the inexpensive software and freeware offerings for iTunes:

EasyView X 1.0 (Mac). A visualization plug-in for iTunes that displays the information for the current song with large colorful text (*www.trinfinitysoftware.com/easyview.shtml*).

iAlarm (Mac). People who use the Mac for everything anyway can now use it as a talking alarm clock. The iAlarm freeware can not only start playing iTunes songs at a specified time, but it can speak the weather and news as well (*http://users.wpi.edu/~isam/iAlarm*).

iTunes SideKick (Windows). This plug-in lets you adjust the opacity of your minibar and keep it on top of your other windows, keeping your music in view at all times. You can also minimize it to the tray and see the current artist and song name in a tooltip (*www.ipodlounge.com/ipodnews_comments.php?id=2195_0_7_0_M*).

iHam on iRye (Mac). Playing music over a network is just as much fun as playing it on your own computer, especially if the other Mac has plenty of hard drive space and can serve as a jukebox. The iHam on iRye program works a remote control for controlling iTunes on another computer on the network, especially older Macs with older versions of iTunes that can't share on their own, from the comfort of your own machine (*www.swssoftware.com/products/iham.html*).

iTunes Watcher (Mac). If you can never remember what song is playing and don't feel like drilling down through your Mac's open windows or constantly clicking into the Dock to find out, the iTunes Watcher is for you. The tiny

program creates an equally tiny information panel that always floats onscreen on top of other open windows (*www.charlesarthur.com/fungible*).

ViewTunes (Mac). Let your chat buddies on AOL Instant Messenger know what you're listening to while you trade instant messages. ViewTunes adds the song information to your AIM profile (*homepage.mac.com/mmurph/murphsoft*).

WhiteCap. With 180 different visual effects, customizable settings, and a morphing slideshow, WhiteCap expands the entertainment possibilities so much you may forget all about TV. Available for Windows, Mac OS 9 and X systems (*www.55ware.com/whitecap/download.html*).

Zoomify Photo Visualizer (Mac). This free iTunes plug-in lets you swap out the program's psychedelic visualizations for a personalized slideshow made up from the photos of your choice (*www.zoomify.com/downloads*).

Avalon (Mac). Think of it as an egg timer for your Mac OS X machine: Set up Avalon to go off at a certain time before you leave, and it fires up iTunes and any other programs you want to have up, running, and waiting when you get back (*www.firestormcreation.com/fsavalon.html*).

Volume Logic (Mac). This $20 audio plug-in for Mac OS X digitally remasters your music as you play it to balance the sound and keep volume levels consistent, while not actually altering your files (*www.octiv.com/index.asp?content=iTunes*).

On Deck (Mac). You can display artwork for the current album in a separate window and also use the program to upload art and track information to an FTP or Web server (*http://verseguru.com/?applications/OnDeck*).

iTunes Visuals Plugins (Mac). You can really dress up your Visualizer (in Mac OS 9 or X) with this free passel of plug-ins (*www.trinfinitysoftware.com/itunesplugins.shtml*).

Turning Off Music Sharing

If you want a little privacy for your music collection, you can easily turn off the Sharing function. Just go back to the iTunes Preferences box (Figure 4-23) and click the Sharing icon. Turn off the "Share my music" box and click OK to disable the feature until the next time you're feeling generous. Your playlists are no longer visible to other people on the network.

Tip: To add audio effects—adding a crossfade between songs when playing, enhancing the sound, or even leveling out different track volumes with the iTunes Sound Check feature—choose iTunes→Preferences (Mac) or Edit→Preferences (Windows) and click the Effects button.

MusicMatch Jukebox for Windows

I f you're using your iPod with Windows, you'll probably have the most fun using Apple's own iTunes program to rip, record, and organize your digital music files. This free program has more features than Napster's software, no deliberately crippled features (like CD ripping in MusicMatch), and exclusive access to Apple's iTunes Music Store.

Even so, there are some very good reasons why you might not want to use iTunes. For starters, it requires Windows 2000 or XP, which leaves several hundred million PCs out in the cold. Or maybe you're perfectly content to keep your music collection in MusicMatch Jukebox Plus. (This might be the case if you were using MusicMatch before you got your iPod or if you started using MusicMatch when it was the only program that could talk to your iPod.)

This chapter explores MusicMatch Jukebox, which still works beautifully as a loading dock for the iPod. (Specifically, this chapter describes version 7.5, the last officially Apple-approved version for use with the iPod, and the edition that MusicMatch.com recommends for iPods. More recent versions of MusicMatch Jukebox work with the iPod, too, as long as you install the iPod plug-in software described on page 116.)

Note: Like Apple's iTunes Music Store, MusicMatch has its own online song store for legal music downloads. However, since MusicMatch.com's downloads are copy-protected using Windows Media Audio format, you can't play them on the iPod.

Introduction to MusicMatch Jukebox

MusicMatch Jukebox has been ripping (converting) CD songs to MP3 files since 1998. The program has evolved considerably, adding features like a music subscription service, faster encoding speeds, and more than 28 million customers.

The basic, free version of MusicMatch Jukebox lets you rip MP3 songs from CDs (convert them to computer files) and download them to portable players. The enhanced version—MusicMatch Jukebox Plus—adds tons of extra features, but costs an extra $20. If your iPod's CD came with a copy of MusicMatch, though, you can upgrade to the more muscular MusicMatch for free, just by entering the serial number from the sticker on the iPod CD's cellophane sleeve.

UP TO SPEED

Mixing and Matching MusicMatch

This chapter is based on the menus and features of MusicMatch Jukebox Plus 7.5 for the iPod. If you have version 7.1, version 8 or later, or iTunes, you may need the following instructions to get the iPod to work.

If you have MusicMatch Jukebox 7.1: Download version 7.5 from *www.musicmatch.com/download/free/index.cgi?OEM=APPLE*.

If you've installed MusicMatch Jukebox 8 or later: If you try to install an even newer version—8.0 for example—you'll discover that MusicMatch no longer recognizes the iPod. The workaround: In MusicMatch Jukebox, choose Options→Add New Features. Make sure you're connected to the Internet, because this command takes you to the New Features page of the MusicMatch Web site. Once there, click the "Portable MP3 Players" link to reveal all the available plug-in software for portable players, iPod included. Click the link for your iPod model to start the download.

If you've installed iTunes: If you were curious enough to download and install iTunes for Windows, you may be alarmed to discover that iTunes has wrested control away from your copy of MusicMatch. Suddenly, MusicMatch doesn't even "see" the iPod.

If that's your situation, here's how to get your iPod popping up in MusicMatch again:

1. Unplug the iPod from the PC.

2. Choose My Computer→Control Panel→Add or Remove Programs.

3. Select and uninstall at least five things: iTunes, iPod for Windows, the MusicMatch iPod Plugin software, the iPod System Software Update (or any other iPod software listed), and MusicMatch Jukebox itself.

4. Close the Add or Remove Programs box and restart the PC.

5. Choose Start→Program Files→MusicMatch→MusicMatch Jukebox. Drag files in this folder (but not the folder itself) to the Recycle Bin. Do the same with the files in the Program Files→iPod folder. Empty the Recycle Bin.

6. Reinstall MusicMatch Jukebox from the CD that came with your iPod. Alternatively, download the iPod version of MusicMatch Jukebox from *www.musicmatch.com*.

7. Restart the PC.

8. Connect your iPod to the computer and start MusicMatch Jukebox, which should work fine now.

Note: You'll have best results with iPod and MusicMatch Jukebox if you have at least a 330-megahertz Pentium computer with 96 MB of RAM or more, running Windows Me or later. You'll also need a hard drive large enough to hold all the music you want to listen to and 50 MB of space for the MusicMatch software itself, plus a FireWire or USB 2.0 port on the PC.

The iPod-compatible version of MusicMatch Jukebox Plus gives Windows iPodders features like automatic synchronization, Volume Leveling to help even out sound levels between songs, digital sound effects, a Super Tagging function that quickly locates song information, and the ability to record CDs right from within MusicMatch. More on all of this on the following pages.

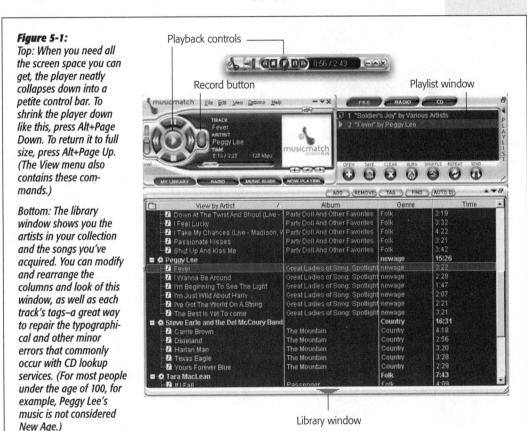

Figure 5-1:
Top: When you need all the screen space you can get, the player neatly collapses down into a petite control bar. To shrink the player down like this, press Alt+Page Down. To return it to full size, press Alt+Page Up. (The View menu also contains these commands.)

Bottom: The library window shows you the artists in your collection and the songs you've acquired. You can modify and rearrange the columns and look of this window, as well as each track's tags–a great way to repair the typographical and other minor errors that commonly occur with CD lookup services. (For most people under the age of 100, for example, Peggy Lee's music is not considered New Age.)

Playback controls

Record button

Playlist window

Library window

A Quick Tour

As shown in Figure 5-1, the MusicMatch Jukebox main window has plenty of buttons and a small menu bar in the upper-left corner. The circular control panel just below the menu bar contains the familiar volume slider, and play, pause, forward, reverse, and record buttons; the song currently playing is identified in the adjacent panel. A small window capable of displaying animated "laser-light shows," album art, and video snippets sits between this area and the Playlists section.

Note: If you've used an MP3 player with RCA Lyra or Creative Nomad Jukebox, then MusicMatch Jukebox may look and feel familiar to you. Lucky you—you've got a lot less software learning to do.

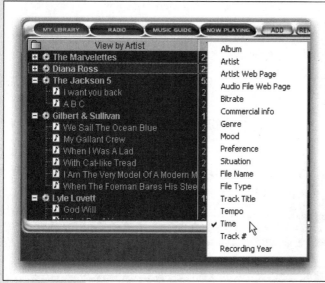

Figure 5-2:
Right-clicking a column heading gives you plenty of choices for substituting a different kind of column—all the better to sort your music by. MusicMatch can display seven columns in the main window at any one time.

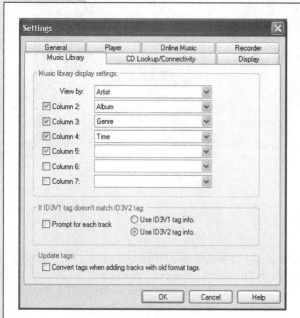

Figure 5-3:
The Settings box lets you set up your My Library columns with just the info you care about, in the order you want to see it. (The bottom two checkboxes let you choose which version of the track-tagging standard you want for your files. The older ID3V1 tag format can't hold as much information as ID3V2, which can display pictures and lyrics in the song's tag file. See the box on page 121 for more about ID3 tags.)

Below this top section are four oblong buttons that each reveal something different in an expanding window below. The buttons, and each of their contents, are:

- **My Library.** Click here to examine the contents of the MusicMatch Jukebox music library. Songs are grouped by performer name, with album information, genre, and track length easily visible.

- **Radio.** This button reveals a list of streaming Internet radio stations in a range of genres.

- **Music Guide.** With a click of this button and an Internet connection, MusicMatch provides links to music downloads, recommendations, charts, and more.

- **Now Playing.** This button brings information about the musician you're currently listening to right into the MusicMatch window for instant gratification.

Window Fun

When you first look at your music library, you'll notice that the View by Artist column groups your music by performer. If you click the + button next to the CD icon, a subcategory unfurls beneath the artist name, showing you all of the songs you have by that particular person or group (Figure 5-1, bottom).

Tip: You don't have to view your music library grouped by artist. You may prefer to organize that first column (the *Folder View*) by album, track title, or any of several other categories. Just right-click anywhere in the Folder View column and choose from the shortcut menu.

You don't have to sort your music alphabetically by artist, however. You can have all kinds of fun with this columnar display. For example:

- Change the order of the columns by dragging. For example, if you want to have Time right before Genre (instead of after), drag the word Time horizontally until it's to the left of Genre.

- To change the identity of just one column—to swap in the Artist column where the Time currently appears, for example—right-click its title. From the pop-up list of column categories (Bit rate, Recording Year, and so on), choose the name of the column you want to replace it with, as shown in Figure 5-2.

- To adjust the width of a column, drag the vertical divider line on its right side.

- To add more information columns (or fewer), choose Options→Music Library→Music Library Settings to produce the dialog box shown in Figure 5-3, where you can turn columns on and off en masse.

- Click a column title (like Artist or Album) to sort the song list alphabetically by that criterion. Click a second time to reverse the sorting order.

  For example, if you're having the girls over for tea and want to have some nice mellow music wafting about in the background, you can sort your music library by genre and select all the music in the Classical section.

Ripping CDs into MusicMatch

If you don't have any music files to move onto that brand-new iPod, it's easy to whip some up with MusicMatch. Just grab those albums and start up the program. Then proceed as follows.

Phase 1: Choose an Audio File Format

When you slide a CD into your drive, Windows XP, if that's what you're running, asks you how it might assist you with the disc you've just inserted. In the dialog box that appears, choose MusicMatch Jukebox Plus to play the CD. (Earlier versions of Windows are not quite as forthcoming as Windows XP. If you've used MusicMatch Jukebox to play CDs before, the program should open right up. But if Windows presents you with a list of programs to consider for the task, choose MusicMatch Jukebox Plus.)

MusicMatch Jukebox Plus starts out set to produce MP3 files recorded at 128 kilobits per second (see Chapter 3), but you can adjust this rate (to produce smaller music files, for example). To do so, press Shift+Ctrl+S or choose Options→Settings, and then click the Recorder tab. Use the Recording Quality controls, as shown in Figure 5-4.

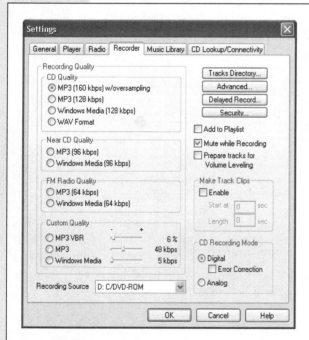

Figure 5-4:
The Recorder Settings window lets you adjust the bit rates of your MP3 files. You can choose a preset one—"CD Quality (128 kpbs)," for example—or use the slider to raise or lower the bit rate. The Settings box is also where you can choose to encode songs in other audio formats like WAV. Although MusicMatch Jukebox can play and rip files into different digital audio formats, not all of them are compatible with the iPod. The MP3 and WAV formats are the iPod-friendly ones.

Phase 2: Download Song Names and Track Information

It turns out that most audio CDs don't include any digital information about themselves. When you first insert a music CD into a PC, you may be disappointed to discover that to the computer, every song on it is called "Track 1," "Track 2," and so on—and the name of the album is "Audio CD." If you don't do anything to solve the problem, after you've ripped, say, seven CDs into MusicMatch Jukebox, you'll find that you have seven songs called Track 1, seven songs called Track 2, and so on—not the easiest way to organize your music.

If you have a high-speed Internet connection (like a cable modem or DSL), the program quickly dashes out and brings back the information by itself (unless you've changed the Deferred CD Lookup setting described next). Behind the scenes, the program is consulting the Internet's massive, comprehensive CD Database (CDDB), which is maintained by a company called Gracenote (*www.gracenote.com*). After MusicMatch sends information from the disc to the CDDB Web site, the database identifies the album and sends back the song titles and other data for MusicMatch to display.

If you have a dial-up modem, you may prefer the Deferred CD Lookup option, which appears on the CD Lookup/Connectivity tab of the Options→Settings box. With Deferred CD Lookup, MusicMatch Jukebox waits to download the information for your songs until the next time you're online.

If your CD has no entry in the CDDB database—if, for example, it's the demo disc for your brother's punk-klezmer quintet—you can also manually enter the track information by clicking in each line and typing the song, artist, and album names. Or you can edit the track's *tag files,* as described in the box on below.

UP TO SPEED

ID3 Tags: The Basics

When you use an option like the CDDB database, MusicMatch (or iTunes, for that matter) matches a code on the CD with the corresponding track information in the online database. That information, which includes artist, song, and album name, is then stored in a part of the MP3 file known as the *ID3 tag.*

Most MP3 and audio-management programs rely on these tags, which have been around since the mid-1990s, to sort and organize song files. Editing ID3 with an MP3 program like MusicMatch is a handy way to fix an occasional typo or incorrect information from an online database (see Figure 5-7).

Although the original tag standard allowed for a limited amount of information to be entered, a newer version of the ID3 tag standard, ID3v2, has room for things like the song's lyrics, elaborate commentary, and pictures. Both MusicMatch and iTunes include an option (in the tag-editing box) to convert a track's ID3 tag to the newer version of the standard. There's detailed technical information on ID3 tags and how to use them at *www.id3.org.*

Note: If MusicMatch tries to download song information and seems to be running into a wall, it might be doing just that—smacking up against your network's firewall. In that case, check the program's settings to make sure you have any *proxy addresses* or other necessary information filled in. Check with your network's system administrator if you're not sure what the settings should be.

If MusicMatch Jukebox Plus keeps causing your *personal* firewall software to complain, consult the program's help files to learn how to let MusicMatch Jukebox pass through without alerting you.

Phase 3: Convert the Song to a Digital Audio File

Once your song information is in place, click the red Record button identified in Figure 5-1. When the Recorder window pops up, showing the list of songs on the CD, pick the tracks that you want to convert to MP3 files (Figure 5-5).

Figure 5-5:
The Recorder lets you select as many songs as you wish from any CD. The second column keeps you updated on MusicMatch's progress as it rips the selected tracks.

When the Recorder first opens, all songs are checkmarked. Turn off the checkbox next to any songs you'd prefer *not* to rip. If you only want one or two songs off the album, clicking None above the song list in the Recorder window unchecks all the songs at once, saving you a few seconds of clicking. This is a great technique when you want only one or two songs in the list; turn *all* checkboxes off, then turn those *two* back on again. (Click All to turn them all back on at once.) The Refresh button

---

FREQUENTLY ASKED QUESTION

Analog or Digital Recording?

I very much enjoyed Figure 5-4. I was puzzled, though, by the choice between analog and digital recording. I thought MP3 files are digital, and so are the iPod and my PC. What's the deal?

The Analog recording mode is slower because it records songs in real time, but it can produce MP3 files with better sound quality, especially if your computer's CD drive isn't equipped to handle digital extraction or doesn't do it very well. If you have an older CD-ROM drive and your MP3 files don't sound very good after digital recording, try switch-

ing to Analog mode by choosing Options→Settings, clicking the Recorder tab, and turning on the Analog box.

Most modern CD drives handle digital recording quite well and can really speed up the recording process, even up to twelve times the normal play speed of the song. A digital recording usually sounds better than an analog recording, but a high-speed processor and good sound card can make analog recordings very close in audio quality to their digital cousins.

---

forces the Recorder to rescan the CD drive for the disc inside (the program sometimes doesn't notice that you've swapped in a different disc).

Once you've selected your songs for ripping, click the Record button at the lower left
(visible in Figure 5-5). MusicMatch gets to work converting the tunes to MP3 files
on your hard drive, keeping you informed of its progress by posting percentages of
conversions completed next to each song title.

Tip: To focus the computer's processing power on the track-ripping task at hand, MusicMatch doesn't *play*
the songs as they're being converted into MP3 files. If you do want to hear the music as it's being converted, though, choose Options→Settings, click the Recorder tab, and turn off "Mute while recording."

The time it takes to convert a CD to MP3 format depends on the speed of the computer and its CD drive, the bit rate you've chosen, and whether or not you've turned
on MusicMatch Jukebox Plus's automatic error-correction feature (in the Settings
box shown in Figure 5-4). On average, a file converted at 128 kbps takes about 20
seconds per minute of audio.

The Recorder window (Figure 5-5) displays the recording speed as you rip along, so
if you see a number like 5.0x in the window, you know you're recording that song at
five times its normal play speed. The program may adjust its speed as it encounters
and corrects errors.

Note: Open, memory-hogging programs like photo-editing software or games can slow down the ripping
process; so can frequently saving files in other programs.

When the program is done converting your songs, it politely hands back your disc
by ejecting it from the computer's drive.

Phase 4: Add Cover Artwork

As shown in Figure 5-6, an accompanying image of an album cover or other evoca-
tive art adds a professional element to your MusicMatch experience. Thousands of
prescanned album covers can be found around the Web on music ecommerce sites
(like Amazon), which you can download to your desktop with just a right-click of
the mouse.

Figure 5-6:
A dash of art in the track's
tag can perk up the window
quite a bit. If you don't
want the album cover, you
can have any picture you
want in the player's art
window.

Here are a few other artwork tips:

- If you have a scanner and a love of art, you can also scan images from the CD insert—or anything else—and attach the image to the track. Save the artwork as a BMP or JPG file in the MusicMatch Jukebox Plus folder on your hard drive.

Then right-click a track in the MusicMatch list and, from the shortcut menu, choose Edit Track Tag(s). In the Edit Track Tag(s) box that appears (Figure 5-7), click the Find Art File, navigate to the correct image, click it, and click OK. The artwork appears in the media window whenever the song plays.

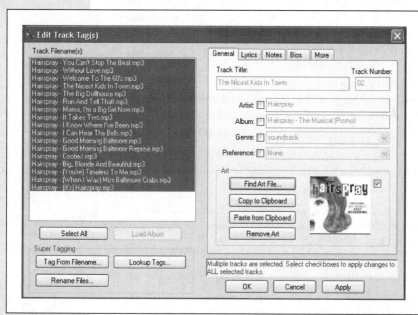

Figure 5-7:
In the Edit Track Tag(s) box, you can add art, adjust the text in the track's tag, paste in lyrics, add notes, and even see where the song file lives on your hard drive. To get started, right-click any song title in your library and select Edit Track Tag(s) from the shortcut menu.

GEM IN THE ROUGH

Autoimporting

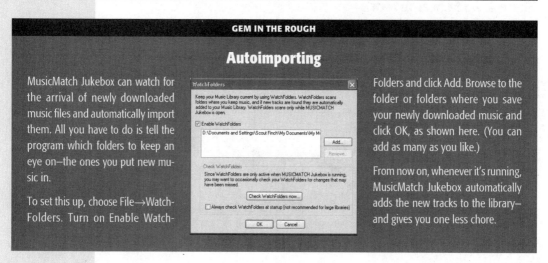

MusicMatch Jukebox can watch for the arrival of newly downloaded music files and automatically import them. All you have to do is tell the program which folders to keep an eye on—the ones you put new music in.

To set this up, choose File→Watch-Folders. Turn on Enable Watch-Folders and click Add. Browse to the folder or folders where you save your newly downloaded music and click OK, as shown here. (You can add as many as you like.)

From now on, whenever it's running, MusicMatch Jukebox automatically adds the new tracks to the library—and gives you one less chore.

- To copy the same piece of art to all the tracks on an album, select a song from it and then open the Edit Track Tag(s) dialog box (see Figure 5-7). When the song is listed in the Track Filename(s) window, click Load Album below it to round up all the tracks ripped from that same album. Click Select All.

  On the other side of the Edit Track Tag(s) box, turn on the checkbox where it says Art. Click Find Art File, navigate to the picture you want to use, and click Open. The art gets pasted into the tag for each track on the album. Click OK.

- Pressed for time but still want your tracks to be artful? MusicMatch Jukebox can hunt down the album's art for you automatically. In the Settings box (Ctrl+Shift+S), click the Display tab and turn on "Look up album art if not already present."

Tip: You can also even make MusicMatch change your PC's desktop wallpaper to match the album art for whatever album is playing. Just turn on "Use album art as wallpaper."

Importing Other Music Files into MusicMatch

Not all sound files come directly from the CDs. If you've had a PC for longer than about two days, odds are you already have some audio files stored on the hard drive: MP3s downloaded from the Internet or ripped in another program like WinAmp, WAV files featuring snippets of dialogue from *Buffy the Vampire Slayer*, sample songs that came with other multimedia software, and so on.

If you're so inclined, you can add these audio files to your growing MusicMatch Jukebox Plus library in any of three ways.

- For a hands-on approach, just drag the icons of your music files right off the desktop (or out of your folder windows) into the MusicMatch Jukebox window.

- For an automated approach, choose File→Add New Music Track(s) to Library. (Alternatively, click Add above your list of songs in the library window, visible in Figure 5-1.)

  A dialog box asks you to find the files you want. If you're in a hurry, feeling lazy, or busy watching the hockey game on the TV, you can have the program do a sweep of your main drive and add any MusicMatch-friendly file formats to the library. Just select your entire hard drive as the directory for MusicMatch Jukebox to search (or choose Options→Music Library→Search and Add Tracks From All Drives. You may wind up with a lot of sonic debris washing up in your library, but you can't beat the convenience.

  If you want to be more selective, you can navigate to folders where you have stored your music files. Click Add when you've found what you're looking for and are ready to add the new songs to the library (Figure 5-8).

Tip: To import a bunch of files at once, Ctrl+click the name of each one, thereby selecting several simultaneously, before clicking Add.

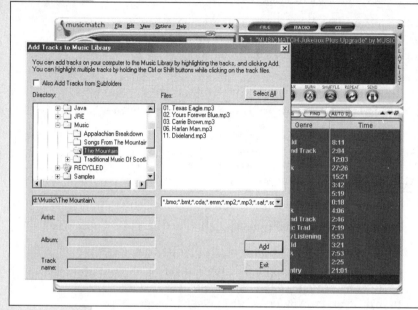

Figure 5-8:
You can add many different types of music files to MusicMatch Jukebox, but remember that Windows Media Audio (WMA) and mp3PRO files are not iPod-friendly. Stick with WAV and MP3 if you want to take those songs on the road. To add the songs in this window, click Select All and then click Add.

Deleting Songs

Music tastes evolve and change, and hard drives get full. If you find yourself in either situation, or just feel like doing a little cleanup, you can remove tracks from your collection with a couple of clicks.

Click the song you wish to delete (or Ctrl+click to select several), and then click the Remove button at the top of the My Library window. MusicMatch asks if you're sure you want to delete the track, and gives you the option of erasing the song from your computer altogether (Figure 5-9).

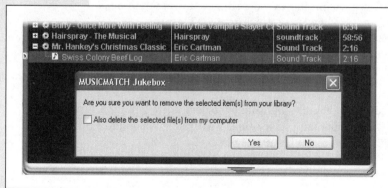

Figure 5-9:
MusicMatch alerts you when you click the Remove button to delete tracks from your library. Turn on the checkbox if you want to erase it from your hard drive, as opposed to just removing its listing in MusicMatch. (Right-clicking the song or album title and selecting Remove Track(s) is another way to dump songs.)

Tip: If you click a track to play it, and all you get is a lousy error message babbling about "path/track could not be found," you may have moved a music file out of its original folder on your hard drive. Fortunately, you can fix it right away. Right-click the faulty track and, from the shortcut menu, choose Repair Broken Links. MusicMatch Jukebox Plus goes on a hunt for busted file paths and gives you the option to fix or remove broken links.

Playing Music

MusicMatch Jukebox Plus is not just mere CD-ripping software, but a full-featured digital audio management program with plenty of ways to customize its look and feel to determine how it presents your music.

Once you've ripped a few tunes, you'll see a list begin to grow in your MusicMatch library window. To turn your PC into a music machine, click the small + icon next to the artist's or album's name in the first column to see all the corresponding songs. (Of course, if you've fooled around with the display settings for this first column, you may already be staring at a big long list of songs.)

There are many ways to play a song or album:

- Click the song title, and then click the triangular Play button in the MusicMatch Jukebox player controls.

- Ctrl+click multiple songs in the library window, and then click the Play button.

- Click a performer's name in the Library window, and then click the Play button to play all of that artist's songs. (The same trick works if you're viewing the main list by album or another category.)

The songs you select end up in the Playlist window, and a red triangle appears next to the song title that's now playing. Use other player controls to pause, stop, rewind, or fast-forward the songs in an album or playlist. You can jump to another part of the same song by dragging the small Tylenol-shaped button on the progress bar. Of course, the volume slider works, too.

Visualizations

As music plays, you can control and manipulate the music and the visuals of your PC in all kinds of interesting ways. As a result, some people don't move from their PCs for months at a time.

Visualizations, for example, are animated graphics that appear in the Media Window, wiggling and pulsating in time to the music (Figure 5-10). You can create your own visual world of music by choosing View→Visualizations→Select Visualization.

In the dialog box that opens, clicking Get New takes you to an area on the Music-Match Web site where you can download new animations. Running the graphics can slow down your PC, though, so if you're running tight on available memory, skip the Visualizing.

Skins

If you're tired of the way your MusicMatch Jukebox Plus window looks, you can give the whole thing a fresh new look by changing its *skin*.

Figure 5-10:
Visualizations can keep dancing long after the music stops. Click the tiny oval button above the frame to make the display slightly larger.

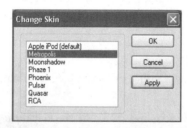

Figure 5-11:
Top: Choose View→Change Skin to produce this dialog box, which makes it easy to give MusicMatch Jukebox Plus a whole new look. (Click a skin name and then click OK—or click Apply to test it out without having to close the dialog box first.) If you get tired of the ones that came with the program, just go to View→Download Skins and snag some more.

Bottom: There are skins available in all kinds of styles, from Earnest Techno to Whimsical Moderne; here, the skins called Xtreme, Starskin, and Phaze are on parade.

"Skin" here has nothing to do with dermatology; it's computerese for "the visual look and design of the program, like its color scheme, window design, font choices, and button shapes." MusicMatch comes with a few alternate skins, which you can try on for size as the mood strikes you (see Figure 5-11).

Note: In the version of MusicMatch Jukebox Plus that came with the 2002 iPods, the Change Skin and Download Skins commands were in the Options menu, not the View menu.

The Graphic Equalizer

On expensive luxury stereo components, a *graphic equalizer* is a control console that lets you adjust the strength of each musical frequency independently.

MusicMatch provides an Equalizer, too, stocked with presets for various styles of music. To adjust the sound quality of your tracks with prefab—or customized—settings, choose Options→Player→Equalizer. Turn on the Enable EQ box in the lower-left corner, then choose one of the preconfigured settings from the pop-up menu at the bottom of the box. From there, you can adjust the sliders to customize the sound for your personal listening pleasure, as described in Figure 5-12.

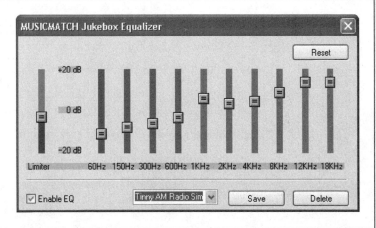

Figure 5-12:
The Graphic Equalizer lets you apply your own sonic boom to songs. The Limiter controls the overall amplification, while the bass frequencies start on the left at 60 Hz and proceed to the high end of the scale at 18 KHz. This Tinny AM Radio setting shows a distinct lack of bass.

Presets of your own

If you've taken advantage of the serial-number sticker on your iPod CD and upgraded your software from mere MusicMatch Jukebox to MusicMatch Jukebox *Plus*, you can create and save your own customized Equalizer presets.

Click the word Custom in the box at the bottom of the dialog box, and then type a name for the preset you're about to create ("Tinny AM Radio Simulator," for example).

Now go to work with the sliders shown in Figure 5-12. You can fiddle with the Limiter (a slider that can keep a lid on the levels at which the frequencies are amplified) and ten sliders that adjust sound frequencies in the bass, treble, and midrange tones of the music.

Once you're done sliding around, click Save to add your new custom preset to the list, where you'll be able to summon it later with a couple of quick clicks.

Note: Equalizer presets from MusicMatch don't transfer to the iPod with your music. Of course, you can always use the EQ settings on the iPod itself when playing your tunes.

Preventing Ear-Blast Syndrome

Volume Leveling adjusts the volume of both loud songs and soft songs to create a middle ground, so you're not straining to hear one track and then deafened by the next one.

To use the feature, select the tracks you wish to work with, in either My Library or Playlist window.

Right-click any one of them and then, from the shortcut menu, choose Prepare Tracks for Volume Leveling. MusicMatch Jukebox asks for confirmation; if you give the go-ahead, it automatically adjusts the recorded volume levels. It adds a green musical note next to the name of each track that's received volume surgery.

These tracks will maintain their adjusted volume settings when transferred to the iPod—*if* you turn on the right switch. Proceed as follows:

1. **Connect the iPod to the PC.**

   Wait for MusicMatch to start up. Eventually, a window called Portable Device Manager appears, displaying the iPod's icon.

2. **Right-click the iPod icon. From the shortcut menu, choose Options.**

   The Options dialog box appears.

POWER USERS' CLINIC

Look, in the Window! It's Super Tagging!

MusicMatch Jukebox not only tags music files, it can Super Tag them. Super Tagging actually means Auto Tagging; it speeds up tagging tasks by analyzing the song's file name on your hard drive. These features are especially useful when the file's name actually reflects the song and performer names. For example, you might have downloaded a song file called, "I Wanna Be Sedated – The Ramones.mp3."

In the lower-left corner of the Edit Track Tag(s) box (Figure 5-7), you'll find these options:

Lookup Tags zips into the MusicMatch online database to search for the full tag information based on just the artist or track name on the file's name.

Tag From Filename analyzes the downloaded file's name and, if possible, creates tags with the Artist and Track names in their proper fields. In the example above, you'd get "I Wanna Be Sedated" in the title box, and "The Ramones" in the Artist box.

Rename Files does the opposite. In songs whose tags are correctly entered, this command changes the song file.

---

3. Click the Audio tab and turn on "Apply volume leveling" (Figure 5-13).

That's it. The next time you sync with the iPod, your PC will transfer all of the newly modified songs to the player.

Note: You may spot an option on the iPod itself called SoundCheck, which also purports to adjust mismatched volume levels between songs. But that's for use with iTunes only. MusicMatch for Windows doesn't work the same way; it adjusts song volumes on the PC and then transfers the whole shebang over to the player.

Figure 5-13:
Grab a magazine next time you sync—applying volume leveling to your tracks makes them take longer to download to the iPod from MusicMatch Jukebox.

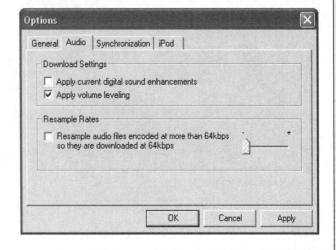

MusicMatch Administration

At its heart, MusicMatch is nothing more than a glorified database. Its job is to search, sort, and display information, quickly and efficiently. Here, for example, are some powerful managerial tasks it stands ready to handle.

Searching for Songs

The Find feature can search out all the songs that have a specific word in their title, album name, or artist attribution. To make it work, click Find at the top of your library window.

In the Find in Music Library box, type the word or name you're looking for, and then click Find First.

For example, in Figure 5-14, typing *love* jumps down the library list to tracks by different performers that all have the word "love" somewhere in the song's information—maybe the title of the song, maybe the band name. Click Add to add the song to the playlist window, and then click Find Next to move on.

Tip: There's another way to find a certain song, too: just start typing the first few letters of the artist or album. MusicMatch highlights the first matching song in the list.

Figure 5-14:
The Find function in MusicMatch Jukebox makes it easy to find love, or rather, songs with the word "love" in their titles within your music library. This sort of thing could be useful for creating themed playlists, like a mix for that Valentine's Day special someone made from songs that all have the word "love" in the title.

Editing Track Tag Information

As described on page 121, the CD Lookup feature saves a lot of time and tendons filling out *tag* information (track names, album names, and so on). But MusicMatch provides space to attach much more information to each song. Only the song title, artist, album, and genre show up on the iPod, but music librarians with an attention to detail can have a ball with the track tags on the PC side.

To change or add more information to your song files, click a track name in the My Library window and then click Tag. The Edit Track Tag(s) box pops up. You can add

---

GEM IN THE ROUGH

Waking Up with "Wake Up, Little Susie"

You already know that the iPod can wake you up to music if you happen to nod off while wearing the earbuds. But what if you fall asleep at the PC?

MusicMatch is there for you. In fact, you can use the little-known Alarm function to play up to five different alarms throughout the day, programmed with different songs and

sound clips—like "Food, Glorious Food" to alert you to lunch hour.

To get to the Alarm Settings box, right-click the MusicMatch Jukebox Plus icon in the Windows system tray. In the Settings box that opens, select the days, times, and songs you wish to use for your musical alarms.

---

lyrics, album art, and personal comments (Figure 5-7). The General tab has all basic information, including a huge selection of genres—but you can also type in genres of your own (Rockabilly Waltzes, anyone?).

Tip: To save time entering the same tag information for all the songs from the same album, open the Edit Track Tag(s) dialog box as described above. Then click Load Album (shown way back on page 124). You've just added to the list all the songs from the same CD, or–if you had already entered the album title by hand for each track–all songs with a matching album name.

If you click the More tab, you'll find that you can apply your own designations for the Mood or Situation fields from a pop-up list as well—or add your own like "Cheery" or "Keg Party at the Delta Upsilon House."

When you've finished filling out your tags, click Apply and then OK.

Internet Radio

Clicking the Radio button on the MusicMatch Jukebox Plus window whisks you off to the company's server, where you can sign up for an account with the MusicMatch MX Platinum subscription service. The service costs $5 a month and offers Internet radio streams from over 8,000 performers, like the one shown in Figure 5-15. A free trial is available on the site, as is a tutorial on how to use it.

Figure 5-15:
MusicMatch MX can bring streams of music flowing from the Internet into your computer. While you listen to the radio over the Internet, you can browse the MusicMatch site for tracks by other artists with a similar sound.

MusicMatch MX has helpful features like Artist on Demand to search for certain musicians, and Artist Match, which purports to find acts that *sound* like your favorites. You can listen to low-bandwidth streams of popular music and programming from online radio stations free of charge—by clicking them in the list at the left side of the window.

Playlists

A *playlist* is a list of songs that you've decided should go together. It can be made up of pretty much any group of songs arranged in any order. For example, if you're having a party, you can make a playlist from the current Top 40 and dance music in your music library.

Unlike the tedious, afternoon-consuming way of making a mix album in the Olden Days of vinyl, cassettes, and a stopwatch, MP3 playlists are a cinch to set up. Once you've got 'em, you can save your playlists, download them to your iPod, or even burn them to CDs for posterity.

Making a New Playlist

The Playlist window at the upper-right corner of the MusicMatch screen (Figure 5-16) is your workspace for making and mixing playlists. (If some technically challenged miscreant accidentally closed it when you weren't around, choose View→Playlist.) The Playlist window tucks itself behind the main MusicMatch Control panel, but leaves a vertical sign reading PLAYLIST on the edge that you can click to slide it out.

Figure 5-16:
You can make a playlist from anything you can drag into the Playlist window–like the song being dragged here. The buttons at the bottom let you Open previously created playlists, Save your new creations, Clear the songs out of a playlist window, Burn the playlist to a CD, Shuffle the play order, Repeat the playlist over after the last track is finished, and Send the Playlist to an external device, like an iPod. The three buttons at the top of the window indicate the source of the songs in the playlist–from audio files, streaming radio, or a CD.

Once you have your Playlist window open, you're all ready to make a playlist. If there are song titles still in the window from the last time you used the program, click the Clear button just below the window to wipe the slate clean.

To add songs to this window, start in the My Library window. Double-click each tune you'd like to add to your new playlist. You can also drag individual tracks—or groups of them—onto the playlist window, as shown in Figure 5-16.

To make a playlist from the entire contents of albums or collected artists' works, use any of these tactics:

- Drag album titles or performer names from the first column (Folder View) up to the Playlist window.

- Right-click a track and then, from the shortcut menu, choose the Add Track(s) to Playlist option.

- Drag sound files directly from your desktop or folder windows into the Playlist window. (Note, however, that these songs don't get automatically added to the library unless you change your preferences. To do so, choose Options→Settings; click the General tab; then, where it says "When double-clicking local music files," turn on "Add to Music Library.")

Don't worry about clogging up your hard drive. When you add a song title to a playlist, you don't *copy* the song; you're just giving MusicMatch instructions about which tracks to play and where to find the files. In essence, you're creating file short-cuts of the originals. You can have the same song on several different playlists without having to worry that you've now got sixteen copies of "Convoy" by C.W. McCall.

Once you have that new playlist just the way you want it, click the round Save button at the bottom of the Playlist window. A dialog box asks you what you'd like to call this new playlist.

Note: After you've created new playlists, don't move your original music files and folders around on the hard drive. The Playlists feature uses the file paths and locations of the music files when you originally saved the playlist, so moving the original files will result in having to redo your playlists.

Once you've saved and stored some playlists, you can call one up again by clicking Open at the bottom of the Playlist window. When the Open Music box pops up, click the icon for Playlists, click the playlist you want, and click the Play button within the Open Music box to start the music.

Modifying a Playlist

To reopen a playlist so you can add to it, shorten it, or rearrange the songs in it, proceed like this:

1. **Open the Playlist window.**

   If it's not onscreen, go to View→Playlist, or click the triangle on the edge of the MusicMatch control panel window to slide open the Playlist window.

---

2. Click the Open button.

   The Open Music dialog box appears.

3. Click the Playlists icon on the left side of the box, and then click the name of the playlist you want to edit.

   It looks like a folder with an .m3u file extension.

4. Click Play to load the tracks into the Playlist window, where you can work on them.

   Now you can drag the song titles up or down within the playlist window to reorder them, drag new songs into the window, delete songs by selecting them and then pressing the Delete key, and so on, until you're happy.

5. Click Save.

   You can give the modified playlist a new name if you like. To retain the old name, click Yes when MusicMatch Jukebox asks if you want to replace the older version.

Deleting a Playlist

You can delete a playlist, but you'd never guess how.

Start by opening the Playlist dialog box. Then, believe it or not, you're supposed to click the playlist name and click *Save*. In the Save Playlist box, click the name of the one you want to delete and then click Delete (Figure 5-17). The playlist disappears from your collection.

Click the red X in the top-right corner to close the dialog box (your other options are Save, Cancel, and Delete, none of which are good for making the escape).

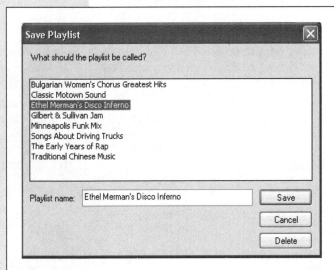

Figure 5-17:
The Save box also holds the key to deleting playlists, which isn't exactly the most intuitive thing in the world, but it works.

AutoDJ Playlists

Computers have automated many a time-consuming mission, and making playlists is no exception. With its AutoDJ feature, MusicMatch Jukebox Plus can compose its own playlists that appeal to your personal tastes. You just have to tell it what your personal tastes *are* for the playlist at hand.

For example, you might tell one AutoDJ Playlist to assemble a two-hour set of songs from your immense jazz collection—but *only* tracks by Louis Armstrong, Ella Fitzgerald, Art Tatum, and Duke Ellington. Doing it the AutoDJ way lets you spend less time picking through your library to find songs that match your mood, meaning you can get on with the music that much faster.

To get started, click the AutoDJ button at the top of the My Library window (or choose Options→Playlist→AutoDJ). As you can see in Figure 5-18, the AutoDJ dialog box asks for your input on the amount of time you want the playlist to last and what kind of music you want on it.

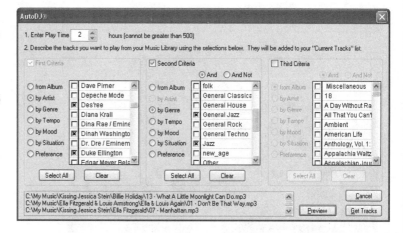

Figure 5-18:
The AutoDJ automatically generates a playlist with the guidelines you provide. Just pick the amount of time you want the playlist to last and then add criteria like albums, artists, or genres. This AutoDJ production, for example, will snag two hours of tunes by selected artists in the Jazz genre. You can give the AutoDJ up to three sets of criteria.

You can get a sneak peek at the computer-generated playlist by clicking Preview. A list of tracks appears in the Preview window. If you like what you see, click the Get Tracks button to sweep all the tunes into the Playlist window.

If you like the AutoDJ playlist enough to transfer it to your iPod the next time you synchronize it, click Save.

Tip: The more information you've added to your track tags during your music-organizing activities, the more detailed and precise you can get when formulating an AutoDJ playlist. What you've done is give yourself more elements to use in the AutoDJ criteria boxes.

Burning CDs

The iPod version of MusicMatch Jukebox Plus comes with a separate CD burning program called Burner Plus. With it, you can record regular audio CDs, MP3 CDs, and data discs. You can even do things like print out CD labels and jewel-case inserts and split up large chunks of data over multiple discs.

Tip: Before investing a lot of time with Burner Plus, check *www.musicmatch.com* for a list of CD and DVD drives that work with the program.

Once you have a CD in your drive, the procedure for making an audio CD of your tunes goes like this:

1. **Click the Burn button under the Playlist window (or choose File→Create CD).**

    The Burner Plus window appears (Figure 5-19). If there's a playlist in the Playlist window, its songs appear in the burner's window.

    If not, your job is to load the songs you want into the Burner window.

Figure 5-19:
The MusicMatch Jukebox Burner Plus program can record everything from audio discs to data backups, and can even help you design a label for the finished disc.

2. **Drag songs, albums, or artist names from the My Library window into the Playlist window.**

    You can also add audio files from your hard drive by clicking the Add button atop the window.

Tip: At the bottom of the Burner Plus window, you can see how much space you have left on the disc as you add more files to it. If you've chosen too much music for an audio CD, you have two alternatives. First, you can select some songs and then click the Remove icon at the top of the window. Alternatively, you can divide the batch and spread it out over multiple CDs by clicking the Split button at the top of the window.

---

3. **Choose Options→Settings in the Burner window. In the dialog box that appears, select the size of CD media you're using.**

   The drop-down menu offers you choices like 74 minute, 650 MB; 80 minute, 700 MB; and even DVD discs and those peewee 50 MB "business card" CDs.

   You can also make other configuration adjustments on the various tabs of this dialog box: selecting the kind of disc you want (standard audio, MP3, or data), adding a two-second gap between songs, and applying volume leveling.

4. **Click OK to close the Options dialog box. Then click the orange Burn button to start the CD recording process.**

   As a final touch, you can click Print to call up the Print CD Insert box, which lets you add art and titles and print out a list of track names to go with your freshly burned CD.

ALTERNATE REALITIES

Using a Mac iPod with a Windows PC

In the beginning, there were no Windows iPods. When it was introduced in 2001, the iPod was a Macintosh-only product. This made many Windows fans feel completely unloved and ignored. Here was this fabulous device they couldn't use with their computers! In short, Windows people found out what it's like to be Mac people.

Not wanting to let this cool gadget slip away because of a minor operating system incompatibility, creative Windows programmers rose to the challenge and came up with software that would let Windows machines connect to Macintosh-formatted iPods.

If you want to give your old Mac iPod a second life as a WiniPod, you can download the Windows iPod software from Apple's Web site and reformat the player's hard drive into a PC-friendly machine. (Just point your browser to *www.apple.com/ipod/download* and pull down a copy of the software designed for your version of the iPod. Once you download and start the installer program with the iPod connected, you need the Restore option to reformat the drive. Full details on using this software are on page 296.)

XPlay makes the iPod look like any other drive in Windows Explorer, so that you can drag music files and con-

tact information right onto the player. It walks you gently through the process of setting up the iPod and includes its own tools for making playlists and tweaking audio files. XPlay, which you can download from *www.mediafour.com/products/xplay*, costs about $30. A demo version is also available.

EphPod is a free program created by Joe Masters, who was a college student when he wrote it. To use it with a Macintosh iPod, you'll also need to buy MacOpener, a program that lets Windows see Macintosh-formatted disks. It's available for $40 for EphPod users; there's a link to it on the EphPod Web site at *www.ephpod.com*. (The program can work without MacOpener if you have a Windows iPod and are just looking for a free, great, user-friendly program to manage your iPod contents.)

The EphPod screen sort of looks like an Excel spreadsheet crossed with an inventory list from a record store, but it's easy to use, especially for transferring songs on and off the iPod. EphPod also includes the ability to download news headlines and create memos, contacts, and calendar information for the iPod. (There's more about the EphPod freeware in Chapters 2, 7, and 9.)

Note: MusicMatch Jukebox Plus is chock full of features that have nothing to do with the iPod. To find out more about the more intricate, Pod-free parts of the program, just select one of the many topics under the program's Help menu.

Resampling for More Room

If your iPod is getting crammed full, one way to solve the problem is to re-rip all your music from the original CDs, this time using a lower bit-rate setting. You'll get smaller files (of course, at lower quality).

That's a lot of effort, though. You may as well mow your lawn with fingernail scissors.

Fortunately, there's a much faster, automatic way. You can make MusicMatch Jukebox do the job for you—without even requiring your original CD collection. With the iPod plugged in, click the Options button in the Portables Plus window,

You'll see an option for *resampling* your songs at a lower bit rate when transferring tunes. Turn on the box for resampling, then drag the slider to a lower bit rate than what's currently used in your library (probably 128 kbps).

The next time MusicMatch transfers the music to your iPod, it will automatically convert each song to a lower, more compact form. This feature adds quite a bit of time to your sync session, of course. But the beauty of it is that your original music collection retains all of its original quality— on the PC. Only what's on the iPod is affected.

The iTunes Music Store

The recent explosion in Internet song swapping presented the recording industry with a paradoxical challenge: to stop music lovers from freely trading files over the Internet, while trying to make money themselves by selling copy-protected music online. The early attempts, backed by the major record companies, featured a monthly fee, a puny song catalog, and no ability to burn the bought music to CDs or save it onto music players. What a deal!

Needless to say, people stayed away in droves. The free (and free-form) world of Napster, Grokster, KaZaA, LimeWire, and similar file-trading services were much more attractive.

Then Apple took a whack at it. In April 2003, the company unveiled its iTunes Music Store, an online component of iTunes 4 that scored the hat trick that other companies had yet to achieve: digital audio downloads that were easy, cheap, and—drum roll, please—legal. At first, it was a Mac-only enterprise: these days, its doors are open to Windows fans, too. Here's a look inside the store, and how to shop it.

Welcome to the Music Store

The iTunes Music Store is a super-simple music download service that has the backing (and the song catalogs) of five big music companies, plus an increasing number of independent ones. Its inventory contains over 500,000 songs from major-label artists like Bob Dylan, U2, Missy Elliott, Jewel, Sting, and hundreds of other musicians in a range of popular styles like Rock, Pop, R & B, Jazz, Folk, Rap, Latin, Classical, and more—and the collection grows by thousands of songs a week. You can also browse, sample, or buy any of 5,000 audiobooks from Audible.com.

Tip: To see what songs have been added recently, click the Just Added link at the left side of the main Music Store page.

Farther down the page, you can also see and hear what famous people are listening to in the store's Celebrity Playlist section. It never hurts to know what Wynton Marsalis and Kevin Bacon are listening to these days.

You can browse the virtual CD racks from the comfort of your own computer, listen to the first 30 seconds free from any track in the store, and download desired songs for 99 cents each with a click of the mouse. There are no monthly fees. And your digitally protected downloads don't go *poof!* into the ether if you decide to cancel your subscription, as they do with certain rival services. All your downloaded songs go right into iTunes, where they are just a sync away from your iPod's traveling music collection.

You can play the downloaded songs on up to three different iTunes 4–equipped Macs or PCs (in any combination), burn them onto CDs, and download them to the iPod. Thousands of people use the Music Store every day, in fact, without even realizing that the songs are copy protected.

Apple's early success with the iTunes Music Store—more than 25 million downloads in the first six months—caught its rivals' attention. These days, Apple's imitators in the dollar-a-song biz include BuyMusic, Napster 2.0, MusicMatch, and even Wal-Mart. (Remember, though, that music from these services come in Microsoft's Windows Media Audio format, which won't work on the iPod.)

Note: The iTunes Music Store is a feature of iTunes 4 and later. If you're still running iTunes 3, you can download the latest version from Apple's Web site at *www.apple.com/itunes/download*.

On the Mac, iTunes 4 requires Mac OS X 10.1.5 or later, a 400-megahertz G3 processor or better, and at least 256 megabytes of RAM. (You also need QuickTime–Apple's multimedia software–version 6.2 or later, which you can also pick up on the iTunes 4 download page.)

On the PC, you need Windows 2000 or XP, a 500-megahertz Pentium-class processor or faster, and 256 megabytes of memory.

A Store Tour

With iTunes 4 running, click the Music Store icon in the iTunes Source list on the left pane of the program's window (Figure 6-1). If you use a dial-up modem, fire it up as you would to check email or surf the Web. If you have a cable modem or DSL, a message about connecting to the store appears in the status display at the top of the iTunes window.

Note: As you can imagine, the whole Music Store business works *much* better over high-speed Internet connections.

Setting Up an Account

After you click the Music Store icon in the iTunes Source list and connect to the store, you land on the home page, which works like a Web page (Figure 6-1).

Figure 6-1:
In the store, the Browse button and Search box in the iTunes window perform their song-locating duties on the Store's inven-tory. Each genre of music listed in the Choose Genre pop-up menu has its own set of pages.

If you're in the mood to buy, you might as well take care of setting up your Apple Account now. To do so, click the Account: Sign In button on the right side of the iTunes window. A box like the one in Figure 6-2 appears.

Figure 6-2:
If you already have an Apple Account, you can sign in here. If not, just click the Create Account button to get started. If you're an America Online member, you can skip the Apple Account and sign into the store using your AOL screen name and password.

If you have ever bought or registered an Apple product on the company's Web site, signed up for the AppleCare tech-support plan, have a .Mac membership, or used another Apple service, you probably have an Apple ID already. All you have to do is remember your user name (usually your email address) and password.

If you've never had an Apple ID, click Create Account. The iTunes Music Store Welcome screen lists the three steps you need to follow to set up your Apple account:

1. **Agree to the terms for using the store and buying music.**

2. **Create an Apple Account.**

3. **Supply a credit card number and billing address.**

As your first step to creating an Apple Account, you must read and agree to the long scrolling legal agreement on the first screen. The 23-part statement informs you of your rights and responsibilities as an iTunes Music Store customer. (It boils down to this: *Thou shalt not download an album, burn it to CD, and then sell bootleg copies of it down at your local convenience store.*)

Click the Agree button to move on to Step 2. On the next screen, you're asked to create a user name, password, and secret question and answer. If you later have to email Apple because you've forgotten your password—hey, it could happen—this is the question you'll have to answer to prove that you're you. Apple also requests that you type in your birthday to help verify your identity.

On the third and final screen, provide a valid credit card number with a billing address. After you click Done, you see a screen congratulating you on your account-setup prowess.

Click Done. The account creation process is complete. From now on, you can log into the Music Store by clicking the Account Sign In button in the upper-right corner of the iTunes window.

The Shopping Cart

Thanks to Apple's 1-Click option, iTunes can instantly download a selected track as soon as you click the Buy Song button. That's a quick and painless experience for people with high-speed Internet connections.

UP TO SPEED

Accounting for Your ID

Technically, an *Apple ID* and an *Apple Account* are two different things. Your Apple ID is the *user name* for your Apple Account. Another element of the Apple Account is your password, which, if you didn't already have one, you chose when you first set up your iPod.

Most Windows fans probably never had an Apple ID before they wandered into iTunes. But Macintosh mavens who buy and register Apple computers and software have had them for years. You may have created your ID and password when you set up a .Mac account, signed up for AppleCare, or bought something from the online Apple Store.

If you do have an existing Apple ID, you can use the same name and password to set up your Apple Account and shop the iTunes Music Store. You just need to add the final ingredient necessary for an Apple Account—a valid credit card number.

If you have a dial-up modem, though, you may not want to sit there and wait for each song to download. Each song may take several minutes, which can severely impede your shopping rhythm.

Figure 6-3:
If you connect with a dial-up modem, you may want to turn on "Buy using a Shopping Cart," so that you won't have to wait for each song to download before proceeding with your next purchase. You might want to turn on "Load complete preview before playing," which prevents gaps and stops in listening to the sound clips because of slow connection speeds or network traffic. Click OK when you're done.

FREQUENTLY ASKED QUESTION

Changing the Information in Your Apple Account

I moved and need to change my billing address for the iTunes Music Store. How do I do that?

You can change your billing address, switch the credit card you have on file for your music purchases, or edit other information in your Apple Account without calling Apple. Just start up iTunes, click the Music Store icon on the Source list, and sign in to your account by clicking the Sign In button.

Once you've signed in, you'll see your account name (email address) next to the Account button. Click it. In the box that pops up, type in your password again and click View Account, then click the Edit Credit Card button. You're ready

to change your billing address or credit-card information. In the main account area, you can also set up an allowance (page 152) or buy iTunes Music Store gift certificates (page 151).

If you want to change your user name, password, or secret identity-proving question, click the Edit Account Info button. (Click Done when you're done.)

Note, by the way, that any changes you make to your Apple Account through iTunes affect other programs or services you might also use with your account, like ordering picture prints with iPhoto.

To solve this problem, iTunes offers a Shopping Cart option. When you use it, all the songs you buy pile up until the end of the session; then iTunes downloads them all at once when you click on the Shopping Cart icon in your iTunes Source list (and then click Buy Now). This way, you can go off and do something productive (or unproductive) while the stack of tracks takes its time squeezing through the dial-up connection.

If this idea appeals to you, choose iTunes→Preferences on the Mac, or Edit→Preferences if you're of the PC persuasion. In the Preferences dialog box, click the Store icon, and proceed as shown in Figure 6-3.

Searching and Shopping

You don't have to log in to browse the store—only when you want to buy music or audiobooks.

And music is everywhere you turn in the iTunes Music Store. Click any album cover or text link to zoom right to it. The upper left corner area of the Music Store home page offers a pop-up menu to jump straight to the Genres you want to explore.

You can also use the Power Search tool, shown at top in Figure 6-4, to zero in on a specific song, artist, album, genre, or composer—or just peruse the text-based lists, as shown in Figure 6-4 at bottom.

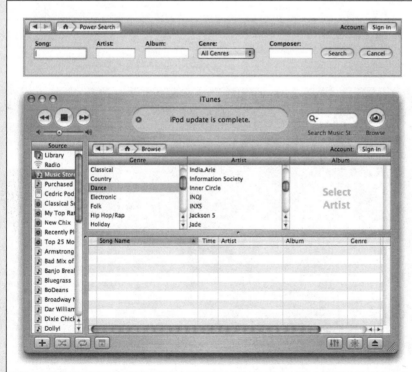

Figure 6-4:
Top: Click the Power Search link on the Music Store's home page to do some serious sleuthing for specific songs.

Bottom: One click leads to another when browsing the iTunes Music Store. Click Browse, then pick a Genre and then click an Artist on the next list to see the albums available by that musician or group. Once you have settled on a genre, the store unfurls a list of all the artists in that category.

When you find a performer you're interested in, click the name to see a list of songs or albums on hand for purchase. If you click an album name, all of the songs available from it appear below in the Details window. Double-click a track to hear a 30-second snippet of it to see how it suits you, or to make sure that's really the song you were thinking of, before buying it.

You navigate the iTunes Music Store aisles just like a Web browser. Most song and artist names are hyperlinked—that is, you can click their names, or album cover images, to see what tracks are included.

Click the Back button in the Store window to go back to the page you were just on, or click the button with the small house on it to return to the Music Store home page.

GEM IN THE ROUGH

Charting History

Quick! What was the Number One song during your senior year in high school? What tunes were topping the music charts during your college years? If you've ever paid attention to any sort of a Top Ten list, odds are you were looking at a Billboard chart.

Billboard, something of an industry bible among music professionals, is a weekly magazine that's been tabulating and reporting lists of the popular songs and albums for over 50 years. These days, the company now uses high-tech methods to chart the hits in several music categories. SoundScan, for example, is a computerized system that tracks retail music sales. The tabulators also keep a close ear on what songs are spilling out of radio stations around the country. All these numbers get crunched together into a formula that's part of the Billboard chart recipe.

In addition to all the other ways to find and buy your favorite songs, the iTunes Music Store lets you riffle through the Billboard top 100 charts going all the way back to 1946. (Missing entries in the song list—like the top three songs for 1968—reflect songs that iTunes doesn't have for sale, usually because the record companies or the bands haven't given permission for online sale yet.)

To see the charts, click the Charts link at the left side of the main page. Glancing at an old Billboard chart can serve as a sonic snapshot of a particular musical era: You see the songs listed, and you're instantly transformed back to the time when you heard them first (if, that is, you were even *alive* then).

Check out charts from the early Sixties, and you learn just how hip the girl-group sound was. Go back a few years further, and you discover the hip-shaking Reign of Elvis. Jump forward several decades, and you see hip hop transforming the cultural airwaves.

Tip: When browsing the store, you may see a small, gray, circular icon bearing a white arrow in some columns of the Details window. That's the "More Info this way!" button. Click it to jump to a page bearing details about the subject, like a discography page next to a singer's name in the Artist column, or to the main page of artists for the genre listed.

The main iTunes Music Store page also displays links to new releases, exclusive songs that can be purchased only from the Music Store, Apple staff favorites, songs scheduled to become available in the near future, sneak peeks at unreleased tunes, and the Billboard Top 100 charts going back to 1946 (see the box on page 147).

Adjusting the Columns

Just as you can modify the look and information displayed for your own music library in iTunes, you can customize your columns in the iTunes Music Store. See Figure 6-5 for an example of how to modify which columns of detail information to display.

Remember, too, that you can drag column headings (like Time, Artist, or Price) horizontally to rearrange them, or drag the divider lines between them to adjust the column widths.

Figure 6-5:
Left: When the Browser is open, choose Edit→View Options to specify which columns of information appear.

Right: Or just right-click (Control-click) any column heading to produce this secret pop-up menu of available columns.

Buying a Song or Album

Making a purchase is as easy as clicking the Buy Song button next to a song (Figure 6-6).

The songs for sale in the iTunes Music Store cost 99 cents each. Most albums cost $10 to $14, which is quite a bit cheaper than the $17 or so you'd pay to buy the same album on CD. Plus, you don't have to worry about finding a parking space at the mall.

Tip: Many musicians in the Featured Artists area also have a free video that you can watch right in iTunes. Depending on your connection speed, it may take a few minutes for the video to download. Unfortunately, iTunes stops playing other songs, so that it can concentrate on snagging the clip. You're forced to download in silence.

The solution: Double-click it in the Source list to open it in a separate window. Now the iTunes tunes can keep away spinning in the background, giving you something to listen to as the video download proceeds.

Figure 6-6:
When you download an album, or even just one song from an album, you get music files in the AAC format (page 69). A color picture of the album cover is attached to the song file, which you can display in the artwork pane of the iTunes program window when you're playing that song.

Once you click that Buy Song button, the iTunes Music Store comes to your service. Now you see an alert box like the one in Figure 6-7.

Figure 6-7:
The iTunes Music Store checks with you via an alert box to make sure you really want to buy the song you just clicked. In the iTunes Music Store, all sales are final. (Besides, it's awfully hard to return a download.)

Click the glowing Buy button to confirm your purchase decision, or Cancel if you suddenly remember that your credit card is a bit close to the edge this month. (You can also turn on "Don't warn me about buying songs" if you feel that there's quite enough nagging in your life already. You'll never see the box in Figure 6-7 again.)

Tip: Don't see a song or album in the iTunes Music Store that you really want to buy? Click the Requests & Feedback link on the Music Store's home page and send your plea to Apple. There's no guarantee they'll add it, but it can't hurt to make your wishes known.

Buying an Audiobook

The iPod has always been compatible with Audible.com's electronic "books on tape" (spoken recordings of books, public radio programs, current newspapers, and so on). Today, though, you can buy many of Audible's most popular selections right from the iTunes Music Store (Figure 6-8). Just select Audiobooks from the genre pop-up menu on the store's home page, and off you go to the listening library.

Figure 6-8:
Since you can't really flip over an audiobook to read the jacket copy, the Audiobooks section of the iTunes Music Store provides both a description of the book's contents and a 90-second sonic preview so you can try before you buy.

Selections range in price from about $3 to $16. (Yes, that's more expensive than a song, but hey—it's a longer recording. And you get a 90-second preview before you buy, instead of a 30-second snippet as you would for music.)

When you click the Buy Book button, your selection lands right into iTunes in standard, iPod-friendly AAC format. (For the record, they're encoded at 32 kbps and have been "sweetened" for human voice recordings.) That's one difference between Audible files that you buy from the Music Store and Audible files you buy directly from Audible.com (which arrive in Audible's own *.aa* format; see page 71).

Tip: Want to browse the Music Store while still fiddling with your own songs and playlists? Although the Music Store usually fills the iTunes windows when you click it in the Source list, *double-clicking* the Music Store icon opens it up into its own window so you can switch back and forth between shopping and spinning tunes.

Gift Certificates

Gift certificates make perfect presents for People Who Have Everything, especially when purchased by People Who Are Lousy Shoppers. In the modern form of redeemable email coupons, the certificates are also an excellent way to save face in potentially unpleasant situations (*"Honey, you may think I forgot our anniversary again, but...check your email!"*).

So in this crazy world, what better than the gift (certificate) of music? With iTunes Music Store gift certificates, available both from the iTunes store or from Apple's Web site, you can send your friends and family $10 to $200 worth of credit to go hog-wild in Apple's music emporium.

Buying

To buy a gift certificate, click the Gift Certificates link on the main page of the iTunes Music Store. After you click to choose delivery by either email or U.S. Mail, the process is like buying anything on the Web: You fill in your address, gift amount, personalized message, and so on.

If you already have an Apple ID (page 144), you can log in and request to have your credit card billed; if not, you have to sign up for one. Once you complete all the pixel paperwork, your gift certificate will be on its way.

Figure 6-9:
Receiving and redeeming an iTunes Music Store gift certificate is as easy as opening your email and clicking Redeem Now to add the gift credits to your account. You can also send paper gift certificates through the U.S. mail.

Tip: Before sending off an iTunes Music Store gift certificate, you might want to discreetly check whether your recipient's computer meets the iTunes 4 requirements. People on Windows 98, Windows Me, and older operating systems may be in for an even bigger pang of disappointment than if you gave them a box of cheap tube socks.

Spending

Whether they come in the mailbox by the front door or the one on the computer, iTunes Music Store gift certificates are meant to be spent. Here's how they work:

- If you're lucky enough to be the recipient of an iTunes email gift certificate (Figure 6-9), redemption is just a click away. The Redeem Now button at the bottom of the message takes you straight to the Music Store, where the certificate's confirmation number pops up automatically. Click Redeem in the Music Store window to credit your account and start shopping.

- If the gift arrived by postal mail, start up iTunes and click Music Store in the Source list. On the main Music Store page, click the link for Gift Certificates. On the next screen, click Redeem Now. Type in the confirmation number printed on the lower edge of the gift certificate and click Redeem.

If you already have an iTunes Music Store account, log in and start shopping. If you've never set your mouse pointer inside the store before, you'll need to create an Apple Account. You have to provide your name and address, but you don't have to surrender a credit card number. If you choose None, you can use your gift certif as the sole payment method—and end your shopping experience once you've burned through it. Once you've created your Apple Account, a friendly screen appears to congratulate you and send you on your way to the virtual record bins.

iTunes Allowance Accounts

Allowance accounts are a lot like iTunes store gift certificates. You, the parent (or other financial authority), decide how many dollars' worth of music or audiobooks you want to give to a family member or friend (from $10 to $200, in increments of $10). Unlike gift certificates, however, allowance accounts automatically replenish themselves on the first day of each month—an excellent way to keep your music-loving kids out of your wallet while teaching the little nippers how to budget their money throughout the month.

Both you and the recipient need to have Apple IDs. To set up a monthly allowance, click the Allowance link on the main page of the iTunes Music Store and fill out the form on the next screen. After you select the amount of credit you want to deposit each month, fill in your recipient's Apple ID and password. (There's also an option to create a new account for the monthly allowance.)

Once the giftee logs into the designated Apple Account, the spending can begin—no credit card required. Once the allowance amount has been spent, that's it for music until the following month. (Of course, if the recipient *does* have a credit card on file, he can always put the difference on the card.) If you need to cancel an allowance account, go to your Account Info page (page 145) to take care of the matter.

Tip: Can't remember how much money you have left on your gift certificate or in your allowance account? Look at your iTunes window the next time you're logged into the store. Your balance appears right next to your account name.

The Interrupted Download

If your computer crashes or you get knocked offline while you're downloading your song purchases, iTunes is designed to pick up where it left off after you restart the program and reconnect to the Internet. If for some reason it doesn't go back to downloading, choose Advanced→Check for Purchased Music to log back into the Music Store to resume your downloading business.

POWER USERS CLINIC

Thinking of Linking?

Web logs—also known as *blogs*—are online journals. You post your blog on the Web, so that anybody passing by can read your deepest thoughts on everything from politics to Saturday morning cartoons. You don't even have to be a Webmaster to create your own blog, since the software usually handles most of the formatting and uploading for you. Movable Type (*www.movabletype.org*) and Live Journal (*www.livejournal.com*) are two of the many companies that sell blogware, and even America Online offers a journal feature to its members.

Like blogs, music is often best when shared. If you've found a hot new band or singer that you just *have* to share with the world via your blog, Apple gives you an easy way to point your pals directly to the artist's song, album, or page in the iTunes Music Store. You're spared the hassle of figuring out the correct URL to type into your blogware.

Just point your Web browser to the iTunes Link Maker page (*www.apple.com/itunes/linkmaker*). Type in the artist, album, or song name into the Link Maker form; it will then crunch out and present you with a complicated chunk of HTML code containing the Internet address that will take your visitors directly to the appropriate page in the iTunes Music Store.

All you have to do is paste that entire blob of text into your blog program, so with just a click, everyone can see the band you're raving about. The code is already in the language of Web pages and blogs. You can even paste it into an email message.

If you know how to turn a graphic image into a link (using a Web-design program), you can also use the Link Maker–generated code as the link for a graphic button, the better to get your readers hooked and spread the joy of iTunes across the land.

Signing Out

If other people have access to your computer when you're not around, consider wrapping up your shopping session by clicking your name (next to the Account button on the Music Store window) and then Sign Out. Unless you're one of those exceedingly benevolent types, you probably don't want anyone else to come along and charge up your credit card with a music-buying marathon.

Locating Your New Tracks

You can find your new tracks by clicking Purchased Music in the iTunes Source list (Figure 6-10). As the dialog box says, you can work with the Purchased Music playlist as though it were any other playlist. That is, even if you delete a track from it, the song itself still remains in the iTunes music library. And behind the scenes, the corresponding music file stays in your Home→Music→iTunes→iTunes Music folder (Mac) or My Music→iTunes→iTunes Music (Windows).

Figure 6-10:
When you click the Purchased Music playlist after buying music, iTunes offers an explanation of how the playlist works (top) and fills out your list with the newly bought songs (bottom). From here, you can play the songs, drag them into other playlists, transfer them to your iPod, or burn them to a CD to play on the stereo.

iTunes on America Online

If you're an America Online member, you can use the iTunes Music Store without having to sign up for an Apple ID. Now, that doesn't mean you can use the Store for free (are you *kidding!?*). It does mean, though, that you'll have one less name and password to keep in your brain.

Now that Apple and AOL are buddies, there's even an "iTunes on AOL" area, as shown in Figure 6-11. You can get there quickly at Keyword: *iTunes*.

To use iTunes with AOL, you need to download the iTunes software, if you haven't already (from *www.apple.com/itunes/download*). Click the Account Sign In button on the iTunes window. But in the Sign In box (Figure 6-2), select the option to use your AOL screen name instead of an Apple Account. Type in your AOL screen name and password.

Figure 6-11:
The iTunes on AOL area of America Online has a music search engine that can take you right to any hits for sale in the iTunes Music Store. AOL members can use the AOL Wallet service to pay for iTunes Music Store binges (it's at Keyword: Wallet *and also accessible from a pop-up menu in AOL 9.0).*

FREQUENTLY ASKED QUESTION

Your Electronic Wallet

What's AOL Wallet? Sounds expensive.

AOL Wallet is America Online's version of the express check-out lane for online shopping: Once you find something online you want to buy, you just invoke your AOL Wallet, which conveniently has all your shipping and billing info stored inside.

You set up your Wallet at AOL Keyword: *Wallet* in your AOL software (Windows or Macintosh). Once you've filled out your address and credit card info, AOL Wallet automatically plops all that same information into merchants' checkout screens when you buy things online from America

Online–associated vendors.

You can use the same credit card you have on file with AOL for your monthly membership charge for your Wallet purchases, or use a different one if you want to spread out your bills. AOL Wallet can store info for up to 10 different credit cards and 50 addresses, which makes it easier to send gifts to friends and family.

The autofill feature saves lots of typing and gives you extra time to buy even *more* stuff. Plus you don't have to keep digging your credit card out of your *non*-AOL wallet.

If you have an AOL Wallet (see the box on the previous page), the bills go there; otherwise, you need to supply fresh credit card information to the iTunes Music Store. But whether you opt for AOL Wallet or fill in a credit card number directly in the iTunes Music Store, you can start shopping once you have iTunes installed and your financials worked out.

In the iTunes On AOL area of America Online, you can search for artists, albums, and songs for sale in the Store; sample a variety of artists on AOL Radio; or even buy an iPod. The AOL Music Search section also has integrated links to music and musicians featured in the iTunes store, as shown in Figure 6-12.

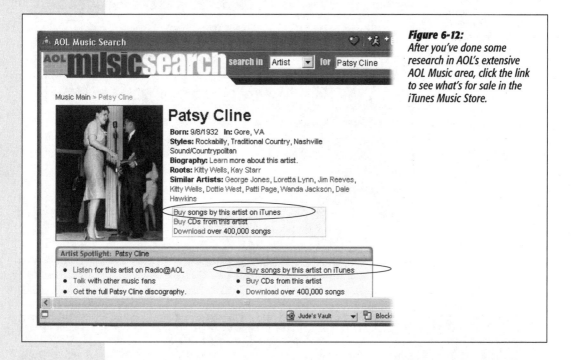

Figure 6-12:
After you've done some research in AOL's extensive AOL Music area, click the link to see what's for sale in the iTunes Music Store.

You can browse AOL to find out more about the artists you're interested in. Once you've zeroed in on exactly what you want and know it's available in the iTunes Music Store, click the iTunes link to go shopping. Your copy of iTunes starts up, and you're swept into the Music Store to complete your purchase and download your music.

Tip: Exclusive tracks from Sessions@AOL—recordings that were made *live* just for AOL—are available in the Music Store alongside the other half million tunes.

What to Do with Music You've Bought

As you know, the iTunes Music store gives you a lot more freedom to use your down-loaded songs than other music services. There are a *few* restrictions, though.

Play It on Three Computers

You can play Music Store–bought songs only on an *authorized* computer. Authori-zation is Apple's copy protection scheme.

Between work, home, and the family network, not everyone spends time on just one computer these days. So Apple lets you play your Music Store songs on up to three computers at once: Macs, PCs, or any combination. You just need to type in your Apple user name and password on each computer. Each must make an Internet connection to relay the information back to Music Store headquarters.

Authorizing Computers

You authorized your first machine when you signed up for an Apple Account for the iTunes store.

To authorize a song to play on another computer, follow these steps:

1. **Find the song you want to transfer.**

   This step, of course, involves *finding* the song on your hard drive.

   Method 1: On the Mac, open your Home→Music→iTunes→iTunes Music folder; in Windows, open My Documents→My Music→iTunes→iTunes Music. Music Store files are easily recognizable by their .m4p file name extensions.

UP TO SPEED

AAC, Copy Protection, and You

Apple's AAC files are copy-protected, but not all AAC files are. Some, which you may have collected from other Web sites, are freely copyable.

How can you tell the difference?

In iTunes, click the questionable track in the music library and then press ⌘-I (Mac) or Ctrl-I (Windows). The Summary tab of the song shows the album cover, technical information about its encoding, who bought it, and where it lives on the computer. If the Kind says "Pro-tected AAC audio file," well, you've got your answer.

(In this picture, the phrase [remote] means that you're checking out a song that's on another computer on the network.)

Incidentally, the suffix on a pro-tected AAC file (as viewed on your desktop, for example) is .m4p. iTunes 4 can play AAC files that were ripped in iTunes, and it can play protected AAC files downloaded from the iTunes Music Store.

But beware: you may have problems playing non-iTunes AAC tracks from another online music service or Web site.

Method 2: Just drag the song you want out of the iTunes window and onto your desktop.

2. Copy the song to the second computer.

Copy the song file onto a CD or USB flash drive; email it to yourself; transfer it across the network; or whatever method you prefer for schlepping files from machine to machine.

Deposit the songs in the iTunes Music folder on the Computer #2. (See "Method 1" above for the location of this folder.)

3. Bring the copied song into iTunes on the second computer.

To do that, you can either choose File→Add to Library (and then select and open them), or just drag their icons right into the iTunes window.

4. In your iTunes list, select a transferred song and click the Play button.

iTunes asks for your Apple Account user name and password.

5. Type your Apple ID and password, and click OK.

This second computer is now authorized to play that song—and any other songs you bought using the same Apple Account.

Note: Although you may feel like AAC stands for Always Authorizing Computers, remember that this whole authorizing business is necessary only to play songs you've *bought.* To play songs you've ripped into AAC format from CDs, for example, or to play everyday MP3 files, you don't have to authorize anything.

Deauthorizing Computers

You won't be able to play the purchased music on a fourth computer if you try to authorize it. When you connect to the authorization system over the Internet, it will see three other computers already on its list and deny your request.

That's a drag, but copy protection is copy protection—and it's three times better than earlier music services, which permit you to play downloaded music only on *one* machine (and only as long as you're still paying the monthly fee).

In any case, you have to deauthorize one of the other computers if you want to play the music on Number 4. To deauthorize a computer, choose Advance→Deauthorize Computer, and then type in your Apple Account user name and password. The updated information zips back to Apple over the Internet.

Tip: Thinking of putting that older computer up for sale? Before you wipe the drive clean and send it on its way, be sure to deauthorize it, so your new machine will be able to play your songs from the iTunes Music Store. Erasing a hard drive, by itself, does not deauthorize a computer.

Copy It to Your iPod

Not only can you download your purchased songs to your iPod, but you can download it to *unlimited numbers* of iPods. Apple placed no copy restrictions on iPod joy.

Tip: If your iPod is a pre-2003 model, you must first update its software to version 1.3 or later. Otherwise, the iPod won't recognize files in the AAC format. (See page 296 for details.)

When you buy a song, it lands in the iTunes playlist called Purchased Music. But you can easily drag it into other playlists you've concocted within iTunes. The songs, artists, and albums appear just like any other tracks in iTunes.

Burn It to a CD

You can also burn purchased tracks to blank CDs, so you can listen to them in the car or on the big component rack in the living room. Here, Apple has put in only one tiny, almost irrelevant form of copy protection: If you've made store-bought songs part of a certain playlist, you can't burn more than ten CD copies of it in a row without making at least one change to the song list.

And if you find *that* limitation restrictive, you must be so dedicated a music pirate that you wear an eye patch and a parrot on your shoulder.

Share it Across the Network

You can also share purchased music tracks with other people on your same office network—by playing them live, not by copying the actual files. Details on page 110.

Back It Up

If your hard drive croaks and takes your entire music library with it, you have three alternatives. (a) Buy all of your Music Store songs all over again. (b) Copy the music *from* the iPod to your hard drive (page 52). (c) Calmly reach for the backup CD or DVD you had the foresight to make before disaster struck.

Backing up your music library

To back up your entire music collection, you want to copy the *iTunes* folder.

- **Macintosh.** This folder is in your Home→Music folder.

- **Windows.** The iTunes folder is in your My Music folder.

Backing up this folder, huge though it may be, backs up not just your songs, but all the other work you've done in iTunes (creating and naming your playlists, organizing your columns, and so on).

You can use any standard backup method for this:

- Copy the folder to another computer via network cable.

- Burn it onto a blank CD (if the folder fits) or a DVD (if you have a DVD-burning computer).

• Use a program like Dantz Retrospect to back it up onto Zip disks, multiple CDs, or whatever you've got.

When your hard drive croaks, restore your backed-up iTunes folder by dragging it back into your Music folder (Mac) or My Music folder (Windows). You're saved.

Backing up playlists

iTunes 4 also has a built-in backup feature. Note, however, that it can back up only one playlist at a time.

This backup procedure isn't the same thing as burning an *audio* CD. Here, you're burning a *data* disc. That's important if you want to preserve the original file formats in your iTunes music library and avoid turning your high-quality AIFF files, for example, into squished-down MP3 files. To make this important change to your Burning desires, see Figure 6-13.

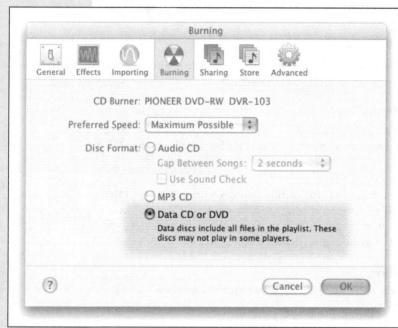

Figure 6-13:
Choose iTunes→ Preferences (Mac) or Edit→Preferences (Windows), click Burning, and click the button for data CD or DVD. Selecting the Data format for your disc will copy your files in their original MP3, ACC, or Audible formats without converting them to standard audio CD files, which would happen if you created an audio CD.

After you've chosen the Data format for your backup disc, make a playlist that includes all the files you want to copy to the CD or DVD. Keep an eye on the total size at the bottom of the window to be sure it will fit on one disc: about 650 megabytes for a CD, 4.7 gigabytes for a DVD. (If not, you'll have to file your songs away into multiple playlists—one per backup disc—to spread out your collection over multiple discs.)

Burn it to disc by clicking the Burn Disc button on the iTunes window. Insert a blank disc when the machine asks for one, and then click the Burn Disc button again to start copying.

If your hard drive ever dies, copy this data disc's files back onto the computer and re-import them into iTunes to rebuild your library from the backup disc.

Backing up non-music data

If you've got a .Mac account (Apple's $100-a-year suite of online services), you can use the handy Backup program to save copies of your personal files to a remote Web site, recordable disc, or external hard drive—including your list of iTunes playlists. See Figure 6-14 for details.)

Figure 6-14:
With the click of a checkbox, Backup's QuickPicks feature saves copies of your iTunes and Purchased Music playlist information—not the song files themselves—to a recordable CD or DVD, to an external hard drive, or to your iDisk (the online backup drive that's also part of the .Mac deal). (Unless you've paid to upgrade it, though, the iDisk holds only 100 megabytes.)

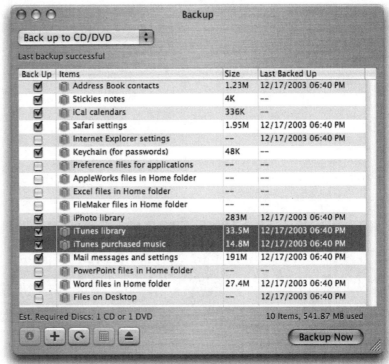

Back Up	Items	Size	Last Backed Up
☑	Address Book contacts	1.23M	12/17/2003 06:40 PM
☑	Stickies notes	4K	--
☑	iCal calendars	336K	--
☑	Safari settings	1.95M	12/17/2003 06:40 PM
☐	Internet Explorer settings	--	12/17/2003 06:40 PM
☑	Keychain (for passwords)	48K	--
☐	Preference files for applications	--	--
☐	AppleWorks files in Home folder	--	--
☐	Excel files in Home folder	--	--
☐	FileMaker files in Home folder	--	--
☑	iPhoto library	283M	12/17/2003 06:40 PM
☑	iTunes library	33.5M	12/17/2003 06:40 PM
☑	iTunes purchased music	14.8M	12/17/2003 06:40 PM
☑	Mail messages and settings	191M	12/17/2003 06:40 PM
☐	PowerPoint files in Home folder	--	--
☑	Word files in Home folder	27.4M	12/17/2003 06:40 PM
☐	Files on Desktop	--	12/17/2003 06:40 PM

Back up to CD/DVD

Last backup successful

Est. Required Discs: 1 CD or 1 DVD   10 Items, 541.87 MB used

Backup Now

Music Store Billing

The iTunes Music store keeps track of what you buy and when you buy it. If you think your credit card was wrongly charged for something, or if you suspect that one of the kids knows your password and is sneaking in some forbidden downloads before you get home from work, you can contact the store or check your account's purchase history page to see what's been downloaded in your name.

The Customer Service Page

If you have general questions about using the iTunes Music Store, have a problem with your bill, or want to submit a specific query or comment, the online Customer

Service center awaits. To get there, connect to the Internet and then choose Help→Music Store Customer Service.

Click the link that best describes what you want to learn or complain about. For billing or credit-card issues, click Purchase Information.

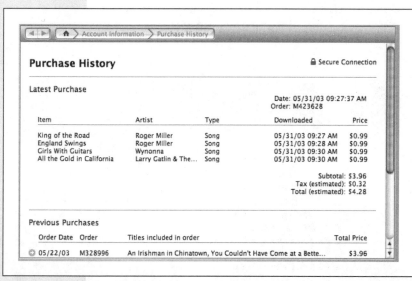

Figure 6-15:
The Purchase History area records all of the songs and albums downloaded and charged to an Apple Account, which can be useful for bracing yourself for the coming credit card bill. The list starts with the most recent ones.

GEM IN THE ROUGH

Back Up Only What Needs Backing Up

They say that backing up is hard to do–but mainly, it's hard to remember what you've already backed up and what still needs attention.

Here, however, is a sneaky trick that makes iTunes help you make backups of all the songs you've bought or ripped since the last time you backed up your iTunes Music folder. This means you won't have to burn the whole darn library to a stack of CDs or DVDs each time, and can just fill a disc with the new stuff you've added.

After you've backed up your music files to disc for the first or latest time, open iTunes and choose File→New Smart Playlist.

In the Smart Playlist set-up box, change the pop-up menus to say *Date Added–is after–[today's date]*. Make sure Live Updating is turned on, and that there's no limit set for the amount of songs on the playlist. When you click OK, give your new playlist a name, like Smart Backup.

The next time you're ready to burn a data backup disc, back up only your Smart Backup playlist to get the only latest library additions.

Then, once you've burned it to CD, choose File→Edit Smart Playlist change the Date Added to today's date, so that iTunes starts keeping track of the new stuff for your next backup.

Note: The iTunes Music Store sends out invoices by email, but they don't come right after you buy a song. You usually get an invoice that groups together all the songs you purchased within a 12-hour period, or for every $20 worth of tunes that you buy.

Your Purchase History

To have a look at just how addicted you've grown to buying songs, open iTunes, click the Music Store icon in the Source List, and sign into the store. When you see your user name appear next to the Account button in the iTunes Music Store window, click it. In the box that pops up, click the View Account button.

When you get to the Account Information screen, click Purchase History. In the list that comes up, you see all of the songs you've bought (Figure 6-15).

If you see songs on the list that you didn't buy, and you're sure that other people who use your computer didn't buy them, contact Apple. Because the account is linked to a credit card, you'll want to take care of the situation right away.

The iTunes Music Store Song

It would be depressing to end this chapter with such a bummer of a warning, so here's a little song parody that appeared on the Web shortly after the iTunes Music Store had its grand opening. It's attributed to filk master Scott Taylor.

Tip: Filk songs are parodies of well-known tunes, or original compositions, with lyrics about computers, TV, movies, science fiction, fantasy, and other crunchy bites of the pop culture universe tossed in. It's a goofy and exuberant art form unto itself. (See *dmoz.org/Arts/Music/Styles/Filk*.)

iTunes Man

To the tune of "Piano Man" (Billy Joel)

It's nine o'clock at the iTunes store,
A phenomenal crowd's logging on,
There's an old man on AOL,
Finding music from ages bygone.

He says, "Steve, can you play me a memory?
I'm not really sure how it goes,
But I typed in a track and got album names back!
And I'm not even wearing my clothes!"

Oh la da da diddy da da, la da diddy da da da.

Sell us a song, you're the iTunes man,
Sell us a song tonight.
Well, we're all in the mood for a melody,
And you've got the pricing just right.

Now Claude at Vivendi's a friend of mine,
And his business is selling CDs.
And he knows the solution for store distribution,
But he's worried about MP3s.

He says, "Steve I believe this is killing us,
All these pirates don't pay us a dime.
Well, I'm sure that you could be a billionaire,
If you could sell music online."

Oh la da da diddy da da, la da diddy da da da.

Sell us a song, you're the iTunes man,
Sell us a song tonight.
Well, we're all in the mood for a melody,
And you've got the pricing just right.

Now Paul is an iPod enthusiast,
Who listens to jazz with his wife.
And he's chatting with Maxine, who's still in the rap scene,
And probably will be for life.

And the waitress is downloading Dixie Chicks,
As the dial-up man slowly gets Stones.
Yes, they're sharing the bandwidth from Akamai,
But it's better than P2P clones.

Sell us a song, you're the iTunes man,
Sell us a song tonight.
Well, we're all in the mood for a melody,
And you've got the pricing just right.

It's a pretty good crowd for just Macintosh,
And the PC guys give me a smile.
'Cause they know that iTunes will be Windows-bound soon,
If they just can hold out for a while.

And the AAC sounds like originals,
And rights management isn't a pain,
And they sit at the screens of their iTunes machines,
And say, "Man, this is worse than cocaine!"

Sell us a song, you're the iTunes man,
Sell us a song tonight.
Well, we're all in the mood for a melody,
And you've got the pricing just right.

Part Three:
Beyond the Music

Chapter 7: iPod as Address Book

Chapter 8: iPod as Calendar

Chapter 9: Games and eBooks

Chapter 10: iSync

Chapter 11: The iPod As Hard Drive

3

iPod as Address Book

When the iPod music player made its debut, many a reviewer compared its pocketable shape to that of personal organizers like PalmPilots. Maybe the physical similarity put the notion in people's minds that the iPod would also make a convenient way to carry around addresses and telephone numbers. Or maybe it's because anything that can be hacked, will. In any case, it didn't take long for the iPod faithful to figure out ways to add nonmusical, life-information features to even the earliest iPods.

Apple took the hint. When it released version 1.1 of the iPod operating-system software in 2002, the company included several basic organizer functions alongside the iPod's music-management features. This chapter guides you through importing information from programs like Palm Desktop and Outlook and then looking it up when you're on the go.

Introduction to the iPod Address Book

Before Apple incorporated the Contacts program into the iPod's software, people went through all kinds of contortions to get their address lists onto the music player. They went so far as to create short, silent MP3 files, named "Bob Smith" from the album "(212) 523-1522" recorded by the artist "23 Broadway, New York, NY 10023," just so that they could look up their phone numbers. Shareware wizards rode to the rescue, but using the iPod as a little black book was still an exercise for geeks. (See the end of this chapter for more about organizer software for the iPod.)

But starting with iPod software version 1.1, all of the extraneous hassle went away. In most cases, you can simply export the contacts list from Palm Desktop, Entourage, Outlook, or another compatible program, and then drag the exported file into the iPod's Contacts folder. Presto: You've got your friends and associates listed right there alongside your Rolling Stones and Little Walter albums. Your little white box is now a little black book.

At this point, you can just use the Extras→Contacts command on the iPod (page 27) and zip down the list with the scroll wheel to the name of the person you want. Click Select to see the person's name, address, phone number, and other information from your desktop program's exported contacts file. Figure 7-1 shows a sample.

Contact

Naomi Cleary

Telephone

home: (650) 555 1234

E-mail

ncleary@apple3.com

Home Address

Figure 7-1:
A contact file on the iPod can display all the basic information on how to reach your friends and associates, including the person's name, job title, company, and so on. Unfortunately, the iPod doesn't pick up more elaborate bits like the photos found in some address book programs.

POWER USERS' CLINIC

Anatomy of a vCard

When it added the Contacts feature to the iPod, Apple included a sample vCard in the technical support area of its Web site (*http://docs.info.apple.com/article.html?artnum =61568*), so curious minds could see what a vCard looks like when opened in a text-editing program like TextEdit or (for Windows) WordPad. If you're not put off by odd-looking punctuation and formatting, you can even make your own vCards. Just reproduce this text, making sure to fill in the proper information where indicated here in italics, and save the file with a .vcf extension.

```
begin:vcard
version:3.0
fn:Sample
n:Sample;;;;
title:Accountant
org:Sample Company\, Inc.
note:Here's a sample to show you all that can be
    displayed in a contact on your iPod.
url;type=work:apple.com/support/ipod
```

```
adr;type=work;type=pref:;;200 Industrial Park
    Circle;Metropolis;CA;98765;USA
label;type=work;type=pref:200 Industrial Park
    Circle\nMetropolis\, CA 98765\nUSA
adr;type=home:;;10201 Fine
    Drive;Smallville;CA;98765;USA
label;type=home:10201 Fine Drive\nSmallville\,
    CA 98765\nUSA
tel;type=home:408-555-9292
tel;type=work:408-555-3131
tel;type=cell:408-555-1010
end:vcard
```

If you want to back up all your vCards in one big file, you can copy and paste the text for each contact one after the other in a text file. Just make sure you have *begin:vcard* as the first line of each new contact and *end:vcard* as the last line.

You can read more about the vCard standard and where it's headed at *www.imc.org/pdi*.

The vCard

A vCard is a special file in a format that many email and Rolodex programs recognize, including Microsoft Outlook and Entourage—and the iPod likes it, too. It's basically a digital business card that you can pass around between email programs, organizer software, Web pages, and handheld computers. It can display all the typical text-based things you'd expect from a business card, like name, title, phone numbers, and addresses—plus goodies like corporate logo graphics and clickable URLs. If you've ever gotten an email attachment with a .vcf file extension, you've got yourself a vCard.

What makes the vCard format especially handy is that it's becoming a standard, so you can set up your own vCard within a program like Outlook or the Mac OS X Address Book and attach it to an outgoing message. You can send it off in Outlook on your PC, and the vCard will arrive in full glory in the Entourage inbox on your friend's Mac. Even better, your recipient can usually add your vCard to his own address book by just dragging it into the list. A vCard can save time and typing on both ends of the message.

So when Apple made the iPod ready for contacts, it made it vCard-friendly. Now you can use the information that's already in just about any popular desktop organizer program without having to retype anything.

Tip: Many contact-management programs these days can export their data to the vCard format. But if you've been using an older program that doesn't deal in vCards, and you're dreading having to retype your list to get it into the Mac OS X Address Book, take a look at a shareware program called vCard Creator (available at the "Missing CD" page of *www.missingmanuals.com*). If you can export your contacts in the form of a tab-delimited database from programs like Microsoft Entourage, Now Contact, Palm Desktop, or several database programs, the vCard Creator shareware can convert it into the vCard format.

The vCard format itself is capable of storing many more *fields* of information (individual info blobs like name, street, city, zip) than the iPod can display, however. The iPod can show only the following information: name, addresses, telephone numbers, email addresses, title, company name, Web address, and your own notes on the person.

Transferring Contacts to the iPod

If you use a calendar/address book/notes program—which nerds call personal information management (PIM) programs—you're not alone. With each passing day, more people switch to a digital method of organizing their calendar, phone book, and note pad. Indeed, a whole generation has never done it any other way.

Some of these PIMs can transfer their data to a Palm or PocketPC organizer. This notion of "yes, you *can* take it with you, especially without having to retype it" helped propel the popularity of handheld computers into the stratosphere.

If you use a current version of one of the popular PIM programs—like Palm Desktop, Microsoft Outlook, Entourage, or the Address Book programs that come with Windows and Mac OS X—you can transfer your contact list to the iPod. There are a number of ways to do this, either manually or automatically, with shareware or software. This chapter covers all those methods. (And if you have a Mac running OS X 10.2 or later, see Chapter 10, which looks at Apple's iSync program.)

Even with manual methods, you have at least a couple of different ways to get those addresses on the iPod. If you want every single contact in your desktop program to appear on your iPod, the process can be very quick and uncomplicated.

Note: To use the Contacts feature, you need to have your iPod set up for use as a FireWire disk. See Chapter 11 for details.

Furthermore, any time you copy contacts onto the iPod from any program, you need to *unmount* it (remove its icon from the computer screen) and then disconnect the FireWire Cable when the "OK to Disconnect" message (or iPod main menu) appears onscreen. 2003-and-later iPod models are ready to go right away, but older models take a moment to reboot (this is what the iPod's doing when you see the Apple logo on the display screen) before you can choose Contacts from the Extras menu.

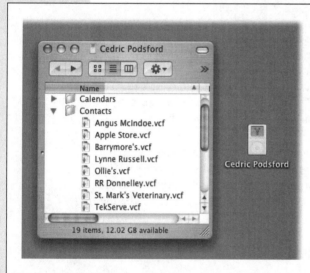

Figure 7-2:
To access your iPod's Contacts folder, have the iPod connected to your computer and set up as a FireWire disk. At that point, you can open the iPod icon and locate the Contacts folder, which houses contacts from various programs in vCard format (.vcf).

Copying Contacts from Windows

One of the first things you need to do to copy your contacts is to find them within the particular program you use. Just remember that you can save time and fumbling by having the iPod connected to the computer, with its main window open on-screen, so that you have a clear view of the iPod's Contacts folder (see Figure 7-2).

Palm Desktop 4.1

In principle, getting contacts out of Palm Desktop should be easy, because it offers an Export vCard command.

In fact, though, you have to export one single contact at a time—not the most pleasant way to spend your next two Saturday afternoons.

Instead, what you want is Palm2iPod, a Palm Desktop 4.1 plug-in. It can synchronize the Palm's address list and date book to the iPod's Contacts and Calendar features automatically. Best of all, it moves all the addresses and events files at once, which can really speed up your export times. If you use the Windows version of Palm Desktop, this program can make you very happy indeed. It's free, but contributions are welcome; it's available from the "Missing CD" page at *www.missing manuals.com.*

Microsoft Outlook, Method 1: EphPod

Outlook, too, has trouble exporting all of your addresses at once into an iPod-recognizable form. And here again, the solution is software that doesn't come from Microsoft.

For example, EphPod, the same versatile free program that can synchronize your music between the iPod and the PC (page 59) can do the same thing with your Microsoft Outlook contacts. Once again, you can download EphPod for free at *www.missingmanuals.com.*

Tip: You can also create contacts right in EphPod. Choose File→New Contact, and fill in the Contact Information box that pops up.

Connect your iPod to the PC and set it up for use as a FireWire disk (page 213) before you begin. To import your contacts list from Outlook, open EphPod and click the Get Outlook Contacts button in the toolbar, as shown in Figure 7-3.

Note: Some versions of Outlook may generate an alert box at this point; that's normal. Security features within Outlook 6, for example, are designed to look out for malicious code like email viruses. If you get such a warning, turn on "Allow Access For" in the box and, from the pop-up menu, choose an amount of time to let EphPod use the Outlook address book. A minute or so should be enough.

Figure 7-3:
Pulling in Outlook Contacts is just a click away in the EphPod toolbar. EphPod can also keep you up to date with the news and provide a calendar function.

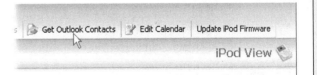

Once EphPod has finished importing the contacts, you can check them right there. Go to the iPod View section of the EphPod window (Figure 7-3) and click Get Outlook Contacts to see a list of the addresses now on your iPod. Your iPod is ready to roll. (Just be sure to eject the iPod properly first, as described on page 215.)

Microsoft Outlook, Method 2: iPodSync

Just as Windows programmers figured out ways to use iPods with PCs long before Apple officially released Windows-compatible models, shareware coders lost no time in making a Windows version of Apple's iSync program (page 205).

With iPodSync, a $12 program available at *www.missingmanuals.com*, you can transfer your Outlook contacts to the iPod, plus your calendar information, notes, and tasks as well.

Once you've connected your iPod to the PC (see page 35) and started up iPodSync, click the Contacts icon, and then turn on Synchronize Contacts. You have a choice of syncing only the contacts in Outlook's Default Contacts Folder, or *all* contacts from all of the Contacts folders in Outlook. Choose the option you want (see Figure 7-4).

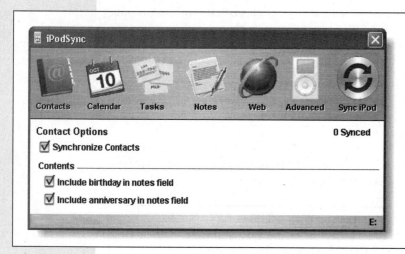

Figure 7-4:
If iSync and Windows XP had an offspring, it would probably look a lot like the iPodSync shareware program. It provides an easy way to copy your Outlook contacts, appointments, notes, tasks, and more over to your iPod.

Once you've made your decisions, click the curiously familiar-looking Sync iPod button in the top right corner. (Can you say, "Copy-and-paste job from Apple's iSync"?)

The program copies your addresses into one big vCard file and places it in the iPod's Contacts folder, ready for consultation on the run.

Microsoft Outlook, Method 3: OutPod

Another homemade programming solution for Outlook addresses is OutPod, shown in Figure 7-5. The software is fairly straightforward and can also import Outlook calendar info to the iPod.

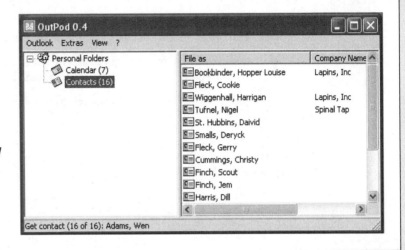

Figure 7-5:
OutPod displays your Outlook contacts and exports them from a command under the Outlook menu. As seen in the next chapter, OutPod can also transfer Outlook calendar events onto the iPod with ease.

You can download OutPod from the "Missing CD" page of www.missingmanuals.com.

After connecting the iPod to the PC (page 35) and opening OutPod, you see a panel with choices for Calendar and Contacts. Click Contacts to see all of your addresses pop up on the right side of the window. From this list, click to select the contacts you wish to copy onto your iPod.

In the Outlook menu of OutPod, you'll find commands for saving selected addresses either as one big file or as separate vCards. Saving the files separately makes it easier to randomly delete outdated contacts from the iPod, since it lets you move the unwanted files from your iPod's Contacts folder into the Recycle Bin. If you save them in one big vCard file, you'll have to open the document in a text-editing program and stumble through the code until you find the unwanted contacts (see the box on page 168).

After you've selected how you want to save the contacts, navigate to the iPod's Contacts folder. If you've chosen to save your Contacts as one big file, OutPod asks you to name it before saving it onto the iPod.

Windows Address Book

With your iPod connected and its window open onscreen so you can see the Contacts folder (Figure 7-2), open your Address Book program. (If you've never actually used the Windows Address Book directly—but have instead typed in your address information through Outlook Express—choose Start→Programs→Accessories→ Address Book.)

If you have multiple *identities* (sets of data, one per person who uses the machine) stored on the PC, log onto the one you want to use (File→Switch Identity). Open up the contacts file for that identity by clicking on the Contacts folder in the left pane of the Address Book box; the contacts appear on the right pane.

Select the names you want. To select multiple files, you can use various tricks like these:

- Select them all at once by pressing Ctrl-A or choosing Edit→Select All.

- Select a swath of them by clicking the first in a batch, and then Shift-clicking the last. All of the contacts in between are highlighted.

- You can add individual names to the selection, or remove individuals, by Ctrl-clicking them.

Drag the selected contacts out of the Address Book window and into the iPod's Contacts folder. You'll see a bunch of separate little .vcf files floating around in the folder once they've been copied over.

Tip: In many versions of Windows, you can also export a contact as a vCard from the Address Book by choosing File→Export→Business Card (vCard).

Outlook Express

Although you may not realize it, Outlook Express on the PC taps into the Windows Address Book for names and numbers. (Many people also don't realize that Outlook and Outlook Express are two different programs. The former is part of Microsoft Office; the latter is free on every PC.)

You can't drag contacts out of the program's small Contacts pane, though. When you have the main Outlook Express window onscreen, click the Address Book link to open its window, and then follow the steps in the previous section to export your contacts as vCard files.

Copying Contacts from the Macintosh

Many of the popular Rolodex/calendar programs for both Mac OS 9 and Mac OS X can export data to vCard format for transfer to the iPod. And for those that don't, there are other ways to extract the information so that your iPod is as *au courant* as your iMac or iBook.

Tip: If you're using Mac OS X with 10.2 or later, you can use Apple's free iSync software to synchronize information with your iPod automatically. If a Mac is the hub of your digital lifestyle, Chapter 10 is for you.

Palm Desktop 4.1

Palm Desktop for Mac OS X lets you export your entire Address List module to a vCard file in a few swift clicks. Just choose File→Export and, in the Export dialog box, select Addresses from the Module pop-up menu, as shown in Figure 7-6.

Then, from the Format pop-up menu, choose vCard. Finally, click Export to copy all the entries in your Palm Desktop Address List into one file. (You can drag the file into the Contacts folder on the iPod or save it there directly when exporting.)

Tip: If you're in the mood for a little light mousework, here's an alternate method that lets you control which names get transferred: Just drag individual names—or clumps of them, using the selection tricks described below—from your Address List, right out of the Palm Desktop window and directly into the iPod's Contacts folder.

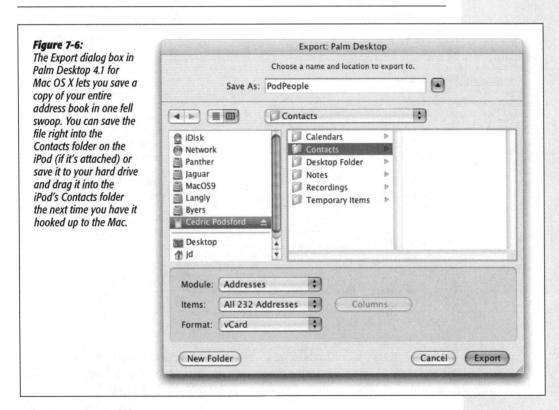

Figure 7-6:
The Export dialog box in Palm Desktop 4.1 for Mac OS X lets you save a copy of your entire address book in one fell swoop. You can save the file right into the Contacts folder on the iPod (if it's attached) or save it to your hard drive and drag it into the iPod's Contacts folder the next time you have it hooked up to the Mac.

Microsoft Entourage

Entourage is the email-calendar-address book part of Microsoft Office for Macintosh.

Connect your iPod (page 213) and double-click its desktop icon to open its window so you can see the Contacts folder. To grab the contacts you want to move there, open Entourage.

• **Entourage X:** Click the Address Book button in the top-left corner.

• **Entourage 2001:** Click the Address Book item in the Folder List area.

Select the contacts you want to copy, using any of these tricks:

• Select them all at once by pressing ⌘-A or choosing Edit→Select All.

• Select a swath of them by clicking the first in a batch, and then Shift-clicking the last. All of the contacts in between are highlighted.

• You can add individual names to the selection, or remove individuals, by ⌘-clicking them.

Once you've highlighted the contacts you want, drag the whole batch over to the iPod's Contacts folder, as illustrated in Figure 7-7.

To see your Contacts, unmount the iPod from the computer (page 215) and detach the FireWire cable. Then, on the iPod, choose Extras→Contacts and scroll away.

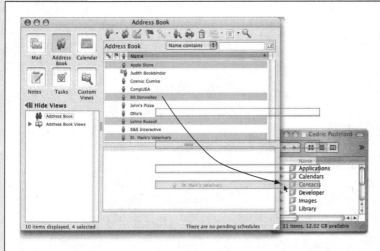

Figure 7-7:
As seen here in Entourage X for Macintosh, you can select specific entries you wish to copy and drag them to the Contacts folder in the iPod's main window while you have it connected to the computer as a FireWire disk (page 213). Most programs that work with the vCard format let you drag and drop your contacts into the iPod's Contacts folder.

Mac OS X Address Book

Moving your contacts to the iPod from the Address Book is quite similar to moving them from Microsoft Entourage. You start by figuring out which contacts you want to copy, and then selecting them using the tricks described above.

Then you can drag the highlighted contacts right out of the Address Book window and into the iPod's Contacts folder. Alternatively, you can choose File→Export vCards and send the .vcf files to a specific destination…like oh, say, an iPod.

Of course, none of this is really necessary. You, the powerful Mac OS X owner, can replicate all of that manual labor with a single click, using iSync (Chapter 10).

Tip: If for some reason, you trashed the Contacts folder on your iPod before you knew what it was for, just make a new folder named Contacts (in the main iPod window) the next time you have the iPod connected to the computer. Drag your contact information into the Contacts folder.

Coaxing vCards out of Other Mac Programs

You can cajole a few other Macintosh programs into working with vCards. If you use the venerable email program Eudora 5.1, FileMaker Pro, or Now Contact, you can usually get your contacts from here to there on the iPod—but you'll need some shareware to help extract and convert the information first.

Eudora 5.1

If your social circle is listed in Eudora 5.1 for Mac OS 9 or X, download a free copy of the Eudora vCard Export program from *www.missingmanuals.com.*

After installing the program on your Mac, you're ready to go. Double-click the Eudora vCard Export icon. The program asks for your preferences about how to sort the contacts stored in your Eudora address book and whether you'd like a separate vCard for each Eudora nickname. (Picking a separate vCard for each name makes it easier to weed out outdated files later during spring cleaning, because you can just trash the individual contacts.) Once you've made your choices, click OK.

Figure 7-8:
Top: Drag your Eudora Folder onto the Eudora vCard Export icon. A progress bar appears, shown here in Mac OS 9.

Bottom: When the Eudora vCard Export software is finished, it announces how many Eudora nickname files it converted, and a folder called Contacts appears on your desktop. Once you've connected your iPod to the Mac, drag the .vcf files out of this desktop Contacts folder and onto the iPod Contacts folder.

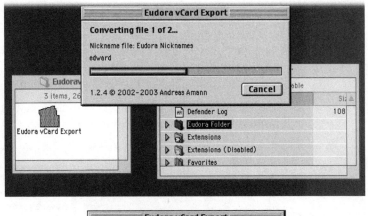

Next, you'll need to track down your *Eudora Folder* folder, which is where the program stores your downloaded mail, address book and nickname files, and program settings. In Mac OS 9, the Eudora Folder is usually in the System Folder. In Mac OS X, it's in your Home→Documents folder.

Once you've located your Eudora Folder, see Figure 7-8 for instructions.

FileMaker Pro

If you've got FileMaker Pro 5.5 or later and want to get your contact files exported over to the iPod, you can download a free XSLT style sheet called "FMP to iPod." The style sheet translates the FileMaker contact database into a version that displays properly on the iPod. Everything you need, including specific instructions for setting up FileMaker and exporting the data to the iPod, is included in the download file.

Two freeware programs specialize in FileMaker 5.5 contacts: FilePod for Mac OS 9 and X (usually available in software archives like *www.macupdate.com*) and FileMaker Pro to iPod for Mac OS X.

Both utilities use AppleScript and a special FileMaker Pro 5 file to convert and transfer the data onto the iPod. To use either, connect the iPod (page 213), launch FileMaker Pro, and then double-click the script icon (that is, FilePod or FileMaker Pro to iPod). Follow the onscreen instructions to import your contact records onto the iPod.

All three of these programs are available at the "Missing CD" page of *www.missing manuals.com*.

Now Contact, Method 1: NowPod

The Now Contact address book program, another longtime pillar of the Mac software community, also needs a little freeware footwork to transform its contacts into vCards. Here are a couple of programs designed to do just that.

First, there's NowPod, which works with both Mac OS 9 and Mac OS X. You can download it for free at *www.missingmanuals.com*.

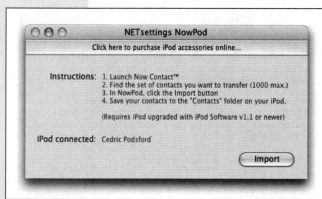

Figure 7-9:
With a quick list of simple instructions, NowPod gets to the point and explains the whole contact-importing tango right up front.

Once you've installed NowPod, connect your iPod to the Mac (page 213) and open Now Contact (you need version 4 or later). Double-click the iPod-shaped NowPod icon. As pictured in Figure 7-9, the program tells you pretty much everything you need to do on the first screen.

Don't miss the NowPod→Preferences command, by the way. Here, you can specify the first name/last name order, set up *automatic* importing of Now Contact names, whether or not to transfer fields like fax numbers and email addresses, and so on.

In your Now Contact address list, select the contacts you wish to import. In the NowPod window, click Import. If you haven't turned the "Automatically save contacts to iPod" option in the Preferences box, NowPod asks you where you'd like to save the exported contacts file. Save the file to the location of your choice and drag it into the iPod's Contacts folder—or save it directly into the iPod's Contacts folder.

Now Contact, Method 2: NowPak

Here's another way for Now Contact fans to sync up with the iPod. Power On Software offers a free utility called NowPak for iPod. (It's available for download at *www.missingmanuals.com.*) If you've purchased Now Contact and Up-to-Date, you already have the NowPak utility; it's in a folder called Additional Documentation & Tools.

NowPak includes components called Now Contact to iPod and Now Up-to-Date to iPod that transfer the respective contacts and calendar information from the two programs onto your music player.

To move your contacts, connect the iPod to the Mac (page 213) and open Now Contact. Double-click the "Now Contact to iPod" icon and select your iPod when requested. Choose how you want your contacts to be displayed (first name or last name first); click Select to start the contact transfer process. NowPak automates the whole process, even doing you the favor of dumping the vCard file into the Contacts folder of the iPod.

Note: If you've previously moved contacts using Now Contact to iPod, you may see an alert regarding an existing entry. You can choose to overwrite the earlier entry, append any new contacts to the existing entry, or cancel the whole thing.

When Now Contact to iPod has finished its work, click Done. You'll need to unmount the iPod (page 215) and disconnect the FireWire cable to see your newly placed Contacts on the iPod.

Outlook Express 5, Method 1: Contact This!

Microsoft's free email program has address book functions, too, but you need a little help prying them out of the program and into a usable form for the iPod.

Contact This! is a $15 shareware program for Mac OS X. It's actually an address book in its own right. But it can also import contacts from Outlook Express for both Mac and Windows, plus contacts exported from Entourage for the Mac and Outlook for Windows. Once you import the files from the other programs, Contact This! can export them back out in vCard format, straight to the iPod.

Outlook Express 5, Method 2: Outlook Express to vCard

The Web is a wondrous thing. Case in point: the friendly page at *http://homepage.mac.com/phrogz/OE2vCard.html*. It can convert your Outlook Express address book into a vCard file with a little cut-and-paste assistance from you. It's more effort than using Contact This!—but it's free.

Here's how to use it:

1. **In the Outlook Express address book, select the names that you want to convert.**

   You can use any of the selection tricks on page 174.

2. **Choose File→Export Contacts. In the Save dialog box, press ⌘-D (so that you'll save the exported file to the desktop), type any name you like, and click Save.**

   Outlook Express dumps your data into a large text file on your desktop (or wherever you saved it).

3. **Double-click the text file you created.**

   It opens into TextEdit or SimpleText, which is fine.

4. **Choose Edit→Select All, and then Edit→Copy.**

   You've just copied all of your address book information.

5. **Open Internet Explorer (this trick doesn't work properly in Netscape or Safari). Go to *http://homepage.mac.com/phrogz/OE2vCard.html*.**

   The instructions there talk about moving data into Mac OS X's Address Book program, but never mind that.

6. **Click inside the upper text box on the Web page, and then choose Edit→Paste (⌘-V).**

   You're halfway home as the text appears in the box.

7. **Click Convert.**

   The Web page itself converts your Outlook Express data into vCard format in the text box below.

8. **Click in the lower text box, choose Edit→Select All (⌘-A), and then choose Edit→Copy (⌘-C).**

   The converted text is now on your clipboard.

9. **Switch back to TextEdit or SimpleText, and paste (⌘-V). Save the text document with a .vcf extension.**

You can save it onto the desktop, for example. (Note: If you're using TextEdit, first choose TextEdit→Preferences, and change the upper-left setting from Rich Text to Plain Text. Do this *before* you save the document.)

10. **Drag the resulting vCard document into the iPod's Contacts folder.**

Of course, this method involves sending your contact information through the Internet via a Web form. If you're concerned with security and privacy in any way, you may want to use a different method.

Tip: Check out the page of conversion software at the ultra-helpful Web site, *www.emailman.com/ conversion*. This site offers all kinds of utilities for converting things like Eudora and Netscape mailboxes.

Manually Deleting Contacts

As with life, contact and address books change with the times. If you find your iPod needs some updating, do like so:

- If you dragged dozens of *individual* vCard files onto the iPod, you can delete individual names by dragging them out of the iPod's Contacts folder and into your computer's Trash or Recycle Bin. You can then drag updated entries back onto the iPod from your desktop organizer program.

- If you originally exported your address list as one big file, and you've made significant changes to it since loading it onto the iPod, you can easily update it. Drag the original file out of the iPod's Contacts folder to the Trash or Recycle Bin, and then re-export the address list from your desktop program, just as you did the first time. Save or drag the new file into the iPod's Contacts folder.

Address Book Settings

Once you get your contacts on the iPod, you can sort them in either of two ways. To change the order in which your contacts appear on the iPod screen, choose Settings→Contacts using the iPod's menus. You'll see settings for Sort and Display.

- **Alphabetically by last name:** Choose the Sort→Last, First option, which lists the entries like this: *Simpson, Bart.*

Tip: Be sure to select the same sorting style for the Display option. Otherwise, your list will have all the last names listed first, but be *alphabetized* by first name, making the whole thing look profoundly confused.

- **Alphabetically by first name:** If you prefer to see the names of your contacts listed like this—*Bart Simpson*—then select the sorting setting of "First, Last" for the Display option.

The beauty part is that even if you choose this option, the contacts can still be *alphabetized* by last name. Just select "First, Last" for your Display setting and "Last, First" for the Sort setting.

If you prefer the first-name basis approach, you can pick "First, Last" for both the Display and Sort options. This will alphabetize and list all your contacts by the first letter of the first name, which means *Bart Simpson* will come before *Ned Flanders* in your contacts list.

Note: If you're using shareware that pulls down news headlines (Chapter 9) or other data that it stores in the Contacts area of the iPod, you'll probably see all that stuff listed at the very top of your address list. Most programs throw in an asterisk to make the news and info files sort at the top, where they're easily located. Your regular addresses start below all the * files.

Even More Organizer Shareware

You've read about a lot of add-on software in this chapter, but you've only just begun. The world's iPod-loving programmers are way ahead of you, as this list of handies suggests.

Tip: As usual, you can download all of the following programs from the "Missing CD" page of *www.missing manuals.com*.

- **PersonaPodX.** This $20 application for Mac OS X lets you manage notes, contacts, and other files on the iPod. One feature lets you rename large groups of files, like those from a digital camera. A small preview window lets you view and organize movie clips before copying them to the iPod's FireWire-enabled hard disk for transferring between Macs.

- **Panorama iPod Organizer.** Before the iPod was granted the power to wield contacts and calendars, programmers took matters into their own hands. The Panorama iPod Organizer, which costs $20 and works with Mac OS 9, perfected the art of using MP3 files to organize and store data. The program comes with a straightforward desktop application that can import text files from spreadsheet or address book programs. The data MP3 files get mixed in with the music MP3 files, and everything shows up in the Songs list.

- **ipoAddress.** Another do-it-yourself option by a German developer for Mac OS 9 and X. The ipoAddress freeware turns addresses into MP3 files. You can decide what information you want to see on the iPod by way of iTunes before syncing up.

iPod as Calendar

"Oh, dear! Oh, dear! I shall be too late!" If the White Rabbit had had an iPod in Wonderland, he would've had not only a built-in clock, but also a convenient calendar program with an alarm to keep himself on schedule. (In any case, the iPod would have matched his fur better than his pocket watch *and* he could have listened to Jefferson Airplane on the go.)

Although the iPod works quite well with Apple's own iCal calendar program, it also displays date-book information and appointments from other programs, like Palm Desktop and Microsoft Outlook. This chapter shows how to get your schedule loaded onto your iPod and keep you from falling down the rabbit hole on the way.

Note: As with the Contacts feature described in Chapter 7, the iPod can only *display* your calendar. You can't record new appointments or edit the ones that are already there. Of course, most people use pocket organizers just to look up their schedules anyway.

Preparing the iPod

Just as with the Contacts feature, you have to set up your iPod as a FireWire disk before using any of the Calendar transfer techniques described here. Chapter 11 has the details.

Calendar Formats for the iPod

The iPod's calendar system couldn't be more basic: Its software displays the contents of any *iCalendar* or *vCalendar* files it finds in the Calendar folder on its hard drive. All you have to do is put them there.

To do that, you'll probably want to export your existing schedule from a Mac or Windows calendar program. Fortunately, most programs can export either iCalendar (.ics) or vCalendar (.vcs) format.

These files are something like the vCards described on page 169: You can make 'em, trade 'em, swap 'em with your friends, even if you use a Mac and they use PCs.

There are some differences between the *i*Calendar and *v*Calendar formats, however:

- The iCalendar format is designed for uploading and using calendars on the Internet; the vCalendar (vCal) format is popular for handheld computers and hardcore scheduling programs.

- Your alarms and reminders (page 187) survive the journey to your iPod if they're in the iCalendar format—but not if they're in vCalendar format.

Calendars from iCal (Macintosh)

If you record your life in iCal, Apple's free desktop calendar program for Mac OS X, you're in luck. Perhaps not surprisingly, the iPod has an excellent rapport with its i-named sibling.

The Easy Way

Getting your iCal calendar onto the iPod is simple: You just use Apple's free iSync program, exactly as described in Chapter 10. It automatically synchronizes and up-

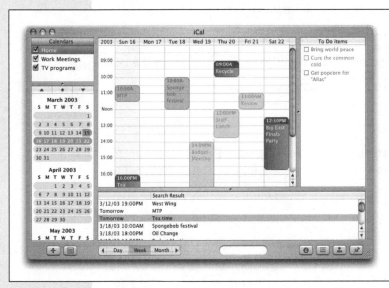

Figure 8-1:
The iCal main window lets you see your life at a glance in several panes, in addition to a main window where you can display events by the day, week, or month. In the Calendars pane, you can create several color-coded calendars for different needs or family members; view coming months in the pane below. The To Do list pane lets you set up a list and check off completed tasks. In the search pane at bottom, you can seek and find specific events.

dates complete iCal calendars between the Macintosh and the iPod. (In iCal lingo, a *calendar* is one category, or set, of appointments. You might have three, called Home, Work, and Rotary Club—or Dad, Mom, and Chris. iCal color-codes your appointments to show what calendar they belong to, as shown in Figure 8-1.)

The beauty of this system is that iSync will keep your iPod updated each time you connect it.

Tip: If your iPod is a 2003 or later model, iSync can send your iCal *To Do* list items (Figure 8-2) to the iPod, too. Once you've synced up, spin your scroll wheel to Extras→Calendars→To Do and see what you're *supposed* to get done today.

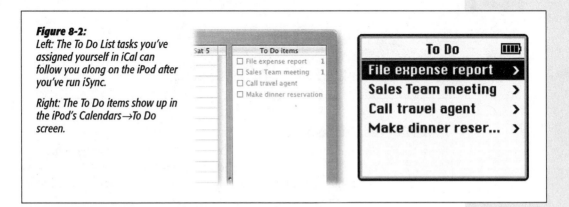

Figure 8-2:
Left: The To Do List tasks you've assigned yourself in iCal can follow you along on the iPod after you've run iSync.

Right: The To Do items show up in the iPod's Calendars→To Do screen.

The Manual Way

If you want to load just a *single* calendar category onto the iPod, you can manually move it without using iSync. To do so, click the category in the Calendars list at the left side of the iCal window, and then choose File→Export. Name the calendar file and save it someplace easy to get to, like your desktop. The exported calendar file's name has *.ics* at the end.

Bring your iPod's icon to the screen and make sure it's set up as a FireWire disk (page 213). Double-click the iPod's icon to open it, and then drag the .ics file into the Calendars folder on the iPod, as shown in Figure 8-3.

Tip: The iPod can display multiple calendars, but you have to export and drag them one at a time. Note, too, that you have to repeat the whole calendar-exporting business each time you want to update the iPod; it's not automatic, as it is when you use the iSync method.

Once your calendar file is safely inside the Calendars folder, unmount the iPod (drag it to the Trash, for example). What happens next depends on which iPod model you have:

• **2003 and later models:** The main iPod screen appears as soon as you unmount the player.

• **Earlier models:** Unplug the FireWire cable and wait for the iPod to start up again.

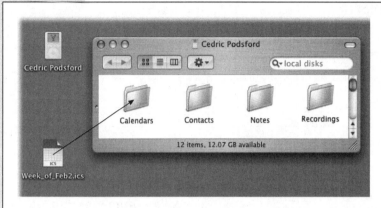

Figure 8-3:
Drag the exported calendar file into the iPod's Calendars folder to load it onto your music player. If you've accidentally deleted your Calendars folder, make a new one on the iPod and name it Calendars.

Inspecting the Calendar

From the iPod's main menu, navigate to Extras→Calendars. If you have just one calendar, you'll see a miniature calendar grid with small dots on days that you have events planned, as shown at the top right in Figure 8-4. If you've imported more

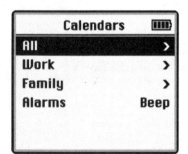

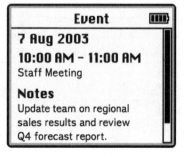

Figure 8-4:
The Calendar view on the iPod is similar to the Month view on a PalmPilot. The dots represent days with events scheduled. Use the iPod's scroll wheel and Select button to see what you have planned.

From top left: Drilling down from the list of "calendars" (subsets of appointments), to the month view, to the day view, to the screen for an individual event.

than one calendar, you must first choose the calendar (subset) you want from the iPod's Calendars menu (top left in Figure 8-4).

Tip: On recent iPod models, you can choose Calendars→All to see *all* the scheduled events on your various iCal calendars, compiled on one grid.

Of course, viewing tiny dots on a calendar grid the size of a Wheat Thin isn't exactly useful. When someone asks if you're free for lunch Friday, you can't exactly say, "No, I'm sorry, I have a tiny black dot that day."

Fortunately, you can zoom in to see your actual schedule for a certain day. To choose the day you want, turn the iPod's scroll wheel; the tiny black highlighting square zooms through the calendar dates until you home in on the one you want. At that point, click the Select button to call up that day's schedule (Figure 8-4, lower left).

In fact, you can drill down even more. You can use the scroll wheel again to highlight a specific appointment, and then click Select again to see detailed information about just that event (Figure 8-4, lower right).

Tip: On the iPod's Event screen, you can advance to the next day's events by pressing the iPod's ▶▶ button. Press the ◀◀ button to go backward in time.

Deleting a Calendar

To delete a calendar file from the iPod, connect it to the computer in FireWire disk mode (page 213), open its icon, and drag the unwanted calendar file from the Calendars folder to the Trash.

Hearing Your Alarms

The amazing part about syncing iCal to the iPod is that any alarms you've attached to iCal calendar items will actually make the iPod beep at the appointed time—*if* you've correctly configured the iPod's settings in advance. It's a simple matter of turning on the Alarms options.

- **2003 and later iPods:** From the main menu, choose Calendars→Alarms.

- **Older iPods:** From the main menu, choose Settings→Alarms.

Either way, you'll find that the Alarms submenu offers three choices. Choose the one you want by pressing the iPod's Select button:

- **Off.** When appointments come due, nothing will happen.

- **On.** At the appointed times, your iPod will wake up, display the name of the appointment, and emit a quick, external, headphones-free beep to get your attention.

- **Silent.** When appointments come due, you'll see a text message on the screen, but you won't hear any sound.

(Unlike the Alarm Clock, you can't choose music as your alarm sound.)

Calendars from Palm Desktop 4

Palm Desktop is the free calendar/address book/to-do program that comes with every Palm organizer. But you don't have to buy a Palm to get it; you can download it from *www.palm.com/software* for free. It's available in separate versions for Mac OS 9, Mac OS X, and Windows.

Mac OS 9, Mac OS X

If you want to copy your entire Date Book to the iPod as quickly and thoroughly as possible, proceed like this:

1. **Make sure your iPod is connected to the Mac as a hard drive.**

    See page 213 for instructions.

2. **In Palm Desktop, choose File→Export.**

    The Export dialog box appears.

3. **Set up the pop-up menus as shown in Figure 8-5.**

    The name of the file you're exporting doesn't really matter.

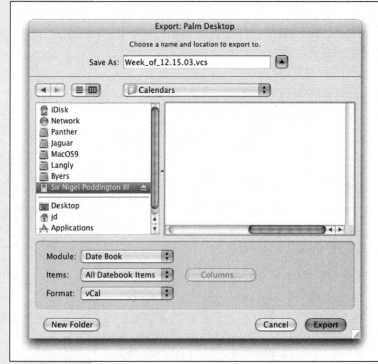

Figure 8-5:
The Palm Desktop Export dialog box lets you move your life quickly onto the iPod all at once. From the Module pop-up menu, choose Date Book. Then, from the Format pop-up menu, choose vCal. The name of the file you're exporting doesn't much matter.

4. **Navigate to the iPod's Calendars folder, and then click Export.**

The deed is done. Disconnect the iPod as described on page 215.

Tip: Although you probably won't use this technique as often, you can also drag individual events out of your Palm Desktop calendar display—clear out of the window—and into the iPod's Calendars folder. Dragging the events creates separate files with the .vcs file extension, which is the mark of a vCal document. It's a quick and dirty way to schedule your day.

Windows

Palm Desktop for Windows can't export your whole calendar file at once, or even multiple appointments at once. Incredibly, you have to export one event at a time, which is tremendously annoying, not to mention lame (see Figure 8-6).

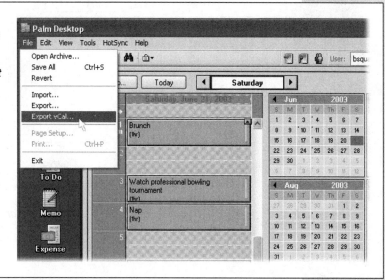

Figure 8-6:
To copy events out of the Palm Desktop Date Book in indows, select the items you want to move and choose File→Export vCal. Give your event file a name in the resulting dialog box, and then click Export. Save the file into the iPod's Calendars folder—or drag it there from wherever you saved the file.

Fortunately, shareware can do the job for you. Download Palm2iPod (from, for example, *www.missingmanuals.com*). Once you install this plug-in for the Palm software, you see two iPod-shaped icons at the top of your Palm Desktop screen. Consult Figure 8-7 for the simple instructions.

Calendars from Microsoft Entourage X

The Mac OS X version of Microsoft's Entourage email, address book, and calendar program also works with the iPod, but its calendar events pose a bit of a challenge.

While Entourage kindly offers a File→Export Contacts command, there's no similar Export Calendars command. You can drag each calendar event out of the

Entourage window and into the iPod's Calendars folder one at a time, but your great-grandchildren will have to finish the job for you.

Solution 1: iCal

Weirdly enough, one way to solve the problem is not to use Entourage at all. Instead, send your data on a detour to iCal (page 184). Within iCal, choose File→Import; you'll be offered the opportunity to import your Entourage calendar. From there, proceed as described on page 185.

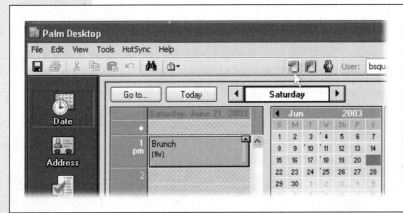

Figure 8-7:
To set up Palm2iPod, click the second iPod icon as shown here, which opens the iPod Export Preferences dialog box. Choose your iPod's drive letter, and click OK. When you're ready to export, click the first iPod icon. All of your Palm contacts and calendars are sent to the iPod in one thunderous mouse click.

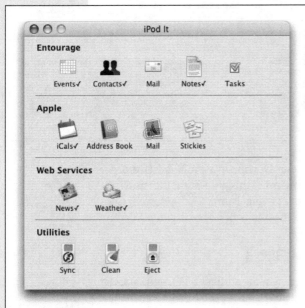

Figure 8-8:
The iPod It program gives you, the Entourage aficionado, a quick way to get your Entourage contacts and calendars moved over to the iPod. The program can also add to the iPod news, weather reports, and even driving directions with just a click of the Sync button.

Solution 2: iPod It

If you have your heart, soul, and desktop neatly organized in Entourage and don't have the patience for a side trip to iCal, consider iPod It ($15 shareware available at *www.missingmanuals.com;* see Figure 8-8). The program can convert and synchronize Entourage X events, contacts, notes, and tasks with an iPod. If you're attached to Apple's Mail, Address Book, and iCal programs, iPod It can sync those, too.

Calendars from Entourage 2001

The Mac OS 9 version of Entourage doesn't work with the .ics or .vcs formats, but if you're comfortable using AppleScripts, you'll find ones that import and export data from Entourage 2001 at *www.scriptbuilders.net.*

Calendars from Microsoft Outlook

If you rely on Outlook for Windows, you can get your appointments out of your calendar and onto your iPod—but here again, there's a manual way and a faster way.

Solution 1: Drag Individual Appointments

If you have just a few appointments to move, the manual method will do fine; see Figure 8-9.

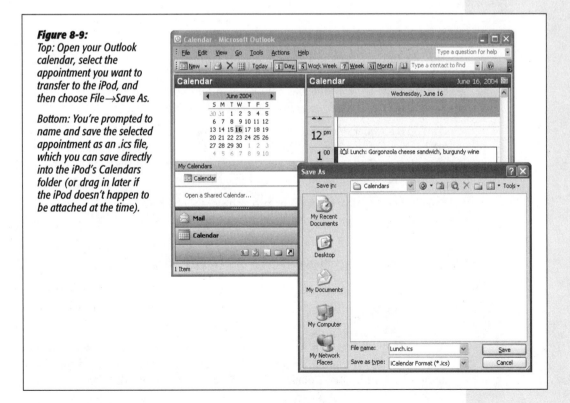

Figure 8-9:
Top: Open your Outlook calendar, select the appointment you want to transfer to the iPod, and then choose File→Save As.

Bottom: You're prompted to name and save the selected appointment as an .ics file, which you can save directly into the iPod's Calendars folder (or drag in later if the iPod doesn't happen to be attached at the time).

Solution 2: iPodSync & Co.

The $14 iPodSync program, described on page 172 and shown in Figure 8-10, can synchronize Outlook appointments, as well as contacts and to-do items, from PC to iPod.

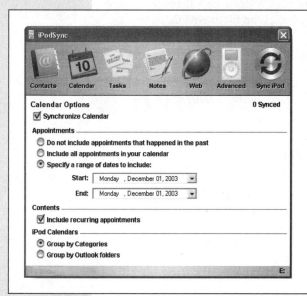

Figure 8-10:
Just as it can shuttle your Outlook contacts over to the iPod, iPodSync can likewise get those important appointments and other information out of your PC and onto your iPod with just a few clicks—and with no nasty format messes to clean up afterward.

Two other outlets for Outlook users are out there. There's iAppoint, a freeware creation. Instead of herding individual appointment files to the iPod, you can use iAppoint, which is a tool that combines all Outlook appointments into one big iCalendar-format file to copy into the iPod's Calendars folder.

OutPod is another shareware program that exports multiple appointments into one big happy vCal or iCalendar file, as shown in Figure 8-11. Once installed, OutPod displays your Outlook calendar and contacts files in its windows and you can select the data you want to move to the iPod.

You can download all three of the programs described here from the "Missing CD" page at *www.missingmanuals.com,* among other places.

Calendars from Now Up-to-Date for Mac OS X

If your life is recorded in the popular Now Up-to-Date calendar program, the free NowPak companion software is all you need to hand off your appointments to the iPod.

You can find a link to it from *www.missingmanuals.com.* Or, if you've recently installed Now Up-to-Date & Contact for Mac OS X, the NowPak for iPod software is in the suite's Additional Documentation & Tools folder. Open the NowPak for iPod folder and double-click the Now Up-to-Date to iPod icon. A box like the one in Figure 8-12 walks you through the process of transferring your appointments from Now Up-to-Date to the iPod.

Figure 8-11:
With OutPod on board, you can see all of your Outlook calendar items and contact files. Select the files you want to move, then go to OutPod→"Save selected items as a single file." You then have the choice of what format to save the files in and the chance to save it right onto the iPod.

Subject	Start	End
Breakfast	6/21/2003 9:00:00 AM	6/21/2003 9:30:00 AM
Lunch	6/21/2003 1:00:00 PM	6/21/2003 1:30:00 PM
Dinner	6/21/2003 7:00:00 PM	6/21/2003 7:30:00 PM
Massage	6/21/2003 4:00:00 PM	6/21/2003 4:30:00 PM
Read Sunday papers	6/22/2003 2:00:00 PM	6/22/2003 6:00:00 PM
Brunch @ Mumbles	6/22/2003 1:00:00 PM	6/22/2003 2:00:00 PM

OutPod 0.4
Outlook Extras View ?

Personal Folders
— Calendar (7)
— Contacts (13)

6 appointments written to G:\Calendars\Wee

Save As

Save in: Calendars

WorkWeekSked.vcs

File name: WeekendSked.vcs   Save

Save as type: vCalendar (*.vcs)   Cancel

vCalendar (*.vcs)
iCalendar (*.ics)
Calendar (*.ics, *.vcs)

Figure 8-12:
Once you click Import, the Now Up-To-Date Importer will ask you how far back and how far ahead you'd like to import your appointments, making it easy to leave your past on the computer while transferring your future to the iPod.

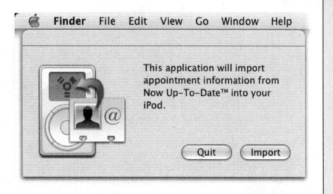

Finder File Edit View Go Window Help

This application will import appointment information from Now Up-To-Date™ into your iPod.

Quit   Import

iPod Games and eBooks

The very first iPod model was all music, all the time—unless you knew the secret Easter egg: the classic breakout Brick computer game, hidden from everyone who didn't know the sequence of button presses that could call it to the screen. Once the secret began to spread across the Internet, Apple's engineers admitted that the jig was up, and brought the game out into the open—or at least into the Extras menu, under a command called Game.

On the 2003 iPod models, the Extras menu command changed from Game to Games, tripling the ways to kill time on the iPod. The Extras menu also picked up a whole new item: Notes. For the first time, the iPod became not just a music player, calendar, Rolodex, and game machine—it also became an electronic book reader. (Don't worry if you have an older iPod model that doesn't have the new text-reading power; add-on shareware brings you the same feature.)

Games

The iPod is a personal entertainment machine on many levels. All models have at least one game: Brick. The iPod 2003 comes with two others: Parachute and—perhaps the most popular program ever in the history of the computer—Solitaire.

Brick

The Brick game has wandered all over the iPod's system software. In the first version of the iPod software, you unearthed it by holding down the Select button for five seconds on the About menu (Figure 9-1). In version 1.1, Brick surfaced in the Legal copyright info area in the Settings menu. Ever since version 1.2 of the iPod software, Brick has lived in an Extras submenu called Games.

To get there on the latest iPod models, choose Extras→Games→Brick.

Wherever it may be on your iPod, Brick is instantly recognizable as a miniature version of the Atari arcade staple Breakout, which Apple co-founder Steve Wozinak created. Your mission, should you choose to accept it, is to use a ricocheting ball to break through rows of bricks at the top of the screen. Press the Select button to start the game; as the small ball rockets in from the side, use the scroll wheel to move the paddle (at the bottom) from side to side in an effort to deflect the ball into the bricks above.

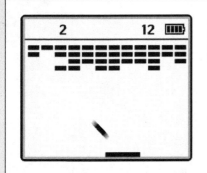

Figure 9-1:
Adventure games and flight simulation programs may come and go, but there'll always be Breakout. The iPod's Brick game, once playfully hidden, is now right up front on the Extras menu.

You get one point for each brick you knock out. If you miss the ball, you lose it (you only get three balls per game). If you manage to knock out all the bricks at the top of the screen, you move up a level, and the game begins again. It continues until you use all your balls—or suffer a horrible thumb cramp.

Parachute

Shooting at things has always been a popular theme for games, particularly computer games. (Originally, this may have been a tactic to help people manage their anger without taking a shotgun to the computer itself.)

On the 2003 iPods, Apple included a new game called Parachute, which lets you assume the controls of a ground-based antiaircraft gun. You're supposed to shoot at the helicopters that fly overhead and drop tiny little parachuting stick-people.

To play Parachute, choose Extras→Games→Parachute, and then press the Select button to start the game. The gun sits in the center bottom of the screen, but you can use the scroll wheel to pivot the barrel and direct your fire to the helicopters that buzz overhead. Press the Select button to fire at either the helicopters or the tiny parachutists. You get points for hitting a helicopter with one shot, but lose points if you miss.

Tip: Once a paratrooper lands safely on the ground, he can lob grenades at you, so it's best to hit those guys while they're in the air. Oh–and if one of the parachuting troops lands on your gun, you lose. Nobody said war is pretty.

Solitaire

This single-player card game has been entertaining the bored and lonely for centuries, and Solitaire's arrival on the iPod is sure to give many people something to do. Although it's not as large and colorful as the versions you can play on a desktop computer, iPod Solitaire (Figure 9-2) has its advantages. For instance, you can play it with one hand while riding the bus or waiting around for a friend to show up.

To begin play, go to Extras→Games→Solitaire and tap the Select button to deal out the first three cards. The game is standard Klondike: You get a row of seven card piles, on which you're supposed to alternate placing black and red cards in descending numerical order. Since you can't physically touch the cards, the iPod provides a helping hand cursor.

Use the scroll wheel to pass the hand over each stack of cards. When you get to the card you want, click the Select button to move the selected card to the bottom of the screen.

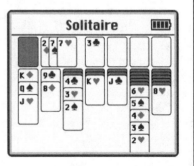

Figure 9-2:
In Solitaire on the iPod, use the scroll wheel to move the hand that plays the cards. Cleaning up after a game of Solitaire is much quicker on the iPod than in real life: Just tap the Menu button. "Fifty-two pickup" has never been easier.

Now scroll the disembodied hand to the pile where you want to place the card and click the Select button again to make the play.

When you need to deal out another three cards, place the hand over the deck at the top of the screen and tap the Select button. After you go through the deck once, it will automatically restack whatever cards are left so that you can continue dealing.

Music Quiz

Fans of the old "Name That Tune" show will recognize the concept behind the latest game in the iPod's toybox. You need iPod Update 2.1 to play it (see page 297).

Put on your headphones, then navigate to Extras→Games→Music Quiz. The game plays the first few seconds of a random song from your iPod's music library. You have 10 seconds to pick out the song's title from the five names listed on the iPod's screen. If you miss, you get an "Incorrect!" message onscreen and a deep sense of shame for not knowing your own music collection. Choosing the correct title adds to your running score and advances you to the next random song.

An iPod stuffed with thousands of songs will make this all the more challenging. And if you've got an exam coming up in Music Appreciation, why not download all the works on the syllabus onto your iPod so you can quiz yourself? Let iPod be your personal tutor!

Notes

The squint factor may be a little high, but the iPod can also lend its screen for displaying text files, which can come in handy if you want to review class notes while relaxing to a little Queen Latifah or skim your talking points before a presentation.

If you have an iPod 2003 or later model, all of this comes to you courtesy of a text-reader program called Notes (Figure 9-3). Notes can hold about 1,000 plain text files and display one at a time onscreen.

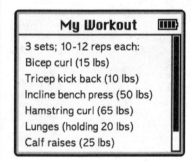

Figure 9-3:
If you can save it as a plain text file, you can read it on your iPod with the recently added Notes feature. If you don't have a 2003-model iPod, see page 200 for several shareware programs that do the same thing.

You create iPod Notes from plain text files—those with a .txt extension. You can't use full-fledged word processing documents from Microsoft Word or AppleWorks, unless you save them as plain text files. (As Chapter 11 makes clear, you can certainly use the iPod as a portable drive to ferry big files from one computer to another, but you can only *display* text files in Notes). Most word processing programs, however, can export a file's contents into Text Only or Plain Text.

For example, if you have a Word or AppleWorks document that you want to read on the iPod, open it and choose File→Save As (or the equivalent command in whatever program you're using). Select plain text formatting for the newly saved copy. Fancy formatting, graphics, and other niceties won't show up in the .txt file, but on the bright side, the file size will get a lot smaller. The iPod Notes program can display files up to 4 KB in size, which is plenty of room for lists, itineraries, or brief chunks of text. The iPod truncates files bigger than 4 KB after they pass the size limit.

To use the Notes feature, attach the iPod as a FireWire disk (page 213). When you've saved your text files as described above, drag the files into the Notes folder on the iPod. To do so, open the iPod by double-clicking its icon on the Mac desktop or in the My Computer window. The Notes folder, as seen in Figure 9-4, appears alongside the Contacts and Calendars folders. (See Chapters 7 and 8, respectively, for the story on what these folders do.)

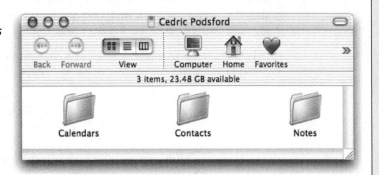

Figure 9-4:
Drag your text files into the Notes folder (right) to read them later on the iPod. To remove files, reconnect the iPod to the computer (page 213) and open the Notes folder on the desktop. Drag the unwanted files into the Trash or Recycle Bin and empty it.

After you've copied your text files, *unmount* the iPod (page 215). When you're ready to start reading, choose Extras→Notes. You'll see the names of your text files listed in the Notes menu. Scroll to the one you want and click the Select button to bring it onscreen.

As you read, you can use the scroll wheel to page up and down through the file. Press the Menu button to close the file and return to the list of Notes files. If you can't find a document you're looking for in the Notes menu, open the Notes folder on the iPod and make sure it's indeed a .txt file.

Tip: Want to compose, format, and link your own Notes files together? A free six-page guide from Apple's Web site gives you the basics. You can download a copy from *http://developer.apple.com/hardware/ipod/ipodnotereader.pdf.*

---

iPod as eBook: The Shareware Way

Even if your iPod model didn't come with the handy Notes feature, you can still read text files. Shareware programs can help you transfer your text files to the iPod, where they show up as entries in the Contacts menu, of all places. That's not quite as seamless as having the built-in Notes function, but it works.

Many text-reading shareware programs can also scavenge the Web for reading material, like news headlines, weather forecasts, and movie listings.

Note: As with any piece of software, check the information page with each program to make sure your computer system and iPod versions will work with the program.

eBooks for Macintosh

Since the iPod came out first for Macintosh, most of the goodies in this category are Macintosh-only. (You can find links to all of the following on the "Missing CD" page at *www.missing manuals.com.*) For example:

• **PodWriter.** PodWriter (for Mac OS X) lets you compose notes and import short bits of text that you can save, open, and read on the iPod.

Tip: You can use the Mac OS X spell checker program to hunt down typos before you transfer the note to the iPod by choosing PodWriter→Edit→Spelling→Spelling.

Once you've composed and titled your PodWriter note (Figure 9-5), save the file and drag it to the iPod's Contacts folder.

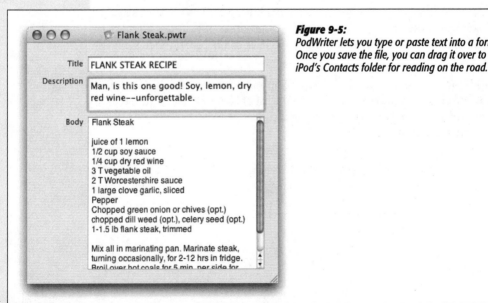

Figure 9-5:
PodWriter lets you type or paste text into a form. Once you save the file, you can drag it over to the iPod's Contacts folder for reading on the road.

- **Text2iPod X.** Early iPod text programs often had limitations on the size of the files they could handle. But size doesn't matter to Text2iPod X. This free Mac OS X program automatically detects a connected iPod. When you drag and drop a text file of any size onto the Text2iPod X icon, the program converts it and prompts you for a place to save it. Once you save it into the iPod's Contacts folder, the text file shows up as a single entry in the list under the Contacts menu.

- **Musicians iPod Tools.** This program helps professional musicians store set lists, song titles, equipment inventory, and other lists. The tool kit includes two programs—ContactsTool and MP3Tool—that, together, let you store your lists all over the iPod (not just in the Contacts folder). The software works for Mac OS 9 and X and requires iTunes and AppleScript on the Mac side.

- **PodText.** Although it can only handle text files in chunks of 2,000 characters or less, this nicely designed piece of freeware keeps track of how much you've got so far and transfers it to the iPod's Contacts folder with the click of a button, as shown in Figure 9-6. It comes in versions for both Mac OS 9 and X.

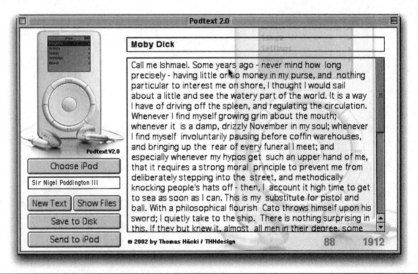

Figure 9-6:
The Podtext counter in the lower-right corner shows you how far you have to go to hit the size limit of the files it can handle. The "Send to iPod" button completes your text transfer.

- **NewsMac.** Serious newshounds might like NewsMac just for its clean desktop interface and ability to keep tabs on many popular computer and world news Web sites. The fact that the program, shown in Figure 9-7, can also sync up your favorite news channels to you iPod with one click makes it even better. NewsMac works on Mac OS X, and its creators would appreciate a PayPal donation if you like the software.

- **Pod2Go.** Pod2Go (for Mac OS X) is great for news addicts who want to keep up with the latest headlines from news outlets like the BBC, CBS, Wired News, and the major iPod news sites. The program can download stock quotes, weather forecasts, and even a daily reading from the Tao Te Ching. The software can also copy over text files to the iPod (as individual entries in the Contacts menu). Pod2Go becomes addictive after only a few syncs, and best of all, it's free (Figure 9-8).

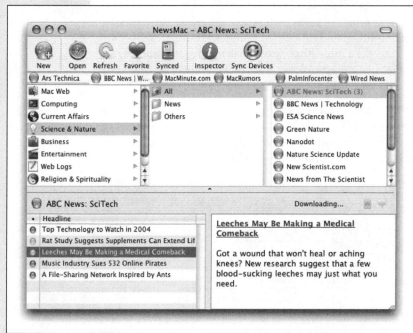

Figure 9-7:
NewsMac provides an efficient way to surf your favorite Web sites and take them with you on an iPod. The Sync iPod icon doesn't appear at first, but a quick trip into the program's settings brings it front and center.

Figure 9-8:
Pod2Go gives news addicts a steady supply of fresh headlines from around the world and can also transfer weather forecasts, movie listings, horoscopes, driving directions, and text files of your choice to the iPod's Contacts folder during a syncing session.

- **iSpeak It.** Talk about weird and wonderful: This program is designed to turn any text, HTML, Microsoft Word, or AppleWorks file into a *spoken-word* soundtrack, using the Mac's synthesized voices. The beauty of this idea is that you can now listen to your favorite Web sites, magazine articles, email messages, and other written material as you drive, jog, or work out at the gym.

  With the click of a toolbar button, iSpeak It converts the document to an audio file (Figure 9-9) and automatically sends it into iTunes, ready for transfer to the iPod. The program can also convert downloaded news headlines and weather forecasts to audio files for the iPod. (You may want to tinker with the Mac's built-in voices in the Speech area of System Preferences until you find a voice that doesn't remind you of the Swedish Chef on *The Muppet Show*.) The shareware by Michael Zapp, who is also the author of iPod Launcher and iPod-It, costs $9.

Tip: Got lots of time and not much money? Hit up the Project Gutenberg Web site (*www.gutenberg.net*) and download great works of literature in convenient electronic form, ready for iPod reading. Project Gutenberg has thousands of free, 100 percent legal eBooks in the public domain—things like the works of Shakespeare and the original Tarzan novels from the 1920s—in plain text format. You can even download some titles as MP3 audiobooks.

Figure 9-9:
With iSpeak It, just import or paste in some text, and the program converts it to an audio track and sends it to iTunes—where it syncs up with your iPod.

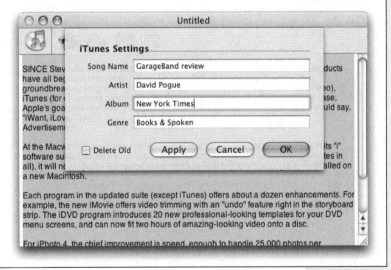

- **Book2Pod.** Unless you're a big fan of haiku or extremely short stories, the 4 KB limit of the iPod's Notes program may put a damper on your eBook reading. As its name implies, the Book2Pod freeware program lets you pack a proper novel onto your iPod by automatically linking those little 4 KB files together into one almost seamless scroll. The program works with Mac OS X 10.2 and later and iPod software 2.0 and later.

eBooks for Windows

Although Mac fans have a few more programs to choose from, Windows shareware for the iPod is beginning to pop up around the Web.

- **EphPod.** The now-familiar wonderware for Windows does more than copy songs and Outlook contacts to the iPod (page 171); it can also fetch news and weather updates. If you have a Windows-formatted iPod, EphPod is free. If you're using a Mac-formatted iPod with your PC, you'll also need a copy of MacOpener by DataViz, which runs about $40.

- **iPodLibrary.** Serious eBook readers who juggle multiple formats (like .lit, .pdf, .html, and .txt) to get their daily literary fix, might want to take a look at iPodLibrary (Figure 9-10). This free program can import your existing eBook files, dice them up into Notes-approved 4 KB bites, and link them together for you automatically.

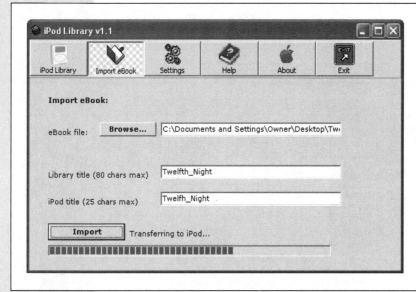

Figure 9-10:
iPodLibrary can convert electronic books in several formats into the iPod's Notes format quickly and easily. Just locate your desired eBook on your hard drive, give it a name so you can find it in your iPod's Notes folder, and click Import.

iSync

H igh-tech gadgets are supposed to make our lives simpler and easier, but sometimes they just makes things more complicated. Think, for example, about how many different places you keep your address book: One copy on your main machine, another on your laptop, another on your Palm or PocketPC, another on your cellphone, and—if you've read Chapter 7—one more on your iPod.

Now then: Are all of these various address books completely identical, or do they vary from device to device? *("Well, Tory beamed me her business card, so I have that on my Palm Tungsten T3. But I haven't programmed her into my cellphone yet, and I have Chris's new office number on my phone but haven't typed it into my Mac's Address Book, and then there's all of Charlie's contact info since he moved…")*

Wouldn't it be great if there were a way to synchronize all of your contacts and addresses books automatically, so no matter which gadget you grab on your way out the door, your data would be fresh, hot, and useful? If you use Mac OS X 10.2 or later, there is: iSync.

The iSync Concept

iSync can synchronize your address book and calendar with your iPod, Palm-based organizers, Bluetooth-enabled cellphones, and even other Macs (if you have a .Mac account). There's only one prerequisite: Your address book and calendar information must already be in Apple's own address book and calendar programs, Address Book and iCal. (See the box on page 209.)

For a quick visual reference, the main iSync window lays out all the devices you've opted to synchronize together, as shown in Figure 10-1.

If you don't have it already, you can download a copy of the free iSync program from Apple's Web site at *www.apple.com/isync.*

Note: Bluetooth (named for a tenth-century Danish king, not some sort of dental condition) is a short-range wireless technology designed to help you rid your life of cables. Gadgets like computers, cellphones, handheld organizers, and printers wired with Bluetooth capability can communicate with each other from up to 30 feet away. To use a Bluetooth phone with your Mac and synchronize any of its information with your other devices, you need a Bluetooth adapter for the Mac. Most Bluetooth adapters plug into the Mac's USB port and sell for around $50. And, of course, certain models have Bluetooth built right in (as do the latest laptops).

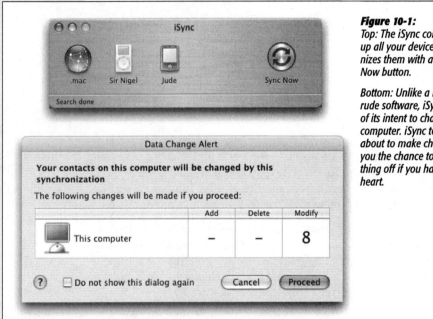

Figure 10-1:
Top: The iSync control panel lines up all your devices and synchronizes them with a click of the Sync Now button.

Bottom: Unlike a lot of rude software, iSync can warn you of its intent to change your computer. iSync tells you when it's about to make changes and gives you the chance to call the whole thing off if you have a change of heart.

iSync Meets iPod

Part of iSync's charm is its ability to keep your iPod in perfect harmony with iCal and Address Book—and you don't have to export, drag, or drop a thing.

To use the dynamic duo of iSync and iPod, you need version 1.2 or later of the iPod system software. (You can download the most current version at *www.apple.com/ ipod/download*).

Once you've installed iSync, connect your iPod to the Mac with the FireWire cable and then start up iSync. In iSync, choose Devices→Add New Device. The iSync program looks around to see what compatible items are connected to the Mac.

When iSync has located your iPod, it invites you to drag the icon into the iSync window to add it to the team (Figure 10-2).

Now the iSync window expands so that you can set up the synchronization process (Figure 10-3). (You can also expand the iSync window by clicking any of the device icons.)

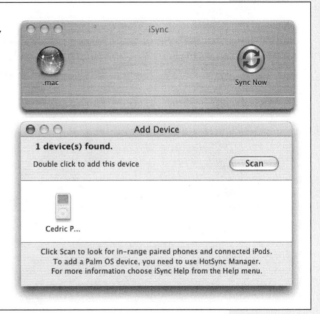

Figure 10-2:
When you first open iSync (top), it doesn't "see" the iPod.

But once iSync has looked around and found your iPod (bottom), you can add it to the brushed-metal toolbar by dragging its icon—or by simply double-clicking it.

In the expanded iSync window, turn on the synchronization function. This is also your opportunity to decide whether or not you want iSync to update your iPod *automatically* each time you connect it to the Mac. You can also pick the specific calendars (that is, subsets of appointments; see page 184) and contact groups you wish to add to the iPod.

UP TO SPEED

Dot Mac, Dot Com

Apple's .Mac service is a members-only society that costs $100 a year. While membership may not get you a preferred tee time, it gives you a bucket of goodies for your Macintosh.

Some of the perks include a *mac.com* email address, a place for your own Web page, antivirus and backup software, and 100 MB of space to back up your files (or upload documents that are too big to email). You can also store your Address Book, Safari bookmarks, and iCal calendars on .Mac, making them available to co-workers, friends, and relatives from any Web-connected computer.

The annual fee may seem steep, but Apple offers a free 60-day trial. Go to *www.mac.com* to see if membership really does have its privileges.

Note: If you're trying to work your Palm-based organizer into the iSync mix, you have to download the iSync Palm Conduit 1.2 software from Apple at www.apple.com/isync. You'll also need iCal 1.5 or later and Palm Desktop 4.0 or later for Mac OS X.

Once you've installed the software, open Palm Desktop, choose HotSync Manager→Conduit Settings, and turn on "Enable iSync for this Palm Device."

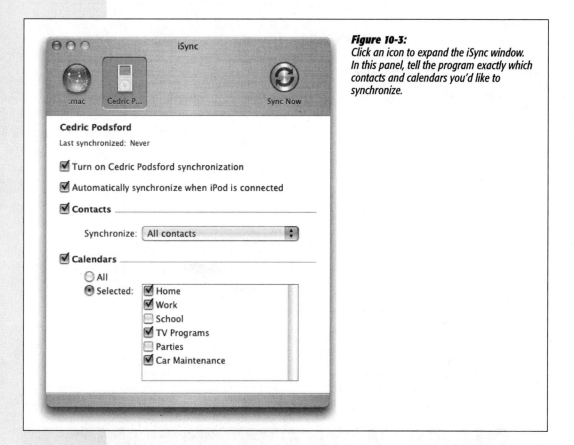

Figure 10-3:
Click an icon to expand the iSync window. In this panel, tell the program exactly which contacts and calendars you'd like to synchronize.

Once you've made your selections, click the round Sync Now button. If this is your first syncing session, iSync may take a few minutes to copy all of the data down to the iPod. You might also see the Safeguard box, like the one at bottom in Figure 10-1, warning you of iSync's activities.

After iSync finishes up, your iPod will be in sync with iCal and your Address Book. You can check the date of your last synchronization for any device by clicking its icon in the iSync window; the first line tells you when you last synced. As shown in Figure 10-4, you can also check your iSync log in Window→View Logs to see what just happened.

Tip: If you've just run iSync only to realize that you didn't *want* to update all that information quite yet, iSync can save your bacon. You can go back in time and restore your data to the state it was in before that last synchronization by choosing iSync→Devices→Revert to Last Sync.

Figure 10-4:
iSync gives you a progress report as it works (top), but in case you're curious, the program also keeps a log of what it did and when it did it (bottom). You can visit the log at Window→Show Logs or by pressing ⌘→L on the keyboard.

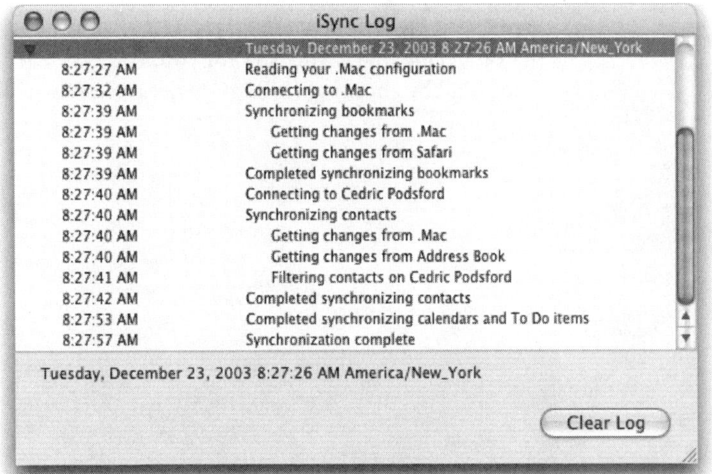

	iSync Log
	Tuesday, December 23, 2003 8:27:26 AM America/New_York
8:27:27 AM	Reading your .Mac configuration
8:27:32 AM	Connecting to .Mac
8:27:39 AM	Synchronizing bookmarks
8:27:39 AM	Getting changes from .Mac
8:27:39 AM	Getting changes from Safari
8:27:39 AM	Completed synchronizing bookmarks
8:27:40 AM	Connecting to Cedric Podsford
8:27:40 AM	Synchronizing contacts
8:27:40 AM	Getting changes from .Mac
8:27:40 AM	Getting changes from Address Book
8:27:41 AM	Filtering contacts on Cedric Podsford
8:27:42 AM	Completed synchronizing contacts
8:27:53 AM	Completed synchronizing calendars and To Do items
8:27:57 AM	Synchronization complete

Tuesday, December 23, 2003 8:27:26 AM America/New_York

Clear Log

FREQUENTLY ASKED QUESTION

Converting Information for iSync

I want to use iSync, but I have never used the Address Book; all my contacts are in another program. How do I move them into the Address Book so I can sync?

If your other address book program can export contacts as vCards, you should be able to get them into the Mac Address Book easily. For example:

Palm Desktop: Choose File→Export and export your entire Rolodex as one big vCard file.

Save the exported file to your desktop, open Address Book, and then drag the vCard file into the Address Book window to add all of your addresses. The next time you run iSync, it'll copy the new contacts in the Address Book over to the iPod's Contacts folder.

Microsoft Entourage: Select all contacts, or individual contacts, and drag them, en masse, completely out of the Entourage window and onto a new folder on your desktop.

You've just created a vCard file for each name.

Now open your Mac OS X Address Book. Switch to the Finder, open the folder you created, choose Edit→Select All, and drag the vCard files into the open Address Book window.

Eudora, Now Contact: See Chapter 7 for details.

iSync's other talent is transferring your *calendar* information into the iPod. Once again, though, it only talks to Apple's own calendar program: iCal.

To get your data from any other calendar program into iCal, the trick is to export it to the *iCalendar* or *vCalendar* format (page 184). Then, in iCal, choose File→Import to bring in the new file. (iCal can also import Entourage calendars from the Import dialog box.)

At this point, syncing your gadgets with iSync blesses them with your whole agenda, too.

If you have several devices in your iSync list but don't have them all connected each time you run iSync, the program throws up a pessimistic alert box saying that the synchronization failed. Remain calm. This doesn't mean your iPod didn't get synced. It just means iSync has failed to synchronize *all* the devices on its list—because they weren't all connected or configured properly.

Removing the iPod from the iSync List

If you decide that iSync isn't for you, you can sever the connection between it and your iPod by choosing iSync→Devices→Remove Device.

The iPod as Hard Drive

There may come a time when the size of your files grows to exceed the size of a blank CD or Zip disk. For many people, that time is *now*. Thanks to the boom in digital audio, photography, and video, our supersized files don't fit on such meager disks anymore, which makes it harder to cart them around from computer to computer.

That's where the iPod's most magnificent hidden feature comes into play. Remember that the iPod is, at heart, essentially a hard drive (which is why it can hold so many thousands of songs). With a single click in Preferences, in fact, the iPod can turn itself into an external hard drive—a real live icon-on-your-screen hard drive. Depending on the capacity of your iPod—and how much music you have on it—you could easily have a spare 2, 10, or 25 gigabytes of space available for backing up your Documents folder, transporting that 800 MB movie of your baby's first steps, or even storing a bootable System folder that you can use if your Mac crashes and can't get up.

The iPod's Hard Disk Format

The iPod's drive is formatted in such a way that it can communicate with a computer much like any other hard drive—depending on which model iPod and computer you're using.

The first iPods, released in 2001, functioned only as *Macintosh* hard disks. The 2002 iPods came in separate Macintosh or Windows versions. And 2003-and-later iPods are compatible with both Mac and Windows (you don't have to pick a format at purchase time; see page 4).

A Windows PC won't recognize a Macintosh-formatted iPod. On the other hand, a Mac can recognize *both* PC- and Mac-formatted iPods. Some people even go back and forth between a Mac and a PC with their Windows-formatted iPods, merrily and manually updating their music collection between iTunes for each platform.

Tip: You can tell if an iPod was formatted for Macintosh or Windows in the About menu on the main iPod screen. If the last item in the list is the iPod's serial number, you've got a Macintosh-formatted iPod. If it says, "Format: Windows" underneath the serial number…well, you can figure it out from there.

You can reformat a Mac iPod for Windows, or a Windows iPod for Macintosh, but only by erasing it completely and reformatting it.

Note: Do not reformat or partition the iPod's hard drive with any utility software other than the iPod installer program that came with your player. These installers format the drive in HFS Plus (Mac) or FAT32 (Windows), which is what the iPod needs to play music. Formatting the drive with, say, the Unix or Mac OS Standard file systems spell the end of your iPod's career as a music player.

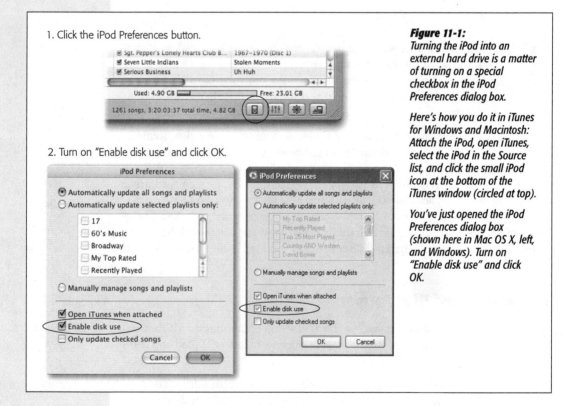

1. Click the iPod Preferences button.

2. Turn on "Enable disk use" and click OK.

Figure 11-1:
Turning the iPod into an external hard drive is a matter of turning on a special checkbox in the iPod Preferences dialog box.

Here's how you do it in iTunes for Windows and Macintosh: Attach the iPod, open iTunes, select the iPod in the Source list, and click the small iPod icon at the bottom of the iTunes window (circled at top).

You've just opened the iPod Preferences dialog box (shown here in Mac OS X, left, and Windows). Turn on "Enable disk use" and click OK.

Turning the iPod into an External Hard Disk

To set up the iPod as an external hard disk, you don't have to jump through compli-cated technical hoops. The days of installing disk drivers, fiddling with jumper switches, SCSI-chain termination, and IRQ settings are long gone.

- **If you use iTunes.** See Figure 11-1 for step-by-step instructions.

- **If you use MusicMatch Jukebox.** If you have a 2003 or later iPod, see Figure 11-2.

    If you have an older model, connect it to the PC. Open MusicMatch Jukebox, if it doesn't open automatically. Once MusicMatch Jukebox senses the iPod, the Por-tables Plus window appears. Right-click the iPod's icon (in the list at the left side) and, from the shortcut menu, choose Options. In the iPod's Options box, click the iPod tab, turn on "Enable disk mode," and click OK.

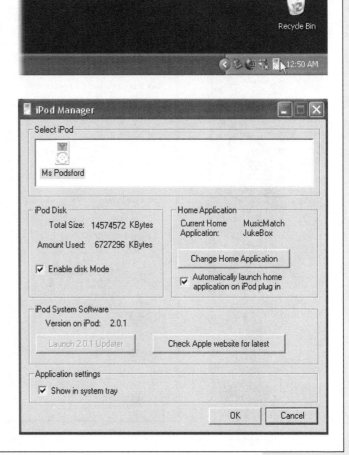

Figure 11-2:
Click the small white iPod icon in the Windows system tray (indicated by cursor, top) to call up the iPod manager box (bottom), where you'll find a strangely capitalized checkbox called "Enable disk Mode."

Turning on this box turns your iPod into a living, breathing external hard drive that shows up in My Computer exactly as though it's, well, a hard drive.

Note: If you've disabled automatic synchronization (page 50), you may notice that the option to turn on the FireWire mode is dimmed out. That's because switching the iPod to manual-update mode *also* enables the FireWire disk mode, whether you like it or not.

If you don't want the FireWire disk option turned on, turn off the button for manual updates, and then turn on either "Automatically update all songs and playlists" or "Automatically update selected playlists only" instead.

Storing Data Files on the iPod

From now on, every time you connect the iPod to your Mac or PC, its icon pops up on the desktop (Mac) or in the My Computer window (PC). You can go right to town using the iPod as the world's shiniest, best-looking, and most expensive floppy disk, as shown in Figure 11-3.

Figure 11-3:
The iPod is reborn—as a disk! On the Mac (left), its icon appears on your desktop, just like the other hard drive. Double-click it to open up its window. On the PC (right), the iPod shows up in Windows Explorer or My Computer as another drive with its own letter (here called Ms Podsford).

The music is kept in a special, invisible place on the iPod, so copying regular computer files onto the iPod doesn't affect them. (And syncing your music with the Mac or PC doesn't affect the computer files, either.) However, remember that the more you fill up your iPod with music, the less room you have to store data files—and vice versa.

Note: Both 2001 and 2002 iPod models use a FireWire cable with a standard 6-pin connector on both ends (with a 4-pin adapter for the FireWire jacks on some Windows computers).

The thinner iPod 2003 cable, however, has a standard FireWire connector on one end and a weird, non-standard, flat rectangular dock connector on the other. If you're going to be regularly using your iPod as a FireWire drive to transfer files between two machines, you may want to get an extra connection cable (about $20) so that you don't have to carry your original cord back and forth. (Apple sells iPod FireWire cables on its Web site.)

Deleting Data Files

Deleting files from the iPod when it's impersonating a hard drive is just like erasing them from any other kind of disk: just drag them to the Trash or Recycle Bin—or use keyboard shortcuts, like the Delete key in Windows or ⌘-Delete on Macintosh—and empty it.

Just remember that this isn't how you delete *songs*. You delete songs in iTunes (or MusicMatch Jukebox Plus).

Note: Don't use a disk utility program like Drive Setup or Norton Utilities to erase the iPod's data files. You could damage its music-playing powers—and then be stuck having to reformat the drive with the iPod software installer and *then* copy all of your songs over again.

Unmounting the iPod Drive

You're not supposed to detach any kind of hard drive just by ripping its cord out of your computer. If it happens to be right in the middle of copying a file, or performing some automatic internal maintenance that you're not even aware of, you risk badly scrambling the data on that disk.

The same goes for the iPod. Yes, you can "eject" it as you would a CD—that, after all, is its whole delicious advantage—but only after first *unmounting* it (that is, removing its icon from the screen) like this:

- **iTunes.** In the iTunes Source list, select the iPod and then click the Eject iPod button (identified in Figure 11-4). On a Mac, you can also use any of the usual disk-ejection methods: drag the iPod icon on the desktop to the Trash, Control-click the iPod icon and choose Eject from the contextual menu, click the Eject icon next to the iPod's icon in the Sidebar (Mac OS X 10.3), and so on.

At this point, if you have iTunes open, the iPod disappears from the Source list and from your desktop. Depending on your iPod model and software, either the main menu or the "OK to Disconnect" message appears on the iPod's screen.

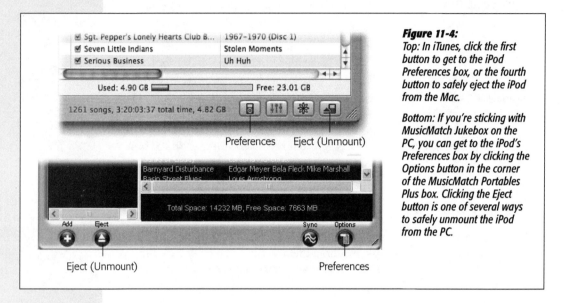

Figure 11-4:
Top: In iTunes, click the first button to get to the iPod Preferences box, or the fourth button to safely eject the iPod from the Mac.

Bottom: If you're sticking with MusicMatch Jukebox on the PC, you can get to the iPod's Preferences box by clicking the Options button in the corner of the MusicMatch Portables Plus box. Clicking the Eject button is one of several ways to safely unmount the iPod from the PC.

- **MusicMatch Jukebox for Windows.** If you didn't have 6,342 different ways to do something, it just wouldn't be Windows.

Here are some of the different ways to detach your iPod from your PC.

Note: In all cases, don't disconnect the iPod until you see the iPod's "OK to Disconnect" message or its main menu appear—which may take as long as 15 seconds.

Method 1: In MusicMatch, click the Eject button at the bottom of the Portables Plus window (Figure 11-4). When MusicMatch asks if you're sure, click Yes. Wait a few seconds while the "Ejecting iPod" and "It is now safe to disconnect iPod" messages flash on the PC screen.

Method 2: See the tiny white iPod icon in your system tray (Figure 11-2)? Right-click it and choose Unmount iPodster (or whatever your iPod's name is) from the pop-up menu.

If this trick doesn't work, it's probably because MusicMatch or Windows is still communicating with the iPod about something. Quitting MusicMatch Jukebox usually clears this up.

Method 3: Click the Safely Remove Hardware icon, which looks like a small green arrow floating above a gray box (Figure 11-5). Choose whatever variation of the "Stop IEEE 1394 Disk Drive" option you see.

When the "Safely Remove hardware" message appears, click OK.

Note: Apple advises that you *not* eject the iPod by right-clicking its icon in the My Computer window and using the Eject option from the contextual menu.

Figure 11-5:
Top left: The icon for the iPod Manager program looks like an iPod. Right-click it to unmount the iPod.

Top right: It's OK to disconnect.

Bottom: Here's another way to release the iPod.

The iPod as Startup Disk (Macs Only)

For years, Mac-heads worldwide have taken comfort in a backup startup disk: a CD or external hard drive containing a working System Folder that can start up the computer when its own copy of the system software gets hosed. Many techies even put copies of their favorite disk utility programs (Tech Tool, Disk Warrior, Norton Utilities, or whatever) on there, too, to make fixing a crashed, cranky, question-mark-flashing Mac as quick and efficient as possible.

Thanks to the iPod, that trick is more convenient than ever. The following instructions guide you through turning your Macintosh iPod into a bootPod. It assumes that you have enough space left on your iPod over and above all your music and other files.

Note: A Windows iPod can't, alas, start up a PC.

Which OS?

Before you begin, consider which version of the Mac OS you want to use. Mac models that debuted after January 2003 can't start up using Mac OS 9 at all. But if your older model can, note that Mac OS 9 is less complicated to get on the iPod, it's easier to take off, and takes up much less drive space than Mac OS X. (A lean Mac OS 9 can take up as little as 300 MB, compared to 2 GB and up for Mac OS X.) Furthermore, top-notch disk-rescue programs like Disk Warrior run fine in Mac OS 9, yet diagnose and fix problems found on both OS 9 and OS X systems.

While you can erase a Mac OS 9 System Folder by tossing it in the Trash, getting a Mac OS X system off your iPod is more of a challenge. That may be a consideration when you one day decide that your bootPod days are over and you want to fill up your iPod with Norah Jones and everybody who sounds like her. Because of its Unix underpinnings, deleting a Mac OS X system from any disk requires hunting down dozens of hidden files and purging the iPod of things like mach_kernel and .DS_Store.

What to Include

Once you've decided about what version of the Mac OS to install, make a list of what you need to use with it. Your list should include both those disk utility programs and things like printer and scanner drivers, special fonts, and network and Internet settings. Also consider adding whatever everyday programs you might need in a pinch (Word? Photoshop?) and other files you might need in a hardware emergency.

Installing Mac OS 9 on an iPod

Use the installation CD that came with your Mac, or one that you bought.

Note: Make sure you that have the CD that says "Mac OS 9 Install"; the ones that say things like "iMac Software Restore 1 of 6" don't contain the right installer program.

Then follow these steps:

1. **Connect your iPod to your Mac as a FireWire disk.**

   The process is described on page 213.

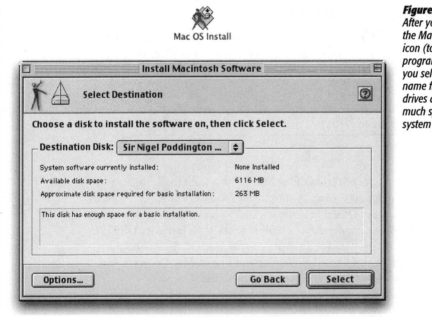

Figure 11-6:
After you double-click the Mac OS 9 installer icon (top), the Installer program (bottom) lets you select your iPod's name from a list of drives and tells you how much space the new system will take up.

2. Insert your Mac OS 9 Install CD into the Mac. Choose Restart from the Special menu or the menu. As the screen lights up again after the chime, hold down the letter C key.

You can release the key when the Happy Mac icon appears. You've just forced the Mac to start up from the CD instead of its hard drive. (The startup process takes longer than your normal Mac startup sequence because it has to read the System Folder on the CD.)

When the Mac has fully started up, it opens the CD's window on the desktop.

3. Double-click the "Mac OS Install" icon (Figure 11-6, top). Click Continue.

The installer asks for a Destination Disk (Figure 11-6, bottom).

4. From the pop-up menu, choose your iPod's name and click Select.

You see a screen of information about the software.

5. Click Continue. Then, on the license screen, click Continue and then Agree. When you arrive at the Install Software step, click Start.

The installer program takes it from here. You don't have to do anything for the next few minutes except quit the program when it announces that it's finished. You can double-click the iPod's desktop icon to see your new System Folder on the drive.

Starting up from an iPod in Mac OS 9

To start up a Mac from the newly enhanced iPod, choose →Control Panels→ Startup Disk. In the Startup Disk control panel, click the icon of the Mac OS 9 System Folder, as shown in Figure 11-7. Click Restart to start up from the iPod. (When you want to switch *back* to the Mac's regularly scheduled System Folder,

Figure 11-7:
Go to →Control Panels→Startup Disk and pick the system disk you'd like to start up from the next time the Mac restarts. This is your opportunity to put the iPod in charge.

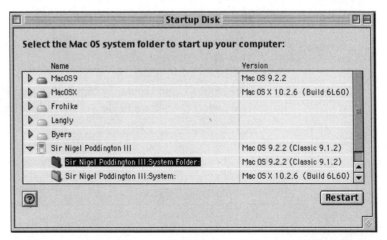

return to the Startup Disk control panel, click the System Folder you wish to use, and then click Restart.)

The Startup Manager

Of course, if your regularly scheduled System Folder is hosed, you can't very well start up your Mac to get to its Control Panels folder. In that case, you have to *force* the Mac to start up from your iPod. To do so:

1. **Connect the iPod to the computer and restart it.**

   On Macs with the Power button on the keyboard, press Control-⌘-Power button to force the Mac to restart. On newer Macs that lack the power button, press Control-⌘-Eject. (If you have no Eject key, press Control-⌘-F12 instead.)

2. **Hold down the Option (Alt) key as the machine starts back up.**

   A series of icons appears onscreen, each representing one startup disk that the Mac has found (Figure 11-8).

Figure 11-8:
The Startup Manager, a secret routine built into most Mac models, appears when you press Option as the computer is starting up. It shows you all available startup disks.

3. **Click the icon representing the iPod's System Folder, and then click the right-pointing arrow button.**

   The Mac starts up from the System Folder stored on the iPod.

Note: This trick works on most, but not all, Mac models.

Once you've repaired your regular System Folder, go back to ⌘→Control Panels→ Startup Disk, select the System Folder on your Mac's hard drive, and click Restart.

Tip: If you're using the iPod to boot up your ailing Mac, take it out of any protective case or sleeve you might be using, as it could overheat and malfunction. Using an iPod to drive your Mac makes the hard disk spin constantly, which generates excess heat that can get trapped inside a case or sleeve. Remember, heat and hard drives don't mix!

Installing Mac OS X on an iPod

Getting a startup version of Mac OS X onto an iPod isn't as straightforward as setting up a Mac OS 9 system. Mac OS X is a whole new ball game, fundamentally and structurally different from the Mac systems that roamed the Earth before.

All you need to start up from Mac OS 9 is a System Folder. In Mac OS X, you need all sorts of additional files, including invisible files, all of which have to be copied—*just so*—for the operating system to work properly. For instance, the Darwin core of Mac OS X requires certain *symbolic links* (the Unix equivalent of alias and shortcut files) to be in certain places around the system.

Mac OS 10.0 or 10.1

If you have a pre-10.2 version of Mac OS X (and if your Mac model can run on those earlier versions), this isn't so bad. Follow the same steps as you would for Mac OS 9 (page 218). When you're offered a Custom Install button, however, click it. You'll be offered the chance to choose which Mac OS X components you want to install—and unless you're absolutely swimming in excess iPod hard-drive space, you should turn off components like Mac OS X programs, foreign-language versions, and other things besides the base operating system.

Once the Installer has finished, the Mac restarts from the newly installed System folder (on the iPod). (If it doesn't, for some reason, see "The Startup Manager" on the facing page.)

If you *don't* want to start up from the iPod quite yet, unplug it before the Mac fully restarts.

As with any brand-new computer, you'll probably have to go through a series of system setup screens with the new Mac OS X system installed, including specifying user accounts and Internet settings. If your iPod is connected to your Mac and your Mac is connected to the Internet, you'll probably see the Software Update application start up and go look for new updates, upgrades, and patches to add to your fresh new system.

Depending on your version of Mac OS X, you may go through several turns of the Download-Install-Restart tango until Software Update is satisfied that it's up to date.

When the day comes that you want to start up your Mac from the iPod's copy of Mac OS X, open System Preferences→Startup Disk, select the iPod, and click Restart.

Mac OS X 10.2 (Jaguar)

Mac OS X 10.2 improved on the existing Mac OS X system in many ways, but one of them wasn't the ability to install the system on an external drive. The Jaguar installer program spans two CDs and requires you to restart the machine between their insertions, which makes it something of a challenge to create a bootable external drive. The Jaguar installer just doesn't want to let go of that midstream restart, and neither does its Panther successor.

So if you can't install the system directly onto another disk, how can you get Mac OS X 10.2 or later onto your iPod? By *cloning* it on! With cloning, you can make an exact duplicate of the entire system in one shot, with everything in its rightful place.

If you're comfortable typing Unix commands in Mac OS X's Terminal window (you know who you are), you can use the *ditto* command to clone a system onto a designated drive.

If you're a normal human being, however, you'll probably find life much less stressful if you use a cloning program like the excellent Carbon Copy Cloner, a $5 shareware program. (Behind the scenes, it uses the same *ditto* command—but it has an attractive, normal-looking Mac OS X control panel.) With it, you can clone a drive without typing in commands like *sudo ditto -rsrcFork /System /Volumes/Backup/System* into the wee hours.

You can download Carbon Copy Cloner from the "Missing CD" page of *www.missing manuals.com*. With Carbon Copy Cloner installed and running, and your iPod connected to the Mac, you're ready to roll.

Note: Depending on what you install, a fully loaded Mac OS X 10.2 or 10.3 system can take up 3 GB of disk space or more. Unless you have an extra-roomy iPod model, cloning a Jaguar or Panther system onto your iPod may make an uncomfortable dent in the space you have available for other iPod content, like calendars, contacts, news headlines, and documents.

Oh, and *songs*.

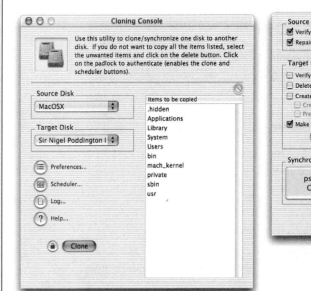

Figure 11-9:
Left: The Cloning Console window of Carbon Copy Cloner takes all the same func-tions performed by typing lengthy Unix commands and puts them into a clean, clickable graphic interface.

Right: Turn on "Make bootable" in the Carbon Copy Clone Preferences box to properly enable the Mac OS X system on your iPod.

1. In the Cloning Console window of Carbon Copy Cloner (Figure 11-9, left), click the hard drive that already contains Mac OS X 10.2.

    That's going to be called your Source Disk.

2. **Choose your iPod as the Target Disk.**

    The program displays a list of files in your System folder in the "Items to be copied" window.

3. **Click each item that you *don't* want copied to the iPod, and click Remove.**

    It's the button above the right side of the list, the one with the familiar circle-with-a-slash-through-it symbol.

    Specifically, you *don't* need .DS_Store, dev, Volume, Network, etc, tmp, var, automount, .vol, mach, mach.sym, Cleanup At Startup, TheVolumeSettingsFolder, File Transfer Folder, Trash, .Trashes, and TheFindByContentFolder.

    Select everything else in the *root level* (what would be the main hard drive window). (You can also choose other things to copy—folders of photos, icons on your desktop, whatever.)

4. **Click the Preferences button. In the box that pops up, turn on "Make bootable" (Figure 11-9, right). Then click the Lock icon at the bottom of the box.**

    The "Enter account name and password" box opens. You won't be able to change Cloner's settings until you've established your trustworthiness by entering the name and password of an Administrator account.

5. **Enter your name and password, and then click OK.**

    Now you're in.

6. **Click Clone.**

    The software proceeds to clone your system files, creating a mirror image of the System folder on the iPod. Depending on how much stuff you're cloning over to the iPod, the job could last 30 minutes or longer.

7. **When the software has finished the clone job, quit Carbon Copy Cloner.**

Mac OS 10.3 (Panther)

Panther people (that is, people using Mac OS X 10.3 and later) have another way to get Mac OS X onto the iPod for use as a startup disk: the Disk Utility program. This convenient software is primarily designed to partition, repair, or erase hard disks, but it can also clone the whole enchilada to another disk, including an iPod's. You'll find Disk Utility in the Applications→Utilities folder.

Once in the program, click the Restore tab. At the left side of the dialog box, you see the names of all your hard drives (and all the *partitions* on those drives). Proceed as shown in Figure 11-10.

Restarting from the iPod in Mac OS X

When it comes time to start up a Mac from a connected iPod, follow the steps in Figure 11-11.

If your Mac can't start up by itself, restart it with the iPod attached, and see "The Startup Manager" on page 220. Having a spare system on the iPod can come in especially handy if your Mac is sick and you can't find your Mac OS X CD, or you're working on a different computer away from your utility discs.

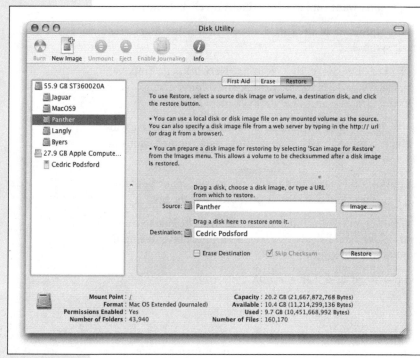

Figure 11-10:
In this example, the hard drive has several partitions. To clone the Panther partition, drag its name ("Panther") into the Source field in the middle of the dialog box. Then drag the name of the iPod ("Cedric Podsford") into the Destination box.

Finally, click Restore. It takes a while to copy everything, but eventually, you get an exact duplicate of the disk on your iPod. Just make sure you have enough room on the player to fit it all.

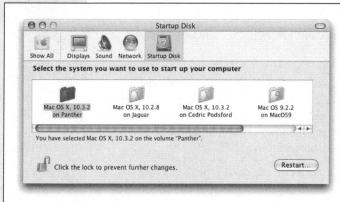

Figure 11-11:
To make your Mac start up from the iPod, choose ⬧→ System Preferences. Click the Startup Disk icon to produce the window shown here. Click the System folder on the iPod, and then click Restart. In the confirmation box, click "Save and Restart."

To make the Mac start up from its own hard drive once again, repeat the steps of Figure 11-11—but this time, choose your main hard drive's System folder.

Uninstalling Mac OS X from the iPod

Mac OS X isn't easy to remove from a drive, but it's not impossible. Unlike the folders in a Mac OS 9 system that you can simply drag to the Trash, all those little invisible files and curiously named pieces of Mac OS X have to be rounded up and deleted.

The quick way

The quickest way is to run the Restore program that came on the iPod installation CD. It erases and reformats the drive.

Of course, you should wait until you're certain that all your songs are safely in the iTunes library, that your contacts and calendars are up to date, and that any files or folders you've stored on the iPod are backed up on another drive—*all* of it will be wiped out on the iPod.

Then, once you've restored the iPod to its innocent state, transfer your iTunes library, contacts, calendar information, and stored files back onto it.

POWER USERS' CLINIC

Software for the Mac's Emergency First Aid Kit

If you're going to all the trouble of setting up a bootable operating system on your iPod to use when troubleshooting your primary Macintosh computer, having at least one disk utility on the iPod can make life a lot easier. Disk utility software can diagnose, defragment, and repair ailing hard disks, and even help recover accidentally erased files.

If you want a thorough arsenal of helpful tools at hand, consider some of the following programs.

Disk Utility (Mac OS X) or Disk First Aid and **Drive Setup for Mac OS 9.** Included with Apple's system software CDs for years, these two free programs can check a hard disk for problems and reformat a disk that needs it, respectively.

Disk Warrior. From daily maintenance to in-depth repair, Disk Warrior is the first choice of many experts to keep a hard disk happy and healthy ($80; *www.alsoft.com*).

Drive 10. Drive 10, one of the first disk utility programs exclusively for Mac OS X, can fix a range of hard drive prob-

lems and *defragment* disks as well (reconstitute files on the disk surface that have been split apart into available nooks and crannies of free space) ($70; *www.micromat.com*).

Hard Disk Toolkit. Compatible with Mac OS 9, the Hard Disk Toolkit makes reformatting and partitioning all kinds of hard drives a breeze ($90; *www.fwb.com*).

Norton SystemWorks. Although you can also purchase the popular Norton Utilities program separately for $100, it's included in the SystemWorks suite. SystemWorks also includes Norton AntiVirus, the data-backup program Retrospect Express, and Aladdin's Spring Cleaning software for sweeping duplicate and unneeded files out of your Mac ($130; *www.symantec.com*).

Tech Tool Pro. Tech Tool Pro can check and repair drives, find lost files, defragment disks, zap viruses, and sort out software conflicts. Versions are available for Mac OS 9 and X ($98; *www.micromat.com*).

The manual way

If you don't want to erase your iPod, you can manually toss out Mac OS X, piece by piece. This is a long, tedious, and worrisome task. You've been warned.

Into the Trash, drag the files and folders labeled *applications, System, Library, Users, mach, mach_kernel,* and *mach.sym* and any other files you cloned originally. You should also throw out the folders labeled System and Applications.

Even then, Mac OS X leaves behind dozens of tiny invisible files. You can see these files by using the TinkerTool procedure described on page 54. Toss them into the Trash once you can see them.

Tip: If Mac OS X won't let you throw some files away, you may have to change their *permissions* so that the Mac thinks that *you* own them. See page 293.

Part Four:
Extreme iPodding

4

Chapter 12: Connecting the iPod to Other Audio Systems

Chapter 13: Hot Hacks and Cool Tools

Chapter 14: iStuff for iPod

Chapter 15: Troubleshooting the iPod

Chapter 16: iPod on the Web

Connecting the iPod to Other Audio Systems

Y ou've labored over ripping CDs and composing playlists for months now, and you just want to share it with the world—or at least with the people at your party. But how? By playing Pass the iPod? And what about all those songs that are perfect for cranking up in the car? Are they locked away in your iPod forever, never to provide the music for impromptu sessions of Stoplight Shimmy?

Absolutely not. If you can load it onto your iPod, you can channel it through most any stereo system or blast it through your car's speakers. This chapter explains the simple procedures for playing your iPod songs through the woofers and tweeters in your life.

Note: The prices, Web sites, and model numbers in this chapter are intended to get your geek saliva flowing—not to serve as an up-to-date catalog. One spec or another has almost certainly changed since this book went to press, or even since you started reading this paragraph. Even so, you'll certainly learn one thing from this chapter: There's a lot of neat stuff out there.

Connecting the iPod to a Stereo System

CD players that can play discs of MP3s cost less than $100. But if you have an iPod, you already have a state-of-the-art MP3 player that you can connect to your existing system for under $20.

When connected to a stereo system, the iPod's wide frequency-response range and 60-milliwatt amplifier give it the audio oomph to fill a room. To link the iPod to your stereo, you need the right kind of cable (page 231) and a set of input jacks on

---

the back of your receiver. Most audio systems come with at least one extra set of inputs (after accounting for the CD player, cassette deck, and other common components). Look for an empty AUX jack, like the one shown in Figure 12-1.

Figure 12-1:
What you want is a cable with a miniplug on one end (which plugs into the iPod's headphone port) and two RCA connectors (which plug into the AUX jacks of the stereo system, shown here). Some cables use color-coding to match the stereo jacks: red for the right channel and white for the left.

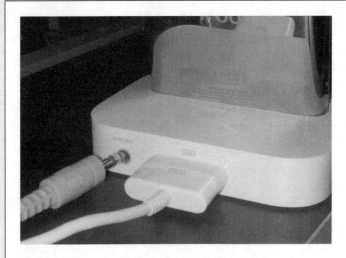

Figure 12-2:
The dock that comes with some iPod models provides a Line Out jack on the back. You can use it to connect the docked iPod to a stereo receiver or other external audio equipment.

The cable you need is a Y-shaped cord with a 3.5mm (1/8") stereo miniplug on one end and two bigger RCA plugs at the other end. The stereo miniplug is the standard connector for Walkman-style headphones (and for speakers and microphones); RCA plugs are standard connectors for linking stereo components together.

You plug the smaller end into the iPod's headphones jack, and the RCA plugs into the left and right channel jacks on the back of your stereo.

Alternatively, if you have a 2003 or later iPod, you can use the Line Out jack on the back next to the charging dock, as shown in Figure 12-2.

Where to find the right stereo cable

At your friendly neighborhood Radio Shack, ask for a Y-adapter audio cable, which costs about $7. You can also visit Radio Shack's Web site at *www.radioshack.com*.

Note: When shopping for audio cables, you may see or hear reference to "male" and "female" plugs. In this case, technology mimics nature: Male plugs are the kind with prongs and female connectors are hollowed out at the end. (No wisecracks, please.) The jacks on both the iPod and the back of the stereo receiver are female, so you want a male-to-male cable.

For a little more glamor, you can buy the Xwire Gold RCA audio cable from XtremeMac. It's sheathed in white Apple-chic plastic with gleaming gold connector plugs on the end. (Gold-tipped cables are supposed to provide better audio quality.) The 7-foot cable costs about $13.

If you need more distance than seven feet, XtremeMac also sells a female-to-male extension cable that you can plug into the RCA cable to double its length. There's a wide selection of audio cables designed to plug the iPod into several different audio sources at *www.xtrememac.com/foripod/cables.shtml*.

Tip: If you and your significant other are dreading the Hollywood C-picture that's sure to be the in-flight movie on your upcoming trip together, why not zone out and share the iPod instead? You just need an adapter like the iShare Earbud Splitter from XtremeMac, which turns one headphone port into two. The Y-shaped white and gold adapter sells for $10 at *www.xtrememac.com/foripod*.

Just make sure to create a playlist full of songs you *both* like.

Figure 12-3:
The miniplug-to-RCA cable from Griffin Technology's iPod Home Connect Kit gets that iPod pumping its playlists through your home stereo in no time. Just plug the small end into the iPod's headphone port and the twin RCA plugs into the audio input jacks on the back of your stereo system.

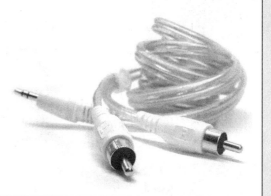

Another option for iPod-to-stereo cabling is the iPod Home Connect Kit. The kit comes with two different gold-tipped cables: the standard RCA audio cable (Figure 12-3) and a model with two *female* RCA plugs, which comes in handy when you want to connect the iPod to external computer speakers. The kit sells for $15 at *www.griffintechnology.com/products.*

Tip: When playing your iPod through another audio system, don't spin its scroll wheel up to the highest volume. You risk distorting the sound by overamplification. Instead, take the volume level on the iPod to about half the maximum and, if you still need more volume, use the controls on the *receiver.* This technique gives you the best audio quality.

Monster Cable, the venerable cordmeisters favored by AV fanatics, has even jumped into the iPod accessory game. Its gold-tipped, 7-foot Monster iCable for iPod goes for about $30. The company's Web site has more information and a link to stores that carry Monster cables at *www.monstercable.com.*

If you're tired of dragging your dock and cables back and forth between the stereo and the computer, look for the iPod Stereo Connection Kit in the iPod Accessories area at *http://store.apple.com.* For $80, you get an extra dock, FireWire cable, iPod AC adapter, and a Monster miniplug-to-RCA cable.

Connecting to a Car Stereo

Since the glorious days of crackly AM radio, music and driving have gone hand in hand. These days, a stereo system with AM/FM radio and a cassette deck is the bare minimum for most cars, and late-model vehicles now cruise around with all sorts of high-end equipment tucked inside, from MP3-compatible CD players to satellite radio. (Whether the music you can play on them has improved over the years is the subject of debate.)

If having your playlists with you is your idea of paradise by the dashboard light, there are several inexpensive ways to get your iPod nestled right in with your car's stereo system.

You have to consider two factors when taking the iPod along to play in the car:

- **How to wire it to your existing auto audio system.** You have your pick of using either a cable or wireless connection.

- **How to power it.** Of course, your iPod can run fine on its battery for short trips. If you're retracing historic Route 66 or barreling down I-95 from Maine to Miami, however, you'll probably want to invest in an adapter that can power your iPod from the car's electrical system.

The Wireless Way

Gadgets that transmit a personal signal over an existing FM frequency have been around for decades. Today, you can hook up an FM transmitter that connects to an

MP3 player's headphone port and broadcasts its sound through an unoccupied FM channel on the car radio—and out through the speakers.

This method offers several advantages. For one thing, you don't have to deal with cables or cords snaking around the dashboard. Also, most FM transmitters are inexpensive, often costing less than $30.

But there are disadvantages, too. The sound quality isn't so great—it depends on the strength of the signal—and radio is frustratingly prone to interference (static). Furthermore, you'll need to keep the iPod physically close to the radio. Some FM transmitters offer a few preset frequencies down on the lower half of the FM band to use for broadcasting your own music, but you might have trouble finding an unused frequency if you live in an area with lots of radio stations at the lower end of the dial.

Still, if you think an FM transmitter is your ticket to ride, you have several choices:

- **iTrip.** This eye-catching gadget is a gleaming white cylinder that plugs into the iPod and rests across the top of the player to transmit the FM signal (Figure 12-4). The iTrip can use any FM frequency, and it uses the iPod's battery for its juice. You can order iTrips for any iPod model for about $35 at *www.griffin technology.com/products/itrip*.

Tip: Check out Griffin Technology's Web site (*www.griffintechnology.com*) for helpful iTrip downloads. They include the iTrip Station Finder Software for both Windows and Macintosh systems, which lets you look up available FM radio frequencies in 240 American cities and 15 countries. If you're traveling abroad with your iPod, you can also download a file of European radio frequencies to use on the road.

Unfortunately, thanks to a 1949 law that regulates broadcasts on FM airwaves, the iTrip has been banned in the United Kingdom and, for similar reasons, in Austria and Iceland.

Figure 12-4:
The iTrip by Griffin Technology has a stereo miniplug that snaps right into the top of the iPod. The iTrip even turns itself off after 30 seconds of silence.

- **The DLO TransPod.** This transmitter also serves as a secure dashboard mount for the iPod (Figure 12-5). For power, it plugs into the car's cigarette lighter, so you don't have to worry about your batteries. For these reasons, this $100 unit may be your best bet if you frequently use your iPod while driving. The TransPod is available at *www.everythingipod.com*.

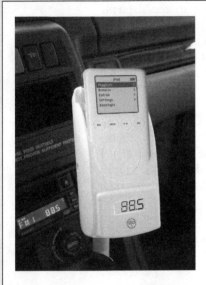

Figure 12-5:
DLO TransPod both powers and cradles your iPod, and the built-in FM transmitter takes care of broadcasting your playlists through the radio. TransPod models are available in both wireless and wired connections, with models available for all three generations of iPod.

- **TuneCast Mobile FM Transmitter.** Here's a gadget on a budget: Belkin sells it for under $40. This small white accessory plugs into the iPod's headphone jack and plays through one of four frequencies on the low end of the FM dial. You can find it at *www.belkin.com*. The company also makes the Belkin Digital FM Transmitter, which can transmit on any frequency from 88.1 to 107.9. It sells for $40 in the iPod accessories area at *http://store.apple.com*.

- **iRock 400FM** and **SoundFeeder SF121.** These less expensive FM transmitters, made by *www.myirock.com* and *www.arkon.com*, respectively, consist of a small FM modulator connected to a cable that plugs into the top of the iPod. Each is available for under $30 from various online music shops. The iRock 400FM (Figure 12-6) can run on two AAA batteries or on the included 12-volt charger. The SoundFeeder SF121, available in black or ivory plastic, runs on two AAA batteries. Arkon's SoundFeeder SF100 model comes with a built-in car charger.

The Wired Way

You may prefer to stick with cables, either because the sound quality is better or because you can't get a consistently clear signal in your part of FM Land.

One solution is an adapter that resembles an audiocassette. An attached cable and stereo miniplug link the iPod to the car's stereo—if your stereo is equipped with a cassette player, that is. You just plug the cable into the iPod, slip the cassette end into the dashboard, and press Play.

Some examples:

- **The Sony CPA-9C Car Connecting Cassette.** The Sony unit is designed for connecting Sony's own portable Discmen and MiniDisc players to the car's stereo, but it also works with the iPod and costs less than $20.

- **XtremeMac iPod Cassette Adapter.** This white cassette adapter matches the iPod and comes with a gold-tipped miniplug (see Figure 12-7). It's about $20 from *www.xtrememac.com.*

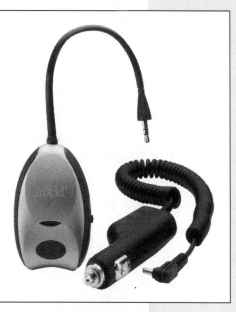

Figure 12-6:
The iRock 400FM wireless FM transmitter runs on two AAA batteries or its own 12-volt adapter that plugs into the car's cigarette lighter. The transmitter gives you the choice of four FM radio frequencies (88.1 to 88.7) to tap into to broadcast your favorite iPod playlists.

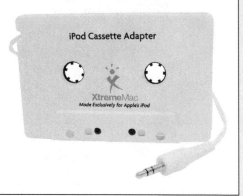

Figure 12-7:
This type of adapter brings your iPod's music through the car's speakers by way of the cassette deck. XtremeMac's iPod Cassette Adapter is available, along with many other iPod accessories, at www.xtrememac.com.

iPod Cassette Adapter

XtremeMac
Made Exclusively for Apple's iPod

• **DLO TransPod II.** This gizmo is quite similar to the TransPod described above, except that it connects through the car's cassette player instead of zapping tunes through the radio. Like the original, the TransPod II can be found at *www.everythingipod.com* and costs about $60. It works with 2001 and 2002 iPod models.

Incidentally, if your car's stereo console has a 3.5mm jack on the front as an auxiliary input, you can use a simple male-to-male miniplug audio cable to connect your iPod (under $10 at Radio Shack or audio stores).

Chargers

Your car's cigarette lighter can provide a far healthier use than its original intention, because it can accommodate an iPod battery charger. You'll live a long, healthy life without ever having to worry about the iPod conking out in the middle of your favorite song. Several companies make these car chargers, including three well-known iPod accessory mavens:

• **PowerPod Auto.** Sporting a black, silver, and white color scheme, this $25 doodad from Griffin Technology satisfies the Mac fan's obsession with sleek looks (Figure 12-8). It comes with a 4-foot cable and has a fuse and filter to protect the iPod from any nasty electrical spikes it may encounter while plugged in. It works with iPod 2001 and 2002 models (by connecting to the FireWire port on top), and you can buy it at *www.griffintechnology.com/products*. (If you have a 2003 iPod, you can also use this charger, but you need to use the FireWire cable from the iPod dock.)

Figure 12-8:
When connected, the PowerPod by Griffin Technology transforms power from the car's cigarette lighter into battery charge for the iPod.

• **AutoPod FireWire AutoCharger.** If you're the proud owner of a 2003 iPod, this appliance powers the iPod and recharges it through the car's cigarette lighter as you travel. The $25 charger comes in either black or white and has a coiled cord that can stretch out to about three feet. A version of the DLO AutoPod FireWire Charger for iPod 2001 and 2002 models is also available for about $18. You can get them at *www.everythingipod.com*.

- **Premium iPod Car Charger.** Like its rivals, this charging cable connects the cigarette lighter socket to the iPod's FireWire connection. It sells for $20 at *www.xtrememac.com/foripod* and features a replaceable fuse and an LED power indicator that lets you keep tabs on your charging situation. Versions are available for all iPod models.

- **Belkin Auto Kit.** Designed for dock-connecting models, the Belkin Auto Kit includes a cable for charging your iPod from the car's power port, plus an audio-out jack and adjustable amplifier that works with Belkin's Tunecast or cassette adapter (neither of which is included) for blasting iPod tunes through the car radio. The kit sells for $40 in the iPod accessories area at *http://store.apple.com*.

All-in-One Kits

If you don't have time to track down all the parts individually, you can buy it all in one box. Several companies have come forth with iPod connection *kits* containing everything you need. Before you click that Buy Now button, make sure the kit you're ordering is designed to fit your particular iPod model.

- **Dr. Bott's iPod Universal Connection Kit** is available with either an FM transmitter or a car cassette adapter, and it works with all iPod models. The kit also includes an auto charger, an adapter for using 2003 iPods with standard FireWire cables, a stereo miniplug-to-RCA cable, a male-to-male miniplug-to-miniplug cable, and a miniplug extension cable with a male connector on one end and a female connector on the other. The good doctor provides an iPod carrying pouch as well. The FM transmitter version sells for $50, and the cassette adapter edition costs $48 at *www.drbott.com*.

- **DLO's iPod Auto Connection Kit** at *www.everythingipod.com* skips the cables and focuses on the automotive needs of the iPod. You can choose between a kit with a cassette adapter or one with a wireless FM transmitter. You also get the AutoPod FireWire Auto Charger, hardware to mount the iPod on the dashboard, and one of the company's sturdy, weather-resistant NeoPod iPod cases. Versions for all iPod models are available for under $50.

- **XtremeMac's Get Connected Audio Kit** gathers the three most needed types of miniplug connections (RCA, male-to-male miniplug, and male-to-female miniplug). The bundle also includes an auto charger, a cassette adapter, and the iShare Earbud Splitter for connecting two sets of headphones to one iPod. The kit, available for all iPod models, sells for $50 at *www.xtrememac.com/foripod*.

Tip: If all of this sounds like a lot of hunting around the Web, keep in mind that the Apple Store sells compatible cables and other iPod-friendly goodies from a variety of manufacturers at *store.apple.com*—all in one place.

Connecting to the Computer

A FireWire cable is the common bond between computer and iPod, but that's for transferring battery power and music files. What about sound?

If that's your goal, you can connect the two directly through their stereo jacks. You'd do that when, for example, you want to sample the iPod's sound (by recording it onto your hard drive) and then tinker with it in an audio-editing program.

Tip: Want to dabble around in audio in search of your inner Moby? Music-mixing programs, many of them free or inexpensive, are all over the Web. The Hit Squad, a vast site for music-related shareware, has thousands of programs for Windows, Macintosh, and Linux at *www.hitsquad.com.* MusicMatch Jukebox Plus for Windows can record music as well: Just choose Options→Recorder→Source and change the Recorder's input settings from CD Player to Line In.

To connect this way, you need a stereo miniplug cable with male connectors on both ends (under $10 at many of the stores mentioned in this chapter). One end goes into the iPod and the other goes into your computer's sound-in port. Once you've cabled the two together, you're ready to record. Start up your audio software and start recording, then press the iPod's Play button to transfer all the snippets, samples, and sound clips you need directly from the device.

Once you've finished weaving your personal aural tapestry, save it as an MP3 file from your audio program, import it into your MP3 music library, and download it right back to your iPod.

Tip: If you're just busting to hear what your iPod sounds like connected to a nice set of multimedia speakers, just pick up a male-to-female miniplug cable at an online iPod emporium or an electronics store. The male end goes to the iPod, and the male connectors on the speakers connect to the female ends of the cable adapter. A $10 adapter like Monster Cable's iPod Mini Stereo Y-Splitter will also do the trick.

Hot Hacks and Cool Tools

I f you've read this book from the beginning, you know that you can do a lot more with your iPod than just play music on it. You can bestow it with palmtop powers to display your contacts and calendar information. You can make it do double-duty as a music player *and* a portable hard drive, as well as wire it up to be your portable jukebox for the car and home stereo.

But the 2003-and-later iPods have even further secret powers, including an undocumented recording feature. And you can make your iPod even more useful with dozens of AppleScripts designed to automate and augment certain iPod-related tasks. This chapter takes your iPod skills—and your iPod—to the next level.

The AppleScripted iPod

AppleScript is a simple programming language that lets Mac fans write mini programs to perform certain tasks. For instance, you could rig AppleScript to make iTunes play "We Will Rock You" at 8:03 every morning. Or you could use an AppleScript to send an email every three hours to your co-workers telling them how many shopping days are left until Christmas.

There are plenty of frivolous uses for AppleScript, too.

Installing the Script Menu

Mac OS X comes with a handful of ready-made AppleScript programs (called *scripts*), including one that checks the current temperature in your Zip code and one that lets you count messages in all your mailboxes.

Most Mac fans never even know they exist, because these scripts are buried in the Application→AppleScript→ExampleScripts folder. Fortunately, they're also listed in something called the *Script menu,* an icon on your menu bar that puts the scripts at your fingertips. To install the Script menu, open your Applications→AppleScript folder, and double-click the folder icon called Script Menu (see Figure 13-1).

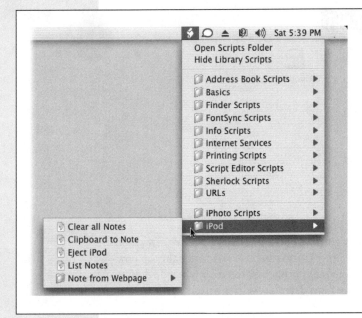

Figure 13-1:
The Script menu, which looks like a little scroll at the right end of the Mac's menu bar, lists dozens of useful AppleScript mini programs. Why perform five or six steps when all you have to do is find and run a script designed to automate the task?

Apple's iPod Scripts

If you want to maximize the potential of the Notes feature (page 198), Apple has a collection of scripts just for you. You can download the collection at *www.apple.com/ applescript/ipod.* (These scripts work with Mac OS X 10.2 and later.)

Install them by dragging the downloaded folder (called iPod) into your Home→ Library→Scripts folder. Magically, they now appear in your Script menu, as shown in Figure 13-1.

Here are the names of the iPod scripts in the collection and the actions they perform:

- **Clear All Notes.** If you've read all the notes on your iPod and want to dump them all at once, use this command to delete all the files in the iPod's Notes folder. You have the option to trash any subfolders within the Notes folder as well.

- **Clipboard to Note.** Whenever your work brings you to a scrap of information you think would be handy to have on your iPod—driving directions, a recipe, a news story, a detailed email message—highlight it, copy it to the Mac's clipboard by pressing ⌘-C, and then choose iPod→Clipboard to Note from your Script menu. In one fell swoop, the script creates a note on the iPod.

Note: If the text is longer than about 4,000 characters, the script chops it up into multiple linked files on the iPod.

- **Eject iPod.** Run the Eject iPod script to safely unmount the iPod (page 215). It's just an alternative to dragging the iPod icon to the Trash.

- **List Notes.** This script shows you a list of all Notes files currently stored on the connected iPod. If you want to revise a note, select it from the list that appears and open it for editing.

- **Note from Web page.** Web pages often contain interesting articles that you want to read later or save for future reference. As long as you're using Apple's own Safari browser, you can grab the text from an open Web page and turn it into an iPod Note just by using this script.

  To copy the article or text to your iPod, visit the "printer friendly" version of the page (which ditches all the ads, blinking banners, Flash files, and other ornaments), if one is offered. Then, from the Script menu, choose iPod→Note from Webpage→Printer Friendly. Another script in the same folder called MacCentral does the same thing with an article you're viewing on the MacCentral.com Web site.

Doug's AppleScripts

Doug's AppleScripts for iTunes has a Wal-Mart–sized inventory of AppleScripts for Mac music adventures—including a section devoted to iPod-related scripts. New scripts appear here frequently, so it's a good site to look in on every so often.

Many of the scripts automate the transfer or deleting of songs between iPod and Mac. For example, the collection called Four iPod Scripts (which actually contains *five* scripts and seems to be designed for people who have far too much music to fit on their iPods) contains AppleScripts like these:

- **Random Albums to iPod, Random Artist to iPod,** and **Random iPod** deletes the iPod's songs and playlists, then randomly adds albums, artist repertoires, or tracks from the iTunes Library to the iPod until it's full.

- **Clean iPod** deletes all songs and playlists on the iPod.

A script called Rip to iPod v1.0, for Mac OS 9 and X, tells iTunes to rip the checkmarked songs from a CD, copy them to the iPod, and then delete the tracks from the iTunes library. You skip the part about saving the audio files on your hard drive first, which can save some disk space. (Just make sure that your iPod isn't set to autosync.)

You'll find a link to the iPod scripts at *www.missingmanuals.com.* They're worth a look by anybody who loves making the Mac do stuff on its own. (The same author has created a library of iTunes-related AppleScripts; see *www.malcolmadams.com/ itunes.*)

More Mac Shareware

AppleScript isn't the only way code warriors have crafted helpful utility programs for the iPod. Here's an assortment of standalone software programs that do wacky and useful things for Mac iPods.

Tip: You can find links to all of these programs on the "Missing CD" page at *www.missingmanuals.com.*

- **iPod Access** can provide a complete backup copy of the iPod's contents, including purchased music, to a designated folder on the Mac. If you didn't find an iPod song-transferring utility you liked back in Chapter 2, iPod Access does that, too. This $10 Mac OS X program copies the songs in a tidy fashion and can even organize them into album and artist folders.

- **Pod 2 Pod** can make an exact clone of one iPod and copy it onto a second one—music, contacts, files, and all. This Mac OS X program, shown in Figure 13-2, can also make a full backup of your iPod and all its contents onto your Mac's hard drive as a slice of security in case your iPod gets broken, stolen, or lost. You can also restore the backup onto a new iPod when the time comes.

Figure 13-2:
Pod 2 Pod offers an easy-to-understand way to make a clone of one iPod and copy it to another. It's ideal for those of you who have too many iPods lying around the house and want all of them to be exactly the same.

- **iPod Launcher** starts up a whole batch of programs and scripts automatically whenever you connect the iPod to your Mac OS X system. You might use it to trigger auto-backups of the data files on the iPod, for example. Or, if you use it in tandem with iPod It (page 191), you can synchronize your Entourage data as well as download news headlines and weather reports without having to think about any of it.

- **VoodooPad** is a notepad with delusions of grandeur, as you can see in Figure 13-3. VoodooPad ($10) works with Mac OS X 10.2 and later.

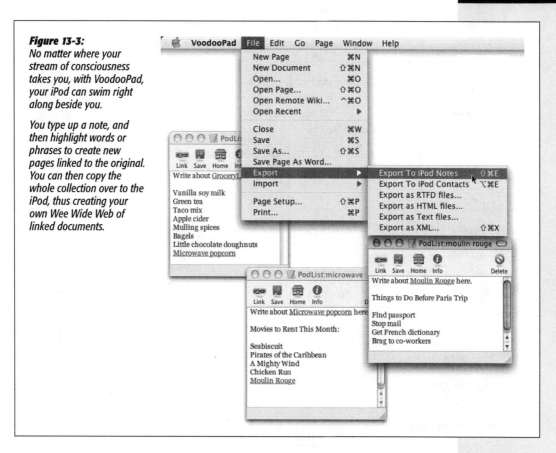

Figure 13-3:
No matter where your stream of consciousness takes you, with VoodooPad, your iPod can swim right along beside you.

You type up a note, and then highlight words or phrases to create new pages linked to the original. You can then copy the whole collection over to the iPod, thus creating your own Wee Wide Web of linked documents.

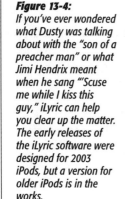

Figure 13-4:
If you've ever wondered what Dusty was talking about with the "son of a preacher man" or what Jimi Hendrix meant when he sang "'Scuse me while I kiss this guy," iLyric can help you clear up the matter. The early releases of the iLyric software were designed for 2003 iPods, but a version for older iPods is in the works.

- **Burn Out.** If you have iTunes 3 or later, an iPod, and a copy of Roxio's Toast program for burning CDs, then Burn Out can make life a little easier. It lets you record CDs right off an iPod by way of iTunes, saving you the time of having to hunt for the original files and drag them into the Toast window. Instead, just select a playlist and burn away (*homepage.mac.com/beweis*). (The site is in German, but it links to an English edition of the program on VersionTracker.com.)

- **iLyric** scans the Internet for the words to the songs in your music library and downloads them to your Mac, as shown in Figure 13-4. You can read them there or copy them over to the iPod's Notes folder for viewing on the go. The program is freeware for Mac OS X 10.2.6 and later.

- **AAChoo** makes it easy to convert your hefty MP3 collection into the new AAC format to save room on your iPod (Figure 13-5). It requires Mac OS X and Quick-Time 6 and costs $15.

Figure 13-5:
Want to convert your music library from the MP3 format to AAC without a hassle? AAChoo lets you convert single files, whole folders, or entire CDs into the AAC format; the program can even automatically update the iTunes library for you.

Windows Shareware

The Mac people may have gotten a head start on handcrafted iPod shareware, but the Windows crew is beginning to develop programs of their own to extend the iPod's abilities. Like the Mac software described earlier, all of these programs are available on the "Missing CD" page at *www.missingmanuals.com*.

euPod Volume Boost

It's not your imagination: European iPods *can't* play as loudly as American ones. Not because Americans are any wilder, but because of government-mandated volume restrictions on European music players.

Hackers to the rescue! euPod Volume Boost lets everyone around the world melt their ears off at higher volumes. The software tinkers with a setting in the iPod's database to alter the sound output.

Weather for Me

Meteorologically obsessed music lovers can bring along ten days of weather forecasts after syncing their iPods with Weather for Me (Figure 13-6). This program grabs its info from *www.weather.com* (home of the Weather Channel) and can also convert temperatures from Fahrenheit to Celsius.

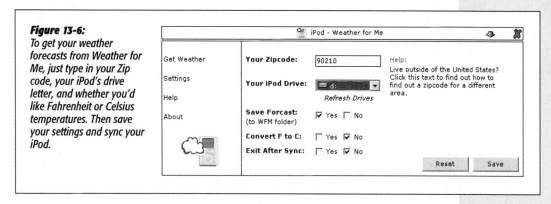

Figure 13-6:
To get your weather forecasts from Weather for Me, just type in your Zip code, your iPod's drive letter, and whether you'd like Fahrenheit or Celsius temperatures. Then save your settings and sync your iPod.

J. River Media Center

The Media Center is designed for media mavens who spend hour after hour organizing and playing with their digital audio and video files. For those looking for alternative music-management software, this $40 program can sync the iPod's contents with the Media Center, adjust song volumes, and bookmark Audible files. (A free 30-day trial version is also available.)

Linux on the iPod

When the Macintosh-only iPods appeared on the horizon, clever programmers created software like EphPod and XPlay that made them Windows-compatible, long before Apple created Windows-friendly iPods.

Not surprisingly, disciples of the Linux operating system weren't far behind. Linux is an alternative operating system for personal computers, created in 1991 by Linus Torvalds of Finland. (It's the system whose official mascot is a cute penguin named Tux.) Instead of starting his own company or selling his code to a large software corporation, Torvalds made his source code available for free on the Internet (as *open source* code) and invited other programmers to help him improve it, which they did.

Over the years, Linux has evolved from a hobby to a formidable operating system in its own right that runs servers and computers all over the world. Here are some of the iPod-related projects that the innovative Linux community has developed.

Note: Linux comes in several slightly different versions (called *distributions* in Linux lingo). Read the fine print on the Linux iPod pages about which distributions work with the software in question.

GNUpod

GNUpod provides a collection of free Perl scripts for power users, which make the iPod work with GNU/Linux systems, FreeBSD Unix, Darwin (that is, Mac OS X), and Solaris 9. Not for the technically faint of heart, the GNUpod tools can prepare an iPod for use with those systems, add and delete song files, make playlists, and carry out other standard iPod activities (*www.gnu.org/software/gnupod*).

gtkpod

gtkpod, a program with a graphical user interface for Linux and Unix, uploads songs and playlists to the iPod, edits ID3 tags on MP3 files, and alerts you to duplicate songs in your music database. The gtkpod program, which builds on some of the code written for the GNUpod scripts, is at *http://gtkpod.sourceforge.net*.

myPod

Not to be confused with the Mac OS utility program MyPod, the myPod program for Linux can create, edit, and transfer playlists to the iPod. It can also edit ID3 tags and organize music files on the computer. Since myPod source is written in Java, it works on any computer that can run Java-based programs and recognize a connected iPod as a hard drive (*http://mypod.sourceforge.net*).

The iPod on Linux Project

Bernard Leach has figured out a way to get Linux to actually run *on* the iPod, in a version of the system called uClinux. Although using the iPod this way hampers its natural abilities for playing music and responding to its own controls, Leach hopes that the iPod might one day do things like function as a storage bin for images from digital cameras. You can follow the project's progress at *http://ipodlinux. sourceforge.net*.

Tip: Several Linus enthusiasts have described their own techniques for getting an iPod up and running with Linux. Two helpful pages, featuring personal stories and lots of links to other resources, are at *http:// pag.lcs.mit.edu/~adonovan/hacks/ipod.html* and *http://neuron.com/~jason/ipod_archive.html*.

Recording Your Own MP3s

In addition to songs downloaded from the iTunes Music Store (Chapter 6) or ripped from CDs (Chapters 4 and 5), the iPod can play digital audio files that you've recorded yourself. This sort of thing can come in handy in situations where, say, you have a recital or music lesson coming up and want to record yourself for analysis later. Or perhaps you have to give a speech and want to record a sample of yourself practicing to weed out the "ums" and "you knows."

You can take either of two approaches. First, you can record on the iPod and transfer the finished recordings to the computer. (You need one of the snap-on iPod microphones described on page 259.)

Second, you can record on the computer and transfer the recording to the iPod. In this case, your Mac or PC needs a microphone, as described in the next sections.

Tip: If you don't already have a microphone or a sound-in port on your computer, you can do it the USB way with the iMic from Griffin Technology. The iMic works with both Windows and Macs through the USB port, as described in Chapter 14.

Griffin Technology also makes the PowerWave (*www.griffintechnology.com/products/powerwave*), a $100 device that works as both a desktop amplifier and audio input box for recording live sound on your Mac or PC.

Windows

Most new desktop systems these days include a small external microphone, and many laptops have built-in microphones. Check your manual.

You can record WAV files using the Sound Recorder program that comes with Windows, of course (choose Start→Programs→Accessories→Entertainment→Sound Recorder). But MusicMatch Jukebox, which, if it didn't come with your iPod, is a free download from *www.musicmatch.com*, is a more versatile option.

Here's how to do it:

1. **In MusicMatch Jukebox Plus, choose Options→Recorder→Source and pick the type of device you want to record from, as shown in Figure 13-7.**

   Since you're not ripping from a CD, you need to tell MusicMatch how you're going to do the recording.

2. **Connect your recording equipment to the PC.**

   For Line In recording, which you can use to record MP3 files from those old vinyl records and dusty cassette tapes taking up space in the attic, connect your stereo receiver, turntable and preamplifier, or tape player to the computer.

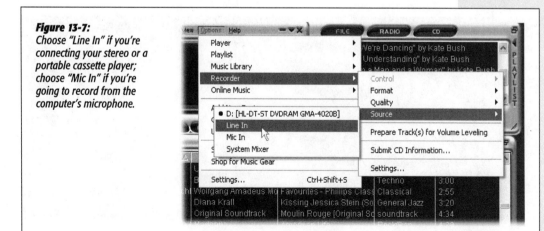

Figure 13-7:
Choose "Line In" if you're connecting your stereo or a portable cassette player; choose "Mic In" if you're going to record from the computer's microphone.

In most cases, that entails a Y-shaped cable with two RCA connector plugs on one end, which you plug into the output jacks of your audio source. Plug the 3.5mm stereo miniplug (page 231) on the other end into the Line In port on your computer's sound card or sound-import device.

3. **On the MusicMatch Jukebox player controls, click the red Record button.**

   MusicMatch asks you to enter a name for the file you're about to record.

4. **Type a name and then click the red Record button. Press Play on the tape deck, record player, or human being.**

   When you're ready to stop recording from the external source, click Stop.

The new file appears in your MusicMatch Jukebox Plus music library under the name you gave it, in whatever format you've chosen for encoding digital audio files. (You can easily change the recording format by choosing Options→Recorder→ Format and picking either MP3 or WAV, both of which play on the iPod.) You may have to adjust the volume level on your equipment and experiment until you find the right balance.

You can now work with it as you would any of your other music library files. The next time you connect your iPod, you can add your newly recorded homemade tracks just like any other music file.

Note: When you've finished recording your own material and want to return to ripping CDs, don't forget to change the recorder's source preference back to the computer's CD drive.

Macintosh

Many recent Macintosh models, including the iMac, eMac, white iBook, and titanium PowerBook, have microphones built into the screens. Older Macs from the Beige Days usually came with an external PlainTalk microphone, and later Power Macs take in sounds with USB microphones from other companies. If you don't

---

GEM IN THE ROUGH

Recording Voice Notes in Mac OS X

If you'd like to make a *voice* recording (as opposed to recording something from your stereo), you don't need any add-on software. Instead, use iMovie to create an audio-only "movie" with no visuals to it.

To do that, use iMovie's narration-recording feature as you speak your piece. (In iMovie 3 and 4, for example, you do this by clicking the Audio button. Then click the round Record button to the right of the Microphone graph.)

When you're satisfied with the recording, save the file and quit iMovie. Inside the movie project folder (a folder that bears the name of your movie), you'll find a folder called Media. Inside *that*, there's a file called, for example, Voice 02. That's the sound file you just made.

Add .aiff to its name, confirming your decision when the Mac asks, and then drag the file into the iTunes window. It's now a standard track, ready for iPodding.

have a built-in microphone or even a sound-in port on your Mac, the iMic and PowerWave (page 247) can pull in stereo sound input through the USB port.

Connecting the Mac to a stereo receiver, cassette deck, or turntable and preamplifier requires audio patch cables. In most cases, you'll need a Y-shaped cable with two RCA connector plugs on one end (for the stereo) and a single 3.5mm stereo mini-plug on the other end (for the Mac's sound-in jack or an iMic). (If you're recording from a portable cassette or Mini-Disc player, you'll probably need a stereo mini-plug-to-miniplug cable.)

When you've connected the cables, direct your Mac's Sound preferences to the correct jack (microphone, line in, or whatever). In Mac OS 9, choose →Control Panel→Sound. In Mac OS X, open System Preferences and click the Sound icon, then click the Input tab.

Once you have the hardware, rustle up some recording software (iTunes doesn't offer recording capability). Plenty of inexpensive Macintosh shareware programs for audio recording await on the Web; visit, for example, *www.osxaudio.com* or *www.hitsquad.com/smm/mac/AUDIO_RECORDING.* Two popular shareware for audio recording for both Mac OS 9 and X are Amadeus II ($25) and Audiocorder ($20), shown in Figure 13-8. (Both are available on the "Missing CD" page at *www.missingmanuals.com.*)

Follow the instructions provided with whatever sound-recording program you decide to use. Once you've recorded your sound files, named them, and saved them,

---

GEM IN THE ROUGH

The iPod's Secret Hidden Recording Feature

If you want to use your iPod to *record* sound and not just play it, $40 or $50 will buy you a small, white, snap-on microphone for 2003-and-later iPod models (page 260). Its self-contained software lets you record hours of voice memos, classroom lectures, and other live-audio opportunities. You can even sync the recordings back to iTunes.

But if you (a) have a pre-2003 iPod and (b) you haven't installed the iPod 2.0.1 software update, you're in for a treat. The iPod can actually record your own six-second Notes to Self all by itself.

Restart the iPod by holding down the Menu and ▶ II buttons simultaneously. When the Apple logo appears on the screen, hold down the I◀◀, ▶▶I, and center Select buttons. When you let go of the three buttons, the iPod emits a loud chirp, flashes a backwards Apple logo, and then displays its secret diagnostic menu.

Press the ▶▶I button to bop down the list until you get to the line that says J. RECORD. Press the Select button.

When the word BEGIN appears on the screen, you have about six seconds of recording time. Speak into the iPod's left earbud, which now functions as a microphone. When your recording time is up, the iPod screen says DONE. Stick the earbud in your ear and press the Select button to hear your six seconds of spoken-word glory.

When you're done, press the ▶ II button to return to the list of diagnostic tests. To return the iPod to its normal menu screen, press the Menu and ▶ II buttons to reset the iPod once more.

Apple's repair technicians use the recording function for troubleshooting ailing iPods. Otherwise, this feature seems to have no purpose in daily iPod activities, apart from tantalizing iPod fanatics the world over.

---

you can add them into the iTunes library by dragging them onto the iTunes window or choosing File→Add to Library. Now you can edit their track tags, add them to playlists, and copy them onto your iPod, just like any other audio file.

Some audio-recording programs may save the sound files in the AIFF format, and if you don't have the option to convert the files to MP3 or AAC there, you can always use the iTunes command Advanced→Convert Selection to MP3 (or whatever format).

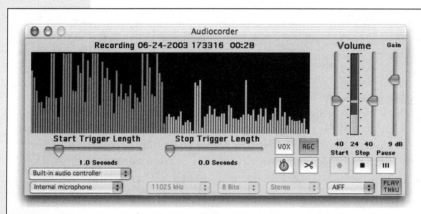

Figure 13-8:
If you have a Mac and a mike and a copy of Audiocorder, you can record yourself practicing that difficult harmonica solo, or hook up your stereo and digitize your old vinyl and copy the files onto the iPod. You'll never have to buy the White Album again.

iStuff

Just as the original iMac's unique rounded shape and Bondi blue plastic case inspired hundreds of brightly colored add-ons from other companies back in the late 1990s, the iPod has similarly energized the MP3 accessories market. Online and in stores, you can find dozens of iPod-themed add-ons created to protect, enhance, and improve your iPodding adventures.

This chapter looks at some of the things you can buy to go with your iPod and where to find them—from a waterproof case to keep out the rain to an attachment that turns your iPod into a storage locker for digital photos.

That's right: you can now buy gadgets for your gadget.

Cases

Once you get your iPod loaded with music, you'll want to take it with you without worrying about scuffs and scratches.

Apple includes a basic black sheath-type case (with belt clip) for some models. Unless you use the iPod's remote control, however, you have to keep taking the player out of the case to operate the controls, which is not only a drag but also an opportunity to drop the iPod on the sidewalk. An iPod taking a face plant onto the concrete is a horrible sight.

When selecting a case, keep in mind the situations in which you tend to use your iPod. If you use the iPod for running, you may prefer a waterproof neoprene case with an armband; if you take it on business trips, you may prefer a more professional-looking covering. Some cases make the scroll wheel and controls easy to get to, while others conceal the front of the iPod to protect it. So take into account how often you use the controls for changing volume, skipping songs, or checking addresses.

Here are a few cases that stand out.

Tip: Some cases are specially designed for 2001 and 2002 iPods, whose buttons surround the scroll wheel. Cases for the 2003 and later models must accommodate the four small buttons across the middle instead. Inquire about which cases fit which models before you buy.

DLO Action Jacket

If you take the iPod along for every walk, run, or workout, take a look at the DLO Action Jacket, a case that cushions the iPod in a thick layer of waterproof neoprene fabric. The case has a clear plastic window that lets the iPod's display screen show through and cutaway panels that make the scroll wheel and controls easily accessible. The Action Jacket, which comes in different versions for old and new iPod models, costs $30 and comes with a belt clip and a Velcro armband. It's available, along with several other iPod cases shown in Figure 14-1, at *www.everythingipod.com*.

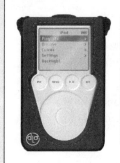

Figure 14-1:
The neoprene Action Jacket by DLO (left) protects the iPod both front and back. The company makes cases for all models of iPod, and in a variety of colors and fabrics including molded rubber (center) and leather (right). You can find an iPod jacket for just about any occasion at www.everythingipod.com.

iSkin

If fear of scratches prevents you from taking your iPod out much, check out the line of form-fitting silicone iSkin sleeves, available in a rainbow of vibrant colors. The washable rubber iSkin cases feature heat-ventilation pores and tiny raised feet on the back to help air circulate around an iPod laid flat on a desk. The new iSkin eXo2 case includes a rotating belt clip and scratch-resistant screen protector. Other case colors in the iSkin line even glow in the dark, making it easier to find your iPod at 3 a.m. Prices range from $15 to $30 at *www.iskinprotect.com*.

Belkin iPod Leather Organizers

The Belkin case for the original iPod resembles those dapper leather cases for Palm organizers. It opens up to reveal the iPod nestled in a black leather sleeve, alongside a pocket for the earbuds and slots for cash and credit cards. The $30 case, which fits the original iPod design, is available on the Belkin Web site (*www.belkin.com*) or in retail stores. The company also makes leather cases for the newer iPod models, including a $25 holster-style belt-clip case and a $30 flip-open sleeve.

Matias iPod Armor

The iPod Armor ensures that *nothing* scars your iPod—even if you fall off your snowboard and tumble downhill over rough terrain. As shown in Figure 14-2, the hard aluminum case completely covers the iPod front and back, leaving only a small hole for the earbud cord; a layer of foam protects what's inside. Your iPod winds up like Han Solo encased in the carbonite block. The company also has a version of the armor that's designed to resemble newer iPods.

Tip: A case is intended to protect your iPod's surface, but scuffs, smears, and scratches can still happen (like when you're pulling it *out* of the case).

If you accidentally gouge your iPod's surface, try the iCleaner Scratch Remover, a nonabrasive solution that can help restore the smooth surface of the iPod. The iCleaner package comes with enough polish for about 20 buffings, plus a cleaning towel and instructions. You can get it for $15 (and often less) at *www.photoline.com.*

Figure 14-2:
The iPod Armor seals in the iPod and keeps out dings and dents with its sturdy aluminum shell. Just pop off the front plate to get to the controls. The iPod Armor fits all models and sells for $50 at www.halfkeyboard.com/ipodarmor.

OWC Pod Protector

The iPod Protector is a snug, black leather jacket—with or without a swiveling belt clip. The no-nonsense look of black leather makes the Pod Protector look at home everywhere from an engineering major's belt to the streets of New York's East Village. It fits original iPod models, and you can find it for $30 at *www.otherworld computing.com.*

XtremeMac Xtremity iPod Case System

If you use your iPod for both walking and driving, consider a multifunction case like the Xtremity case shown in Figure 14-3. It hitches to your belt or mounts on your car's dashboard, and even has room to store accessories. A flexible plastic cover shields the front of the iPod from dirt and weather. It also comes with a plug to keep dust out of the dock connector. The case sells for $30 at *www.xtrememac.com.*

Marware SportSuit Convertible

Some activities are higher impact than others, and the SportSuit Convertible case comes prepared for a variety of sporting occasions. The neoprene case has a hard removable lid that you can snap on when the going gets rough. The SportSuit Convertible comes in six different colors and includes an armband and a belt clip. It sells for $40 at *www.marware.com/iPodType.html,* where a handsome leather "CEO Classic" iPod case is also available. Most case styles come in versions for old-style iPods and the newer dock-type iPod models.

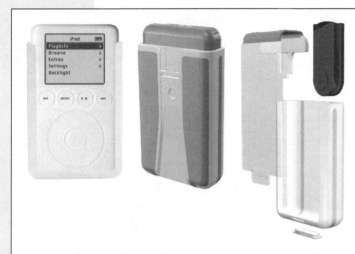

Figure 14-3:
Seen here from the front, from the back, and with all its various snap-on sections, XtremeMac's Xtremity iPod Case goes to extremes to protect your iPod. The company also sells designer iPod cases in everything from preppy plaid to military-style camouflage.

WaterField Designs iPod Cases

The WaterField case design features a pocket for the earbuds and a protective flap that shields the iPod's controls. The iPod's ports are accessible through a slit in the top or bottom of the case, which comes in red, white, or blue and sells for $40 with sizes for all iPods. The company also makes small Gear Pouch bags (useful for toting things like iPod docks, remotes, and cables) for $35. All are available at *www.sfbags.com.*

iSleeve

Crafted from molded rubber, the iSleeve from Terforma (Figure 14-4) doesn't slow you down with flaps, snaps, or zippers that get in the way of the iPod's display screen and control panel. The case's raised edges and rounded corners protect all sides of the player from a drop at any angle, yet leaves the headphone jack and Hold switch exposed.

Tip: Many women find the belt clip option just doesn't work with their wardrobe, especially the clean lines of a Donna Karan suit. Enter the Groove Speaker Purse for iPod, which not only serves as an iPod carrying case, but also incorporates built-in speakers into a large handbag. Two different purse styles are available, and each costs about $145 at *www.welovemacs.com/ipodcarrybags.html*.

Figure 14-4:
Terforma's iSleeve creates a protective rubber bumper all around the iPod and has a place to tuck away the earbuds and headphone cord. The iSleeve comes in black or white and sells for $50 at www.isleeve.com. *It's available for all iPod models.*

Speakers

You can hook up your iPod to a home or car audio system to share your sounds, as noted in Chapter 12, but sometimes, it's more convenient to get the iPod a set of speakers to call its own. Most speakers designed to take input from a portable CD or MP3 player work fine with the iPod, but here are a few notable options.

inMotion Portable iPod Speakers

Portable, self-powered, and supremely Podly, Altec Lansing's inMotion speakers let you blast your playlists all over the room with style and ease. The lightweight, folding speakers, shown in Figure 14-5, can run for 24 hours on four AA batteries. Plus, if you have a 2003 or later (dockable) iPod, the included AC adapter can charge up your iPod.

Tip: Want a personal trainer to help you get into shape, but don't want to pay those personal-trainer prices? Try the MP3 Gym Personalized Workout Sessions, a set of 60 prerecorded exercise routines that you download to your iPod as MP3 files. You can order the $20 CD at *www.mp3gym.com*, where you'll also find some free samples.

Cambridge SoundWorks PCWorks

The PCWorks Amplified Multimedia/Computer speaker system was designed to offer big rumbly sound to computers at an affordable $36. A compact subwoofer booms from the floor; two desktop cubes handle the higher frequencies. The PCWorks system and other audio components for portable players are available at *www.hifi.com*.

Figure 14-5:
Altec Lansing's inMotionPortable iPod speakers quickly go from flat and folded to proud and loud. The speaker unit is about eight inches wide and weighs about 15 ounces, making it easy to take almost anywhere. It works with all full-sized models of the iPod and costs $150 at www.apple.com/ipod/accessories.html.

Sony SRS-T55 Folding Travel Speakers

Whether your journey is long or short, these speakers won't take up much room in your bag, because you can *fold them in half* and tuck them away until you want to turn on the music. The speakers take four AA batteries or an optional power adapter. They're at *www.sonystyle.com* for $50.

JBL Creature 2.1 Speakers

It may look like a family of alien turtles creeping across the desk (Figure 14-6), but the three-piece JBL Creature speaker set for desktop computers can also give your iPod its own voice.

Figure 14-6:
The three-piece JBL Creature set ($130) has a large domed subwoofer and two small satellite speakers. It comes in several colors, including white to match the iPod. You can get Creature speakers at www.harman-multimedia.com, audio shops, or the online Apple Store.

Sony SRS-RF90RK Wireless Speaker System

If you have enough cables in your life and seek to zing your iPod's music through the air no matter where you are, consider Sony's SRS-RF90RK 900 MHz RF Wireless Speaker System. The battery-powered speaker can last about 3.5 hours between recharging sessions and has a range of 150 feet. Both the silver receiver and transmitter have a futuristic design and blue illumination. Available at *www.sonystyle.com* for $180.

Tip: Truly discerning audiophiles can adjust the iPod's sound with the Koss eq50 three-band stereo equalizer instantly and without interrupting the music. The small black equalizer, with controls for bass, midrange, and treble levels, plugs into the iPod's headphone port and has its own jack for the iPod earbuds or speakers. It runs on two AA batteries and costs $20 at *www.koss.com*.

Stands

You can put your iPod on a pedestal at your desk or in your car with a specially designed stand. A good solid stand not only keeps your iPod in full view and above the desk clutter, but also makes the control panel easily accessible, so you can input figures into a spreadsheet with one hand while cranking up the volume on your Budget Report Hot Jam playlist with the other.

Desk Stands

Here are a few stands that prop up your Pod with style.

DVBase Nickel-Plated iPod Stand

This stately and elegant stand has nickel plating to match the back of the iPod, creating a seamless look when you park the iPod majestically on your desk. The DVBase comes with a $55 price tag at *www.thinkdifferentstore.com*.

The iPodDock

Not to be confused with the charging dock that comes with the latest iPods, this iPod stand (Figure 14-7) does double duty as both a stand and docking cradle for 2001 and 2002 iPod models. Place the iPod upright in the front slot, and it's an unassuming stand. Flip the iPod over and plug it into the FireWire and audio ports in the back of the Dock, and you can now recharge the iPod or connect it to your stereo system using the proper cables (Chapter 12).

PodHolder

The clear plastic PodHolder sports an uncluttered design and holds your iPod up at an easy-viewing angle. Small rubber pads keep the iPod from slipping out of the stand. The PodHolder sells for $10 at *www.PodShop.com*.

Mod Pod iPod Stand

This laser-cut acrylic easel for the iPod brings to mind Apple's own approach to industrial design, as the Mod Pod props up the player in graceful Lucite curves. It comes in four colors and sells for $15 at *www.macskinz.com.*

Figure 14-7:
BookEndz was making iPod docks long before Apple released the dock-connectable iPods of 2003 and later. If you have an older iPod and want to dock it, browse on over to this page at www.bookendz docks.com. The iPodDock comes in two versions (one for newer iPods with FireWire port covers and one for original models), each costing $45.

PodStand

This modern-looking Pod platform comes in white or clear acrylic with a wide base to keep the iPod steady. Four rubber feet keep the PodStand from scooting across the desk, and the $15 price makes it an inexpensive way to keep your iPod from drowning in paperwork. It's available at *www.marware.com/stand.html.*

PodPerch

For those who think Apple's white charging dock is a bit too boxy, there's the PodPerch, a clear acrylic cradle for the 2003 iPods. Nestled in the perch, the iPod reclines at a sloping angle, and there's even space at the bottom for the flat FireWire connector to slide in without bending the cable. The PodPerch costs $20 at *www.macmice.com/podperch_1.html.*

iPod Extenders

There are so many new add-on gadgets for the iPod, the average consumer might be forgiven for forgetting all about its music-playing abilities.

Belkin Media Reader

If you have a digital camera, you know that once your memory card is full, the fun's over. You can't exactly duck into a drugstore to buy a new SmartMedia card to tide you through the rest of the day at Disney.

So what does this have to do with the iPod?

Plenty, thanks to the Belkin Media Reader (Figure 14-8, left; $100). You attach this device to a dock-connectable iPod, and then insert your camera's memory card (Compact Flash, Secure Digital, Smart Media, or Memory Stick format).

On the iPod's main screen, go to Extras→Photos→Import Photos→Import. (You don't see the Photos option except when the Media Reader is attached.) When you choose Import All, the iPod begins slurping in the photos from the card—a process that can take anywhere from 6 minutes to 20 minutes, depending on the size of the photos and the size of the card.

When the importing is complete, the onscreen commands offer you the chance to erase the memory card so that you can insert it back into the camera for more shooting.

Note: In general, the Media Reader doesn't import movies or sounds—only still photos. So be careful with the Erase Card option, which carries the risk of nuking movies and sounds before you've rescued them from the card.

You can't look at the photos on the iPod itself—black-and-white screens are funny that way—but if you choose Extras→Photos, you can see a list of the *rolls* you've imported. (Each batch of transferred pix is one roll.) The roll number information also tells you things like the number of photos and size of the roll.

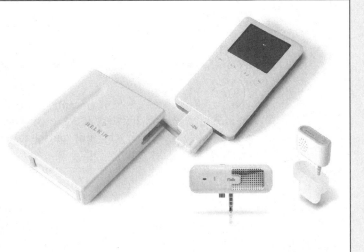

Figure 14-8:
Left: Thanks to the Belkin Media Reader, the iPod can take a load off your digital camera by transferring photos from its overloaded memory card to the iPod's hard drive for safekeeping.

Below: The Griffin iTalk (left) and Belkin iPod Voice Recorder (right, snapping into its protective prong cover) fit into the iPod's headphone jack and record your dulcet tones—or anyone in range of its microphone. Once the iPod is connected to the computer, you can move all your stored photos and voice memos back to the mother ship.

To get the pictures onto your computer, connect the iPod. If you're on a Mac, the images arrive in iPhoto, exactly as they would from a digital camera. If you're using a PC, grab your pictures from the iPod's drive just as you would from any other removable hard drive. (Open it up in My Computer, for example, or use Windows Explorer to locate and copy them over from the DCIM folder.)

The Belkin Media Reader runs on four AAA batteries, so it doesn't draw its power from the iPod's battery (although copying files onto it may drain a little iPod juice as its hard drive whirs away). Depending on the size of your iPod's hard drive, you can save thousands of pictures on it at a time between pit-stops back at your computer.

Tip: The rap against the Media Reader is that it's bulky (bigger than the iPod, thanks to that big battery compartment), and it's slow. By mid-2004, Belkin plans to release the Media Reader's successor, which is smaller, cheaper, and faster—and it doesn't require pulling the memory card out of the camera. The new gadget plugs directly into your camera, connecting it to the iPod.

Voice recorders from Griffin and Belkin

The white, oval-shaped Belkin iPod Voice Recorder (Figure 14-8, lower right) and its rival, the Griffin iTalk (*www.griffintechnology.com;* Figure 14-8, lower left), plug into the top of the iPod (2003 and later models, though not the iPod Mini). Presto: You've got yourself a handheld recording studio for voice memos, classroom lectures, and other audio opportunities. You can listen to yourself through the recorder's built-in speaker or on your computer.

Tip: At least as of this writing, the Griffin iTalk offers three advantages over its rival from Belkin. First, it has a microphone jack that can accommodate a fancier external mike. Second, it has a headphone jack, so you can monitor your recording as you make it (or privately review that art history lecture you just slept through). And third, it costs $40 instead of $50. They're both offered at *www.apple.com/ipod/ accessories.html.*

All your vocalizations will sync up and land back in iTunes when you hook up your iPod, whereupon you can store, edit, or even email your thoughts to unsuspecting people.

These voice recorders create mono audio files in the WAV format—not exactly booming rich stereo sound, but look at the bright side: you can save hundreds of hours of recordings on your iPod. Why limit yourself to a mere hour or two of Deep Thoughts to Myself like those wimpy digital recorders offer, when you can recite your life story *and* still have room for the complete works of Smokey Robinson and the Miracles?

You plug the Belkin or Griffin voice recorder to the iPod's headphone and remote jacks. To start recording, go to Extras→Voice Memos→Record Now on the iPod, and press the ►❚❚ button. (Press it again to pause.)

When you're all done, press the iPod's Menu button. Your new sound file gets saved with the date and time and stored on the iPod. To play back one of your recordings, go to Extras→Voice Memos and select the one you want to hear.

If you have the iPod enabled as a hard drive (page 213) and it's connected to your computer, you can find your voice memo sound files in the iPod's Recordings folder. Drag and drop anywhere you'd like to save them.

Tip: Want to use your iPod and Voice Recorder together as an alarm clock? Just connect them and then turn on the iPod alarm the usual way. (Go to Extras→Clock→Alarm Clock→Alarm and choose On. Set your desired alarm time at Extras→Clock→Alarm Clock→Time.)

Then go to Extras→Clock→Alarm Clock→Sound and pick the song you want to wake up to—or better yet, a voice recording of your mother yelling, "You get out of bed THIS INSTANT!!" When the alarm goes off, the sound or song will play through the Voice Recorder's speaker until you hit the Play/Pause button on the iPod to turn it off.

NaviPod

Sure, everyone knows that you can hook up the iPod to a home stereo (at least, they do if they've read Chapter 12). But how are you supposed to control it? Surely you're not going to get up off the couch and *walk across the room.* Let's not be absurd!

No, what you need is the NaviPod remote control from Ten Technology (Figure 14-9). It comes with a chrome stand, an infrared receiver that plugs into the top of the iPod, and a round, five-button remote control that lets you command your wee white jukebox from a comfy chair.

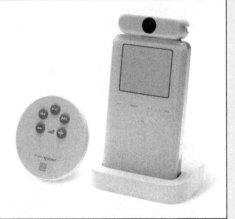

Figure 14-9:
The NaviPod lets you command your iPod from across the room. Its distinctive round white remote stands out among the typical bouquet of magic wands for the TV, DVD, VCR, cable box, and TiVo. NaviPods for all iPod models cost $50 at www.drbott.com or www.apple.com/ipod/accessories.html.

Digisette iPod 5430 FMXT FM Radio
Complete with neck strap and earphones, the Digisette 5430 FMXT radio offers another option for supplementing your own music collection with live FM radio.

Its stereo miniplug fits in the iPod's headphones jack (any model), and its radio can automatically scan for stations. $30 at *www.welovemacs.com/lovemacs/ipod-stuff.html*.

Dashboard Stands

Several companies make mounting hardware to secure the iPod to your car's dashboard. The auto mounts keep your iPod within comfortable reach of the driver's seat and also keep it stable, so you don't have to worry about it sliding off the passenger seat or bouncing out of the cup holder when you drive through road construction.

Gripmatic iPod Mount Kit

The Gripmatic cradle holds the iPod in place with cushioned pads on either side and mounts on the console or dashboard. The kit comes with a choice of methods for attaching it to the car—adhesive or screw-in, depending on your preference. $30 at *www.everythingipod.com*.

Tip: Some iPod casemakers also sell swivel clips that mount on the car's dashboard, so that you can detach the iPod from your belt clip and stick it on the dash without taking it out of its case. Check the manufacturer or dealer's Web site to see if your model has this option.

If you want to outfit your car all at once, you can get a case and dash-mount swivel clip, plus an FM Transmitter and a car charger, in the $40 DLO iPod Auto Connection kit at *www.everythingipod.com*. There are kits for all iPod models and a version that comes with a cassette adapter instead of a wireless transmitter. See Chapter 12 for more iPod car accessories.

Cup Holder iPod Car Mount

If you can spare a cup holder slot between the front seats, try the Cup Holder iPod Car Mount: an adjustable plastic stand that plugs into most standard-size cup holder

Figure 14-10:
Just plant the Belkin TuneDok in the nearest available cup holder (shown here with and without the iPod bracket), and you and your iPod are ready to hit the road. Belkin also sells FM transmitters and cassette adapters that let your iPod's playlists pour forth from the car radio.

holes. It holds the iPod up for use by both driver and shotgun-seat passenger. The iPod rests firmly in the cushioned Gripmatic cradle atop the stand. $35 at *www.everythingipod.com*.

Belkin TuneDok

The iPod snaps into the cradle, and the TuneDok's suction cup anchors the mount firmly into your car's cup holder. The TuneDok lets you adjust both the height and angle of the iPod and has a clip to keep cables out of the way. Shown in Figure 14-10, it works for both old and new iPod models and sells for $30 at *www.belkin.com*.

Tip: Just in case you don't have enough wires coming out of your head already, meet the Skullcandy LINK. When a call comes in on your cellphone, the LINK throttles back the iPod music volume automatically, so you can still groove to your tunes while chatting away. (Your conversation partner, of course, doesn't hear the music.)

The gizmo attaches to a pair of headphones or earbuds (your choice) and is available to fit five different types of cellphone audio connector jacks. $30 at *www.skullcandy.com*.

Power Adapters

It never hurts to have a spare power adapter, so that you don't have to keep hauling the iPod's cable and AC adapter when you need to recharge on the road. (If you're looking for an automobile charger to use for powering the iPod through the car's cigarette lighter, see "Connecting the iPod to a Car Stereo" on page 232.)

- **iPod AC Adapter** has an AC plug on one end and a FireWire Connector on the other. For pre-2003 iPods. $25 at *www.everythingipod.com*.

- **The Apple World Travel Adapter Kit** works with the iPod's included AC adapter for electrical outlets in North America, the United Kingdom, Continental Europe, Australia, Japan, China, Korea, and Hong Kong. (As international travelers know, all electrical outlets are not created equal. Not only is the voltage often different in other countries, but the outlets have differing plugs.) $40 in the Music & Audio section at *http://store.apple.com*.

- **SiK FireJuice** is a connector contraption for iPods that connect to 4-pin (unpowered) FireWire jacks or CardBus laptop cards that don't supply power to the iPod. The FireJuice box provides an extra FireWire jack right when you need it so you can use your AC adapter to charge up the iPod simultaneously while syncing your music and not have to wait around for your battery to get itself together. The FireJuice also lets iBook users connect their iPods without having to worry that it's siphoning off the laptop's battery. It works with Apple's iPod AC adapter or SiK's auto charger (which, like the FireJuice, is available at *http://store.sik.com*) and comes in models for 6-to-6 pin or 4-to-6 pin cables. FireJuice costs about $25 to $40, depending on the type of iPod.

Tip: If you need a spare AC adapter, or replacement FireWire or USB 2.0 cables for your iPod, you can find them at the online Apple Store (*http://store.apple.com*), along with several other iPod-friendly products.

Battery Boosters

An iPod with a dead battery is no fun at all. Here are a couple of items designed to keep the music playing, even when the battery is not.

• **Belkin Backup Battery Pack** can supply 15 to 20 hours of music even after the iPod battery has run down. You put four regular AA batteries into this pack, and then clamp it onto the back of the iPod with suction cups. The flat FireWire connector connects to the bottom of the music player to feed it energy. $60 at *www.belkin.com*.

POWER USERS' CLINIC

Two for Tunes

While lots of these good-looking goodies are purely for the iPod, a couple of hardware items from Griffin Technology can enhance the digital music experience on the desktop side of things. Both devices work with Windows and Mac, and are available at *www.griffintechnology.com*.

The Power-Mate USB Controller & Input Device, pictured here at left, looks like a plain old volume knob from a stereo console. But when you plug it into the computer's USB port, you can spin the dial to control the contents of just about any window on your screen. You can program the PowerMate to control the iTunes or MusicMatch Jukebox Plus volume level, scroll through insufferably long Web pages and documents, or advance quickly through camcorder footage in a video editing program. You can even program it to perform key commands

The controller, which sells for $45, works with just about any application.

Not all computers, especially laptops, come with an audio-input or microphone jack for recording your own sounds and songs directly onto the computer's hard drive. For those without, the iMic ($40) universal audio adapter, pictured here at right, connects to the USB port and provides the computer with stereo input and output jacks.

Because the iMic is outside the loud, whirring computer, it often gets better audio quality than an internal microphone going through the sound card. (Software included can further customize the device's audio settings.)

The iMic uses a standard stereo miniplug jack and can record from other music sources, like a MiniDisc player or stereo system, making it possible to record some of those old vinyl albums onto the computer and convert them to MP3 for use on the iPod.

- **Replacement Battery for iPods.** The iPod's internal rechargeable battery is intended to last the life of the player—but on occasion, extremely heavy use might cause the battery to slow down or conk out. Although Apple has its own $99 battery-replacement service (take a deep breath and read down the page at *www.info.apple.com/support/applecare_products/service/ipod_service.html*), there's a way to do it yourself for less money if you don't mind voiding the warranty—especially if it's already out of date anyway.

Laptops for Less sells rechargeable replacement batteries designed to fit both the original and dock-connecting iPod models. Illustrated instructions on its Web site let you see what you're getting into before you buy the battery. (Warning: It involves screwdrivers, rulers, and the forcible prying-open of iPods.) The replacement iPod battery sells for $50 at *www.ipodbattery.com*.

PDASmart.com sells $60 replacement batteries for older iPod models as well. (If you're squeamish about cracking open the iPod case, mail it to them, and they'll do if for you for the mere fee of $68 for parts and labor.) Check out *www.pdasmart.com/ipodpartscenter.htm* for more information.

Troubleshooting

The iPod is a fairly uncomplicated device, at least compared with towering desktop machines with printers and scanners attached, or even one of your more sophisticated microwave ovens. But a number of things can temporarily trip up your iPod—hard-drive glitches, wonky cables, or a wrong turn at the crossroads where hardware meets software.

At least three generations of iPods and a Mini-Me now stalk the earth. Some problems may apply only to certain models, but many of the hardware-oriented issues are universal. You can remedy some problems by simply pressing a couple of buttons, but others require a little more time and effort.

This chapter covers all of the above, and includes a section devoted to troubleshooting the iTunes Music Store. And if you don't find the answer, turn to the last section, which lists iPod repair resources.

The iPod's Self-Help Modes

If you've used a computer for any length of time, you know that hard drives can sometimes crash, lock up, or have days when they're just not feeling well. Unlike most MP3 players, which use memory chips to store 64 or 128 MB of music, the iPod uses a hard drive to store its music and data. Accordingly, sometimes you need to use hard disk diagnostic and repair tools, like ScanDisk or Disk Utility. All you have to do is push the right sets of buttons.

How to Reset an iPod

If your iPod seems frozen, locked up, confused, or otherwise unresponsive, you can *reset* it without losing your music and data files. You may lose some personalized settings and preferences, though. On the 2003 and later iPods, for example, any custom configurations of the main menu and the Alarm Clock revert to their original, factory-set states, and the On-The-Go Playlist gets purged from the iPod's memory.

Here's the iPod's reset sequence:

1. **Connect the iPod to its power source.**

   Use the AC adapter and FireWire cable that came with the player, or you can plug the same FireWire cable into the computer's FireWire port.

Note: Hooking up to external power isn't technically necessary, but it rules out the possibility that a dying battery is the cause of the lockup.

---

2. **On 2003 and later iPods, slide the Hold switch on and off again.**

   If you have an earlier model, go straight to step 3.

3. **Press the Menu and ▶︎❚❚ buttons on the front of the iPod simultaneously. (On the iPod Mini, press the Menu and center Select buttons instead.) Hold them down until you see the Apple logo appear on the screen.**

If the technology gods are smiling, the iPod goes through its little boot sequence and then returns you to the main menu.

Scan the iPod's Hard Disk

If the iPod's having hard disk difficulties, you may see what Apple calls the iPod Disk Scan icon when you turn it on (see Figure 15-1). That's an indication that the iPod has noticed its own flailing. It's running a built-in disk-fixing program automatically. Life is sweet.

If your hard drive seems to be acting up (freezing, skipping songs, and so on), you can force the iPod to do a Disk Scan self-exam on your command, like this:

4. **Reset the iPod as described in the previous section.**

   Wait until you see the Apple logo appear, then go on to step 2.

Figure 15-1:
The iPod's screen scans its own hard disk for any problems or potential problems.

5. **Press the ⏮, Menu, ⏭, and Select buttons all at once.**

If your fingers are contorted in a yoga-like position, you're doing it right.

The icon shown in Figure 15-1 appears. It may take up to 20 minutes for the horizontal progress bar to creep along, so you may want to just let the iPod do its disk introspection and go buy some new tracks from the iTunes Music Store.

You can interrupt the disk scan by holding down the round Select button for a few seconds—but the next time you turn on the iPod, it will begin to scan the disk again. (The "interrupted disk scan" icon looks like an X over the disk icon.)

Once the test has finished completely, you should see one of four icons on the screen. These are:

- **Checkmark on a disk.** Your iPod has aced the exam and everything's fine. No worries, mate.

- **Exclamation alert triangle on a disk.** The disk scan test failed, but will try again the next time you boot up or reset the iPod.

- **Arrow on a disk.** The scan found some disk problems and fixed them, but the show's not over. You should now download the latest version of the iPod software from Apple's Web site and run the Restore program to reformat the iPod's hard disk (page 296).

  (Make sure you have all your music and files backed up before you do, because running Restore wipes the drive clean.)

- **Exclamation alert triangle on sad iPod.** This one's bad, really bad. The iPod's hard disk is damaged. About all you can do is send it to Apple for repairs. Go to the iPod Service page at *http://depot.info.apple.com/ipod*.

Force the iPod into FireWire Disk Mode

It's usually easy to put your iPod into FireWire Disk Mode, as described on page 213. However, if your computer seems to have amnesia and doesn't recognize your iPod, or if you're trying to connect your iPod to a computer with an unpowered FireWire port, you may need the "forced FireWire" maneuver.

Caution: Before you use this method with an unpowered FireWire port, make sure the iPod's battery is fully charged. Otherwise, your little buddy could run out of juice while you're transferring songs.

It goes like this:

1. **Reset the iPod.**

   Use one of the methods described on page 268.

2. **When the Apple logo appears, press the ⏮ and ⏭ buttons simultaneously until you see the "Do Not Disconnect" message on the screen.**

   On the iPod Mini, press the ▶︎❚❚ and Select buttons instead.

Either way, the computer gets the message from the iPod and recognizes it as a be-loved friend and FireWire device. The iPod shows up as a disk on your desktop or in the My Computer window shortly thereafter.

Run the iPod Diagnostic Tests

Many Podheads got very excited when gadget-guru Web sites—like Slashdot.org and iPoding.com—reported that Apple had buried a super-secret *debugger program* in the iPod software: a mode for programmers that could run sixteen different diag-nostic tests on the iPod to make sure all its systems were Go.

Now, you, as a mere mortal who's never been to electronic-engineering school, prob-ably won't learn much from these tests. They're designed for Apple technicians try-ing to fix ailing iPods.

Still, some of them may help you narrow down certain iPod problems, and all of them are enlightening—a glimpse into just how technical this apparently simple gadget really is.

To get to the diagnostic mode, reset the iPod. When the Apple logo appears, press the ▐◀◀, Select, and ▶▶▌ buttons simultaneously. When you let go of the buttons, the iPod lets out a tweet and flashes a quick screen giving the version of the tests being used.

Then it displays a long alphabet-soup list of test titles (Figure 15-2). You've arrived at the Diagnostic Mode menu.

For 2001 and 2002 iPods running iPod Software 1.3, the tests include:

- **A. 5 IN 1.** Runs five tests (described individually below): LCM, RTC, SDRAM, FLASH, and OTPO.

- **B. RESET.** Restarts the iPod.

- **C. KEY.** Tests all the buttons on the front of the iPod (press them all within 5 seconds to see if they pass).

- **D. AUDIO.** Examines the iPod's audio circuitry. You'll see "0X00000000 DONE" on the screen if it passes the test.

- **E. REMOTE.** Gives you a chance to push each button on an attached remote to make sure it's working right. (If you don't have the remote hooked up, you get a RMT FAIL message.)

- **F. FIREWIRE.** If your FireWire bus tests okay, you get an FW PASS.

- **G. SLEEP.** Puts the iPod to sleep—deep sleep. The Low Battery icon appears on-screen and you'll have to reset the iPod to wake it up again. (If it does take the snooze, then it passed the Sleep test.)

- **H. A 2 D.** Tests the iPod's internal power system and then shows you a voltage reading, along with a string of numbers and codes comprehensible only to iPod engineers.

- **I. OTPO CNT.** Spin the scroll wheel during this test to see its response presented in hexadecimal code. If the value onscreen changes as you spin, your wheel is working. (*Hexadecimal* is how computers count on their 16 "fingers." They count like this: 0, 1, 2, 3, 4, 5, 6, 7, 8, 9, A, B, C, D, E, F. Programmers know how to read it.)

- **J. LCM.** Push the Select button through three different screen patterns to test the iPod's screen.

- **K. RTC.** Most iPodologists think this test performs a system check of the iPod's internal clock. (You can see more hexadecimal code each time you push the Select button—in case you just can't get enough of that hexadecimal code.)

- **L. SDRAM.** Checks whether your iPod's memory is OK. If so, you see SDRAM PASS.

- **M. FLASH.** Displays a hexadecimal number that identifies the iPod's *ROM* version. (ROM is *read-only memory*, a stash of permanent memory that holds startup instructions and other vital info.)

- **N. WHEELA2D** or **OTPO.** iPods with the immovable, touch-based scroll wheel use the WHEELA2D test; iPods with the moving scroll wheel (and software before version 1.2) use the OTPO test. (You need to reset the iPod at the end of the wheel test.)

- **O. HDD SCAN.** This is the hard drive test mentioned on page 268.

- **P. RUN IN.** This test runs several of the diagnostic tests mentioned above repeatedly until you press the Play/Pause button to stop it.

Figure 15-2:
It's not just the secret diagnostic menu; it's a glimpse deep into the lingo and the lives of hardware programmers. Only they, for example, comprehend the purpose of all of these commands.

The Diagnostic Menu for the 2003-and-later models and iPod Software 2.1 is almost the same. Different or renamed items include:

- **F. LIN REC.** This test, which supposedly dealt with the iPod's Line In recording function when placed in the iPod Dock, appeared in iPod Software 2.0 but was replaced with a FireWire test in 2.0.1 and later.

- **J. RECORD.** The secret recording feature described on page 250 made a cameo appearance in iPod Software 2.0, but was gone with the iPod 2.0.1 software.

- **K. CHG STUS.** The iPod shows STATUS TEST across the top, and lists information about the player's USB, FireWire, and battery charge.

- **L. USB DISK.** Running this test flips the iPod into Disk Mode and displays the big "OK to Disconnect" checkmark onscreen. Resetting the iPod gets you out of it.

- **M. CHK SUM** presents another hexadecimal number across the screen, and Apple isn't saying what it means.

- **N. DISPLAY.** This was a test for the Display, but it changed to the CONTRAST test for the screen in iPod Software 2.0.1.

No matter which iPod model you have, press the ▶▶I and I◀◀ buttons to scroll through the list of tests; to start the highlighted test, press Select. Press the ▶ button at the end of the test to go back to the main list.

When you want to stop testing and go back to listening to music, press the iPod's reset button combination (Menu and ▶) until the Apple logo appears.

Note: The iPod Mini's diagnostic screen has a few new tests of its own, including STATUS, AUDIO, AND DISKMODE. To get to the tests, reset the iPod and then simultaneously press Select and I◀◀.

---

iPod Hardware Problems

If your iPod syncs up fine to the computer and only seems to misbehave when you're out trying to listen to your Rockabilly Workout playlist at the gym, the problems could lie within the iPod itself.

The iPod Keeps Freezing Up

Inside the iPod spins a busy hard drive, just like the one inside a desktop computer. Hard drives have been known to freeze, crash, and lock up when you least expect it, and the iPod's is no different.

Rebooting (resetting) usually thaws a freeze, so grab the iPod and reset it as described on page 268. But if a simple reset doesn't solve the problem, read on.

Restoring the iPod software
If the iPod still freezes up again after you reset it, restoring its software may help smooth things out; see page 296.

The iPod Won't Turn On or Wake Up from Sleep

Some days you just don't want to get out of bed. In its own way, the iPod has days like that, too. If you're pushing its buttons and nothing's happening, run through this troubleshooting checklist:

- **Make sure the HOLD switch isn't on.** Yes, this is obvious, but it's surprisingly easy to overlook in a panic. If it's on, slide it so that the orange band doesn't show, and then try to turn on the iPod again.

- **Check your battery charge.** Even if you're sure you recently charged it up, your iPod could have gotten bumped inside a backpack or purse and run itself down. The iPod can't turn on if the battery doesn't have enough juice. You may even see a flash of the Low Battery icon, or a message. Plug the iPod into the computer or AC adapter to get some power flowing, wait a few minutes, and then try to turn it on while it's recharging.

- **Reset the iPod.** See page 268.

The iPod Won't Reset

If the iPod doesn't respond to any amount of poking and prodding, and you can't even reset it, you may have to take more drastic measures.

First, unplug it from power and put it away for at least 24 hours to let the battery's power drain. Once the iPod has had its little time-out, reconnect it to the AC adapter (or your computer) so it can draw power, and then try to reset it again.

Also make sure the iPod is actually getting power when you plug it in. The AC adapter that came with the iPod could be plugged into a dead power outlet, or a turned-off power strip could be at fault. Look for the charging-battery icon to confirm that your iPod's power cell is getting filled up.

Note: The iPod's battery won't charge when connected to a computer in Sleep mode. Make sure the computer is up and running.

If you charge the iPod via its FireWire cable, note that a bent or damaged FireWire cable may fail to deliver power to the iPod. Make sure you're using the FireWire cable that came with the iPod, too, because a different cord may not work properly. Finally, try plugging the iPod's FireWire cable into a different port (most modern Macs and FireWire add-in cards have two).

Tip: Check the FireWire port on the iPod to make sure it's free from anything that might block some of the connector pins. Some iPod models have a small plastic cover for the FireWire port to help prevent these situations, but early iPods have exposed ports. (The FireWire port is on the bottom of the 2003 and later iPods.)

If you've managed to revive the iPod with any of the above steps, updating or restoring its software may help prevent this situation from happening again. See page 296 for the restore instructions.

Alas, if none of these methods revive the iPod, your next step should be having Apple look at it (see page 302).

Tip: If you're having problems getting any of your iPod or other FireWire devices to show up on the Mac, a little time out may help matters. Unplug all the FireWire devices and then shut down the Mac. Unplug the power cord from the wall for a few minutes. Then plug it back in, start it back up, and after it boots up all the way, try plugging in the iPod again.

Weird Icons When iPod Boots Up

If you turn on the iPod one day and see odd icons instead of the familiar menus, the iPod may be trying to tell you something. Here are explanations for the typical icons you may see (Figure 15-3).

Figure 15-3:
May you never see these icons except right here in this book. They let you know that your iPod is concerned for its own health.

Folder icon with exclamation point

Longtime Mac fans may remember the dreaded Disk Icon With Flashing Question Mark, which indicates a corrupted System Folder or a hard drive problem. This icon on an iPod could have similar meanings. Among the possible causes of this icon:

- **You have the wrong version of iPod software.** If you inadvertently installed a version of the iPod software that's earlier than the software it came with, download and install the latest version (page 296).

- **The battery is too low.** Plug your iPod into its AC adapter or a powered FireWire cable to see if juicing it up makes the icon go away.

- **The iPod's hard drive was formatted incorrectly.** If you were just tinkering and decided to wipe the iPod's drive and reformat it with your favorite Mac or Windows disk utility instead of the iPod Software Updater, the iPod might have a hissy fit. Download and use the Restore option to install the latest version of the iPod Update software on your iPod.

If none of the above seems to mirror your situation, try resetting the iPod to see if the folder icon goes away. If not, it may be time to contact Apple or the holder of your extended warranty about repairs.

Apple logo and iPod name won't go away

If you turn on your 'Pod and see only the Apple logo (Figure 15-3, middle), and it seems like your poor machine is stuck in a continuous loop of restarts, try one of the following steps:

- Plug the iPod into your computer's powered FireWire port, if you have one. (If it's an iPod Mini, you can plug it into your computer's USB 2.0 port instead.) Then reset the iPod as described on page 268.

- Go into forced FireWire mode, as described on page 269. As soon as you see the Apple logo, press and hold the ⏮ and ⏭ buttons until you see the "Do Not Disconnect" message on the iPod's screen. (In early versions of the iPod software, you see the Y-shaped FireWire icon instead.)

- Download and use the Restore option to install the latest version of the iPod Update software on your iPod. Remember, doing a restore wipes the iPod's drive; you'll have to copy all of your songs, contacts, and other data back to it.

- If your iPod is so trashed that it never even displays the "Do Not Disconnect" message, try the first two steps above again to see if you can get to the point where you can restore the iPod software.

If nothing works, contact Apple (page 302) to inquire about repair options.

Hard disk icon with magnifying glass
If you see the disk-scan icon shown at right in Figure 15-3, the iPod suspects trouble with its own hard drive. See page 268.

Battery Life Issues
Since the iPod's introduction, the subject of battery life has consistently lit up online forums and message boards around the Internet. For one, owners of the 2003 iPods were dismayed to see that these new models only had a maximum battery life of eight hours.

Excessive Clock appetite
Even with the 10 hours of battery time promised on the 2001 and 2002 iPods, owners found that they weren't even getting that much. Some iPodders also noticed that the battery charge seemed to run down far more quickly after Apple introduced the Clock feature in version 1.2 of the iPod software.

Many tech-savvy iPod owners concluded that the clock and the alarms used with the Calendar were gulping down juice unnecessarily. People who didn't care about the new organizer functions, and just wanted to play music for as long as possible between charges, fought back by refusing to set the iPod's clock—or even reverted to the pre-Clock version 1.1 of the iPod software that they kept around.

Update 1.2.6 of the iPod software in March 2003 was specifically designed to address battery problems; Apple recommends installing it (or whatever the current version is; see page 296) on all iPod models. A battery that still refuses to maintain a charge—especially with normal usage—may have internal problems that an Apple repair technician should take care of.

Charging the battery
Remember how you were taught that certain kinds of batteries (in laptops and camcorders, say) worked better if you occasionally fully drained and then recharged them? Forget it. You want to keep the iPod's lithium-ion battery charged *always*, or else you'll lose your clock, date, and other settings.

Many dedicated iPod People prefer to charge the player only when the AC adapter is connected. That's because connecting the player to a computer makes its hard drive spin, which uses up the battery juice faster.

Battery life

Apple has posted various recommendations on its Web site for treating the iPod battery to help ensure a long life, including:

- Don't expose the iPod to extreme hot or cold temperature ranges. (In other words, don't leave it in a hot, parked car, and don't expect it to operate on Mt. Everest.)

- Take the iPod out of any heat-trapping cases or covers when you charge it.

- Put the iPod to sleep to conserve battery power. (Press the ▶‖ button until the iPod display goes blank and the iPod settles into slumber.)

- Even when you're not using the iPod, charge the battery every 14 to 18 days to keep it powered even while it's sleeping. (It still needs power in sleep mode.)

- When you see the Low Battery icon or message, plug the iPod into the computer or an electrical outlet with the AC adapter. The iPod battery indicator shows roughly how much charge is left in the battery.

Note: The Battery Indicator icon in the upper-right corner of the iPod screen is an approximation of the battery's charge, not the ultimate authority. It may even tell you that you still have power when the battery has run down, although recent iPod software updates were designed to help with this problem.

Replacing the battery

The iPod uses a rechargeable lithium-ion battery. It's rated to last for 500 chargings. If you use and charge your iPod daily, you'll get two or three years out of it; if you use it more moderately, you're looking at nine or ten years. Since the iPod has only been around since 2001, however, there are no definitive long-term case studies.

That answer wasn't good enough for two brothers who, following a less-than-satisfying adventure in Apple tech support in the fall of 2003, spray-painted a stenciled slogan, "iPod's unreplaceable battery lasts only 18 months" across iPod posters all over Manhattan, and then released a Web movie documenting their revenge.

It wasn't exactly accurate—you'd have to be a serious ten-hour-a-day iPodaholic to burn out the battery in 18 months, and most people's original 2001 iPod batteries are still going strong. Still, the incident caused panic among prospective and current iPod owners. At just about the same time, Apple introduced the $99 battery-replacement program described on page 301. (Coincidence? You decide.)

If your iPod battery clearly isn't retaining its charge, and you've taken all of the other steps described here, and it's out of warranty, you can find replacement batteries for sale on the Web. (Check out *www.ipodbattery.com* or *www.pdasmart.com/ipodpartscenter.htm*, for starters.)

Of course, installing them voids the warranty (if indeed your iPod is still under warranty at all). If it's still covered, or if the thought of opening your iPod gives you the wiggins, let Apple's repair crew take care of it instead.

Tip: The iPod's battery has become such a hot topic that a helpful fan created a Web site—*www.ipodbattery faq.com*—specifically to collect all the latest news and technical documentation on the portentous power cell.

The Backlight Turns on by Itself at Midnight

If you have at least version 1.2 of the iPod software, then you have the Clock feature. When the Clock strikes midnight, it makes an internal adjustment that may pop the white backlight on for a second. This flash doesn't consume much power, but it can be annoying. Turning off the backlight stops the midnight flashing (choose Settings→Backlight timer→Off).

That Little Plastic Flap Came off the FireWire Port

If the FireWire port cover popped off your 2002 iPod but isn't torn, you might be able to reattach it. Position the end of the plastic tab over the slot for the cover flap and push down firmly.

If your port cover is torn or damaged, contact Apple's repair service about getting a replacement.

The 2003 iPods come with a thin plastic cap to snap into the port on the bottom of the player, plus an extra in case you lose the first one.

The Touchwheel is Out of Control

In 2002, Apple replaced the iPod's turnable scroll wheel with a nonmoving "touchwheel" that works like a laptop trackpad. The move to the touchwheel made sense; the moving wheels were so easily tripped up by dirt or sand, using the iPod at the beach was no day at the beach. (The iPod Mini's "click wheel" kept the touchy-feely scrolling action but moved the buttons underneath. You chunk down on the edge of the wheel when you want to hit one of the buttons.)

But even with no moving parts, the touchwheel can be prone to jumpy behavior. It works by translating the electrical charge from your finger into movement on the menu screen. The wheel is very sensitive, and it's not uncommon to hear the iPod jump ahead or skip a song if you accidentally brush it when putting it back in your pocket.

Other factors that could confuse the touchwheel and make it behave erratically include:

• Using the touchwheel right after applying lotion or moisturizer to your hands.

• Using more than one finger on the touchwheel, or resting another finger near it that might confuse its sensors.

- Using pencil erasers or pen caps instead of your finger.

- Getting moisture on the touchwheel from a humid environment or damp hands. (If that happens, wipe off both the wheel and the finger with a soft dry cloth or tissue.)

- Wearing heavy jewelry like bracelets or rings, which may also throw off the touchwheel. If your wheel is acting wacky, try taking off your ring or charm bracelet.

The wheel and *all* the buttons on the front of the 2003 iPod buttons are made of touch-sensitive nonmoving parts. If you've upgraded from a first- or second-generation iPod, it may take a few days to get the feel for the new iPod. Even the Select button is touch-sensitive, so even a light finger brush across it while scrolling can dump you into a menu you weren't intending to visit.

Tip: The touchwheel works best when you use strong, deliberate strokes. Instead of a running-hamster approach—making short little movements all in the same place—slide your fingertip all the way around it.

Some Idiot Set the iPod Menus to Korean

Changing the iPod's operating system language to an unfamiliar alphabet is an obvious trick used by jealous co-workers and older brothers. Fortunately, you have a couple ways to get the iPod back to English.

One quick way is to click the Menu button until you get back to the iPod's main menu screen. You'll see "iPod" in English at the top, and five lines of text in whatever language your wisenheimer pal picked out for you.

1. **Scroll down to the fourth line.**

   If you can't read Korean, you've actually highlighted what would have been the Settings menu.

2. **Select this item. Scroll to the end of the list to the words, "Reset All Settings," which are conveniently in English.**

   Here, you can make a decision.

   Option 1: The *third* menu item from the bottom of the list (two up from Reset All Settings) is the Language setting. Click there to get to the list of languages, then scroll all the way to the top to get back to English (or whatever language you were using before this incident).

   Option 2: If you're tired of your iPod settings anyway, you can wipe them out and start over. Press the Select button on Reset All Settings. You now come to a screen that gives you a choice: Cancel or Reset.

3. **Scroll to and choose Reset (also in English) to get back to the Language menu, where you can select "English" for the iPod.**

Broken Screen Glass

A smashed and broken iPod is a sad sight indeed. Wrap it up gently and contact Apple to inquire about the repair procedure. A list of resources appears at the end of this chapter.

Problems with Song Quality

The sound quality of your digital audio files is affected by a number of things. If you find that your MP3 files sound thin and tinny no matter what you play them on, check the bit rate you used to rip them from the original CDs (page 74). Bit rates below 128 kilobits per second generally don't have CD-quality sound. If you've downloaded songs from Web sites, you're usually at the mercy of whoever encoded the songs in the first place.

Some Songs Skip

If the same songs always skip, the song files themselves may be damaged. Maybe a hiccup or power fluctuation while you were ripping the tune from a CD dinged up the file, or maybe you had several memory-hogging programs open and running while you were recording songs. Try deleting the song files from iTunes or MusicMatch Jukebox and then reripping and reimporting fresh copies.

Shaking or banging the iPod while it's playing can cause its hard drive to skip while playing a song. (Shaking and banging are two things you want to avoid with *any* hard drive.)

True, the iPod comes with a memory stash designed to prevent skipping for at least 20 minutes. But as noted on page 70, enormous song files—either hugely long pieces of music or files encoded in uncompressed formats like AIFF—could be maxing out the iPod's RAM buffer. Here are your options:

- **Rerip AIFF or WAV files into the smaller, compressed MP3 format.** They may not sound as pure, but they're less likely to skip.

- **Break down larger files into smaller ones.** If you've used the Join Tracks feature of iTunes (page 101) to create a sonic tapestry or simulate that live concert feeling, try re-encoding the songs in smaller chunks.

- **Reset the iPod.** Performing a reset or, as a last-ditch effort, running a restore with the latest version of the iPod Software Updater (page 296) may also help stop the skipping.

Noise in Quiet Parts of Songs

Most people don't want to hear high-pitched squealing noises during quiet, emotional parts of songs. This was, unfortunately, what happened with some early versions of the iPod software. Updating the iPod software to version 1.1 or later, as well as lowering the volume a tad, usually helps this situation.

Tip: Ever notice your iPod sometimes seems to skip the first song in a list? Long-time iPodders have been griping about this alleged bug in the iPod's software for years.

One popular workaround: Start your playlist or song by scrolling to it and pushing the Play button, rather than using the round Select button in the center of the scroll wheel.

Problems with the Headphones or Remote

If you're having sound-quality issues with your headphones, check to make sure that they're firmly plugged in. Some headphone cords are notoriously fragile, and the wires encased in the plastic sheathing can break if the headphone cord is bent, twisted, yanked out roughly, slammed in a car door, or chomped on by a pet rabbit (Figure 15-4).

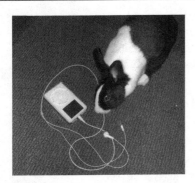

Figure 15-4:
Pets and iPods don't mix! If your headphones don't sound very good, check for teeth marks along the cord.

If you are getting patchy, scratchy sound from your iPod headphones, try using them with another portable player or stereo to confirm that it's the headphones having the problem and not the iPod's headphones port.

The iPod Remote Won't Work

The remote control cable for the 2003 model year iPod is a two-pronged affair, with a smaller connector attached to the regular 3.5 mm stereo miniplug. The twin prongs fit into adjoining remote and headphone ports on top of the iPod. If you've ordered a remote control from the Apple store, make sure you have the right one for your iPod; the remotes for the 2002 and 2003 iPods use different plugs.

If you've connected the small remote control for the 10 and 20 GB 2002 models to your headphone jack, but can't get it to respond when you push its buttons (even though the controls on the front of the iPod work OK), take a closer look. Specifically, look at the top of the iPod where the remote's connector plug meets the headphone jack. Is it pushed *all* the way in, or is a thin bit of the connector's silver ring visible between the white plastic casing and the top of the iPod (Figure 15-5)?

If there is, the remote isn't fully connected. Apply firm pressure and give the connector a slight twist to push it into the headphone jack until it's flush with the top of the iPod.

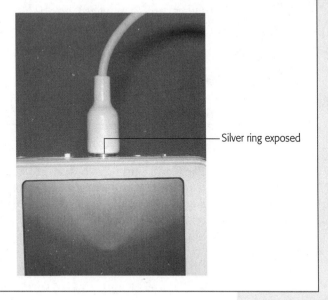

Figure 15-5:
The thin ring of silver between port and plug indicates that the remote cable is not fully connected to the iPod. You need to push the plug all the way in for the remote to work.

Silver ring exposed

iTunes Blues

The iPod and iTunes were designed to work hand-in-hand to manage your music, but occasionally, certain things may come between them. Here are a few of the common issues and problems that may interfere with that good old syncing feeling.

The iPod Doesn't Show Up

Communication is a vital part of any relationship, and the partnership between the iPod and iTunes is no different. If the iPod doesn't show up as a disk on your computer (or in iTunes) when it's connected, ask yourself:

- Are you plugging the iPod's cable firmly into a built-in FireWire or Windows USB 2.0 port? If you added the FireWire or USB 2 card yourself, is it an Apple-approved expansion card, or some cheap third-party card that hasn't been certified to work with Windows or the Macintosh operating system?

- Does your computer meet the system requirements (page 4)?

- If you're running Mac OS 9, do you have the FireWire Enabler, FireWire Support, and iPod FireWire Enabler extensions all loaded and turned on in your Extensions Manager control panel?

Other reasons the iPod may be shy and not showing up:

• **A bad cable or connector (FireWire or USB 2) on either the computer or iPod.** Try a different port on the computer and make sure the iPod's FireWire or USB 2.0 port is unobstructed. If your cable is bent or crimped, it may not be working properly, and you may need to replace it.

• **Other hardware plugged into the FireWire chain may be butting in.** Try unplugging the other FireWire devices and plug the iPod directly into a FireWire port on the back of the computer.

Tip: One way to test the FireWire cable is to plug it into the iPod on one end and the AC adapter on the other, then plug the AC adapter into an electrical outlet. If your iPod begins to charge, you know signals are getting through.

• **The iPod is frozen and needs resetting.** See page 268.

• **The iPod's hard drive is damaged and unable to communicate.** If you recently reformatted it with software other than Apple's iPod Software Updater, the iPod might not be able to recognize its best friend iTunes. Performing the software restore procedure described on page 296 might help. If the iPod doesn't respond to a reset, you may have to try the "forced FireWire mode" procedure described on page 269.

Note: In some combinations of iTunes 2 and Mac OS X, the iPod doesn't show up in the iTunes Source list—if the program is on a partition or hard drive other than the startup disk. Reinstalling iTunes in the Applications folder on the Mac's startup disk usually fixes this problem.

Figure 15-6:
In the iPod's Preferences box, you control how much music is autosynced with your computer (all, just selected playlists, or none). You can also turn your iPod into a FireWire disk here, as described in Chapter 11.

Songs Don't Automatically Update

Make sure the iPod is connected to the computer, select it from the iTunes Source list, then click the iPod Preferences button in the corner of the iTunes window. Make sure the "Automatically update all songs and playlists" option is turned on, as shown in Figure 15-6. If the iPod's preferences are set to "Manually manage songs and playlists," then the iPod is waiting for you to make the first move. (Details on page 50.)

iTunes Program Doesn't Open when I Plug in the iPod

Click the iPod button in the iTunes window and turn on the "Open iTunes when attached" box, shown in Figure 15-6.

iTunes Killed My Windows 2000 PC

Some early versions of iTunes for the PC didn't play nice with some Windows 2000 PCs. If iTunes 4.1 made your Windows 2000 machine fall and it can't get up, reboot and hold down the F8 key. When you see the Windows 2000 Advanced Options menu, pick Last Known Good Configuration; press Enter. Windows now goes back to a time before the software installation scrambled it.

Once Windows comes up, download iTunes 4.2 or later from Apple's Web site (*www.apple.com/itunes/download*), and install *that* version instead.

iTunes Doesn't Open

If you try to open iTunes, but get only an error message ("Not a Valid Library File" or "Error -208 Cannot Open iTunes Music Library"), you might experience a mighty stomach lurch as you imagine your entire digital audio library disappearing in a puff of bytes. Fortunately, it refers only to the database file that iTunes uses to keep track of the *library entries and playlists*, not the actual music files.

In most cases, you can get iTunes to start up again by opening your iTunes folder and dragging the problematic iTunes Music Library file to the desktop. (On the Mac, the iTunes folder is in your Home→Music folder; in Windows, it's in your My Documents→My Music folder. If the iTunes Music Library file isn't where it's supposed to be, search your computer for "iTunes Music Library.")

When you restart iTunes, it creates a fresh, untarnished Music Library file. It's so untarnished, in fact, that it probably shows a completely empty music library, or one that is way out of date. The following Apple-recommended quick fix should get iTunes up and running, but alas, it involves having to recreate playlists.

To save yourself some of this grief, back up your playlists and Music Library file every once in a while.

To back up your playlists:

1. **In iTunes, select a playlist you wish to back up. Choose File→Export Song List.**

   In the Export Song List box, there are a few file format options to choose from.

2. **Pick the XML format. Save the playlist to a folder on your computer or on an external hard drive, so that you can easily find it if something ever goes kablooey with iTunes.**

XML is the language of the iTunes Library.

3. **Repeat Steps 1 to 3 until you've exported all your playlists.**

It may take awhile if you have a ton of playlists. (You can skip the playlists called 60's Music, My Top Rated, Recently Played, and Top 25 Most Played; those are Smart Playlists that iTunes generates on its own.)

Now your playlists are safely backed up for safekeeping. Cut to the unhappy day that you start up your computer and iTunes is either spewing library-related error messages at you or just crashing. If that happens, you'll need to recreate your Library file, add your music back in, and import your saved playlists.

Here's the routine:

4. **Quit iTunes, if it's open. Find your iTunes folder.**

By default, the iTunes folder lives in your Home→Music folder (Macintosh) or the My Documents→My Music folder (Windows).

5. **Open the iTunes folder. Find the files called *iTunes 4 Music Library* and *iTunes Music Library.xml*. Drag them to the Trash or Recycle Bin.**

These are the messed-up versions of the files that are causing iTunes its internal grief. When you start iTunes again, though, the program automatically generates fresh new, empty copies of the files. These new files have nothing to do with what's in your library—*yet*.

6. **Open iTunes. Choose File→Add Folder to Library.**

Now it's time to get that massive collection of songs back in the library's listings.

7. **Locate your iTunes Music Folder (usually inside your iTunes folder). Click the Choose button to import all the music back into iTunes.**

Now you're actually reintroducing iTunes to your music files. Depending on the size of your audio collection, this step may take a few minutes.

New library file—*check*. Songs added back to the new library file—*check*. Now you just need to get those backed-up playlists back into the program; then all will be as it was before this little incident. (If you *didn't* back up your playlists, you need to recreate them by hand at this point, which can be a colossal pain if you had one for every possible occasion.)

Here's how you reimport your playlists:

1. **In iTunes, choose File→Import.**

The Import dialog box appears.

2. Navigate to the location where you safely exported your playlists. Double-click the first one to bring it back into iTunes.

You've just restored the first playlist.

3. Repeat for each playlist you need to restore.

This process can be tedious, but not nearly as tedious has having to recreate them all from scratch if you *didn't* back them up.

If you have a Mac.com account and have recently taken advantage of the service's Backup program for easy iTunes library file backups, log onto the service and use the program's Restore function to place the saved copy back on your Mac.

"Another User" Error Message

Windows XP and Mac OS X 10.3 have a feature called Fast User Switching that lets people who all use the same computer quickly log into their own accounts without making other people log off first. If you have iTunes open in one account, and somebody else—possibly your little sister who wants to start yakking on AOL Instant Messenger—logs onto her account with Fast User Switching, iTunes gets locked up in *your* account. If Sis wants to listen to tunes while she talks, she gets an error message that says, "You cannot open the application 'iTunes' because another user has it open. Ask the other user to quit the application, then try again."

To fix the problem, switch back into your account and quit the program. Now your sister can switch back into her account and start iTunes from there.

iTunes Won't Play a CD or Import Music from It

Newfangled compact discs in fancy formats like Super Audio CD and DVD-Audio are designed to excite audiophiles who live to hear every pick-scrape on Bob Dylan's guitar in 5.1 Surround Sound. Alas, these discs usually have built-in copyright protection that prevents you from ripping them to digital audio files on your computer. Some computers, in fact, can't read these discs at all. So if you've got yourself one of these new formats, you'd better stick to playing it on your expensive stereo system.

Worse, these days, even some non-SACD and DVD-A discs include copy protection that prevents a computer from ripping or even reading the songs on the CD. To confirm that this is the problem, try playing the troublesome disc on another computer, to rule out the possibility that something is funky with your own drive.

If you're having trouble with a regular old CD that you've played successfully before on your computer, proceed as shown in Figure 15-7.

If you've *never* been able to get iTunes to play CDs on your computer, and you're up to date on software upgrades from your drive's manufacturer, it's remotely possible that your drive simply doesn't work with iTunes. If this is the case, submit your drive's make and model number to Apple via the iTunes Feedback page at *www.apple .com/feedback/itunes.html* to make the company aware of the issue.

AppleScripts Won't Import Contact Files

Back in Mac OS X 10.1, you could use several AppleScripts to import contacts to the iPod automatically. However, these scripts don't work after version 1.2 of the iPod software, and they don't work with Mac OS X 10.2 and later.

Chapter 7 explains how to import contact files to the iPod from a variety of different programs.

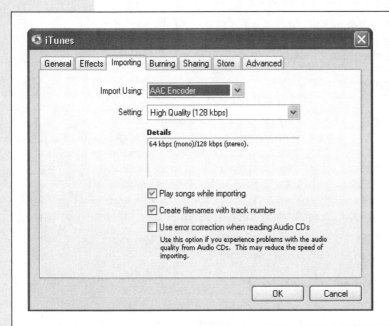

Figure 15-7:
Choose iTunes→Preferences→ Importing (Mac) or Edit→ Preferences→ Importing (Windows) to open the Preferences dialog box shown here. Once you get there, turn off "Use error correction when reading Audio CDs" and click OK. That option might be interfering with the song importing process.

"iPod Is Linked to Another Library"

If you're trying to plug your iPod into a different computer, an alert box may tell you that this particular iPod is already linked to another iTunes music library. iTunes then offers to *replace all of the music* on your iPod with whatever is in *its* library.

Click No here (unless, of course, this second machine's music library is much better than your own).

You can avoid this message by turning on "Manually manage songs and playlists" in the iPod's Preferences box (which appears when you plug the iPod in and click the iPod-shaped icon at the bottom of the iTunes window).

Tip: If you're not the only person who uses a certain Mac or PC—or if you're not the only person using the iPod—turning on "Manually manage songs and playlists" should make everybody happy (page 50). This way, the iPod won't alert you to other iTunes music libraries each time you plug it in, and the rest of the family can manually drag their own choice of music to the iPod without accidentally erasing anything.

The iPod *Always* Says "Do Not Disconnect"

If you've turned on the "Enable disk use" box in iTunes' iPod Preferences panel, the "Do Not Disconnect" message appears on the iPod at *all times*. You have to unmount the iPod from the computer manually to make the message go away (page 215).

Even if you haven't set up the iPod to work as a FireWire disk, its hard drive may not have spun down properly. If it's stuck in a loop, the "Do Not Disconnect" message may also appear. Try clicking the Eject iPod button in iTunes, or dragging the iPod icon on the desktop to the Mac's Trash, to see if you get the "OK to Disconnect" message.

If that doesn't work, try resetting the iPod as described on page 46 and then try ejecting it.

Note: If you live in a cross-platform household and have both Macintosh- and Windows-flavor iPods lying around, make sure you're plugging the WinPod into the PC. Macs are generally friendly towards PC-formatted 'Pods, but not vice versa. Mixing them up can lead to several error messages, including the "Do Not Disconnect" message (even as the computer won't mount or recognize the iPod) and the "This iPod is linked to another Music Library" message.

Windows Woes with MusicMatch Jukebox

If you've decided to stick with MusicMatch Jukebox as your music collection's headquarters (rather than Apple's iTunes program), you may occasionally run into problems unique to this software.

iPod Doesn't Show Up

It can be frustrating: You know the iPod is plugged into the PC because you did it yourself, yet it refuses to show its face in the Portable Device Manager (Portables Plus) window (page 46). If that's your problem, check for the following before grasping at straws (or your hair).

- **Check the basics.** In many cases, just quitting and reopening MusicMatch Jukebox Plus, unplugging and then replugging the iPod's computer cable, or restarting Windows can clear up the problem.

- **The iPod software plug-in is missing.** Exit MusicMatch Jukebox. If you're running the iPod for Windows 1.0 software (the version that came with the 2002 models), follow this path:

  At the desktop, open the My Computer→C: drive→Program Files→iPod→Bin folder. Make sure you see the files called *iPodDB.dll, iPodSongInfo.dll, iPodSrv.exe,* and *ipodwatcher.exe.*

In the 2003 iPod 2.0 software, look in the My Computer→C: drive→Program Files→ iPod→Bin folder for these files: *iPod20DeviceLog.txt, iPodService.exe,* and *iPod Manager.exe.*

Finally, check in My Computer→C: drive→Program Files→Music Match→Music-Match Jukebox→Plugins→Portables and make sure you have a folder called Apple or Apple_2 with the *PortDev.dll* and *unmatch.dll* files inside. As Microsoft veterans know, Windows is very particular about its DLL files.

If you're missing any of these files, reinstall the iPod desktop software from the CD that came with your iPod, or from the MusicMatch Web site (do a search for *iPod software*).

- **A bad FireWire/USB 2.0 cable or connector.** Try a different FireWire port on the PC, and make sure the iPod's FireWire port is unobstructed. If your cable is bent or crimped, it may not be working properly. Replace it with an Apple-approved FireWire cable.

   If you're syncing your 2003-or-later iPod with a USB 2.0 cable, make sure you have the correct, undamaged cable firmly plugged into both iPod and PC.

   Note, too, that Apple released the USB 2.0 software for PCs as a separate download in June 2003; it wasn't on the CD with the first batch of 2003 iPods. So if you've never downloaded the update, your PC may not have the software it needs to use USB 2.0 with the iPod. Check Apple's Web site for the software update.

- **The FireWire/USB 2.0 card you have is incompatible.** Make sure the card you're using with your PC is certified to work with Windows and has the Windows Hardware Quality Labs (WHQL) certificate of approval.

- **Other hardware plugged into the chain may be butting in.** If you've got several devices strung together along the FireWire or USB line, try unplugging everything but the iPod.

- **The iPod is frozen.** Reset it as described on page 268.

- **The iPod's hard drive is damaged and unable to communicate.** Performing the software restore procedure described on page 296 might help. If the iPod doesn't respond to a reset, you may have to try the "forced FireWire mode" procedure described on page 269.

- **The battery has run down.** If the iPod won't turn on, or if you see the Low Battery icon (or a low-battery message), plug the iPod into the AC adapter and let the iPod gather some power for an hour or so before reconnecting it to the PC.

Error Reinstalling the iPod 1.0 Software

If you're merrily reinstalling your iPod software, only to encounter a "Could not find file" alert box, don't panic. For some reason, the installer program couldn't complete the job.

If at first you don't succeed, choose Start→Settings→Control Panel→Add/Remove Programs. Double-click Add/Remove Programs, and on the list of programs, click "iPod for Windows." Remove the program and any shared files.

Once you've gotten rid of the incomplete version of the iPod software, reinstall the components again. You can find them on the MusicMatch Web site (search for *iPod software*).

"Missing Theme" Message

Nobody wants to see an error message right after installing a new program, but you may get an error that says "Missing theme.ini" the first time you open MusicMatch Jukebox. The program is telling you that the special iPod skin for MusicMatch Jukebox didn't make the trip in one piece. Download and install a new copy from *http://techsupp.musicmatch.com/techtools/Apple_iPod_ENU.mmz*.

Songs Don't Automatically Update

In the MusicMatch Portable Device Manager window, with the iPod attached, click Options. Then click the Synchronization tab and make sure the "Automatically Synchronize on device connection" option is turned on.

Sync Seems to Work, but No Songs Transfer

You've probably chosen "Selected playlist synchronization" in the Synchronizations tab of the iPod Options box (page 49)—but have *not* checkmarked any items in the list to synchronize. The iPod is doing just what you told it to do: Synchronize nothing.

To fix it, click Options in the Portable Device Manager window (page 46), go to the Synchronize tab, and turn on some of the playlists in the list.

MusicMatch Doesn't Automatically Open when iPod Connects

Click the Options button on the MusicMatch Portables Plus box (page 49), and then click the iPod tab. In the Settings panel, turn on "Automatically Launch MusicMatch Jukebox on device connection."

If you have a 2003 or later iPod model, you can get to the same checkbox a little faster by clicking the tiny white iPod icon in the Windows system tray. The resulting iPod Manager box offers the same option.

Synchronizing Takes Forever

Some of the bells and whistles you can apply to your digital audio tracks can increase the time it takes to get those same tunes shuttled over to the iPod. For example, two things known to slow song-transferring considerably are Volume Leveling (page 130) and the resampling feature (page 140).

If you prefer speed to song improvements, click the iPod icon in the Portable Device Manager window and then click Options (or right-click the iPod icon and choose Options on the shortcut menu).

Then, in the Options window, click the Audio tab and turn off "Apply volume leveling" and "Resample rates."

The iPod Always Says "Do Not Disconnect"

If you've turned on "Enable FireWire disk use" in MusicMatch Jukebox Preferences (page 213), you'll always see "Do Not Disconnect" on the iPod until you manually unmount the iPod from the PC. Enabling it as a FireWire disk makes the iPod seem like any other external hard drive to Windows, and you have to separate the two correctly—or both may complain.

To eject the iPod correctly, see page 215.

It's also possible that the iPod's hard drive is simply caught in a loop, even if you haven't enabled it for use as a FireWire disk. If you've tried ejecting it correctly, but the iPod is still spinning its wheels, reset it as described on page 268. If the iPod restarts OK, try ejecting it.

Blue Screen of Death

Squabbling among Windows device drivers can cause a system crash, so if your iPod was working just dandy before you installed a new program on your PC, there may be a conflict between something in the iPod software and something in the software you just installed.

For example, in Windows 2000, there's a conflict between the iPod software and the software drivers for the Easy CD Creator 5 Take Two backup program—in fact, it's a Screen of Blue conflict. A technical note on the MusicMatch site recommends uninstalling the Take Two software and its drivers to avoid the problem.

Error Message About Some Other Player

MusicMatch Jukebox Plus works with a number of different portable MP3 players. Because each device uses its own plug-in software, they could all be jockeying for position when you plug in the iPod and MusicMatch Jukebox Plus starts up. The version of the program that came with the iPod works *only* with the iPod. If you (or someone else who uses the computer) were playing around with another player, it probably installed software that conflicts with the iPod.

If you suspect this situation, quit MusicMatch Jukebox. Open My Computer→C: drive→Program Files→MUSICMATCH→MUSICMATCH Jukebox→Plugins→ Portables. (This is where all your plug-ins hang out.)

When you've found it, drag all the folders to the Recycle Bin except the ones called Apple or Apple_2. Restart the PC.

Once you've landed back on your desktop, open MusicMatch Jukebox Plus. Check whether you can now see your iPod, and send it some music.

Songs Ripped with MusicMatch Don't Sound Very Good

A huge number of hardware manufacturers make computers that run Windows, and a huge number of manufacturers make CD/DVD drives for them.

Some combinations of PC, disc drive, and Windows versions work better than others, and some produce MP3 files that sound better than others. Clicks, pops, jumpy playback, and songs that sound like they're being played at the wrong speed can be symptoms of a CD drive that isn't quite in tune with Windows.

To help compensate, MusicMatch Jukebox lets you adjust some settings for better sound quality. Choose View→Settings→Recorder, and on the right side of the Recorder settings panel, click Advanced.

On the right side of the Advanced Settings box are the Digital Audio Extraction (DAE) settings, which give you some control over how your ripped music sounds. For example:

- **DAE Speed.** The speed is factory set to MAX, but if your freshly ripped music sounds a bit on the chipmunky side, try lowering the setting to one of the numbered speeds (4,3,2,1). Of course, the slower the speed you pick here, the longer it will take each track to convert when you're ripping tunes.

- **Multipass.** The CD drive normally makes one pass when encoding a track, but sometimes, once isn't enough to get good quality tracks out of certain drives. Using the pull-down menu to turn on *multipass* lets the program read each song track more than once for better audio results. (Recording music takes a little bit longer, so bring a magazine.)

- **Block Size.** If your tracks sound wobbly and jittery, try increasing the number in this box. The factory setting is 20, and you can go up to 100 in your quest for better-sounding songs.

- **Overlap.** If you're hearing snaps, crackles, and pops in your recorded audio files (and the CD is in unscathed condition), increasing the Overlap value can even out and improve the recording. It starts out set to 3, but you can move it up to 10 in pursuit of smoother sound.

- **Max Mismatches.** If you have a CD that just doesn't want to record, try increasing this value, which starts at 0 and goes up to 255. The higher the number, the greater your chances for getting that track to record. (Strive to find a balance, since higher numbers introduce a greater possibility for a corrupted or bad-sounding recording.)

Problems with the iTunes Music Store

The iTunes Music Store arrived on the scene in April 2003. As with any new product, a few glitches and gaps popped up as shoppers stampeded the store. Here are a few of the more common issues or errors you might occasionally encounter when using the service.

-9800, -9815, or -9814 Error

The Music Store is quite persnickety about punctuality and being on time. If you get this negative-sounding numerical error when trying to play a song you bought from the iTunes Music Store—or even when trying to connect to the store—quit iTunes.

Set your computer's clock to the correct time (use System Preferences on Mac OS X; the Control Panel in Windows).

Music Store Window Is Blank

If you're using iTunes, but clicking the Music Store icon produces only a blank window, then one of these problems is probably afoot:

- You're using an ad- or privacy-filter program, a firewall program, or "Web acceleration" software. Updating to iTunes 4.2 or later should help.

  So should configuring your privacy or security software to permit access to specific Web sites, if it offers this feature. Put *phobos.apple.com* and *phobos.apple.com.edgesuite.net* on the list. Now you should be able to get into the iTunes Music Store even when your moatware is enabled.

- You're using McAfee Privacy Service, which doesn't work well with the iTunes Music Store.

-5000 or -35 Error when Downloading (Mac only)

This error refers to scrambled Mac OS X permissions for the iTunes Music folder. (*Permissions* are behind-the-scenes Unix settings that permit only some people and not others to open and inspect certain folders.) This problem occurs (and recurs) if several people are sharing the same copy of iTunes. It can also happen if someone trashes the iTunes Music folder, or if there's a broken alias for the iTunes Music folder.

If you're using an alias for the iTunes Music folder (page 104), make sure that it works and knows where to find the iTunes Music folder. If the folder has disappeared completely, it's time to make a new one.

How to make a new iTunes Music folder

1. In iTunes, choose iTunes→Preferences.

   The Preferences dialog box appears.

2. Click the Advanced icon. On the Advanced panel, click Change.

   A window called Change Music Folder Location pops up.

3. Navigate to, and select, the disk or folder where you'd like to store the new iTunes Music folder.

   Make sure your new place has enough room on the drive to store all of the digital audio files in your collection. (If you don't specify, iTunes puts a folder called iTunes Music in your Home→Music→iTunes folder.)

4. Click New Folder. Name the folder and click Create. At the bottom of the Change Music Folder Location box, click Choose.

   You've just blessed this new folder as your music vault.

5. **Click OK to close the Preferences window.**

   A message advises you, "Changing the location of the iTunes Music Folder requires updating the location of each of the songs in your music library. This update will not move or delete any of your song files."

6. **Click OK when you're done reading.**

   In the next step, you'll actually move your songs to the new folder.

7. **Choose Advanced→Consolidate Library.**

   A message pops up with the warning, "Consolidating your library will copy all of your music into the iTunes Music folder. This cannot be undone."

8. **Click Consolidate to copy all of your music files into this new folder and location.**

   Since this action copies all of your music files to the new folder, it might take a few minutes. It also makes *duplicates* of any song files found outside the iTunes Music folder, so mind your hard drive space.

How to correct permissions for the iTunes Music folder

Mac OS X, which is based on Unix, uses *permissions* to allow different people different access to files. If they get messed up for a certain file or folder—especially the iTunes Music folder—you can wind up with a real six-aspirin headache.

Note: To perform the following steps, your account must be an Administrator account (not a Standard or Normal account). If your Mac won't let you perform these steps, ask the technical whiz who set it up for help. (That person almost *certainly* has an Administrator account.)

---

1. **In the Finder, locate your iTunes Music folder.**

   It's usually in your Home→Music→iTunes folder. If it doesn't seem to be there, open iTunes, choose iTunes→Preferences, click Advanced, and check the folder map listed in the middle of the box. It tells you where iTunes believes your music to be.

2. **When you've found the iTunes Music folder, click it once and choose File→Get Info.**

   Of course, you can press ⌘-I instead. Either way, the Get Info dialog box appears.

3. **Click to open the flippy triangle to expand the Ownership and Permissions panel.**

   If you're running Panther (Mac OS X 10.3), also expand the Details triangle.

4. **Change the Access and Others pop-up menus so they look like Figure 15-8.**

   Of course, your name should appear where it says Owner. (This, by the way, is where you may be asked for your account password, to prove that you're technically competent—an administrator.) The Group Access and Others pop-up menus should say "Read only."

5. Click **"Apply to enclosed items,"** and close the Get Info box.

If you're not having any luck with the permissions-correction approach, making a whole new iTunes Music folder, as described on page 292, may fix the problem.

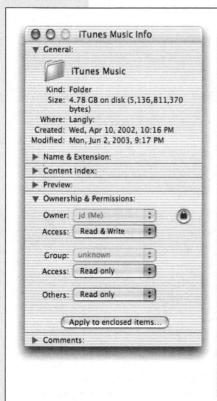 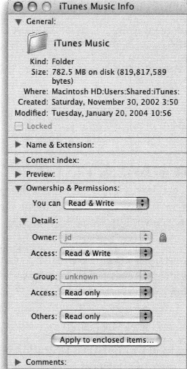

Figure 15-8:
Resetting the permissions on the iTunes Music folder can clear up certain Music Store error messages. The trick is to use Get Info on your iTunes Music folder (shown here in Mac OS X 10.2, left, and 10.3). If you're still getting grief from the Music Store (or its wares) after correcting the permissions, you may have to make a similar correction to the folder for the particular band or singer you were trying to listen to when the trouble started. Go into the iTunes Music folder, locate the folder named for the artist in question, and repeat steps 2–5 above.

"Required File Not Found" Error Message

Some early versions of iTunes for Windows were easily bamboozled by Internet Explorer's "Work Offline" option, resulting in this error message when you tried to visit the iTunes Music Store. Updating to iTunes 4.2 or later is the best way to solve the problem.

Bought Music Doesn't Play

If you've purchased some Music Store songs that refuse to play, first make sure that the computer you're using is *authorized* to play the purchased music. Also make sure that you haven't exceeded your three-computer iTunes Music Store limit (page 157).

There's one other remote possibility: the permissions for your Shared folder (a standard Mac OS X folder, designed for sharing documents among account holders) may have become scrambled or even deleted. The Music Store relies on this Shared folder to store the authorization information for your Mac.

Open your hard drive icon, and open the Users folder inside. If you don't see a Shared folder there, create one (File→New Folder). Follow up by setting its permissions as described in the previous steps—except this time, the Owner should be System.

Now try to play your purchased music, or buy a song from the iTunes Music Store.

Can't Buy Music

If you can't complete purchases in the iTunes Music Store, follow the steps described above for replacing a missing Shared folder. Also, make sure your Internet connection is live and working (not to mention your credit card).

Music Doesn't Download Automatically

You can download your purchases from the iTunes Music Store in one of two ways: either with the 1-Click method, which downloads the songs right away as you buy them, or with the Shopping Cart feature, which collects your songs and then downloads them all when you're done shopping. (See Chapter 6 for details.) If you're expecting instant song downloads, choose iTunes→Preferences on the Mac or Edit→Preferences on the PC, click the Store icon, and make sure the option for 1-Click purchasing is turned on.

Can't Burn My Purchased Music to CD

If iTunes finds an unauthorized Music Store track on your playlist, it will stop burning the CD in progress and scold you ("One or more of the songs on this playlist are not authorized for use on this machine"). Authorizing the song with your Apple or AOL account name and password will fix it, but remember, you can only burn the same playlist containing purchased music 10 times.

Can't Burn My Purchased Songs to an MP3 Disc

While the iTunes Music Store allows you to burn a playlist containing purchased music up to 10 times, you must burn it as an audio CD (page 108) and not an MP3 CD. If you've tried to make an MP3 CD out of purchased music, you've probably seen the foreboding error message, "None of the items in this playlist can be burned to disc."

The songs from the iTunes Music Store are in AAC format and protected from conversion into other file formats like MP3. You can, however, burn them to a regular audio CD or back them up to a data disc. Choose another disc format by choosing iTunes→Preferences, and then clicking the Burning icon.

Note: When you buy a song or album from the iTunes Music Store, it's yours to keep forever—but you can only download it *once* from the store. Additional downloads mean additional payments, so it's a good idea to back up your purchased music files as described in Chapter 6.

Reinstalling and Updating the iPod's Software

What Apple maketh, Apple shall updateth. Like any other software company, Apple constantly fixes, enhances, and fine-tunes the operating systems it writes—including the iPod's.

In general, Apple updates the iPod's system software a few times a year, but the amount of new stuff varies in each revision. Some updates just fix bugs and improve existing functions (like battery life), while other updates add a whole new world of possibilities (like the ability to play AAC files or use calendars on your iPod).

For example, Apple's big April 2003 rollout of the iTunes Music Store (Chapter 6) was the occasion of two big iPod software updates, one each for the old and new models:

- **For 2003 (and later) iPod models,** Apple unveiled iPod software 2.0. Its key features were reorganized menus and the ability to customize the iPod's main menu screen; an Alarm Clock and a redesigned Clock menu; an On-The-Go Playlist for making spontaneous playlists on the iPod itself; the ability to rate songs and update Smart Playlists on the iPod; the new Parachute and Solitaire games; the new Notes program that can store and view text files on the iPod's screen; a display of To-Do Lists from iCal; easier-to-use update and restore software; and the elimination of the "OK to Disconnect" message. (Now, when it's OK to disconnect, you just see the main menu.)

- **For earlier models,** Apple created iPod software version 1.3. Its feature list isn't nearly as long, much to the disappointment of iPod fans ("What would be so difficult about giving us Solitaire?" they wondered).

  Still, it offered a few new goodies, like AAC file playback for home-ripped files and iTunes Music Store purchases; a menu command to flip the iPod's backlight on and off; and improved battery management (for longer life per charge).

How to Know when It's Time

Notification that a new iPod software version is available may come to you in any of several ways:

- **Macintosh Software Update.** If you've got the Mac's built-in Software Update feature turned on in your System Preferences or Control Panels, it can regularly check Apple's servers for updates to all your Apple software, including iTunes, iSync, iCal, and the iPod system software. Just pick the software you want from the Software Update list and click Install.

- **iPod Manager.** This nifty little app comes with the Windows MusicMatch software for the 2003 iPods (see page 46). It has a convenient button you can click to check Apple's Web site for the latest iPod system software.

Finally, if you regularly browse iPod-themed Web sites in Chapter 16 or tech-oriented forums like Slashdot.org, you'll hear about any new iPod update (software *or* hardware) about five seconds after Apple posts it.

Downloading the Updater

When you get the word, aim your Web browser at *www.apple.com/ipod/download*. Usually, Apple provides updates for both the Macintosh and Windows versions. If you've just purchased a brand-new iPod, load the iPod system software included on the CD that came in the box, and then check to see if there's an updated version. The iPod download page (Figure 15-9) explains what the new software does.

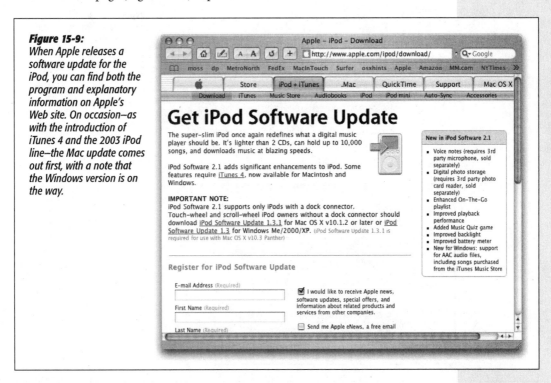

Figure 15-9:
When Apple releases a software update for the iPod, you can find both the program and explanatory information on Apple's Web site. On occasion—as with the introduction of iTunes 4 and the 2003 iPod line—the Mac update comes out first, with a note that the Windows version is on the way.

Running the Updater

iPod software updates are relatively painless: You download the installer file from Apple's Web site, connect the iPod to the computer, and then run the installer program. You may be asked to unplug the FireWire cable once or twice during the process to get the new system up and running. Just make sure you download the right installer for your particular iPod: original flavor, slimline 2003-era, or Mini.

Updating the Macintosh iPod

1. **Connect iPod to your computer using its FireWire or USB cable.**

   Unless you've changed the factory settings, iTunes opens and autosyncs its music with the iPod. Quit iTunes when the iPod's music library is updated.

2. **Open your Home Directory→Applications→Utilities folder. Open the iPod Software Updater application that you downloaded with Software Update.**

   (If you downloaded it to a different folder on your Mac, find the file and double-click the iPod Software Updater icon.)

   As shown in Figure 15-10 at top, the updater software checks your iPod and lets you know if you need to update.

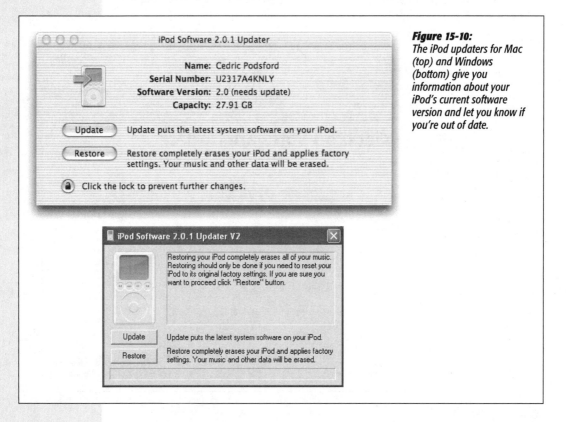

Figure 15-10:
The iPod updaters for Mac (top) and Windows (bottom) give you information about your iPod's current software version and let you know if you're out of date.

3. **If you're told that your iPod needs updating, click the Update button.**

   You'll probably be asked to type in your Administrator name and password before you can proceed. Let the updater program run.

4. **Quit the updater after it's run its course.**

   If you have iPod Software 2.0 or later, the update is now complete. If you have an earlier model, read on:

5. **Unplug the cable from the iPod, then plug it right back in.**

   The iPod screen asks you to replug if you don't do it right away.

   Once you reconnect the cable, the Apple logo appears, with a horizontal progress bar inching along underneath. When the updater says it's done, you're done.

Updating the Windows iPod

1. **Connect the iPod to your PC with its FireWire or USB cable.**

   Unless you changed the factory settings, MusicMatch Jukebox opens and updates the iPod with any new songs or playlists you've created since the last time you synced PC with Pod. Quit MusicMatch Jukebox when it's done.

2. **Choose Start menu→Programs→iPod→Updater.**

   The update program shown in Figure 15-10 at bottom appears.

3. **Click the Update button.**

   (If it's grayed out, you're already up to date.)

   A progress bar creeps along the screen as the update runs. If you have a 2003 iPod running iPod Software 2.0 or later, your work is done here.

   If not, a message appears asking you to unplug the iPod's cable.

4. **Unplug the iPod's cable. Plug the cable back in when the iPod requests it.**

   The iPod loads its new software. When it's done, close the Updater box.

Compared to Windows service packs or Mac OS system updates, the iPod upgrades go very quickly. (If anything goes wrong, check the iPod support area of Apple's Web site for troubleshooting articles; see Appendix A.)

Restoring the Software

Restoring the iPod software isn't the same thing as updating it. Restoring is a much more drastic procedure, like reformatting the hard drive on your Mac or PC. For one thing, *restoring the software erases the iPod's hard drive entirely.*

Of course, you won't lose any of your music, or your calendars, contacts, or notes, because all of that is nothing more than a reflection of what's on your Mac or PC. What you'll lose are the random computer files you've manually dragged onto the iPod's hard drive. If your iPod has been freezing, crashing, or behaving erratically, a good solid software restore may be just the thing it needs to feel better.

Note: If you think there might be a more recent version of the iPod software than what came with your iPod CD, go to *www.apple.com/ipod/download* and snag yourself a piping fresh copy of the iPod updater posted there.

Make sure you get the correct updater for Windows or Mac, whatever you're using.

Before you begin, insert your iPod software CD or have an update installer on your desktop. Then restore the iPod software (also called its *firmware)* like this:

1. **Connect the iPod to the computer with its FireWire or USB cable.**

   Let iTunes or MusicMatch Jukebox Plus automatically synchronize and update the iPod's library, if it seems to want to.

2. **Double-click the iPod Software Updater icon on your desktop, or the installer on your iPod CD.**

   If your iPod software is a version or two behind the current one, you'll see buttons labeled Restore and Update; if the Update button is dimmed and unavailable, then you're already up to date. (If Update is available, run Restore to clean off and reformat the iPod's hard drive, and *then* run Update.)

3. **Click Restore.**

   An alert box pops up asking if you really want to do this. Assure it that you do. (If you're using Mac OS X, Windows 2000, or Windows XP, you may be asked to confirm your technical prowess by typing in your Administrator account password.)

   After you affirm your decision, the installer program gets down to work completely erasing the drive and returning your iPod's factory settings to their original, untouched state.

4. **If the screen requests it, unplug the computer cable from the iPod. Replug it when you're asked to do so.**

   (The 2003 and later iPods skip this cable-unplugging part.)

   As the iPod completes the restoration process, you see the "Do Not Disconnect" message on its screen. iTunes or MusicMatch Jukebox Plus leaps back into action.

5. **Follow your computer's onscreen instructions through the set-up process, just as you did when you first got an iPod.**

   Here's where you give your iPod a name, for example, and choose whether you want to have the player updated automatically when you connect it to the computer. (You don't have to answer these questions the same way you did originally.)

6. **Refill the iPod with your music library from iTunes or MusicMatch Jukebox.**

   Since your iPod is empty now and all of your music is still on your computer, this may take a few minutes.

7. **When you see a message stating that the iPod update is complete, unmount or eject the iPod and quit the iPod Software Updater program.**

   See page 51 for details on unmounting the iPod.

8. **Unplug the computer cable from the iPod and let it start itself up again.**

You'll have to go through the setup process on the iPod as well, doing things like picking the language you wish to use with it.

Once you've gone through all these steps, check the iPod to make sure all your songs and playlists are back where they belong. Then use it as you normally do and see if that nasty freezing problem was fixed.

Tip: After this kind of reset, check the iPod's clock to make sure it's keeping time after resetting the device. You may have to set the clock, too.

Where to Get Help Online

Apple keeps an online library of technical help articles for the iPod on the Web, along with manuals and details about each new iPod hardware and software update.

- The **iPod Support** page, which includes a Frequently Asked Questions document, is at *www.info.apple.com/usen/ipod*.

- There's also an **iPod Troubleshooting** page on the site at *http://www.info.apple.com /usen/ipod/tshoot.html*.

- Information about Apple's own **$99 Battery Replacement Service** for out-of-warranty iPods with dead or dying batteries is at *www.info.apple.com/support/ applecare_products/service/ipod_service.html*.

- If you have questions about **Apple's standard iPod warranty** and have lost the copy that came in the box, you can find a copy of the information at *http:// store.apple.com/Catalog/US/Images/ipodwarranty.html*.

- In case you want pay $59 to extend your iPod's warranty to two full years, information on **AppleCare for the iPod** is at *www.apple.com/support/products*.

- The **technical specifications** for the current iPod models are at *www.apple.com/ ipod/specs.html*.

- You can post a specific question or a "Hey, is anybody else getting *this…*" query on the **iPod Discussions Board** on Apple's site at *http://discussions.info.apple.com/ webx/ipod*.

- For problems with billing, downloading, and computer authorization, the direct link to the **iTunes Music Store Customer Service Center** is *www.info.apple.com/ usen/musicstore/musicstore.html*.

Specific help for Macintosh fans
- The Mac operating system (especially OS X) has built-in help not only for the iPod, but also for iTunes, iCal, and iSync. In the Finder, choose Help→Mac Help

(or press ⌘-?) to open the Mac Help Center. You can search for keywords or type in questions for any of the programs listed in the Help Center panel.

- The **iTunes Support** page lists a number of troubleshooting articles and technical notes about the Mac music program at *www.apple.com/support/itunes/index.html*.

Specific help for Windows fans

- The **iTunes for Windows Support** page has many helpful tips, tutorials, and articles at *www.apple.com/support/itunes/windows*.

- MusicMatch Jukebox Plus comes with **built-in help** that can answer common questions about using the software: choose Help→MUSICMATCH Jukebox Help. Here, you can also find help files for using the iPod. The Help menu also offers a tutorial on using the program, a beginner's guide to getting started, tips, and a link to the MusicMatch Web site, where you can find the latest technical support articles.

- Apple's own **iPod for Windows Support** page, which includes a Frequently Asked Questions document, is at *www.info.apple.com/usen/ipodwin*.

- If you want to go straight to the Web site yourself, try the searchable technical support library for MusicMatch Jukebox at *www.musicmatch.com/form/support*. Information about the company's technical support options is at *wwws.musicmatch.com/faq/MISC020.htm*.

- For help with some aspect of Microsoft Windows, visit the technical support area of Microsoft's vast site at *http://support.microsoft.com*.

Specific help for sick or damaged iPods

The Apple Web page for iPod Service is *www.info.apple.com/support/applecare_products/service/ipod_service.html*. Repairs are free for the iPod's first year (or two, if you bought the extended iPod AppleCare warranty).

Standard repairs and prices for out-of-warranty iPods are listed on the page, but if you're experiencing an iPod problem that's not listed or just won't go away, scroll down to the link for iPod Troubleshooting and Service (*www.info.apple.com/support/applecare_products/service/ipod_service.html*). Click the link and after you've scrolled down to the bottom of *that* page, fill in the form. You need to type in your iPod serial number and set up an Apple ID if you don't already have one, and so on.

If you accept the company's price quote, you'll be asked to fill in your credit card number and to make arrangements for getting the iPod into good hands for repairs.

iPod on the Web

The World Wide Web evolved at hyperspeed. What was once a system that computer scientists developed to share electronic documents has exploded into an entity that contains the collective consciousness of everyone who's crafted a bit of HTML code and uploaded the file. The Web is many things to many people: a carnival of commerce, the world's biggest library, a news medium, a software distribution network, a creative canvas, and a virtual community for people with similar interests, like the finer points of *Star Trek: Deep Space Nine*.

This global geek community took to the iPod like ducks to water, so the Web turns out to be a huge part of the iPod fan's experience. Since its introduction in 2001, the iPod has inspired a number of sites where enthusiasts share information, tips, tricks, and news about their favorite music player. In this chapter, you'll find out where you can get the most recent iPod software, latest news, and coolest tricks.

Points of Interest at Apple.com

In addition to the software updates described in Chapter 15, other notable pages await on Apple's Web site to enhance your iPod experience:

- **The iPod home page.** You can see all the latest models and features listed here, along with short video demonstrations, technical specifications, and a link to the feedback area (*www.apple.com/ipod*).

- **Macintosh iPod Support.** The Mac iPod support page provides easy access to many of the most popular iPod articles in Apple's Knowledge Base (its collection of tech-help writeups), plus details about using one with a Macintosh (*www.info. apple.com/usen/ipod*).

- **Windows iPod Support.** PC people can find answers to technical questions or issues unique to the Windows-formatted iPod family here (*www.info.apple.com/usen/ipodwin*).

- **The iTunes home page.** Information about the newest version of Apple's iTunes software for Macintosh and Windows resides here, along with instructional videos and a link to download the software. You can also find a link to lists of CD recorders that operate with iTunes, as well as a place to offer feedback (*www.apple.com/itunes*).

- **The iTunes Music Store.** Apple's music emporium, where you set up an online account to buy songs to play in iTunes 4 and on your iPod. Much more detail awaits in Chapter 6 (*www.apple.com/music/store*).

- **Audiobooks on the iPod.** Audiobooks from Audible.com—plus popular shows from public radio and spoken-word versions of magazines and newspapers—are now available for download right in the iTunes Music Store (*www.apple.com/itunes/store/books*).

- **Technical Discussions.** Apple's forums give both veterans and newbies a place to discuss support issues and directly ask technical questions about the iPod and iTunes. Go here if you haven't been able to find the answer in the Knowledge Base (*http://discussions.info.apple.com*).

- **The Apple Store.** You can buy an iPod, iPod accessories, and a variety of other Apple hardware and software right from the source (*http://store.apple.com*).

Software Updates for iTunes

For Mac OS 9, Apple stopped upgrading iTunes at version 2.0.4. If you need a copy, type *iTunes 2.0.4* in the Knowledge Base search box at *www.info.apple.com* to find the page with the Read Me file and download link.

If you use iTunes for Windows, you can tell the program to alert you to newly available versions by choosing Edit→Preferences→General and turning on "Check for iTunes updates automatically." If you prefer to check yourself, choose Help→Check for iTunes Updates or visit *www.apple.com/itunes/download*.

If you're in Mac OS X, life is just as easy. The Mac's Software Update program is designed to alert you, via a pop-up dialog box, about new updates for iTunes.

If you've turned Software Update off (in System Preferences), however, you can always hit up the iTunes download page at *www.apple.com/itunes/download* to see whether your version is the latest and greatest. The page lists all of the new features and may include some special offers, like a free sample from Audible.com or the chance to buy even more Apple software.

If you're having technical troubles, go to the iTunes Support page at *www.info. apple.com/usen/itunes*.

Tip: You can download the latest versions of iTunes, iSync, and iCal at *www.apple.com/software.*

Software Updates for MusicMatch Jukebox Plus

The safest bet for getting MusicMatch and the iPod to make beautiful music together is to use the version that came on the iPod's CD. Still, some later versions of the jukebox program work with the iPod, provided you download an iPod plug-in file for it. In MusicMatch Jukebox Plus, go to Options→Add New Features to find the iPod plug-in to install.

If your iPod didn't include MusicMatch Jukebox but you want to use it anyway, you can locate the link to the latest iPod-compatible version at *www.musicmatch.com/ form/support*; do a search for "iPod." You can also try the horrendously long address at *www.musicmatch.com/download/free/index.cgi?OEM=APPLE*, where the company usually posts its most recent iPod-approved versions of the software.

Figure 16-1:
You can download the iPod-approved version of the program from the MusicMatch Web site. You can make other versions of MusicMatch Jukebox Plus work with the iPod if you install the proper plug-in software, but check the support area of the site to see which versions are compatible with the iPod and its plug-in.

Fun and Informative iPod Web Sites

Official Web sites are fine for software updates, hardware news, and technical information. But for truly passionate commentary, you just can't find more love, hate, and strong opinions than on the iPod fan Web sites.

iPoding

iPoding (*www.ipoding.com*) satisfies the need (if you have one) for breaking news, industry gossip, shareware sharing, and technical discussions about taking iPods apart to see how they work (Figure 16-2). The site has a great section of tips for maintaining your iPod and learning how to use it better, especially with Windows and Linux computers.

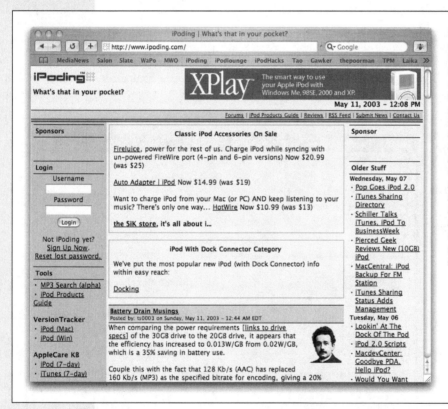

Figure 16-2:
iPoding keeps tabs on all the latest shareware and news. An iPod product guide, links to the VersionTracker site for iPod shareware, and sections covering everything from iPod repair to iPod humor make regular iPoding an entertaining yet educational adventure.

Opinionated and sometimes delightfully snarky, iPoding's registered members post articles and lively personal commentary about what's going on in the iPod world. For example, this is the site that first discovered and explained the iPod's secret diagnostic mode (see page 270).

Tip: Rumor sites are dishy and fun. Sometimes they post accurate leaks of upcoming products (like the 2003 iPod models). Sometimes they post nothing but wishful thinking.

If Apple gossip makes you happy, point your browser to ThinkSecret (*www.thinksecret.com*), MacRumors (*www.macrumors.com*), or Apple Insider (*www.appleinsider.com*).

iPodLounge

The iPodLounge (*www.ipodlounge.com*) tag line is "All Things iPod," and they're not kidding (Figure 16-3). Its fans discuss the iPod in detail on the site's message forums. The site posts links that lead directly back to Apple's technical library articles for troubleshooting issues, but iPodLounge also has its own Tips & Tricks section and Frequently Asked Questions list. If you're looking for software and shareware, the Downloads page has links to Apple's iPod software updaters, plus scads of iPod shareware for Macintosh, Windows, and Linux.

Figure 16-3:
iPodLounge is not only one of the earliest independent iPod sites around the Web, it's also one of the most well designed and organized. The site is a comprehensive, regularly updated electronic magazine with sections for news about the iPod, original articles, and reviews of accessories and other merchandise.

iPodHacks

iPodHacks (*www.ipodhacks.com*) has about 10,000 registered members, many of whom contribute their favorite tips, tricks, and hacks to the message boards. The site has a live iPodChat forum for members from around the world to discuss whatever's on their minds and iPods.

iPod Anonymous

iPod Anonymous (*www.ipodlaughs.com*) is a rib-tickling collection of Podly Web programming that bills itself as "a growing collection of time-passing utilities" for people addicted to their iPods. Once of the site's most humorous areas is iAshamed, a place where readers can post the titles of the most awful songs they are embarrassed to admit they have on their iPods. Other sections include a weekly photo-manipulation forum called iPocalypse Photoshop and the iPod Engraving Utility (Figure 16-4), where you can electronically engrave your favorite phrase on a virtual iPod for fun (or as a preview of what it might look like if you want to fork over $19 and have Apple engrave your next Pod).

Tip: Thanks to Apple's global reach, the iPod has developed quite an international following and inspired Web sites in several languages. If you're into languages and want an interesting worldview, try *www.ipodfanatic.com* for a French perspective, the iPod sections at *www.macnews.de* for German notions, iPod inspirations in Italian at *www.ipod.it,* or go Dutch at *www.macosx.nl*. Google.com can even translate for you.

Figure 16-4:
Just type in your words of wisdom, click the button, and see your saying virtually carved in chrome. You can also read the words of those who came before you from a link on the iPod Engraving Utility page on the iPod Anonymous site.

MacInTouch

Known to many diehard Macintosh fans for its Apple-related news and reasoned analysis since 1994, the venerable MacInTouch site has a section devoted to the iPod at *www.macintouch.com/ipod.html*. Written mostly as an epistolary exchange among the site's readers, the iPod Reader Report starts at the beginning when the iPod was first announced and follows the reactions, observations, and comments from MacInTouch contributors as they discover new things about Apple's music player.

Part Five: Appendixes

Appendix A: iTunes, Menu by Menu

Appendix B: MusicMatch Jukebox Plus, Menu by Menu

5

iTunes,
Menu by Menu

W hile you can do almost anything in iTunes by clicking buttons or pressing keys, some functions are available only in the menus at the top of the screen. This appendix covers each menu command—left to right, top to bottom.

This appendix assumes that you're using the latest version of iTunes 4 for Mac OS X and Windows. (Differences between the Mac and Windows versions, and between the Mac OS 9 and Mac OS X versions, are noted where necessary.) If you find clicking around in menus too slow to bear, there's a list of keyboard shortcuts at the end.

Application Menu (Mac); Help Menu (Windows)

In Mac OS X, commands that pertain to an overall program—like Hide and Quit—appear in the Application menu, the one bearing the program's name, just to the right of the menu.

In Windows, most of the equivalent commands appear in the Help menu (or at least they do in iTunes).

About iTunes

The information in this menu tells you what version of the program you're using, along with the software's creator and copyright information. (In Mac OS 9, About iTunes appears in the menu only when iTunes is in front.)

iTunes Hot Tips

This little nudge from Apple takes you to a Web page where you can read up on tips and tricks that make using iTunes a little more fun and a lot more efficient.

Preferences

The iTunes Preferences dialog box has seven panels, accessible by icons along the top of the window, which you can use to get the program looking and sounding just the way you like it. *Keyboard shortcut:* ⌘-comma (Mac), Ctrl+comma (Windows).

Note: In iTunes for Windows, the Preferences box is the last command in the Edit menu.

Here are the names of the specific preference panels, and what they do for iTunes:

General

Click the General icon to change the size of your Source and Song list text and make other adjustments to iTunes' overall appearance and behavior. You can turn on the "Show genre when browsing" checkbox to add the third Genre column alongside Artist and Albums in your iTunes Browser window (page 97). You can also tell iTunes what to do when you insert a CD, and give the program permission to go on the Internet by itself to get track information by turning on the "Connect to Internet when needed" box. Turning on the "Use iTunes for Internet Music Playback" box makes iTunes launch automatically when you open an Internet radio station or other streaming audio.

Effects

The Effects panel is where you customize the sound of your music. The Crossfade Playback control lets you blend one song into the next and set the amount of time it takes to blend. The Sound Enhancer slider improves the depth of the audio and lets you adjust it to your personal taste for sonic highs and lows. Turning on the Sound Check feature more or less levels out the different volumes of your songs so you're not straining to hear one soft track only to be deafened by the really loud one right after it.

Importing

The Importing panel lets you pick the file format (AAC, MP3, AIFF, or WAV) to use for encoding the songs copied from CDs, as well as the bit rate (page 74). You can also choose to have the songs play while you're ripping them. Turn on the "Create file names with track number" checkbox if you want your songs to fall in the same order as on the original album, even if you don't rip them all at the same time. (iTunes adds the track numbers to the names of the song files in the iTunes Music folder.)

Burning

The Burning preferences let you pick the model of CD recorder you use with iTunes, as well as the type of CD you want to create—either a standard audio disc or an MP3 CD (page 108). (Remember, even though computer drives can handle them, not all CD players and car stereos can play back MP3 CDs.) With iTunes 4 or later, Mac OS X 10.2.4 or later, and an Apple SuperDrive, you can opt to burn copies of your songs to a blank DVD and archive 4.7 gigabytes of music at a time.

Sharing

Here you can set up iTunes to allow other people to sample your songs over the network, or have your computer seek out music collections on other connected computers (page 110). You can choose how much of your music library you wish to share, whether that's everything or just a few specific playlists. If you want to put a password on your playlists, you can set that up here, too.

Store

In the Store preferences, you can decide whether you want to invite temptation and display the Music Store icon in your Source list or not. With the Music Store displayed, you have two options for buying music: download each song as you buy, or download in one batch (page 144). You can also instruct iTunes to play the songs as soon as it downloads them or load a complete preview before playing.

Advanced

The Advanced preferences panel (not to be confused with the Advanced *menu;* see page 321) helps you redirect iTunes to its iTunes Music folder in case you move it onto another drive or partition. If you find your Internet radio stations plagued by gaps and rebuffering messages, you can choose to increase the size of the buffer here, too. You can also name your preference for shuffling (by the album or by the song list).

The last two options deal with the iTunes Music folder. Turn on the "Keep iTunes Music folder organized" checkbox to have each artist and album neatly tucked away in a properly labeled subfolder when you add songs to the library. Turning on this box also lets iTunes automatically refile a song in the correct folder if you edit the text in the Song Information box (page 99). If you want to make sure that the iTunes Music folder always has a copy of each song you drag or import into the program, turn on the "Copy files to iTunes Music folder when adding to library" box.

Shop for iTunes Products

If you're hankering to accessorize your iTunes setup with items like speakers and headphones, let this menu command (and a live Internet connection) whisk you away to Apple's site of iPod-friendly audio products. (In Mac OS 9, this command is in the File menu.)

Provide iTunes Feedback

If you have something to say about iTunes, why not say it directly to the company that makes the program? Selecting this command opens your Web browser and transports you to the iTunes Feedback page on Apple's Web site.

(Don't expect Steve Jobs to read your note and call you right back. Someone at Apple does, however, read and collate these requests—and the biggest choruses of complaint get attention.)

Register iTunes

This menu item, which plops you onto Apple's site to fill out a software registration form, may not make much sense if you downloaded the program for free from Apple.com. If you acquired iTunes for $50 as part if the iLife software suite, though, you can get that feeling of completeness by filling out the online version of a registration card. Telling Apple that you've purchased its wares usually ensures that you get new product announcements and special offers from them, along with an occasional free subscription to *Macworld* magazine.

Services (Mac OS X Only)

These commands are the standard Mac OS X services (see *Mac OS X: The Missing Manual*), like Make New Sticky Note and Reveal Finder. Very few of them work in iTunes, but there are a few surprising exceptions:

- **Mail** opens up a new, outgoing piece of email and attaches the selected MP3 file, ready to address and send to someone.

- **Make New Sticky Note** opens the Stickies program, creates a new empty note, and pastes into it a little chart of the selected songs: Title, artist, album, time, and genre. Kind of a cool way to make a label or a list of your collection.

- Speech→**Start Speaking Text** command makes iTunes read *out loud* the artists, album names, timings, and genres of the selected songs. How weird can you get?

- TextEdit→**Open Selection** works just like Make New Sticky Note, except that it creates the table of song information in TextEdit.

Hide iTunes (Macintosh Only)

This command makes the iTunes window disappear. Click the iTunes icon in the Dock (or choose Show All) to bring it back. *Keyboard shortcut:* ⌘-H.

Hide Others (Macintosh Only)

All open program windows onscreen except iTunes disappear when you choose this command. *Keyboard shortcut:* Option-⌘-H.

Show All (Macintosh Only)

Selecting the Show All option brings any program windows hidden by the last two commands into view again.

Quit iTunes (Macintosh Only)

This is the polite way to close down the iTunes program. *Keyboard shortcut:* ⌘-Q.

File Menu

As its name implies, the File menu in iTunes (and any other computer program, for that matter) is where you go to do things with files: open them, export them, create new ones, and so on.

New Playlist

The iTunes program was made for music, and the first item on the menu creates a new, empty playlist file that you can fill with the songs of your choice from your music collection (page 104). *Keyboard shortcut:* ⌘-N (Mac), Ctrl+N (Windows).

New Playlist From Selection

When strolling through your library, you can quickly make instant playlists by selecting an artist or album and selecting "New Playlist From Selection" on the File menu (page 104). To select only certain songs from the artist or album shown in the song details window, press ⌘ while clicking song titles. (Pressing Shift highlights all the songs between your first and second selection clicks.) *Keyboard shortcut:* With the desired songs highlighted, Shift-⌘-N (Mac), or just Shift-click the Add button; Ctrl+Shift+N (Windows).

New Smart Playlist (iTunes 4 and later)

As described in Chapter 4, Smart Playlists work like this: You give iTunes a set of rules, like the bands you want to hear or the genre you're in the mood for (*"No Air Supply or other '80s Lite on this one, iTunes!,"* and the program goes shopping through your music library to create a customized playlist. The list even updates itself when you add new music to your collection. *Keyboard shortcut:* Option-⌘-N (or Option-click the Add button in the iTunes window) on the Mac; Ctrl+Alt+N (or Shift-click the Add button) on the PC.

Add (File) to Library

If you've just downloaded the new MP3 single that a hot new band posted for free on its Web site, you can get it into rotation on your playlists by choosing File →Add to Library and selecting the song file from your download location. The Add to Library command is just one way to add new songs to your iTunes music library (for others, see page 91). *Keyboard shortcut:* ⌘-O (Mac), Ctrl+O (Windows).

Add Folder to Library (Windows Only)

This command lets you add an entire folder's worth of sound files to iTunes for Windows.

Close Window

If you have a bunch of open playlist windows and need to get some screen real estate back in a hurry, use File→Close Window to close the active iTunes window. *Keyboard shortcut:* ⌘-W (Mac), Ctrl+W (Windows).

Tip: Many people find the keyboard command for Close Window (⌘-W) to be much more efficient than taking the mouse for a joyride through the File menu. See page 325 for a list of other keyboard shortcuts.

Import (iTunes 4 and later)

If you have a playlist of which you're particularly proud on one computer and want to copy it to another computer, you can export it (see the next item) from iTunes. Then you copy it to a disk or email it to yourself and use File→Import to pull that playlist into iTunes on the second computer. *Keyboard shortcut:* Shift-⌘-O (Mac), Ctrl+Shift+O (Windows).

Export Song List

You can save copies of your masterful iTunes mixes in three different formats: plain text, Unicode text, and XML (Extensible Markup Language, which is, among other things, the new wave of the Web). Saving a song list in one of the text formats is useful for making a printed list for a CD cover or importing into a database. Saving the song list as XML allows you to import it into iTunes on another computer.

Export Library (iTunes 4 and later)

If you want to export all of the playlists in your library at once, choose the Export Library option to create a large XML file containing all the information.

Get Info

Much like the old standard Macintosh command, selecting a song from the library or a playlist and choosing File→Get Info in iTunes opens the Song Information box (page 99). In the Summary tab, you can see such trivia as the name, size, length, and location of the file, plus the last time you played it. Click the Info tab to edit the labels on the songs in the library, and the Options tab to make adjustments like adding a specific equalizer preset or song rating (which are features of iTunes 3 and later). Click the Artwork tab to add photos and graphics to your iTunes files (page 87). *Keyboard shortcut:* ⌘-I (Mac), Ctrl+I (Windows); see page 326 for keyboard shortcuts for navigating the Get Info window.

Edit Smart Playlist

Even Smart Playlists can start to sound dumb after awhile. If you want to go back and make some adjustments to your automatic song-selection requirements, click the desired Smart Playlist in the iTunes source list and then choose Edit Smart Playlist. The Preferences box for that particular playlist pops up so that you can adjust its settings. *Keyboard shortcut:* Option-click the + button below the Source list (Mac); Shift-click the + button (Windows).

Show Song File

The song titles listed in the Library and playlists windows are only pointers that link to the actual digital audio file in the iTunes Music folder on your hard drive. The Show Song File command pops open the folder, revealing the actual song file in the Finder or in Windows Explorer. *Keyboard shortcut:* ⌘-R (Mac), Ctrl+R (Windows).

Tip: If you originally ripped the song from a CD, the folder name is usually the same name as the album, which itself is typically buried inside another folder or two, like Russian nesting dolls.

To cut to the chase and see the file path of the song on the Mac, ⌘-click the *window name* in the title bar. You get a pop-up menu that shows your nested-folder hierarchy, revealing the exact location of the actual audio file.

In Windows XP, just glance up at the address bar to see the file's complete path.

Show Current Song

If you want to name that tune but can't remember what it is, choose Show Current Song to refresh your memory. Whatever you're playing at the moment—whether a radio station, MP3 file, or CD track—is highlighted in the song list. *Keyboard shortcut:* ⌘-L (Mac), Ctrl+L (Windows).

Burn Playlist to CD

You can make a home-cooked compact disc from the current playlist in your iTunes window by selecting Burn Playlist to CD. Right away, the circular Burn CD button in the top right corner of the iTunes window spins open to reveal its yellow and black icon, and the status display window asks you to insert a blank CD. (To back out of the deal if you change your mind, click the small gray X in the status display window.)

Update Songs on iPod

If you have the iPod connected while you're ripping new songs or composing new playlists, this command sends the new data directly to the iPod without your having to disconnect and reconnect the player to jump-start the autosync function.

Note: As with just about every Mac program before the arrival of Mac OS X, the last item on the iTunes File menu in Mac OS 9 is the Quit command to close the program.

Exit (Windows only)

Mac fans *quit* their programs; in Windows, you *exit* them by choosing this command from the File menu.

Edit Menu

Like the Edit menus in almost every Mac program, this menu houses the commands that help you move and manage selected bits of information. In iTunes, it also lets you control how information is displayed.

Undo

The Mac's Undo feature reverses the last menu command or keyboard action you took. *Keyboard shortcut:* ⌘-Z (Mac), Ctrl+Z (Windows).

Cut, Copy, and Paste

These familiar text-editing functions come in quite handy for moving around misplaced album titles and artist names in the Song Information box and elsewhere in iTunes. *Keyboard shortcuts:* ⌘-X, -C, and -V on the Mac, Ctrl+X, +C, and +V in Windows.

Clear

Selecting a playlist in the Source list or certain songs on a playlist and then choosing Edit→Clear removes the item from the iTunes window—without deleting it from your music library (page 104). *Keyboard shortcut:* Delete. Or, to bypass the confirmation box, press ⌘-Delete (Mac) or Ctrl+Delete (Windows).

Select All

Select All does pretty much what it says it does. For example, if you want to select all the song titles in the window at once, click in the window and choose Edit→Select All. *Keyboard shortcut:* ⌘-A (Mac), Ctrl+A (Windows).

Select None

Choose Edit→Select None to release any song titles from selection. *Keyboard shortcut:* Shift-⌘-A (Mac), Ctrl+Shift+A (Windows).

Show / Hide Browser (iTunes 4 and later)

The Browser, a secondary song-finding tool, is described on page 97. This command lets you bring it to your screen or hide it again. *Keyboard shortcut:* ⌘-B (Mac), Ctrl+B (Windows).

Show / Hide Artwork (iTunes 4 and later)

The Artwork pane shows the CD album cover of whatever song is currently highlighted. When the Artwork pane is showing, the Source list can display only about half as many playlists, which is why iTunes offers you this command to reveal or hide the artwork at will. *Keyboard shortcut:* ⌘-G (Mac), Ctrl+G (Windows).

View Options

After you select View Options, a box pops up that lets you customize the columns and categories shown in the iTunes song window. If you decide that you don't want to see, say, the Bit Rate setting listed in the window, choose Edit→View Options and turn off the Bit Rate checkbox. Turn on the boxes for the categories you do want to see in your iTunes Details window. *Keyboard shortcut:* ⌘-J (Mac), Ctrl+J (Windows).

Tip: Contextual (shortcut) menus are a wonderful thing, once you remember they're there. They list useful options that are especially relevant to whatever you're clicking. For example, the contextual menu for a song offers choices like Get Info and Convert to MP3; for a playlist, you get choices like Export Song List and Burn Playlist to Disc.

To produce these menus, right-click onscreen items (if you have a two-button mouse) or Control-click them (if not).

Controls Menu

This menu can perform many of the same actions as fiddling with buttons and sliders on the iTunes window—or even on a home stereo system.

Play

With a song or playlist selected in your iTunes window, choose Play to start the music. *Keyboard shortcut:* Space bar.

Next Song, Previous Song

The next two items on the Controls menu let you skip to the next song or back to the last one on the playlist or album you're listening to. *Keyboard shortcut:* ⌘-left or -right arrow (Mac), Ctrl+Left or +Right (Windows).

Shuffle

The Shuffle command tells iTunes to get randomly funky with the order of the songs currently listed in your iTunes window at the time—an album listing, a single playlist, or all the songs in the library. A checkmark next to the Shuffle command means that the setting is already turned on; select Shuffle again to toggle it off. *Shortcut:* Click the Shuffle button in the iTunes window.

Repeat Off, All, One

The next three choices on the Controls menu make iTunes automatically play current playlists or albums over and over (Repeat All) or just once (Repeat One). Repeat Off command disables the repeat function. You can only choose one at a time, and the checkmark shows you which setting is active.

Volume Up, Down

Incrementally increase or decrease the iTunes volume with these two menu items. *Keyboard shortcut:* ⌘-up and -down arrow (Mac) Ctrl+Up or +Down (Windows).

Mute

If you need to take a conference call, or your boss is coming down the hall while you're rocking out at your desk to your Black Crowes playlist, get thee to Controls→ Mute as fast as your mouse can take you. *Keyboard shortcut:* Option-⌘-down arrow (Mac), Ctrl+Alt+Down (Windows).

Eject Disc / Eject iPod

Choosing the Eject Disc command unmounts whatever disc is in the CD or DVD drive and ejects it. If you've got the iPod attached and selected in the source list, you have the option to gently release it from iTunes instead. *Keyboard shortcut:* ⌘-E (Mac), Ctrl+E (Windows).

Tip: If you have an extended Macintosh keyboard, you may find the four buttons across the top row of the numeric keypad a quicker source of volume control. They feature self-explanatory icons for Volume Down, Volume Up, Mute, and Eject).

Visualizer

If you get tired of looking at playlists and just want to zone out, the Visualizations feature (page 93) can provide colorful animations in the main iTunes window. This menu lets you make adjustments to the visualization display. Once you've turned on the visual display, click Options in the top-right corner of the iTunes window to adjust things like frame rate and song-title display.

Turn Visualizer On/Off

The first menu item toggles off and on the iTunes Visualizations feature (page 93). Choosing Turn Visualizer On transforms your iTunes window into a psychedelic animation that can make you feel like you're snowboarding down the DNA helix in living color. *Keyboard shortcut:* ⌘-T (Mac), Ctrl+T (Windows).

Small, Medium, Large

These are the three sizes you can choose for the colorful onscreen animations (see previous command). Choosing Small or Medium leaves a black letterbox frame around the animation, while Large fills the entire iTunes window.

Full Screen

Visualizations can become a full-blown screensaver when you select Full Screen (as well as Turn Visualizations On). To get your monitor back to normal, click anywhere onscreen to toggle off the Full Screen mode. *Keyboard shortcut:* ⌘-F (Mac), Ctrl+F (Windows).

Note: If you've installed any iTunes slideshow shareware or new modules (page 113), you'll see them listed at the bottom of the Visualizer menu. To pick the one you want, select it from the menu. A checkmark next to the name tells you which one is currently in use.

Advanced

The Advanced menu deals with several tasks that might appeal to power users, including adjusting ID3 tag formats (page 121) and downloading track information from the Internet.

Switch to Mini Player (Windows Only)

Instead of minimizing the iTunes program window completely into the taskbar, you may sometimes prefer to shrink its window down to convenient minibar size. That way, the essential controls are still visible. This command does that trick. *Keyboard shortcut:* Ctrl+M.

Open Stream

The Open Stream command opens a dialog box where you can type or paste in a URL to go directly to a streaming audio site. If you've never listened to radio streams over the Internet, iTunes has plenty of preprogrammed links for you to check out (page 102). Just click Radio in the Source list and click the kind of music or radio programming you wish to listen to. *Keyboard shortcut:* ⌘-U (Mac), Ctrl+U (Windows).

Convert Selection to AAC (or MP3 or AIFF or WAV)

Depending on the file type (AAC, MP3, AIFF, WAV) you've designated in Preferences for importing songs into iTunes (page 84), you can use the Convert Selection command to convert a selected item into your preferred format. For example, if you have some WAV clips on your computer but have chosen MP3 as your preferred import setting, use the Convert Selection to MP3 command to select and convert the files to MP3 and import them into iTunes all in one shot.

Consolidate Library (iTunes and later)

If you have songs scattered around the computer in any folders other than the iTunes Music folder, you can use the Consolidate Library command to seek out the scattered songs and put copies of them in the iTunes Music folder. This command puts your entire collection conveniently in one place, but it means you'll have the same song in two places on your computer, possibly even duplicated within the iTunes Music folder.

Get CD Track Names

If you don't have iTunes configured to automatically dash out to the Internet and download track information for the songs on the CD you just inserted (page 84), use the Get CD Track Names command to go fetch those song titles from the Gracenote CDDB database. If you have a dial-up Internet connection instead of an "always on" one, this command lets you connect to the Internet only when you're prepared to dial up.

Submit CD Track Names

The Gracenote CDDB database is a wonderful thing (page 84), but it's far from error-free. This command lets you help make things right.

Make corrections in the Song Information box (page 99), and then choose the Submit CD Track Names command to upload the fixed track information to the Gracenote CDDB database. (Of course, you need to be connected to the Internet to use this command.)

Join CD Tracks (iTunes 4 and later)

Sometimes you don't want two seconds of silence between songs you import from an album. The Join CD Tracks command imports all selected songs as one big track without those mood-breaking sounds of silence (page 101).

Authorize / Deauthorize Computer (iTunes 4 and later)

Apple allows you to authorize up to three different computers to play the songs purchased from the iTunes Music Store (or Audible files). As described on page 157, this system lets you hear your music on more than one computer, while still helping curb the illegal copying of copyrighted works.

If you push your luck and try to authorize a fourth machine, this feature will kick in and force you to deauthorize one of the previously authorized computers.

Check for Purchased Music (iTunes 4 and later)

If you bought some songs in the iTunes Music Store but couldn't download them at the time, Checked for Purchased Music lets you back to get them. (You need to enter your Apple ID and password.)

Convert ID3 Tags

There have been several versions of the ID3 tag format over the years, and earlier versions of the format can store less information than the newer standard. If a song's information doesn't look right, try selecting the song and using Convert ID3 Tags to change the tag format.

Window Menu (Macintosh Only)

The Window menu is where you go to open certain windows as well as expand or collapse the main iTunes window.

Minimize (iTunes 4 and later)

This command sends the iTunes window swirling down into the Mac OS X Dock. As with any Mac OS X program, its windows return to the screen when you click its Dock icon. *Keyboard shortcut:* ⌘-M.

Tip: When iTunes is minimized, hidden, or in the background, you can still control it. Hold your cursor down on the iTunes program icon (which looks like a CD with musical notes on it) to produce a pop-up menu filled with commands like Shuffle, Play, Next Song, and so on. You can even rate the song in progress using the My Rating submenu.

Zoom (iTunes 4 and later)

The Zoom command is the menu bar equivalent of clicking the green circle at the top of the window—it shrinks the full iTunes window down into a tiny compact silver bar. To expand the window back to its full size, choose Zoom again from the menu.

iTunes

You can hide or reveal the program's window—whether in full-screen view or the silver mini control bar—by selecting iTunes from the Window menu. Reselect iTunes from the menu to toggle the window on or off. *Keyboard shortcut:* ⌘-1.

Equalizer

Equalizer toggles the graphic equalizer window onscreen or off. *Keyboard shortcut:* ⌘-2.

Bring All to Front (iTunes 4 and later)

If your iTunes window is buried behind your Web browser, email inbox, and spreadsheet project, you can pop it to the front by selecting Bring All to Front. (This command brings the equalizer and any open playlist windows to the front as well.)

Note: Any open playlist windows also appear in the Window menu. A checkmark indicates which playlist is the currently active and visible window. No checkmark next to the playlist name means it's open but buried under other windows. A diamond in front of the name means the playlist or window is open but minimized.

Help Menu

You can find answers to basic questions about the program's features or functions in the iTunes built-in help files. This menu also gives you access and assistance for the iTunes Music Store (iTunes 4 and later).

Note: If you're running iTunes 2.0.4 on Mac OS 9, your Help menu also offers Balloon Help. As the About Balloon Help command makes clear, you can make little comic-book style dialog balloons magically appear onscreen when you pass the mouse over a menu or window. The Show/Hide Balloons item switches this feature on and off.

Balloon Help is at its most helpful when you're just learning the Macintosh operating system, but after a few hours, the constant text-filled balloons popping up may have you reaching for sharp objects.

iTunes & Music Store Help

Selecting this item launches Apple's iTunes Help program. Several topics are readily available, and you can search the program for specific words or phrases for technical support articles about how the program works. *Keyboard shortcut:* ⌘-? (Mac), F1 (Windows).

Music Store Customer Service

This command takes you to the iTunes Music Store's online Customer Service department. The team can answer questions about your account, passwords, and so on.

iPod Help

The iPod Help program works just like iTunes Help, except that you can search for iPod-specific words and phrases like "scroll wheel."

Keyboard Shortcuts

One item in the Help menu is the list of iTunes keyboard shortcuts, which also appear below in a handy list. Memorizing the shortcuts for the commands you use most often can give you a faster, smoother iTunes experience.

Check for iTunes Updates (Windows)

Although iTunes can be set to automatically check for its own updates, Windows users can also take a manual approach to seeking out the latest versions of the program with this handy menu item (and an Internet connection).

Keyboard Shortcuts for iTunes 4

Shortcuts for playing songs	Keystroke
Play the selected song right now	*Mac:* Return or Space bar. *Windows:* Enter or Space bar.
Play next or previous album	*Mac:* Option-right arrow or -left arrow (or Option-click the ◄◄ or ►►| buttons in the upper-left corner of the iTunes window). *Windows:* Shift+Ctrl+Alt+right arrow or +left arrow.
Next/previous song	*Mac:* ⌘-left arrow or -right arrow (or ⌘-click the ◄◄ or ►►| buttons). *Windows:* Ctrl+left or +right arrow (or Ctrl-click the ◄◄ or ►►| buttons in the iTunes window).

Shortcuts for Library and playlist windows

Create a playlist from selected songs

Mac: Shift-click the + button (or drag songs to an empty spot in the Source list).
Windows: Ctrl+Shift+N (or drag songs to an empty spot in the Source list).

Create a new Smart Playlist

Mac: Option-click the + button beneath the Source list.
Windows: Shift-click the + button.

Reshuffle the current playlist

Mac: Option-click the Shuffle button.
Windows: Shift-click the Shuffle button.

Delete selected playlist without confirmation box

Mac: ⌘-Delete.
Windows: Ctrl+Delete.

Delete selected playlist and all songs in it

Mac: Option-Delete.
Windows: Shift+Delete.

Delete selected song from library and all playlists

Mac: Option-Delete.
Windows: Shift+Delete.

Shortcuts for files and windows

Select or deselect all the songs in a list

Mac: ⌘-click any checkbox in the list.
Windows: Ctrl-click any checkbox.

Change the song information columns

Mac: Control-click a column title to summon pop-up list of possible columns.
Windows: Right-click a column title.

Expand or collapse all the triangles in Radio list

Mac: ⌘-click a triangle.
Windows: Ctrl-click a triangle.

Smoother, outline-only window resizing

Mac: ⌘-drag the resize box in the lower-right corner of the iTunes window.

Expand iTunes window to optimal size

Windows: Shift-double-click the iTunes window title bar.

Go to the next/previous track in Get Info window

Mac: ⌘-N, ⌘-P.
Windows: Ctrl-Left Arrow (Artwork tab only).

Next/Previous pane of Get Info or Prefs window	*Mac:* ⌘-left bracket ([ ) or -right bracket ( ]). *Windows:* Left or Right Arrow key (Get Info box only).
See more options for a visual effect onscreen	Press / or ?, then press the desired key to use its option (not all visual effects can do this).

iPod shortcuts

Prevent iPod from automatically updating	*Mac:* Press ⌘-Option as you connect the iPod to your Mac until it appears in the Source list. *Windows:* Press Shift+Ctrl+Alt as you connect the iPod to your PC until it appears in the Source list.

Music Store

Previous/Next Music Store page	*Mac:* ⌘-left bracket ([ ), -right bracket ( ]). *Windows:* Ctrl+right bracket ( ]), +left bracket ([ ).
Return to the Music Store home	Home key

Audible files

Previous/Next chapter	*Mac:* Shift-left arrow, -right arrow. *Windows:* Ctrl+Shift+left arrow, +right arrow.

Application menu (Macintosh)

Open iTunes Preferences	⌘-comma.
Hide iTunes	⌘-H.
Quit iTunes	⌘-Q.

File menu

New playlist	*Mac:* ⌘-N. *Windows:* Ctrl+N.
New playlist from selected songs	*Mac:* Shift-⌘-N. *Windows:* Ctrl+Shft+N.
New Smart Playlist	*Mac:* Option-⌘-N. *Windows:* Ctrl+Alt+N.
Add file (from hard drive) to the Library	*Mac:* ⌘-O. *Windows:* Ctrl+O.

Close iTunes window

Mac: ⌘-W.
Windows: Ctrl+W.

Import a song, playlist, or library file

Mac: Shift-⌘-O.
Windows: Ctrl+Shift+O.

Open Info window for selected song or CD

Mac: ⌘-I.
Windows: Ctrl+I.

Show hard drive location of a song file

Mac: ⌘-R.
Windows: Ctrl+R.

Show the currently playing song in the list

Mac: ⌘-L.
Windows: Ctrl+L.

Controls menu

Play/Stop

Space bar

Play previous/next song in the playlist
(Mac). *Windows:* Ctrl+left arrow, +right arrow.

Mac: ⌘-left arrow, -right arrow.

Volume down/up
Windows: Ctrl+down arrow, +up arrow.

Mac: ⌘-down arrow, -up arrow.

Mute
Windows: Ctrl+Shift+down arrow.

Mac: Option-⌘-down arrow.

Eject a CD

Mac: ⌘-E.
Windows: Ctrl+E.

Visualizer menu

Visual effects on/off

Mac: ⌘-T.
Windows: Ctrl+T.

Expand visual effects to full screen

Mac: ⌘-F.
Windows: Ctrl+F.

Advanced menu

Stream audio file from a specific URL

Mac: ⌘-U.
Windows: Ctrl+U.

Switch to Mini Player (Windows only)

Ctrl+M.

Window menu (Macintosh only)

Minimize iTunes window to the Dock

⌘-M.

View the main iTunes window

⌘-1.

View the Equalizer window

⌘-2.

Help menu

Open iTunes & Music Store Help

Mac: ⌘-?.
Windows: F1.

MusicMatch Jukebox Plus, Menu by Menu

Before there was iTunes for Windows, MusicMatch Jukebox Plus was the iPod's official gateway to the PC. MusicMatch Jukebox Plus is a muscular music management program that's been slinging MP3 collections around Windows machines for years. You may be using it instead of iTunes because you prefer it, or because you don't have Windows XP or 2000 (the minimum system requirement for iTunes).

This appendix details all of the commands on MusicMatch's menus and highlights some notable features along the way. The menus described here refer to the last officially sanctioned version for use with the iPod, MusicMatch Jukebox Plus 7.5.

File Menu

The MusicMatch Jukebox File menu offers commands for moving your files around the computer, onto a CD, or to the iPod. It also contains tools for working with your music library.

Open

When you choose Open, a dialog box lets you open audio files (in recognized formats), playlists (with an .m3u file extension), tracks from the CD player, or the My Computer window. You can also get to this box by clicking the round Open button below the Playlist window.

Open Music Library

Whether you have one or several music libraries, this command lets you choose a music collection and load it into MusicMatch. Music Library files have a .ddf file extension, and you can also open files with the 3.x Database file extension of .mmd.

Add New Track(s) to Music Library

Lets you scan your drives and directories to gather up any music files hanging around your computer and add them to your Jukebox library. Turn on the "Ignore system folders" and "Skip tracks smaller than [100] KB" boxes to keep the program from displaying things like system alert sound files and other sonic crumbs.

WatchFolders

Wouldn't it be great if every song you downloaded from the Web would just show up in MusicMatch Jukebox Plus without you having to do any work? That's exactly what the WatchFolders feature does, as described on page 124. Since MusicMatch Jukebox Plus can check for new music only when it's running, choose this command and click the Check WatchFolders Now button so the program can look around for any music that you've acquired since you used the program last.

Convert Files

If you have music tracks that you want to convert from one digital audio format to another, use File→Convert Files to transform your WAVs into MP3s (page 66). You select the files to convert from the Source directory and send them on to the Destination directory. There's also a slider to adjust the bit rate of the converted MP3 files.

Export Playlist Tracks

Once you've created that perfect playlist, you can use this command to export the tracks to a portable music player. Or, if it's a really good playlist, you can convert the exported tracks to higher quality WAV files in preparation for burning them to CD.

Send to Portable Device

When it's time to load up the iPod, you need to summon up the Portables Plus window (which MusicMatch sometimes calls its Portable Device Manager). First, connect your iPod to the computer with the FireWire or USB 2.0 cable (page 35). Choose File→Send to Portable Device to open the Portables Plus window and select the iPod in the list. You can drag and drop music files from your computer onto the Portables Plus window to add songs to the iPod. Other ways to add music include clicking Add in the Portables Plus window (and browsing to the tracks you wish to add), and clicking the Sync button to update the iPod with everything that's in your MusicMatch library.

Create CD

Launches the Burner Plus program that comes with MusicMatch Jukebox Plus and then automatically adds all the songs on your current playlist to the CD recorder's window. Just pop in a blank disc and click the Burn button to start making the CD.

Print

Brings up a dialog box that lets you lay out and print a list of the songs and track information for a playlist—or your entire music library—if you want a hard copy of the music you have on your PC. Click Print Preview for a sneak peek at what will come out of your printer.

Exit

When it's time to close up the program for the night or move on to other things, choose Exit to close the program.

Edit Menu

Unlike the typical text-oriented Cut, Copy, and Paste commands on the Edit menu in most programs, MusicMatch Jukebox Plus offers tasks that are more relevant for digital audio files and playlists.

Playlist Track Tag(s)

Use this command to edit the track information file that comes with each song in your music library. You can retype album names; add labels for the song's mood, genre, and tempo; paste in lyrics; and even add album cover art for each song.

Super Tag Playlist Track(s)

If you have a whole bunch of track tags you need to modify (page 130), the Super Tagging feature can make the chore easier and faster. The Lookup Tags function on this submenu locates and adds the correct tag information by scanning the song file names. Choose the Tag from Filename option if you want to turn the existing file name into a tag or Rename Files to do the reverse and change the file's name to match that of its tag.

Copy Art to Clipboard

If you have some album art on display in the Media Window that you'd like to use for your song tags, click it and then choose Copy Art to Clipboard. From there you can paste it into the song's track tag (page 123). If you've scanned in art from a CD cover, you can right-click the GIF or JPG file to copy it onto the clipboard.

Paste/Tag Art from Clipboard

You can use this Paste command to stick a copy of the album art or graphic from the clipboard into the MusicMatch Jukebox Media Window or in the Art area of the Playlist Track Tag dialog box. *Keyboard shortcut:* Ctrl+V.

Select All in Playlist

If you want to highlight all of the songs in the Playlist window at once, use this command to select them all.

Clear Playlist

When it's time to bring some fresh tunes into the MusicMatch Jukebox Plus window, you can clear the list of songs currently in the Playlist window with the Clear Playlist command. You can also get to this dialog box by clicking the round Clear button below the Playlist window (page 134).

Note: Clearing a playlist from the Playlist window does not delete the saved playlist file from your computer. Use the Open command (page 135) to load it in the Playlist window the next time you want to listen to it.

View Menu

The choices on the View menu allow you to control how many different parts of MusicMatch Jukebox you have visible onscreen, along with other visual elements of the program.

Small Player View / Full Player View

Selecting Small Player View shrinks the MusicMatch Jukebox window down to a slim, space-saving bar of controls for music playback. Choosing Full Player View expands the window to its full-size, normal view. *Keyboard shortcut:* Alt+Page Down, +Page Up.

Playlist

Shows or hides the program's Playlist window. In addition to being a workspace to create, edit, and view playlists, the window features a number of shortcut buttons along the bottom frame for saving a playlist, sending it to the iPod, or burning it to a CD. You can also adjust playlist behavior with the Shuffle and Repeat buttons.

My Library

Opens the library window, revealing all of the encoded songs that MusicMatch Jukebox has filed away for your digital audio collection. Another way to pop open this window is to click the My Library button below the playback controls in the program's main window.

Online Music

Whisks you to the MusicMatch MX site, where you can listen to dozens of preprogrammed streaming radio stations and browse some of the offerings from the MusicMatch subscription music service. Access to all of the service's features—including the Artist on Demand area that hosts the works of 8,000 popular musicians—costs $5 a month. A more limited pass to just the service's radio stations and a few other basic areas costs $3 monthly.

Music Guide

If you're connected to the Internet, this command leads you to a special area of the MusicMatch site, where you can browse for free music and more information about the bands and singers you're interested in. The site can give you listening recommendations based on your music preferences and even sell you CDs. The Music Guide button below the song playback controls is another route to this feature.

Now Playing

Displays information like album art and reviews, videos, and discographies related to the current song and artist. To use this feature, you need to have properly tagged your home-ripped music files and be connected to the Internet. There's a shortcut Now Playing button in the MusicMatch Jukebox window.

Recorder

When you're ready to rip a CD to MP3 files (or whatever digital audio format you favor), call up the Recorder to convert the files. The CD Lookup feature attempts to get the track information from the Internet to save you typing song tags. *Keyboard shortcut:* Ctrl+R.

Media Window

Opens the Media Window—the small display where you see album art, video clips, and visualizations (page 127)—into its own detached window. Clicking the tiny dual-window icon directly above the Media Window next to the song playback controls also produces the free-range Media Window.

Change Skin

If you're bored or tired with the way your MusicMatch Jukebox Plus software looks onscreen, you can whip off the old skin (visual interface, that is) and give it a whole new look.

Download Skins

If you don't like any of the skins included with the program, choose View→Download Skins to trundle out to the Web and find a skin that suits you.

Visualizations

Visualizations are wiggly, colorful animations that bop and groove along with the beat of your music (page 127). With the commands on the Visualization submenu (listed next), you can pick the one you want to see and adjust its look to your liking.

Select Visualization

Lets you choose the animated pattern you wish to see in your Media Window. Click the Get New button to download new visualizations from the MusicMatch Web site.

Start/Stop Visualization

Starts the animation or stops a visualization that's running.

Configure Visualization

Lets you add sequences of effects and different graphics to customize visualizations.

Sound Enhancement

After you've added eye candy to your music with visualizations, you can mix in ear candy with plug-ins that let you modify and improve the sound of the player.

Select

Lets you download and install a DSP (digital sound processor) plug-in from the MusicMatch Web site. (Plug-in software often costs money, but you can usually get a free trial period to see whether the additional component suits you.)

Enable

Activates any DSP plug-in you've installed. To disable it, return to this menu item.

Show UI

Displays the digital sound processor control window, with slider bars to adjust effects like 3-D sound and bass levels, as shown in Figure B-1.

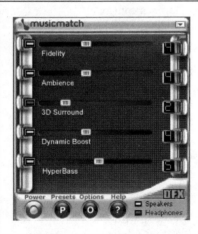

Figure B-1:
The DFX plug-in that you can download to use with the Sound Enhancement feature gives you more effects and control over your audio. The additional software costs about $20.

Auto Arrange Components

If you've detached and shifted various windows of the MusicMatch Jukebox program across your screen, this menu command snaps them back together into the original formation.

Always on Top

Prevents windows from other programs from covering the MusicMatch Jukebox window. *Keyboard shortcut:* Ctrl+T.

Tip: If you don't want to give up that much of your monitor territory, changing to the Small Player View *and* selecting Always on Top will keep the miniature control bar within easy reach on top of other windows but take up much less space.

Options Menu

The Options menu lets you change your preferences for the look and feel of the program as well as controlling the actions within playlists, changing the settings for your Recorder and Radio, and working with your music library.

Player

From this one submenu, you can control most basic aspects of playback, including record, play, pause, volume, and mute. Other commands open more sophisticated dialog boxes.

- Previous track (*Keyboard shortcut:* Alt+left arrow)

- Record

- Play (*Keyboard shortcut:* Ctrl+P)

- Pause (*Keyboard shortcut:* Pause/Break key)

- Stop (*Keyboard shortcut:* Ctrl+S)

- Next track (*Keyboard shortcut:* Alt+right arrow)

- Increase volume (*Keyboard shortcut:* Alt+up arrow)

- Decrease volume (*Keyboard shortcut:* Alt+right arrow)

- Mute (*Keyboard shortcut:* Control+M)

- Seek backward (*Keyboard shortcut:* Shift+Alt+left arrow)

- Seek forward (*Keyboard shortcut:* Shift+Alt+right arrow)

- Skip back tracks

- Skip forward tracks

Volume Leveling

Lets you balance overall sound levels between different songs in your music library. To use this feature, you have to wait for the program to process all the tracks you want to level, which could take awhile.

Equalizer

Turns on the graphic equalizer feature so you can adjust individual frequencies in your songs or use configured presets (page 129) for different styles of music.

Recorder

Another way to summon the MusicMatch Jukebox Plus Recorder controls (page 120).

Settings

Takes you right to the Player tab in the MusicMatch Jukebox program Settings box, where you do things like modify the amount of time and number of tracks the Seek feature uses, or set your MusicMatch desktop wallpaper to change with each album played.

Playlist Menu

Offers several commands for working with playlists (page 134) including:

• Open Music (that is, open a playlist)

• AutoDJ (*Keyboard shortcut:* Ctrl+D)

• Save Playlist

• Clear Playlist

• Shuffle

• Reorder by Album/Track

• Repeat Playlist

• Prepare Tracks for Volume Leveling

• Create CD from Playlist

• Create Radio Station From Playlist

• Print Playlists

• Submit CD Information

• Settings (*Keyboard shortcut:* Shift+Ctrl+S)

Note: The Create Radio Station function analyzes the type of song you've selected in your library or a playlist and then streams in similar sounds through your Internet connection. (If you're not a subscriber to the MusicMatch MX service, though, you get a lower sound quality and more ads on your screen.)

Music Library

The Music Library submenu lets you work with your music collection on a grand scale. You can view everything in your collection by genre, mood, artist, and other categories. You can add tracks, import entire music libraries, export libraries, and delete unwanted tracks from MusicMatch Jukebox. This is also where you can get to the menus that let you edit track tags and choose how you want to sort and search your collection. Many of these commands appear in other menus around the program as well.

Tip: If you have a long afternoon ahead of you and don't want to stop and change playlists, you can play every song in your entire music collection in a random order by choosing Options→Music Library→Play My Library.

Recorder

The Recorder command has several submenus that let you prepare the program for recording music. *Keyboard shortcut:* Ctrl+R.

Control

Sends commands like Stop, Start, and CD Info Refresh to the Recorder program as you prepare to rip CD tracks. You can select all of the tracks or none in the recorder list to rip.

Format

Lets you select the digital audio file format you want to use for ripping your tunes. You have your choice of MP3, WAV, mp3PRO, and Windows Media Audio, but only the first two are naturally iPod-friendly.

Quality

Lets you select the bit rate for recording digital audio files.

Source

Lets you choose where you're recording your music or audio from: the computer's CD drive, a tape deck or turntable, or a microphone. (Certain recording sources like a turntable may require the use of a stereo preamplifier or other audio equipment to record decent-sounding MP3 files.)

Prepare Tracks for Volume Leveling

Evens out major shifts in the volume to create a more consistent level of loudness from track to track in your music collection.

Submit CD Information

Upload new or corrected track information to the CD Lookup database on the Internet.

Settings

Opens the Recorder tab of the MusicMatch Jukebox Settings box, where you can adjust many of the above features.

Online Music

If you have even the slightest interest in exploring the MusicMatch MX online music service, this part of the Options menu and a live Internet connection can help you explore the offerings. If you already have a MusicMatch MX account, you can log in, change your settings, modify your WishList of tracks that you like or want to buy, or get help with using the service.

Add New Features

Takes you to a page on *www.musicmatch.com* where you can find additional plug-in software like extra visualizations or sound-enhancement goodies for MusicMatch Jukebox.

Get Music Recommendations

If you just don't know what to listen to anymore, you can choose this command to get some ideas from the folks at MusicMatch.com. (This service requires that you sign up and register with the site.)

Update Software

Searches for and downloads updated MusicMatch Jukebox software with just a couple of clicks. But be careful: You may accidentally download and install a version of the program that's not compatible with your iPod software (page 43).

Shop for Music

If you absolutely, positively must purchase some new music *right this very instant*, choose View→Shop For Music to browse albums for sale online. (These are physical CDs that come to you by mail, not instant downloads like the iTunes Music Store.)

Shop for Music Gear

This is another menu item designed to take you online to spend more money.

Settings

Opens the multi-tabbed Settings box, where you can choose your preferences for just about every element of MusicMatch Jukebox Plus that you'd want to modify.

Note: Other parts of the MusicMatch Jukebox Plus program, like the Burner Plus component for recording CDs from music library files, have their own settings and options within their program windows.

For example, to get to the settings for the built-in alarm clock feature, right-click the MusicMatch Jukebox icon in the Windows system tray and select Alarm Settings.

Help

This command opens a set of interactive guides that walk you through just about every aspect of the program. Many of the submenus take you to MusicMatch sites on the Internet for technical support, program upgrades or registration, and other interactive features.

Tip: If you've lost your registration key for MusicMatch Jukebox Plus, choose Help→Registration→Retrieve Lost Key. You can also re-enter your key or check your registration information in the Registration submenu.

Keyboard Shortcuts

You can do many of the functions listed in the MusicMatch Jukebox Plus menus with just a few quick keyboard commands.

Shortcuts for Playing Songs	Keystroke
Play the selected song	Ctrl+P
Stop playing the song	Ctrl+S
Pause the song	Pause/Break
Listen to the next track	Alt+right arrow
Listen to the previous track	Alt+left arrow
Seek Forward	Shift+Alt+right arrow
Seek Backward	Shift+Alt+left arrow

Volume Controls	
Increase Volume	Alt+up arrow
Decrease Volume	Alt+down arrow
Mute	Ctrl+M

Player Window Controls	
Full Size View	Alt+Page Up
Small Player View	Alt+Page Down
Jukebox Always on Top	Ctrl+T

General MusicMatch Jukebox Commands	
Open	Ctrl+O
Open Settings box	Shift+Ctrl+S
Open Recorder	Ctrl+R
Open AutoDJ box	Ctrl+D
Find Tracks in Music Library	Ctrl+F
Make Playlist Active	Ctrl+F5
Paste Art	Ctrl+V

IPOD & ITUNES: THE MISSING MANUAL

Index

.Mac accounts, 207
6-pin-to-4-pin adapter, 37

A

AAC files
converting from MP3, 244
defined, 69
impact on battery life, 19
ripping from CDs, 84
versus MP3, 74
AAChoo, 244
About iTunes, 311
About menu, 28
AC adapter, 15
prong adapters for
international use, 18
replacements for, 263
adapter for FireWire cable, 37
address book, 167-182 *see also*
exporting addresses
deleting addresses, 181
exporting addresses to,
169-181
history of, 167-168
opening, 167-168
address book
sorting settings, 181
AIFF files, 70
impact on battery life, 19
ripping from CDs, 84
alarm clock, 26
using iTunes as, 113
your own recordings, 261
alarms (in calendar), 187-188
America Online
and iTunes Music Store,
154-156

AOL Wallet, 155-156
Anapod Explorer, 60
"another user" error
message, 285
Apple help sources, 301-302
Apple ID (account)
.Mac accounts, 207
editing information, 145
setting up, 143-144
Apple logo icon, 274
won't go away, 274-275
Apple music store *see* **iTunes**
Music Store
Apple World Travel Adapter
Kit, 263
AppleCare, 302
AppleScript, 239-241
won't import contact files,
286
arrow notation, 5-6
artwork (CD covers)
hiding or showing (iTunes),
318
in iTunes, 87-90
in MusicMatch, 123-125
Audible files, 103
defined, 70-71
for Macintosh, 72
for Windows, 73
audio books *see also* **Audible**
files
make your own, 203
Audiocorder, 250
authorizing computers, 157-
158
Authorize Computer
command, 322

auto stereos *see* **car stereos**
AutoDJ playlists, 137
automatic synchronization
turning off, 47
autoplay CDs setting, 92
Avalon, 113

B

backing up, 159-162
iTunes Music Store songs,
159-162
onto DVDs, 108-110
backlight, 33
customizing, 29-30
turning on (shortcut), 33
turns itself on at midnight,
277
battery, 16-18
Apple replacement
program, 19
battery-life problems, 275-
277
capacity per charge, 18-19
car Chargers, 236-237
charging via AC adapter, 17
charging via dock, 17, 41
charging via FireWire, 16
charging via USB, 16, 41
checking the charge, 17
customizing the backlight,
29-30, 33
external battery packs, 264-
265
replacing, 264-265, 276-277
responsible for hardware
problems, 273
slow drain, 17, 19

time to charge, 16
tips for extended life, 19, 276
Belkin iPod Voice Recorder, 259-261
Belkin Media Reader, 259
belt clips, 251-255
Billboard charts, 147
bit rates, 74
    importing preferences, 312
    resampling in MusicMatch, 140
    specifying in MusicMatch, 337
blog links to Music Store, 153
blue screen of death, 290
Bluetooth, 205
Book2Pod, 203
books on tape *see* **Audible files**
Brick game, 195-196
Browse menu, 24-25
Browser pane, 318
Burn Out, 244
Burn Playlist to CD command, 317
burning CDs
    auto-Eject (iTunes), 110
    Burn Playlist to CD command, 317
    from iTunes Music Store, 159
    in MusicMatch, 138-140, 330
    in iTunes, 108-110
    preference settings, 313
    troubleshooting, 295
buttons, 13-15
    click sound, 31

C

calendar, 183-193 *see also*
    exporting appointments
    alarms, 187-188
    deleting, 187
    file formats, 184
    looking up a date, 186-187
    preparing iPod for, 183
car chargers, 236-237
car stereos, 232-238
    cassette adapters, 234-236
    wired connections, 234-236
    wireless connections, 232-234

Carbon Copy Cloner, 222
carrying case, 21-22, 251-255
cassette adapters, 234-236
CD burning *see* **burning CDs**
CDDB (Internet CD database), 85, 121
CDs *see also* **burning CDs; cover art; ripping CDs**
    auto-play, 92
    history of, 65-66
    iPod software, 42-45
    missing track names (iTunes), 84-85
    missing track names (MusicMatch), 121-122
checkmark disk icon, 269
cigarette-lighter Chargers, 236-237
classical music
    classification concerns, 25
    EQ (equalizer), 30
    sorting to keep pieces together, 81
click sounds from buttons, 31
clicking, 6
clock, 25-27
    alarm clock, 26
    battery-life problems, 275
    setting, 31-32
    sleep timer, 27
Clutter, 90
compression, 66
Consolidate Library command, 321
contrast adjustment, 31
Control-clicking, 6
copy protection, 68
    iTunes Music Store, 157-161
copying songs *see* **synchronization**
copyrights, 68
cover art (CDs), 87-90, 123-125
    hiding or showing (iTunes), 318
    in iTunes, 87-90
    in MusicMatch, 123-125

D

dashboard stands, 262-263
deauthorizing computers, 158-159, 322
deleting
    everything from the iPod, 241

songs from iTunes, 92
songs from MusicMatch, 126-127
songs or playlists, 52
diagnostic mode, 270-272
dial *see* **scroll wheel**
digital audio
    bit rates, 74
    compression, 66
    formats, 65-76
    history of, 65-66
disconnecting the iPod, 51
    AppleScripts for, 241
    as hard drive, 215-216
    Eject iPod command, 320
Disk First Aid, 225
disk mode, 53, 211-226
    copying files, 214
    deleting files, 215
    Disk Utility, 225
    forced, 269-270
    iPod as startup disk, 217-226
    offloading digital camera pictures, 259
    setting up, 212-214
    uninstalling Mac OS X, 225-226
    unmounting the disk, 215
disk utilities, 225
DiskWarrior, 225
dismounting the iPod *see* **disconnecting the iPod**
"Do Not Disconnect" message, 16, 51
    won't go away, 287, 290
dock, 3, 15, 17
    connecting to home stereos, 230-231
"Don't steal music," 52
Doug's AppleScripts, 241
Drive 10, 225
Drive Setup, 225
DVD-Audio, 285
DVDs
    burning in iTunes, 108-110

E

e-books, 200-203
    free sources of, 203
earbuds (earphones), 20-21
    Apple in-ear style, 21
    sound quality problems, 280

splitters (for 2 listeners), 231
standard, 20
substituting your own, 21
EasyView X, 113
Eject Disk command
in iTunes, 320
Eject iPod command
in iTunes, 320
ejecting the iPod *see*
**disconnecting the
iPod**
engraved iPods, 13
EphPod, 59, 139, 204
exporting addresses, 171
EQ (equalizer), 30
euPod, 244
exclamation-point disk icon,
269
**exclamation-point folder
icon,** 274
Export Song List Command,
316
exporting playlists
from iTunes, 316
from MusicMatch, 330
exporting addresses
from Eudora for Mac, 177-
178
from FileMaker Pro, 178
from Mac OS X Address
Book, 176-177
from Macintosh, 175-181
from Microsoft Entourage,
175-176
from Microsoft Outlook,
171-173
from Now Contact, 178-179
from Outlook Express for
Macintosh, 179-181
from Outlook Express for
Windows, 174
from Palm Desktop for
Mac, 175
from Palm Desktop for
Windows, 171
from Windows address
book, 173-174
from Windows PCs, 170-
174
exporting appointments
from iCal (Mac), 184-186
from Microsoft Entourage,
189-191

from Microsoft Outlook,
191-192
from Now Up-to-date, 192-
193
from Palm Desktop, 188-
189
via iCal, 190
Extras menu, 25-26

F
fast-forward button, 14
FAT32 format, 4-5, 44, 212
FireWire, 4 *see also* **disk mode**
6-pin vs. 4-pin cables, 36-
37
AC adapter cable, 18
damaged cable, 273
defined, 35-36
FireWire 400 vs. FireWire
800, 41
installing FireWire card, 37-
39
iPod connector, 15
powered FireWire
accessory, 263
speed of, 36
to charge battery, 16
FM transmitters, 232-234
forced disk mode, 269-270
frequency response, 20 *see
also* **graphic equalizer**
front panel, 13-15

G
games, 195-198
Brick, 195-196
Music Quiz, 197-198
Parachute, 196
Solitaire, 197
**Get CD Track Names
command,** 321-322
Get Info command, 316
GNUpod, 246
Gracenote CD database, 85,
121
graphic equalizer, 323
in iTunes, 95-96
in MusicMatch, 335
MusicMatch, 129-130
Grokster, 68, 141
gtkpod, 246

H
Hard Disk Toolkit, 225

hard drives *see also* **disk
mode**
converting Mac ↔
Windows format, 212
disk mode, 211-226
formats, Mac versus PC, 4-
5, 44, 212
iPod as startup disk, 217-
226
offloading digital camera
pictures, 259
startup manager, 220
headphone jack, 15-16
help
Help menu, 323
MusicMatch, 338
help online, 301-302
Hewlett-Packard iPod, 3
HFS Plus format, 4-5, 212
history of iPod family, 3
Hold switch, 15-16
iPod won't wake, 272-273
home stereos, 229-232
HP iPod, 3
i.Link *see* **FireWire**
iAlarm, 113
iCalendar files, 184
icons on iPod screen, 268-269
during startup, 274
ID3 tags, 121
auto-tagging in
MusicMatch, 130
converting (iTunes), 322
IEEE-1394 *see* **FireWire**
iHam on Rye, 113
iLyric, 244
iMic, 264
iMovie, 248
importing
Add to Library command
(iTunes), 315
format preferences, 312
Import command, 316
songs from CDs (iTunes),
83-90
songs from CDs
(MusicMatch), 120-125
sound files from the hard
drive (iTunes), 91
sound files from the hard
drive (MusicMatch),
125-126
Internet radio
in iTunes, 102-104
in MusicMatch, 133-134

iPod *see also* **buttons;
    earbuds; dock; screen;**
    etc.
  AppleScripts for, 239-241
  as address book, 167-182
  as alarm clock, 26
  as calendar, 183-193
  as e-book reader, 200-203
  as hard drive, 211-226
  as startup disk, 217-226
  auto accessories, 232-238
  backing up, 159-162
  backlight, 29-30, 33
  buttons, 13-15
  carrying cases, 251-255
  connecting to stereo
    systems, 229-232
  contrast adjustment, 31
  copying music off of, 52-61
  dashboard stands, 262-263
  defined, 1-2
  desktop stands, 257-258
  diagnostic tests, 270-272
  doesn't show up in iTunes,
    281-282
  doesn't show up in
    MusicMatch, 287
  EQ (equalizer), 30
  FireWire port, 15
  frequency response, 20
  games, 195-198
  generations, -4
  getting help online, 301-302
  hard drive repair, 268-269
  hardware accessories, 251-
    266
  hardware tour of, 11-34
  headphone jack, 15
  Help command, 324
  history of, 1-4
  Hold switch, 15-16
  home stereo accessories,
    229-232
  incompatible with WMA
    files, 115
  laser engraving, 13
  menu system, 22-34
  model lineup, 3
  Notes program, 198-200
  original model, 3
  packaging, 12
  parts of, 11-20
  plugs and connectors, 15-
    16
  professional paint jobs, 12

  purse systems, 255
  reformatting a Mac iPod for
    Windows, 139
  reinstalling and updating
    the software, 296-300
  renaming, 52
  resetting, 268
  restore factory settings, 33
  restoring (erasing) the iPod
    software, 296-300
  screen, 11-12
  secret recording feature,
    248
  sleep timer, 27
  software CD, 42-45
  Sound Check, 31
  speakers, 255-257
  synchronize selected
    playlists, 49-50
  synchronizing by hand, 50-
    51
  synchronizing with
    computer, 35-62, 45-46
  system requirements, 4
  to store digital photos, 259
  troubleshooting, 267-302
  turning off and on, 14
  voice recorders, 259-261
  Windows model, 3
iPod Free File Snc, 56
iPod It shareware, 191
**"iPod linked to another
    Library" message,** 286
iPod Manager, 217
iPod Mini, 3
  armband, 22
  battery life, 19
  belt clip, 21-22
  buttons on, 14
  FireWire cable, 37
  FireWire connector, 15
  Hold switch, 15-16
  remote-control, 16
  USB cable, 41
iPod preferences, 48-50
  what to synchronize, 47-48
iPod software
  error installing, 288
  installers, 42
  reinstalling and updating,
    296-300
  restoring (erasing), 299-301
iPod Viewer, 53-54
iPod.iTunes, 56
iPodAddress, 182

iPodLibrary, 204
iPodRip, 57
iPodSync, 172, 192
iPod_Control folder, 53-54
iRock, 232
iSpeakIt, 203
iSync, 205-210
  defined, 205-206
  syncing with iPod, 206-210
iTalk microphone, 259-261
iTrip, 232
iTunes, 77-114 *see also*
    **playlists; iTunes Music
    Store**
  adjusting windows, 80
  and Mac OS 9, 43
  arbitrary music sorting, 81
  backing up, 108-110, 159-
    162
  Browser pane, 79, 97, 89,
    318
  Burn Playlist to CD
    command, 317
  burning CDs, 108-110
  burning preferences, 313
  Consolidate Library
    command, 321
  Controls menu, 319
  Convert Selection, 321
  converting file formats,
    100-101
  customizing columns, 80-
    81
  deleting songs, 92
  disconnecting the iPod,
    215-216
  doesn't auto-open, 283
  downloading CD cover art,
    87-90
  editing song information,
    99
  features of version 4, 78-79
  File menu, 315-318
  Get CD Track Names
    command, 321-322
  Get Info command, 316
  graphic equalizer, 95-96
  history of, 77-78
  ID3 tags, 322
  importing from
    MusicMatch, 83
  importing preferences, 312
  installing, 42-45
  Internet radio, 102-104

iPod won't show up, 281-282
joining songs, 101
joining tracks, 322
location of music library, 104
Mac vs. PC version, 5
menu commands, 311-328
minimizing the window, 82-83
Multiple Songs Information dialog box, 89-90
music sharing on the network, 110-114
Open Stream command, 321
playback effects, 312
playing music, 92-96
providing feedback, 314
registering, 314
ripping CDs, 83-90
searching, 96-97
shareware add-ons, 113
Show Song File command, 317
Smart Playlists, 106-107
song ratings, 97-99
songs don't auto-synchronize, 283
Sound Check, 31, 95-96
Source list, 45, 79-80
synchronize selected playlists, 49-50
synchronizing by hand, 50-51
synchronizing for the first time, 45
system requirements, 78
taking over from MusicMatch, 77
tour of, 79-83
tricks for selecting in a list, 86
trimming song starts and endings, 101-102
troubleshooting, 281-286
turning off auto synchronization, 47
Update Songs on iPod command, 317
upper right button, 82
View Options command, 319
visuals (light show), 93-95, 320-321

won't open, 283-285
won't play a CD, 285
iTunes Hot Tips command, 312
iTunes Link Maker, 153
iTunes Music folder, 104
correcting Mac OS X permissions, 293-294
re-creating, 292-293
relocating, 313
repairing, 283-285
iTunes Music Store, 140-164
allowances, 152-153
and America Online, 154-156
authorizing computers, 157-158
Billboard charts, 147
billing and customer service, 161-163
buying a song, 148-150
buying an audio book, 150
copying restrictions, 157-161
copying songs to iPod, 159
customer service, 324
customizing the columns, 148
deauthorizing computers, 158-159
finding purchases, 154
gift certificates, 151
Help menu, 324
history of, 141
interrupted downloads, 153-154
music won't play, 294-295
preference settings, 313
purchase history, 163
"required file not found" message, 294
searching and shopping, 146-148
setting up an account, 143-144
sharing on the network, 111
shopping cart, 144-145
song parody, 163-164
system requirements, 142
tour of, 142-146
troubleshooting, 291-296
iTunes preferences, 86, 312
autoplay CDs settings, 92
CD burning formats, 109

downloading missing track names, 85
for disk mode, 212
Internet music playback, 103
music sharing, 112
music storage location, 104
Sound Check leveler, 96
VBR (variable bit rate) files, 75
iTunes Sidekick, 113
iTunes Visuals Plugins, 113
iTunes Watcher, 113

I

Kazaa, 68, 141
keyboard shortcuts
defined, 6
visuals (light show), 93-95
keyboard shortcuts (iTunes), 324-328
Eject, 320
Get Info, 316
graphic equalizer, 323
Hide iTunes, 314
Import, 316
Mini player, 320
Mute, 320
New Playlist, 315-316
Next Song/Previous Song, 319
Preferences, 312
Show Current Song, 317
Show Song File, 317
View Options, 319
visualizer on/off, 320
volume controls, 320
keyboard shortcuts (MusicMatch), 339-340
for playback, 335
Next/Previous Track, 335
Play, Stop, Record, 335
volume, 335

L

language
changing, 278
setting, 32
laser engraving, 13
legal issues, 68
LimeWire, 141
Linux, 245-246
basics of, 245
iPod on Linux Project, 246
iPod shareware, 246

lyrics, 244

M

Mac OS 9
  and iTunes, 43
  installing on iPod, 218-219
Mac OS X
  installing on iPod, 221-224
  Jaguar (10.2), 221-222
  Panther (10.3), 223
Macintosh
  copying music from iPod,
    53-57
  e-book software, 200-203
  for playing iPod audio, 238
  getting help online, 301-302
  iPod AppleScripts, 239-241
  iPod as startup disk, 217-
    226
  iPod shareware, 242-244
  iPod software CD, 42-43
  iSync, 205-210
  mixing up Windows iPod's,
    287
  recording sound, 248-250
  reformatting a Mac iPod for
    Windows, 139
  startup manager, 220
  synchronizing for the first
    time, 45-46
  updating the iPod software,
    298-299
  vs. Windows iPods, 4
magnifying-glass disk icon,
  268, 274-275
main menu, 22-23
  customizing, 28
Menu button, 14
menu notation, 5-6
menu system
  changing the iPod
    language, 278
menus, 22-34
  the very basics, 6
Microsoft Word files
  Notes program, 198-200
  read aloud, 203
missing track information
  Get CD Track Names
    command, 321-322
  getting from Internet
    (iTunes), 321-322
  submitting to Internet
    (iTunes), 322

  submitting to Internet
    (MusicMatch), 337
models (iPod family), 3
MP3 files
  and copyrights, 68
  defined, 67
  free and legal sources, 75-
    76
  history of, 67-68
  idea behind, -1
  impact on battery life, 19
  MP3 CDs (iTunes), 108-110
  MP3 CDs (MusicMatch),
    139
  recording your own, 246-
    250
  ripping from CDs, 84
  versus AAC, 74
MPEG-4, 69
Multiple Song Information,
  89-90
music files *see also* **iTunes;**
    songs; synchroniza-
    tion
  bit rates, 74
  converting formats
    (iTunes), 100-101, 321
  converting formats
    (MusicMatch), 330
  formats, 65-76
  free and legal sources, 45,
    75-76
  history of, 65-66
  importing into iTunes, 91
  importing into
    MusicMatch, 125-126
  locating on the hard drive,
    317
  missing track information,
    321-322
  resampling in MusicMatch,
    140
  tricks for selecting in a list,
    91
Music Quiz, 197-198
music sharing via network,
  110-114
  from iTunes Music Store,
    159
  preference settings, 313
music store *see* **iTunes Music**
    Store
Musician's iPod Tools, 201
MusicMatch Jukebox, 115-140
  "another player" error

  message, 290
  auto-tagging, 130
  burning CDs, 330
  compatible versions, 115-
    116
  compatible versions, 44
  customizing columns, 118
  disconnecting the iPod, 216
  doesn't auto-open, 288
  editing tag information, 331
  File menu, 329-332
  finding songs, 131-132
  graphic equalizer, 129-130,
    335
  installing, 43-44
  Internet radio, 133-134
  iPod doesn't show up, 287
  iPod plug-in, 116
  menu commands, 329-340
  Mini viewer, 332
  Online Music command,
    332
  online store, 338
  playback effects, 334
  playing music, 127-131, 335
  Playlist window, 332
  playlists, 134-137, 335
  Portables Plus window, 46,
    330
  preferences, 49
  reasons to use, 115
  recording sound, 247-248
  ripped CDs sound bad, 290
  ripping CDs, 120-125, 333
  Settings dialog box, 118
  skins, 129, 333
  songs don't synchronize,
    288
  synchronize selected
    playlists, 49-50
  synchronizing by hand, 50-
    51
  synchronizing for the first
    time, 46
  syncing takes forever, 289
  tour of, 116-118
  troubleshooting, 287-291
  visuals (light show), 127-
    128, 333-334
  Watch Folders, 330
mute
  in iTunes, 320
myPod, 246

N

naming the iPod, 52
Napster, 68, 141
NaviPod remote control, 261
neodymium, 20-21
network music sharing, 110-114
  from iTunes Music Store, 159
  preference settings, 313
NewsMac, 201
Next/Fast-forward button, 14
Nomad, 118
Norton System Works, 225
Notes program, 198-200
  AppleScripts for, 239-241
  viewing song lyrics, 244

O

OmniWeb, 54
On Deck, 113
On-the-Go playlists, 24
on/off switch, 14
Open Stream command, 321
OutPod, 173

P

painted iPods, 12
Palm2iPod, 190
Panorama iPod Organizer, 182
Parachute, 196
pausing playback, 14
PCs *see* **Windows PCs**
permissions, 293-294
PersonalPodX, 182
PIM (personal information management) software, 169
piracy considerations, 52, 68
Play/Pause button, 14
Playback *see also* **visuals (light show); volume**
  adjusting volume, 13
  Controls menu (iTunes), 319
  crossfades between songs, 312
  EQ (equalizer), 30
  graphic equalizer in iTunes, 95-96
  graphic equalizer in MusicMatch, 129-130
  in iTunes, 92-96
  in MusicMatch, 127-131

navigating a song, 14
Now Playing menu, 33-34
repeat mode, 29
rewind and fast-forward, 14
shuffle mode, 29
Sound Check, 31
playlists
  iPod playlist menu, 23
  On-the-Go, 24
playlists (iTunes), 104-108
  burning to CDs, 108-110
  creating, 104-105, 315
  deleting, 106
  modifying, 105-106
  Smart Playlists, 106-107, 315
playlists (MusicMatch), 134-137, 335
  AutoDJ playlists, 137
  creating, 134-135
  deleting, 136
  modifying, 135-136
plugs and connectors, 15-16
Pod2Go, 201
PodText, 201
PodUtil, 60
PodWorks, 56
PodWriter, 200
Portable Manager *see* **Audible files**
Portables Plus window, 46, 330
power adapter *see* **AC adapter**
power button, 14
Previous/Rewind button, 14
printing
  playlists (MusicMatch), 336-337
  song lists (iTunes), 314
purse system, 255

R

radio
  in iTunes, 102-104
  in MusicMatch, 133-134
  receiver for iPod, 261-262
ratings in iTunes, 97-99
RCA cables, 230-231
RCA Lyra, 118
Recording Industry Association of America (RIAA), 68
recordings
  from iPod microphones, 259-261

from Mac or PC, 246-250
secret iPod microphone, 248
remote control, 16, 21
  wireless, for living room, 261
  won't work, 280-281
renaming
  iPod, 106
  songs or albums, 99
repeat mode, 29
  in iTunes, 319
  in MusicMatch, 335
"required file not found" message, 294
resetting the iPod, 268
  all factory settings, 33
Rewind button, 14
ripping CDs, 83-90
  choosing audio formats (iTunes), 84
  choosing audio formats (MusicMatch), 120
  cover artwork (iTunes), 87-90
  cover artwork (MusicMatch), 123-125
  defined, 66
  directly to iPod, 241
  in MusicMatch, 120-125, 333
  into iTunes, 83-90
  missing track names (iTunes), 84-85
  missing track names (MusicMatch), 121-122
  MusicMatch commands, 337
  ripping (defined), 66

S

sad iPod icon, 269
screen, 11-12
  backlight, 29-30, 33
  broken glass, 279
  cleaning, 12
  contrast adjustment, 31
Script menu, 239-241
scroll wheel, 13
  moving versus touchwheel, 13
  pros and cons, 13
  touch wheel out of control, 277-278
scrubbing, 14

Select button, 14
Services menu, 314
shareware, 239-250
**sharing music on the
      network,** 110-114
   from iTunes Music Store,
      159
   preference settings, 313
shuffle mode, 29
   in iTunes, 319
   in MusicMatch, 335
skins (MusicMatch), 129, 333
skipping, 279-280
sleep timer, 27
Smart Playlists (iTunes), 106-
      107, 315
   editing, 316-317
Solitaire, 197
songs *see also* **iTunes; music
      files; synchronization**
   backing up, 159-162
   converting to other formats,
      86
   deleting (MusicMatch), 92
   deleting (MusicMatch), 92,
      127
   editing information
      (iTunes), 99
   editing information
      (MusicMatch), 132-133
   Internet radio, 102-104
   joining, 322
   joining together, 101
   locating on the hard drive,
      317
   missing track names
      (iTunes), 84-85
   missing track names
      (MusicMatch), 121-122
   printing a list of, 314
   ratings, 97-99
   recording your own, 246-
      250
   searching (MusicMatch),
      96-97
   searching (MusicMatch),
      131-132
   tricks for selecting in a list,
      86, 91
   trimming, 101-102
   troubleshooting playback,
      279-280
Sony Vaio
   6-pin-to-4-pin adapter, 37

sorting
   address book entries, 181-
      182
   columns (iTunes), 80
   columns (MusicMatch),
      118-119
   in iTunes, 80-81
Sound Check, 31, 95-96, 312
speakers for iPod, 255-257
speech
   text-to-speech software,
      203
   Start Speaking command,
      314
stands for iPod, 257-258
startup disk, 217-226
   in Mac OS X, 224
   startup manager, 220
startup manager, 220
stereo systems, 229-232
Super Audio CD, 285
synchronization, 35-62
   by hand, 50-51
   for the first time, 45-46
   full automatic, 47-48
   random songs or playlists,
      241
   selected playlists only, 49-
      50
   troubleshooting, 283
   turning off, 47
   Update Songs on iPod
      command, 317
system requirements, 4

T

Tech Tool Pro, 225
temperature considerations,
      19
text files *see* **Notes program;
      speech**
Text2iPod X, 201
time *see also* **clock**
   setting the time, 31-32
TinkerTool, 54
Toast, 244
touchwheel *see* **scroll wheel**
tracks *see* **songs**
TransPod, 232
troubleshooting, 267-302
   -35 error (music store), 292
   -5000 error (music store),
      292
   "another user" error
      message (iTunes), 285

"another player" error
      message (MusicMatch),
      290
AppleScript won't import
      contact files, 286
backlight turns itself on at
      midnight, 277
battery-life problems, 275-
      277
blue screen of death, 290
broken glass, 279
burning Music Store songs
      to CD, 295
buttons don't work, 16
changing the iPod
      language, 278
check the battery, 273
corrupted iTunes folders,
      283-285
diagnostic tests, 270-272
disk mode, 269-270
"Do Not Disconnect"
      message, 51, 287, 290
earphone problems, 280
European Union volume
      limitations, 244
firewall software (iTunes),
      85
firewall software
      (MusicMatch), 122
FireWire cover pops off, 277
iPod doesn't show up
      (iTunes), 281-282
iPod doesn't show up
      (MusicMatch), 287
iPod freezes, 272
iPod hard drive, 268-269
"iPod linked to another
      Library" message, 286
iPod remote control, 280-
      281
iPod won't reset, 273
iPod won't wake, 272-273
iTunes problems, 281-286
iTunes doesn't auto-open,
      283
iTunes Music Store glitches,
      291-296
iTunes Music Store window
      is blank, 292
iTunes won't play CD, 285
missing track names
      (iTunes), 84-85
missing track names
      (MusicMatch), 121-122

music folder permissions,
    293-294
Music Store songs won't
    download, 295
Music Store songs won't
    play, 294-295
MusicMatch problems, 287-
    291
MusicMatch doesn't auto-
    open, 288
MusicMatch sync takes
    forever, 289
re-creating iTunes music
    folder, 292-293
replacing the battery, 276-
    277
"required file not found"
    message, 294
restoring (erasing) the iPod
    software, 299-301
ripped CDs sound bad
    (MusicMatch), 290
song playback, 279-280
songs don't synchronize
    (iTunes), 283
songs don't synchronize
    (MusicMatch), 288
touch wheel out of control,
    277-278
TuneCast FM transmitter, 232
turning on and off, 14
unmounting the iPod *see*
    disconnecting the
    iPod

U

Update Songs on iPod
    command, 317
USB 2.0, 4, 40-41 *see also* **disk**
    mode
    cable, 41
    defined, 40-41
    speed of, 40-41
    system requirements, 41
    to charge battery, 16
    versus USB 1.1, 41

V

VBR (variable bit rate) files,
    75
vCalendar files, 184
vCards
    anatomy of, 168
    defined, 169
    for use with iSync, 209

ViewTunes, 113
viruses, 76
visuals (light show)
    in iTunes, 93-95, 320-321
    in MusicMatch, 127-128,
        333-334
voice recorder, 28
volume *see also* **Sound Check**
    controlling with scroll
        wheel, 13
    European Union limita-
        tions, 244
    in iTunes, 320
    iTunes volume leveling, 95-
        96
    leveling commands
        (MusicMatch), 335
    MusicMatch volume
        leveling, 130-131
Volume Logic, 113

W

warranty, 12, 302
WAV files, 69
    from iPod microphones,
        259-261
    ripping from CDs, 84
weather, 244
Web pages
    converting to Notes, 241
    read aloud, 203
WhiteCap, 113
Windows PCs
    6-pin-to-4-pin adapter, 37
    blue screen of death, 290
    copying music from iPod,
        57-61
    e-book software, 204
    exporting address book
        from, 170-174
    first iPod for, 3
    for playing iPod audio, 238
    installing FireWire card, 37-
        39
    iPod shareware, 244-245
    iPod software CD, 43
    mixing with Macintosh
        iPods, 287
    powered FireWire
        accessory, 263
    reformatting a Mac iPod for
        Windows, 139
    reformatting iPod Drive,
        44-45

synchronizing for the first
    time, 45-46
updating the iPod software,
    299
vs. Mac iPods, 4
Windows 2000 killed by
    iTunes, 283
WMA files, 115
    defined, 69
    iPod incompatibility, 142
World Traveler Adapter Kit,
    18

X

XPlay, 60, 139

Z

Zoomify Photo Visualizer,
    113

Colophon

This book was written and edited in Microsoft Word X on various Macs.

The desktop-software screenshots were captured with Ambrosia Software's Snapz Pro X *(www.ambrosiasw.com)* for the Mac, and TechSmith's SnagIt for Windows *(www.techsmith.com)*. Adobe Photoshop 7 and Macromedia Freehand were called in as required for touching them up.

The book was designed and laid out in Adobe PageMaker 6.5 on a PowerBook G3 and Power Mac G4. The fonts used include Formata (as the sans-serif family) and Minion (as the serif body face). To provide the and ⌘ symbols, and the iPod button symbols (like ▶▶ and ◀◀), custom fonts were created using Macromedia Fontographer.

The book was generated as an Adobe Acrobat PDF file for proofreading and indexing, and finally transmitted to the printing plant in the form of PostScript files.